Music and Mythmaking in Film

Music and Mythmaking in Film

Genre and the Role of the Composer

TIMOTHY E. SCHEURER

McFarland & Company, Inc., Publishers
Jefferson, North Carolina, and London

An earlier version of Chapter 7 was published in the *Journal of Popular Film and Television* 32.4 (Winter 2005): 157–166. Reprinted with permission of the Helen Dwight Reid Education Foundation. Published by Heldref Publications, 1319 18th Street, NW, Washington, DC 20036–1802, www.heldref.org. Copyright © 2005.

LIBRARY OF CONGRESS CATALOGUING-IN-PUBLICATION DATA

Scheurer, Timothy E.
Music and mythmaking in film : genre and the role
of the composer / by Timothy E. Scheurer.
p.   cm.
Includes bibliographical references and index.

ISBN-13: 978-0-7864-3190-8
softcover : 50# alkaline paper ∞

1. Motion picture music — History and criticism.
2. Film genres.   I. Title.
ML2075.S346   2008   781.5'4209 — dc22   2007041981

British Library cataloguing data are available

On the cover: Kevin Costner as Robin of Locksley
in *Robin Hood: Prince of Thieves*, 1991 (Warner Bros./Photofest);
background ©2007 Shutterstock

Manufactured in the United States of America

*McFarland & Company, Inc., Publishers
Box 611, Jefferson, North Carolina 28640
www.mcfarlandpub.com*

Table of Contents

Films are fantasy and fantasy needs music. — Jack Warner

Preface

I can't remember exactly when I became a lover of film music. I was fortunate enough to grow up in an era in which when one attended movies the lights went down, the curtain opened, and one heard the distinctive fanfares of the studios preceding the titles rolling across the screen. At home, I would stay up till almost any hour to watch a musical biopic, my favorite being *Rhapsody in Blue*, which chronicled the mythical life of George Gershwin. But the biopic is less about film music and more about pop music in general. I think my fascination with and passion for film music started with Max Steiner. I vividly remember the first time I saw *The Charge of the Light Brigade* on late night television, and I recall being struck by Max Steiner's symphonic approach to scoring the great charge at Balaclava. A few years later, it was Percy Faith's recording of Max Steiner's theme from *A Summer Place* that led me to try and find more Max Steiner music; there wasn't much available at that time but a couple of years later I purchased an odd Warner's recording of the soundtrack from *Parrish*—odd because it was done in the style that Henry Mancini had pioneered, i.e., not cues but full blown musical themes, and the B side was piano versions of the music performed by George Greeley (the Warner Brothers house pianist). That may have been my first official soundtrack purchase. It was as a graduate student at Bowling Green State University that I began to seriously study film music. The confluence of the freedom to study popular culture and in particular film music and the release of Charles Gerhardt's wonderful recordings of Max Steiner's film music on RCA records (it seems that Max is a leitmotiv in my scholarly life!) spurred my scholarly interest in the field. So movies and film music have been a passion in my life for over 40 years. I suppose it has helped that, although I am a lover of classical music, I was never a musical elitist. I have no problem going from a recording of a Mahler symphony or a Bach cantata to Hendrix's "Purple Haze" to Tony Bennett's wonderful *Songs for the Jet Set* album to John Williams's soundtrack for *Star Wars*. In fact, I think the reason I have been drawn to film music is that it draws on both the popular and classical realms; the music, moreover, is generally scored in the romantic (or post–Romantic) tradition, which is yet another love of mine.

So, after many years of collecting soundtrack albums, listening to them, and reading and researching the lives and careers of film music composers, I decided I wanted to write something myself. A number of factors influenced the writing of the book you have in front of you. There is my great admiration for film music composers and musicians in general (for instance, I don't know if we fully appreciate the great skill that the studio musician brings to a recording session). Over the years, I learned that being a composer for films is a tough job and one that does not garner the same kind of respect that even a pop songwriter earns, much less his or her serious music counterparts. There are a number of fine studies of the work of

1

the individual composers, including the pioneering work of Tony Thomas and Darby and Dubois. I hope that this book will joins the ranks of those works that help film lovers appreciate the work of the Hollywood composer. Moreover, as a hopelessly amateur and occasional composer, I was fascinated by the factors that influenced certain compositional choices on the part of the composer. And I was particularly interested in what musical elements contributed to the effectiveness of motifs and cues in film scores. Why is there this sense of rightness about the melodic and harmonic elements that Jerry Goldsmith employed to create the theme "Coach" for the film *Hoosiers*? What is at work in those wonderful Korngold love themes in historical romances like *Captain Blood, The Sea Hawk,* and *The Adventures of Robin Hood*? Why and how do they capture the emotions of love and devotion shared by the leads? Personally, I never had a problem freely admitting that I was moved by such musical-cinematic moments. I also arrived at the conclusion, based on continuing practice within genres, that composers must have known that not only I but thousands of others were similarly moved. I wanted to understand that phenomenon a little better. Over the last two decades more and more musicologists and practitioners have dealt with some of these topics, notably Royal Brown, Claudia Gorbman, James Buhler, Irwin Bazelon, George Burt, and Roy Prendergast. But none have focused exclusively on or paid a lot of attention to genres and conventions of scoring in genre films.

Consequently, I was drawn to the idea of looking exclusively at genres. Growing up when I did, as a baby-boomer, and being exposed to classic Hollywood films (both through the movie theater and television), I found, like most moviegoers, that I had some favorite film genres. That interest eventually turned into a scholarly preoccupation when I entered graduate school and began my formal study of popular culture at Bowling Green State University. When I began my study and research into film, I quite naturally then gravitated toward genres, my first article being devoted to the movie musical. Over the years I have written on the music in science fiction and sports films and, in television studies, the variety show. As I explored the music of genre films, I was continually struck by how little had been done with scoring in film genres as genres. What seemed to be at work in film music scholarship were two factors: one, an assumption that somehow we all knew inchoately what the conventions of scoring were; second, a tendency for elitism to lead most scholars to seek out the best scores and composers, relegating generic convention to the background or negating the demands (commercially and artistically) of the genres completely. Growing up as I did and teaching in an educational culture that exalted "art" and that viewed the popular arts with suspicion and, frankly, contempt, I sometimes wondered if scholars were dissuaded from dealing head on with generic convention because it would have been seen as validating the evils of a system (capitalist, studio, etc.) as well as an admission that composers were subject to forces other than their own creativity. Embedded in this tendency, there seemed to be another unspoken assumption: that if composers did indeed conform to generic conventions and industry practice, they could not possibly produce quality work. Although the notion of the aesthetics of film music composition is an important one, I felt that I needed to focus on how the scores work as part of the films, on how they function as part of the mythmaking process of the genre film and, in general, on how well they complement the construction of theme and meaning in films.

And so what I have done is identify some major film genres (one commentator refers to them as the royal genres), and I have attempted to explore the conventions of scoring that complement the narrative conventions. Those narrative conventions, moreover, are framed and analyzed in light of another research interest of mine: popular mythology. In this book, I am in a sense demonstrating how the composers engage in a type of musical mythopoesis when they score genre movies by merit of underscoring the narrative conventions of the genres, which are, after all, the building blocks in the narrative myths being presented on the screen.

As I note in the introduction, my interest in myth stems from my fascination with the dual — or perhaps better, ambiguous — nature of myth. On the one hand, there are those who say myths are pervasive and, some contend, essential to the life of a culture; on the other hand, there are those who view myths less sanguinely, seeing them as traps, delusions, and potentially fraught with evil implications. This book touches on that debate but is, ultimately, more concerned with the interplay between musical and narrative mythopoesis in genre films.

As with any major work of research, there are a number of people I want to thank for their help and support over the years. I want to thank my colleagues at Shawnee State University, Darren Harris-Fain and Roberta Milliken, for taking the time to read selected chapters of the book; their insights, encouragement, and suggestions are most appreciated. I also want to thank my friends and former Bowling Green colleagues Michael Marsden and Jack Nachbar for encouraging my interest in genre films and giving me the opportunity to publish my first article while still a grad student at Bowling Green and for their ongoing interest and support of my scholarship over the years. My thanks to James D'Arc at Brigham Young University for helping me secure the music for the trailer for *The Big Sleep* and to Keith Zajic at Warner Brothers music for giving me permission to look at the score. I also want to thank John W. Waxman for granting me access to Franz Waxman's score for *Rebecca*, which is housed at the Syracuse University Library; and I especially wish to thank the people at the Syracuse University Library Special Collections Research Center for making Roy Webb's scores for *Murder My Sweet* and *Cat People* from the Christopher Palmer Collection of Roy Webb Scores available for study. My thanks as well to James Fitzpatrick at Tadlow Music who made conductor's scores of James Bernard's music for the Hammer Dracula films available to me. John Wagstaff, head of the Music Library at the University of Illinois at Urbana-Champaign, was particularly helpful in supplying information on Frank Skinner's score for *All That Heaven Allows*. I am very grateful to Michael Field, provost at Shawnee State University, for allowing me to pursue the research and writing of this book as part of a summer chairperson's project in 2004. I very much appreciated having the time to bring the writing of the book near conclusion.

I owe a particular debt of gratitude to Tony Bremner, a talented performer, composer (of serious and film music), and conductor, for his encouragement, support, and friendship during the writing of this book. In addition to helping with transcriptions of cues, sharing insights into scoring, and providing information on certain composers, he read the entire manuscript, asked thought-provoking questions, and made many valuable suggestions to improve the manuscript. I do not know how I can ever repay him for his wisdom, creativity, sense of humor, and helpfulness in this process.

Finally, none of this would have been possible without the love and support of my family. My son Andy helped out with a number of transcriptions and could be counted on to double-check my own efforts. My wife Pam read selected chapters, but more than that has encouraged and supported me throughout this entire process, especially during a difficult job transition a few years ago when it looked as though this book would never see publication.

We have shared many memorable moviegoing experiences over the years and we have seen most of the movies in this book together. Consequently, she has been not only the best "date" anyone could wish to see a movie with, but also the major sounding board for my ideas. Thankfully, she has never allowed me to be lax in any part of the scholarly enterprise. My successes as a teacher, administrator and scholar are largely the result of her friendship, love and unflagging support of my dreams and ambitions. In short, I could not have done this without her.

Part One

❧

Major Genres

1

Introduction

Film Genre/Film Music

There's a long, dark passageway, lit only by an artificial source of light coming through a cloudy window at the end. The character enters the hallway, a silhouette against the light. The sound of low staccato notes played softly at first by a piano is heard as the character begins to walk down the corridor. It is a throbbing but irregular pulse that tells you that something is not quite right. As the character walks down the hall, the camera steadily pulls in on him and you hear a pattern of subtly intoned and sustained chords coming from muted low brass. We hear a trilling from the high strings and then we hear a discordant melody picked up by the woodwinds. At this point you might shift uneasily in your seat or mumble to your companion, "This gives me the creeps!" The music grows steadily louder as the camera tracks in on the face of the person until there's a flash of light from the left; the camera pans quickly, accompanied by a screaming glissando in the strings countered by a rapid figure in the bass notes, the character turns, and...

If you had to guess what kind of film this scene was taken from, I'm sure the answers would vary to some degree, but common responses might include a *film noir* thriller, a mystery, or a horror film. The scene could fit into any number of films — even a musical — but the scene as described with that particular kind of music is one we most often associate with the three genres just mentioned. The key element in identifying the genre here was the combination of the visuals and the music that underscored the scene. This book is about that relationship.

My objectives in this analysis of film music are twofold. First, using ideas drawn from new musicology and semiotics, I will analyze the musical conventions and inventions that underscore the narrative conventions of film genres. Second, I will explore the dialogic relationship that exists between the fundamental (or kernel/nuclear) narrative components of film genres (what Rick Altman has described as "the dual correspondence" of film semantics and film syntax) and the musical leitmotivs, topics, and gestures that underscore those self-same narrative-generic conventions. I am particularly interested in the relationship between genre, cultural myths (especially popular myths), and musical mythopoesis (i.e., mythmaking). Like most critics who study genres, I couldn't help but observe patterns in scoring, and like most film music scholars, I began wondering what determined on a largely formalistic scale the musical choices made to underscore characters (the cowboy, the detective, the alien), settings (the West, the city, outer space), and bits of narrative action (gunfights in Westerns, spectacle in historical romances, the first encounter with the alien in science fiction).

Film Genre: A Transformational Approach

Always the same but not in the same way.— Heinrich Schenker, *Free Composition*

The study of genres has been an important focus in film studies ever since critics and scholars began writing about film as art. Genre films rightly or wrongly have been seen as the life's blood of the Hollywood studio system from the early days of the silents (one of the first significant American narrative films, *The Great Train Robbery* [1903], was a Western) and through its heyday in the 1930s, 1940s and 1950s. Although changes in the production and distribution system within in the industry in the '50s and '60s radically altered some genres, these forces did not diminish the need for genre films; in fact, some of the biggest films since the late '90s have been genre films: *Titanic* (disaster film and also historical romance), *L.A. Confidential* (detective mystery), *Gladiator* (historical epic), and the *Lord of the Rings* trilogy (fantasy). Genre study, moreover, has passed through almost as many transformations as the genres themselves. In general, one might say genre study began by focusing on the stable elements (or conventions) and constructing theories and analyses predicated on the belief that genres intrinsically and transhistorically adhered to a largely formulaic — or stable — structure. More recently, scholars have questioned concepts of generic stability as well as the nature and boundaries of film genres, broadening the scope of genre to include analyses of women's films, sports films, blended genres, and the like. Theory, correspondingly, has shifted to deconstructive approaches, focusing more on change (some would characterize it as evolution) and instability within genres. Scholars have, moreover, begun to take an interest in industry factors like production, distribution and discourse to understand the interplay of stability and flux within genre films. Consequently, anyone choosing an approach to study the films or, like myself, the music, must deal with this evolution of theory. What I hope to do here is suggest an approach to analyzing the musical conventions (leitmotifs, topics, gestures) that accounts for narrative conventions as well as for what Rick Altman terms "semantic changes" that occur in the films and, consequently, in the musical scores within genres and across generic boundaries. Because of the comprehensive studies of genre by Rick Altman and Steve Neale, it is not necessary for me to engage in a thoroughgoing historical overview of the topic, but I will cover some of the main points in the debate as I outline my approach to the transformational genre.

Most of us who have written about genre or taught it over the years probably were trying to account for and understand patterns that emerged in the narrative and the visual iconography unfolding on the screen. As I stated in the preface, that is what led me to this place. One goes to see a Western and one expects certain things to happen on the screen — plain and simple. Cowboys behave in specific ways and are possessed of specific hero-skills; women assume certain culturally encoded roles as representatives of civilized or "wilderness" values; the range of villains seems at times quite diverse, but they are also linked by certain values — values, we find moreover, not in accordance with the culturally sanctioned values that have been communicated to us through parents, church and school. Thomas Schatz, drawing on Claude Levi-Strauss and Roman Jakobson, states: "Like language and myth, the film genre as a textual system represents a set of rules of construction that are utilized to accomplish a specific communicative function" (*Film Genre Reader* 96). In many early analyses, the critic and scholar saw in redundancy narrative and thematic significance and pursued that premise. Consequently, we began to place great stock in the stability of generic elements to the exclusion of what they call in semiotics "marked" elements, unusual or anomalous elements which in time might play increasingly greater roles and result in significant transformations of genres. General studies of film and early specialized studies by people like Stanley Solomon, Thomas Schatz, Stuart Kaminsky, and Barry Grant place strong emphasis on generic conventions and provided us with a good roadmaps to begin our journey of generic exploration.

Film criticism itself, however, has evolved over the years and as a discipline has become increasingly more complex. No longer is it English teachers applying literary criticism to an alien medium; instead the field has attracted brilliant scholars who have challenged what Altman calls "the neo-classical model's straight line nature" and have looked more closely at genres and dared to ask if those conventions are indeed all that stable. Are Bogart and Powell (*The Big Sleep* and *Murder My Sweet*) really the same detective as Glenn Ford in *The Big Heat*? Does the comedy of *Destry Rides Again* subvert the mythic roots of the Western? Is *Them* science fiction or horror? How did genres get their finalized names? Recent overviews by Altman and Neale, moreover, reveal a fascinating industry discourse in which films are generically "branded" by *Variety* reviewers and PR people at the studios, often so inconsistently that one wonders if it's the same genre you are studying or watching on TCM. Reception studies have asked us to assess what audiences go for and get out of the moviegoing experience: did Johnny even give a damn if it was a Western or was he there to see Gene Autry? And what do we do with those hybrids (the horror movie set in the 19th century West)? And why haven't we allowed "women's films," sports films, and even melodrama into the generic "canon"? Barbara Klinger, in her analysis of the "progressive genre," cites examples of genre films from the '40s and '50s where one might assume a body of stable conventions and an affirmation of dominant cultural values, but where, in fact, there is an atmosphere of the "bleak, cynical, apocalyptic, and/or highly ironic ... in such a way as to disturb or disable an unproblematic transmission or affirmative ideology" (*Cinema/Ideology* 81). The conclusion that critics have come to is that, as Altman states, "Genres are not just *post facto* categories, then, but part of the constant category-splitting/category-creating dialectic that constitutes the history of types and terminology" (*Film/Genre* 65). In short, cultural studies and other approaches have forced us to look beyond text alone for meaning and significance in film genres. Rick Altman's argument for a "broader understanding" of genre is rooted, as he notes, in the significant changes that have attended "the break-up of the social, economic and political structures subtending the neo-classical system" (*Film/Genre* 180). It would be foolish to think that such cultural tremors would not be felt in the industry and by filmmakers. Scholars, consequently, have felt compelled to illuminate the generic elements that support instability. As Barbara Klinger writes, "The progressive generic text is ... antirealist, as it rattles the perfect illusionism transmitted by a major sector of classic cinema. Assessments of progressive texts/genres generally establish the features of departure from convention in this way and subsequently endow those features with the edifying effects of 'rupture'" (78). Yet, as Klinger herself notes in the article, there still are those pesky patterns that just don't seem to want to go away. Jason isn't the Wolfman but he still is scary, threatening, and conceivably elicits similar emotions from the audience when he goes on the attack. Apparently, the lapse of 40 years, the breakup of the studio system, two major wars (and a number of troubling minor ones), presidential resignation and scandal, stock market meltdowns and terrorist attacks haven't completely exorcised the spirits of Frankenstein, Dracula, and the Wolfman from the body generic of the contemporary horror film. This has not gone unnoticed by critics and scholars.

Today we are at a point where critics seem to acknowledge the persistence of certain stable elements (even though transformed or altered) coexisting with a persistent inclination toward generic instability. Both Rick Altman and Steve Neale have, moreover, provided expert overviews of this phenomenon and suggestions for how we reconcile the various theories of genre. Altman, in his influential article "A Semantic/Syntactic Approach to Film Genre," proposed an approach that would reconcile stable and progressive elements or what Klinger terms "equilibrium" and "disequilibrium" (88). Altman notes that the approaches had at one point existed (and perhaps still do) as separate approaches: "The semantic approach thus stresses the genre's building blocks, while the syntactic view privileges the structures into which they are arranged" (30). He argues for combining these approaches in order to get at a better insight into what films or corpus of films constitute genres. As he states, in his later *Film/Genre*: "At its most forceful, then, genre is located neither in a common semantics nor in a common syntax, but in the intersection of a common semantics and a common syntax in the combined power of a dual correspondence" (70). The result for him is that "genres arise in one of two fundamental ways: either a relatively stable set of semantic givens is developed through syntactic experimentation into a coherent and durable syntax, or an already existing syntax adopts a new set of semantic elements" ("A Semantic/Syntactic Approach" 34). Steve Neale, similarly, has tackled what he sees as the fluidity and "transience" of genres (217) and offers an insight which echoes the Schenker epigram that opened this section: "The repertoire of generic conventions available at any one point in time is always *in* play rather than simply being replayed, even in the most repetitive of films, genres, and cycles." (219). John Wayne's two big army officer roles in *Rio Grande* and *She Wore a Yellow Ribbon* are decidedly different characters in spite of their similar rank and position in the military and placement on the plains in conflict with the Indians.

Critics perennially propose metaphors to describe this interplay or "dual correspondence" between stable and progressive or semantic vs. syntactic elements in the films. Altman discusses the geologic metaphor ("the simultaneous presence of phenomena formed in radically different periods" [*Film/Genre* 68]) and the evolutionary (which should be self explanatory) and, finally, he offers a metaphor that resonated most with me and that was a cartographic one: "The process of genre creation offers us not a single synchronic chart, but an always incomplete series of superimposed generic images" (*Film/Genre* 70). For me, however, the metaphors, with the exception of Altman's, seemed too orderly or too linear. Geology suggests stratification and a progression through time. Evolution suggests too strongly that genres are moving in a purposeful, linear manner and in a direction that might also suggest constant improvement. I found the term progressive problematic because it seems to suggest that a genre is moving toward a state of perfection or an omega point at which the filmmaker and audience and, I guess, all of genre history might achieve apotheosis (forgive me, Teilhard de Chardin!). The cartographic, on the other hand, allows for the simultaneous existence of older (read stable) conventions while accommodating newer invented (or progressive) elements.

Ironically, opposing views by Altman and Neal on the idea of basic elements or "narrative components" prompted me to begin thinking of film genres in transformational terms. Altman believes that "an approach reducing genres to their narrative components fails to capture generic specificity" (*Film/Genre* 151); while Neale, after his discussion of conventions being "in play," notes that it is "difficult to define genres in anything other than basic terms." (219). Neale's point struck me because it seemed to lead me back to what started me on this whole inquiry: why am I hearing similar motivic elements in genre films on synchronic and diachronic planes? There's a blues motif in a '40s detective film and one in the '60s, and they function similarly in similar dramatic situations. And that was the key for me: dramatic situations. Whatever else may happen and whatever elements or conventions may be layered into the narrative in any genre, film is at heart a dramatic work: it contains characters who are in conflict, and that conflict moves toward some sort of resolution. "The same but not in the same way!"

Perhaps it was because I was largely focusing on music as I began this study, but what struck me as I reflected on different genre films and on Altman's and Neale's assessments was that genre films bore some resemblance to two musical subjects: one was improvisation and the other was theme and variations. Uneasy as I was with trying to find my own metaphor for what I saw in the development of genre films, I kept coming back to these two analogies from music. First, *improvisation* suggests that a performer will be inventing, generating or transforming given melodic materials over a relatively stable musical core (usually it will be a song's harmonic progression). What I saw happening in genre films and the music in genre films was not unlike Charlie Parker's reworking of the progressions from Gershwin's "I Got Rhythm" to create his own "Anthropology."[1] Of course what he fashions is something new, but, if you have what Anahid Kassabian (and others) call "competence," you will also recognize the older (archetypal) progression. Second, the concept of *theme and variations* functions much in the same fashion. A composer takes a basic melody and then reworks the melody, augmenting rhythms, adding notes, altering tempi but always retaining some element of the original tune in the variation. The following excerpt from Mozart's "Variations on 'Ah vous dirai-je maman'" K. 265 will illustrate the idea. Figure 1.1 shows the basic theme and Figure 1.2 is the first variation. In the figure of the first variation, I have designated the notes from the original theme with inverted carets.

This led me to conclude that what I saw happening in improvisation and theme and

Figure 1.1.

Figure 1.2.

variations and genre is not a matter of evolution or progression as much as it is transformation or generation of new ideas from a core of stable elements. The idea of transformation in genres had been broached by Alastair Fowler in his book *Kinds of Literature: An Introduction to the Theory of Genres and Modes* (Oxford: Oxford University Press, 1982). As I further reflected on this idea of generic transformation, I was reminded of the basic tenets of Noam Chomsky's early theories of transformational grammar, and I investigated to see if there might be something in the concept of transformational grammar that would help me frame my approach.

I will begin this discussion of my approach to the transformational genre with a caveat: analogies, metaphors, and conceptual frameworks borrowed from other arts or scientific disciplines provide us with but a provisional understanding of how something functions. I have read enough now in genre theory and musicology to arrive at a simple conclusion: film is not language or literature or a mural, and music is not a language or — in its absolute forms — a narrative. Consequently, I can say up front that my approach borrows only the most rudimentary concepts from transformational grammar; concepts, moreover, that help me understand the interplay of musical elements and visual elements and how they change or do not change over the years. What came to mind from Chomsky that resonated with me was the idea of the deep structure and the kernel sentence. A typical example of this is provided by John Lyons in his overview of Chomsky's work: "All the following sentences are related in that they derive from the same underlying string:

1. The man opened the door.
2. The man did not open the door.
3. Did the man open the door?
4. Didn't the man open the door?
5. The door was opened by the man.
6. The door was not opened by the man.
7. Was the door opened by the man?
8. Wasn't the door opened by the man?" [82–83]

Most will recognize the first sentence here as the "kernel sentence" and as, Lyons notes, the remaining sentences differ based on the application of different transformational rules to each. Similarly, a transformational approach to genre study suggests that we are aware of a deep structure in *all* films, a deep structure that is akin to the kernel sentence in Chomksy's theory or the harmonic progression in jazz or even the "fundamental structure" that informs Heinrich Schenker's theories of tonal music outlined below:

This, Schenker posited, is the underlying foundation for most musical compositions and the structure that led Schenker to his aphoristic insight, "The same but not in the same way." The task in genre analysis is to identify a kernel structure that functions the "same but not in the same way" intragenerically and transgenerically, the generic equivalent to what Raymond Monelle

Figure 1.3. Schenker's two part contrapuntal progression.

identifies as a "*semic nucleus*" in music (99–100). To briefly return to jazz: the following may be the chord progression in the "head" of my song: C-Am6-F-Dm-G7-C. If I choose to alter the harmonies as such: Cmaj.7-Am9-F11-Dm6-G7-C13, the potential for melodic transformation is enhanced to be sure, but the "kernel structure," the nucleus, remains the same. I think this roughly corresponds to Altman's thoughts on changes in the semantic and syntactic components of genres. In looking at film genres, I would stress that this kernel structure, as I suggested above, must be rooted in the fundamental dramatic conventions of film in general. Were I talking about real "progressive" films, I would be more hesitant about suggesting that we can (or should) identify a kernel structure or nucleus of the film; but I think there is consensus that the persistence of conventional elements in major genres, even though they may be "in play," suggests the presence of a traditional dramatic archetype. A transformational approach to genre and genre film music that grounds the analysis in the "narrative components," first, allows us to privilege the dramatic elements of the narrative (important, as we shall see, for myth and audience expectations) and, second, provides us with relatively stable dramatic "benchmarks" to determine, interrogate, and evaluate generic transformation. The following diagram illustrates the kernel structure of the Western.

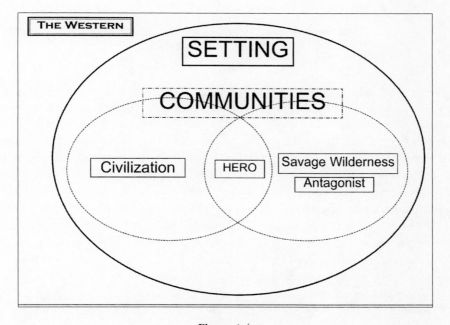

Figure 1.4.

Every film has a setting and that setting is going to generate a certain set of characters, potential conflicts, and other iconographic elements. The L.A. of *The Big Sleep* will not generate Colonel Nathan Brittles! But a Western setting does generate Colonel Brittles and John Dunbar of *Dances with Wolves*. That they are different army men is part of the transformational nature of genre. Dunbar is a variation or, if you will, an improvisation on Brittles; how he came to be transformed will be discussed in time here. The following Venn diagram illustrates the transformational nature of the "cowboy-military" hero in two films:

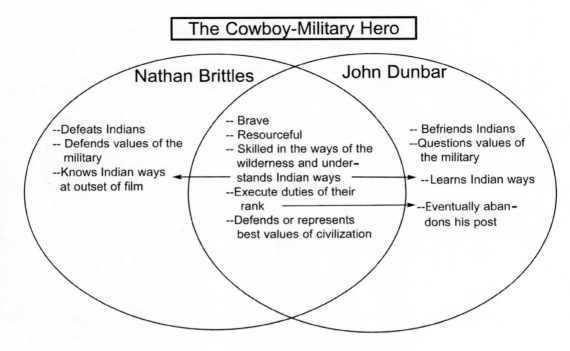

Figure 1.5.

Like Altman's semantic/syntactic approach, thinking of genres as generative and transformational art forms enables us to reconcile the persistence of stable conventions with new perspectives on conventional elements as well as newly imagined elements (i.e., what John Cawelti calls inventions). In the above diagram, we could actually (cartographically speaking) layer in another circle with a different cowboy hero; it would reveal a field of shared characteristics and two fields of inventional elements. Thinking of genres in syntactic/semantic terms or transformational terms emphasizes fluidity over linearity. It, moreover, does not make essentialist claims for the specificity of generic conventions but only for a fundamental structure shared by a large majority of films (and theatre). It is for that reason that each chapter will feature a comparative analysis of at least two scores; by doing this we should be able to see which conventions have indeed remained stable and which conventions (and possibly even whole genres) have been transformed by what I call contextual agents.

Genre/Myth

My interest in a transformational approach to genre is rooted in my belief that the element of generic stability is in great measure attributable to the mythic foundations and formations in the major genres. Leo Braudy states: "Like fairy tales or classical myths, genre films concentrate on large contrasts and juxtapositions. Genre plots are usually dismissed with a snide synopsis (a process that is never very kind to drama that employs conventions, like Shakespeare's plays). But, amid the conventions and expectations of plot, other kinds of emphasis can flourish" (*Genre* 668–669). Rick Altman has observed that the "pleasure of genre film spectatorship ... derives more from reaffirmation than from novelty. People go to genre films to participate in events that somehow seem familiar" (*Film/Genre* 25). Myths reinforce that familiarity by articulating and validating a community's beliefs through dramatic narratives. Nimmo and Combs, for instance, define myth as a "credible, dramatic, socially constructed representation of perceived realities that people accept as permanent, fixed knowledge of reality while forgetting (if they ever were aware of it) its tentative, imaginative, created, and perhaps fictional qualities" (16). Genres and myth share two important and related functions. First, they present beliefs and values in narrative frameworks that are grounded in history but that in fact may not validate historical or sociological accuracy. We may say, borrowing from Barthes, that a genre in its mythical depiction of history "deprives the object of which it speaks all History. In [myth] history evaporates. It is a kind of ideal servant: it prepares all things, brings them, lays them out, the master arrives, it silently disappears: all that is left for one to do is to enjoy this beautiful object without wondering where it comes from" ("Myth Today" 140). Barthes suggests that myths evoke this kind of response as a result of the way in which we "read" or "focus" on them. My semiotic reading of motifs, topics and gestures in genre film music correlates well with this approach to myth and genre and the way music and image dialogically create signs in the films. Barthes discusses three ways in which myth can be read and, in discussing the third, he states: "The third type of focusing is dynamic, it consumes the myth according to the very ends built into its structure: the reader lives the myth as a story at once true and unreal" (115). He goes on to note that "if I focus on the mythical signifier as on an inextricable whole made of meaning and form, I receive an ambiguous signification: I respond to the constituting mechanism of myth, to its own dynamic" ("Myth Today" 115). So if we apply this to a classic historical romance, like *Captain Blood*, we would discover this: viewers are not engaged in Barthes's first type of reading or focusing where they watch the film and say "Errol Flynn is an example of a romantic hero in the form of Captain Blood"; nor would they engage in a second type of reading or focusing where they are providing an "alibi," "distinguish[ing] the meaning and form" and thus consciously realize that Errol Flynn is playing the romantic hero Captain Blood (thereby "undoing" the signification); however, the third reading, and the one that probably comes closest to capturing the film experience of the viewer, finds the viewer standing in the "very presence" (115) of the romantic hero Captain Blood.[2] Needless to say, with this reading comes the entire mythic baggage of the genre: the hero battling forces of oppression to restore individual rights and dignity to members of the realm. Would an audience read this film the same way today? Probably not in the same way as an audience in 1939. There may be, however, enough power in the basic conflict in the narrative (free people seeking to overthrow oppressors) to mitigate some of the demythologizing potentialities of other contextual agents and possible interpretants (in Peirce's approach to semiotics) that viewers may still find themselves in the "very presence" of Captain Blood. In short, an audience's reading may be the same but not in the same way. In its generative or transformational mode, generic mythology is always provisional. Barthes, in fact, notes that "there is no fixity in mythical concepts: they can come into being, alter, disintegrate, disappear completely. And it is precisely because they are historical that history can very easily suppress them" (106).

A second function that genres share with myth is, as Joseph Campbell notes of myth, "the enforcement of a moral order: the shaping of the individual to the requirements of his geographically and historically conditioned social group"; he goes on to note that, "moreover, it is in this moral, sociological sphere that authority and coercion come into play" (*The Masks of God: Creative Mythology* 4–5). If we think of film genres in mythic terms, we come to understand their power and durability over time. Campbell has astutely observed that that "integrity and cogency of [the] supporting canons of myth have been central to the rise and fall of civilizations." He adds, moreover, that "not authority but aspiration is the motivator, builder, and transformer of civilization. A mythological canon is an organization of symbols, ineffable in import, by which the energies of aspiration are evoked and gathered toward a focus" (4–5). The foregoing speaks to what Altman describes as a "generic contract" that involves adherence to particular codes, and, through that adherence, identification with others who so adhere" (*Film/Genre* 157–58). One particular code that "powers" the effectiveness of myth and genre is their ability to resolve some fundamental cultural conflicts. Both myth and drama are concerned with conflict and cultural contradictions and the resolution or reconciliation of those conflicts and contradictions. James Oliver Robertson, echoing Claude Levi-Strauss's notion that myth progresses "from an awareness of oppositions toward their resolution" (*Structural Anthropology* 221), notes that myths "provide good, 'workable' ways by which the contradictions in a society, the contrasts and conflicts which normally arise among people, among ideals, among the confusing realities, are somehow reconciled, smoothed over, or at least made manageable and tolerable" (xv). Referring specifically to genre, Altman similarly notes that genres permit "viewers to consider and resolve (albeit) fictively contradictions that are not full mastered by the society in which they live" (*Film/Genre* 26). This concern for the resolution of conflicts is another reason why focus on the kernel dramatic structure is central to exploring the role of music in genres. As we shall discuss presently, one of the key functions of music in film is to underscore character and conflict.

A second dimension of popular mythology, and by extension genre, is the manner in which these cultural conflicts are resolved. Here we also encounter conflicting theories. On the one hand, there are those who focus on the stable elements in genre and then see how the films conform to a predetermined resolution (rooted in the very codes that I cited in Altman's quote above); on the other hand, are those who look more to what Steve Neale calls "variation and change" (208) in the resolution, the bottom line being not that there is a predetermined resolution but only that we can expect a resolution. Genres, like myths, are indeed sites where cultural conflicts are worked out and resolved, oftentimes reaffirming the values and ideologies of the dominant culture. Consequently, during the '30s, '40s, and '50s the majority of Westerns, as John Cawelti notes, dealt with the struggle of the forces of civilization (settlers, farmers, business people, church) coming into contact with the forces of the wilderness (Native Americans, greedy land barons, outlaws of various sorts) and, through the agency of the cowboy hero, civilization triumphing over the forces of the savage wilderness. The resolution of the conflict, moreover, is a validation (or reaffirmation) of values held by predominantly white middle class viewers: Dance hall girls give way to schoolmarms; greedy land barons make way for simple farmers; paganism and sin give way to Christianity; the way of the gun gives way to the way of the law book or the marshal's badge, e.g. law and order, etc.

We need also to consider the *manner* in which the conflict is resolved. Here we may find that genre, unlike myth, takes a simpler route to reconciling oppositions. Judith Wright Hess notes, "These films [genre films] came into being and were financially successful because they temporarily relieved the fears aroused by a recognition of social and political conflicts" (41). She goes on to state that the resolution to these political, social, and economic conflicts is handled "in a simplistic and reactionary way" (41). Taking Neale's tack, however, we might see this resolution a little less simplistically. For instance, if we take *The*

Maltese Falcon and *The Big Sleep* and examine their respective resolutions, we find that in the case of the former, the resolution is not really all that pat. Justice, indeed, is triumphant, but Sam Spade does not walk away with any ostensible rewards, and one might conclude that he actually, to quote Chico Marx, loses in the deal: no Falcon, no girl, and probably no retainer. But he walks away with his integrity intact and with the audience assured that crime can be solved and justice can prevail. Phillip Marlowe, on the other hand, walks away with it all — a very satisfying conclusion: he gets the girl, probably a nice settlement from Colonel Sternwood, and he can take some comfort that he may have been instrumental in the tentative healing within the dysfunctional Sternwood clan; all this and he keeps his integrity and the bad guys get it. The latter resolution very much supports Warner's contention that films are fantasy while the former seems to reassert the problematic nature of justice in the modern world. We should not be surprised, then, if we find critics questioning Jack Warner's notion that genre films are fantasy, owing to their tendency to portray a world in which difficult conflicts and contradictions are resolved to the viewer's satisfaction. Klinger notes that one of the consequences of the "progressive genre" is that "the overall narrative structure is refined toward an exposure — rather than a suppression, as in the classic text — of ideological contradictions and tensions" (*Film Genre Reader* 83). In short, as she adds, the genres almost seem to "'refuse' closure" (83). This is debatable: as we shall see in my analysis of *Chinatown*, the film does reach closure; it is not as pleasurable as the outcome in the two abovementioned detective films, but it does resolve the conflict and does indeed validate a more widely held belief about justice and law and order in the culture of the 1970s (and probably in 2005).

Another important element in the relationship between genre, myth, and music is ritual. This is where the conventions of the genre (that set of "rules of construction" of which Schatz speaks) come into play. John Cawelti uses the term formula to describe this phenomenon (*The Six-Gun Mystique* 29). Genres use certain elements (conventions) repeatedly because they achieve a desired response. The response works on two levels: first, from a purely artistic and formalistic viewpoint the conventions are assembled in a set pattern that satisfactorily brings the conflict to a resolution; second, the working out of that conflict satisfies the viewer's expectations — this does not mean the viewers walk away happy but only secure in having their values validated. For instance, if a film opens with a dead body (and mysterious circumstances) or a crime (robbery), one can assume that there is a killer and that the killer will have to be brought to justice; hence, it's a detective or mystery story. From that point on the conventions of the genre will be introduced until the crime is solved and the killer is apprehended; justice will triumph and law and order win out over lawlessness and violence. Although there may be variations in future films in the detective corpus (or any genre corpus for that matter), the viewers pretty much know what's going to happen as the plot unfolds, much as they would at a church service. Inventions, as Cawelti calls them, (*The Six-Gun Mystique* 27). or Altman's semantic changes will be introduced into works to breathe new life into the formulas and also to better reflect current beliefs, values, or ideologies. In time, inventional elements may contribute to the transformation of the genre by altering the fundamental conflict, at which point the viewing ritual faces a test among "the faithful": do the transformations allow for a satisfying viewing experience or has the ritual been so altered that the "ceremony" is no longer recognizable and, consequently, rendered an alienating as opposed to an affirmative experience? One example of this would be the role of women in historical romances: as we shall see, the Maid

Marian of the '90s version of Robin Hood is a different woman than Olivia de Havilland's Maid Marian from the 1938 version of the legend. The '90s Maid Marian is an equal match for Costner's Robin intellectually and physically, demonstrated clearly in her ability to hold her own in a sword fight with Robin early in the film. In short, one will still find a love interest in the historical romance but the heroine will probably be fundamentally different from her studio system forebears, reflecting not only improved historical scholarship but also a stronger feminist perspective in contemporary society. A key thing to emphasize here, however, is that in spite of changes in our historical knowledge and how we choose to portray women in film, the convention is still part of the genre and the formula; the ritual largely remains intact. As we shall see, music plays an important role in this ritual aspect. It is a necessary adjunct to the mystery and suspense which underlies the uncertainty of the detective's quest to get the killer — oh, we know he or she is going to get the person, but we also expect some uncertainty: it's one of the conventions. Over time, moreover, one comes to expect a certain type of music to underscore the swashbuckling derring-do of the hero of a historical romance or the first glimpse of the alien in a science fiction film or a gunfight in the streets of Dodge City or, as in my opening illustration, a spooky or eerie scene in a mystery.

In conclusion, in keeping with my philosophy that we cannot conveniently apply a theoretical construct from one discipline to another, I will reiterate that my borrowing of the transformational concept must be read in terms of film alone. Therefore, I will not, like grammarians, be offering a set of rules that would influence the transformation of musical conventions in the films. In keeping with genre theory, however, I will suggest that a host of what I call contextual agents, intrinsic and extrinsic elements that act on the collaborative filmmaking team, influence generic transformations. The notion of agency strikes me as more flexible, less rule-bound, and more in keeping with the fluid nature of generic transformation. Consequently, industry economics may work in concert with trends in music composition (serious music composition) to influence the sound and style of a contemporary horror film. The figure on the following page presents just some of the contextual agents that might influence genre film music composition.

Let us first begin with agents within music and film music in particular and then move on to extramusical agents.

Film Music: Myth, Leitmotif, Topic and Gesture

The music of most genre films largely conforms to the model of film music we associate with the classic Hollywood film. Because the subject of the classical Hollywood film score has been expertly handled by others, ranging from early works by Roger Manvell and John Huntley and Tony Thomas to more recent works by scholars such as Kathyrn Kalinak, Claudia Gorbman and Royal S. Brown and practitioners such as Irwin Bazelon and Fred Karlin,[3] it is not necessary for me to go into great depth about the history, conventions, theories and practices of scoring these films. However, let me briefly summarize some of the main theories about music in the classic Hollywood film that I feel are particularly relevant to genre films.

Let's begin with the function of the film score. Film music evolved rapidly from the days of the silents, when the musical accompaniment was as much a way to cover up projector noise as it was an integral part of the drama unfolding on the screen, to a time when movies of the studio era moved into palaces and orchestral accompaniment became the order of the

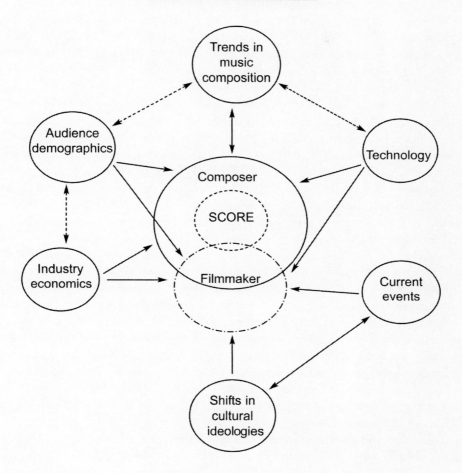

Contextual Agents

Figure 1.6.

day. In the silent era, the scores for most films largely remained a pastiche of musical selections culled from classical and light classical libraries, but musical accompaniment to films would soon become its own industry with, initially, composers and Tin Pan Alley songwriters supplying theme songs for silents. With the dawn of the "talkies," composers were hired to supply complete scores for the films, and during the 1930s composers such as Max Steiner and Erich Wolfgang Korngold put their indelible stamp on the motion picture score. Through their efforts (and that of other composers) the film score began to assume some clearly defined parameters and functions. Kathryn Kalinak describes the conventions of the classic Hollywood film score as follows:

> These conventions included the use of music to sustain structural unity, music to illustrate narrative content, both implicit and explicit, including a high degree of direct synchronization between music and narrative action; and the privileging of dialogue over other elements of the soundtrack. The medium of the classical Hollywood film score was largely symphonic; its idiom romantic; and its formal unity typically derived from the principle of the leitmotif [*Settling the Score* 79].

The film score now had a very definite dramatic function in the film. Kalinak adds: "The starting point for the creation of a musical cue[4] was the image. Its content was gauged in two ways: that which was explicitly in the image, such as action, and that which was implicit, such as emotion or mood" (83–84). Music now not only seemed to accompany action but, in a sense, seemed to comment on it as well: bugle calls and militaristic music underscored the charge of the cavalry; lushly orchestrated and soaring melodies accompanied the lover's embrace; even settings, like Tara in *Gone with the Wind* (1939), might have their own motif or theme — in the case of the aforementioned a soaring four note opening motif with a dramatic opening leap of an octave followed by a leap downward of a third and then resting on the fifth: all in all, good, solid and inspiring writing that effectively captured Gerald and Scarlett O'Hara's noble and passionate feeling for the plantation. Claudia Gorbman states that the film score helped ward off the "displeasure of uncertain signification.... It *interprets* the image, pinpoints and channels the 'correct' meaning of the narrative events depicted" (*Unheard Melodies* 58). Royal S. Brown says something very similar when he notes that "nondiegetic film music functions on at least three levels: (a) as a wallpaper soporific to allay fears of darkness and silence; in the silent era, it also helped mask the sound of the projector; (b) as an aesthetic counter-balance to the iconic/representational nature of the cinematic signs which, although they do not require music to validate the language they create as artistic, get that help anyway; (c) as a cogenerator of narrative affect that skews the viewer/listener towards a culturally determined reading of the characters and situations" (*Overtones and Undertones* 32). It is Gorbman's comment and Brown's functions "b" and "c" that are particularly relevant to my semiotic analysis of music in genre films. Throughout this study I will examine how leitmotivs, topics and gestures provide this "aesthetic counterbalance to the iconic" image on the screen. I will simultaneously focus on the element of expressivity in the music and on identifying distinct generic musical conventions (leitmotivs, topics and gestures) that support and explicate the kernel structure of the film (the mythological functions) and clarify the role of other narrative conventions.

Music, then, helps the viewer delineate and interpret conflict, characters and symbols in the films. Claudia Gorbman, for instance, notes that one of the "Principles of Composition" is "Narrative cueing" which, she says, can be *referential/narrative:* music gives referential and narrative cues, e.g., indicating point of view, supplying formal demarcations, and establishing setting and characters." And it can be *connotative:* music 'interprets' and 'illustrates' narrative events" (73). Music plays an important role in the construction of the mythology that informs genre films by signification of emotional states, cultural codes, and symbols associated with conventions like setting, iconography and character. Music also does this in certain prescribed ways, hence the ritual aspect; musical cues are indeed musical cues: one hears a particular musical gesture or topic and one is cued to interpret that filmic moment in a certain way by merit of the music's ability to engage the emotions of the viewer. For instance, Irwin Bazelon writes of the film score: "It is essentially dramatic, not descriptive, adding an extra emotional dimension to the cinematic assault already being waged on the visual senses" (77). Similarly, Leonard Rosenman has talked about "supra-reality" in film music: something that goes beyond the image, so that "elements of literary naturalism are perceptibly altered. In this way the audience can have insight into different aspects of behavior and motivation not possible under the aegis of naturalism" (qtd. in Prendergast 217). Music then transforms the viewing experience from a purely observed (viewed) or even intellectual thing to a felt thing; to quote Royal Brown, "It is, then, the merging of the cinematic object-event and the musical score into the surface narrative that transforms the morphological affect of music into specific emotions and allows us to 'have them' while also imputing them to someone and/or something else, namely the cinematic character and/or situation" (*Overtones* 27). For example, we shall see that composers from Wagner to Korngold to Horner have relied upon certain musical topics and gestures to accompany or underscore the actions of heroes on the stage and screen; however, the topics and gestures are bound to vary somewhat from genre to genre: in short, the music to underscore the setting in historical romance will differ from that of the cowboy hero depending on the historical backdrop and time period, with, for instance, the historical romance employing the "minuet" topic and the Western employing the "pastoral."[5] But at the heart of these topics and gestures is the element of expressivity.

Expressivity, the affective phenomenon described by Brown, is central to the mythic foundations of genre film scores and, consequently, to the mythic "reading" of the films themselves. Myth and expressivity in film genre are entwined with the concept of the leitmotiv in films scores because they are fundamental to the topics and gestures that function as building-blocks in leitmotivs. Let me first begin with a brief overview of the debate about the ability of music to communicate ideas and emotional states. Eduard Hanslick's influential *On the Musically Beautiful: A Contribution towards the Revision of the Aesthetics of Music* (1854) was one of the first volumes to question the affective and, from an expressivity standpoint, the signifying power of music. He forced musicologists to question whether a piece of absolute music could actually express grief, happiness, longing and the like. His arguments even forced critics to question the signifying ability of program music: does the music in the third movement of Beethoven's Sixth Symphony (the *Pastoral*) really communicate the idea of a storm (or do we know that only because of program notes), and does the "Liebestod" really express eroticism and yearning and is that what we feel when we hear it (regardless of what action is being played out on the stage)? There was long period of time when Hanslick's and Stravinsky's anti-affective stance seemed to dominate most theory and interpretation of music. Recently, owing to the theorizing of individuals like Naomi Cumming, David Lidov and Robert Hatten, musicologists working in the field of musical semiotics have generated an impressive body of literature dealing with expressivity in music. I hope to demonstrate that their ideas are particularly relevant to film music and the music of genre films in particular.

Film music lends itself well to the discussion of the expressivity in music because we are not dealing with "absolute" or non-referential music, the music we might hear in a concert setting. John Sloboda states: "It is arguable that music shows the greatest stability in cultural contexts where it is the vehicle for some non-musical activity (the recounting of verse, ritual, etc.)" (38). Thus, when it comes to film music we are reminded that the viewer — notice I said viewer, not auditor — is *hearing* the music as part of a filmic event and not really *listening* to it as a purely musical one. When we hear these notes in a concert hall they may indeed just be that, notes, or maybe pretty notes, or some such other relatively innocuous description.

Figure 1.7. Main title, *Legends of the Fall.*

Might they move you in any way? Perhaps, but perhaps not. These same notes employed in a scene from *Legends of the Fall* (1994), however, will have a better chance of signifying an emotional state as well as communicating something about the theme of the film because they are in service of the development of character and conflict in the film. Another factor in the ability of film music to express affective states is when redundancy is wedded to cultural coding, a phenomenon that results in what Kofi Agawu terms "listener-competence" (49).[6] Redundancy, quite simply, is repetition. If we repeatedly hear a particular style, motivic figure and so forth embedded in a specific context, we will more than likely associate that music with that context. So, how do we come to associate a style of music with, let us say, grief? There is a chance that if we hear this example below we might associate the music with "grief":

Figure 1.8.

If I, however, print the same notes with a score expression of "Marche funebre," interpretive parameters are definitely narrowed.

Figure 1.9. Beethoven, Symphony no. 3, the *Eroica*.

So we know that the composer's intention was to communicate the emotion of grief. However, the filmgoer is not privy to printed scores, so for the person to experience the music as expressive of grief, the expressive capabilities of the music must be contextualized. If you were to hear this entire passage over footage of a funeral cortege, your response and interpretation of the meaning of the music will be further qualified and constrained as a result of it being wedded to a potentially sad image. The redundant hearing of musical elements (the topics and gestures I referred to earlier) that signify emotional states, allied with what I call contextual agents (which could also perhaps be designated as "interpretants" in Peirce's terms), will result in "listener-competence." Kassabian states: "Competence is based on decipherable codes learned through experience. As with language and visual image, we learn through exposure what a given tempo, series of notes, key time signatures, rhythm, volume, and orchestration are meant to signify" (23). In short, repeated hearing of the music from Beethoven's *Eroica* and other music employing minor keys and "tragic" gestures in funereal settings leads us to associate those pieces with the feeling of grief. In the context of film music, the elements of redundancy and expressivity are necessarily studied in the context of leitmotif, topic and gesture.

Myth and Music

If popular myths inform the themes and structure of genres films, it stands to reason that music will play a role in generic mythopoesis. I should begin with a qualification: in terms of musical signification in genre films I think it is important to state that myth can be a secular phenomenon and does not have to be rooted in a spiritual or transcendental experience. Reading Tarasti's analysis of absolute or program music and James Buhler's analysis of the score for *Star Wars*, I got the impression that they interpreted the mythically referential aspect of music rather narrowly, seeing myth as always pointing toward what Buhler describes as "metaphysical significance" ("*Star Wars*, Music and Myth" 42). This may be attributable to two things: One, the writer is working with the old-fashioned notion that myth is a religious phenomenon associated with ancient or primitive cultures. This is a "classic" religious paradigm in myth studies that assumes myth to be part of a spiritual quest or transcendental experience, seeking heavenly (other-worldly) correlatives or explanations for human problems and historical phenomenon. Two, these writers (and others dealing with myth in music) have been influenced by the Romantic approach to myth and, more specifically, Wagner's form of mythmaking in his music dramas. And the culprit in this Romantic approach is the role of the leitmotif. James Buhler, for instance, states, "The primary purpose of Wagner's leitmotif is the production of myth not signification" ("*Star Wars*, Myth and Music 42). Apparently, he means that the leitmotif is used to create and develop the role of the gods of the Niebelung; mythmaking then become an act of creating gods and telling fantastic tales that bring us into contact with the transcendental and supernatural. My approach, however, is much more secular and in keeping with scholarship on myth in communications and popular culture studies. In this vein, I side with Ernst Cassirer, who has observed that the "'mythical' is not a fixed objective quality, but a certain ideal attitude" (qtd. in Tarasti, *Myth and Music* 52); but, it should be noted, "ideal" should not be construed as synonymous with the supernatural or even the transcendent. One of the key factors that attracted me to new musicology as a critical framework for this study is that it is not afraid to entertain the notion of the referential power of music, that music can indeed refer to "something" beyond the arrangement of notes; but just because it refers to the mythic, it does not of necessity have to refer to the spiritual.

One of the first mythopoeic functions of film genre music is the role it plays in reconciling cultural conflicts and contradictions in the film narrative. Eero Tarasti has stated that "myth and music have another common function: they strive for a resolution of contradictions" (33). Absolute music does this through formal and stylistic elements (ABA form; consonance/dissonance, etc.), and film music does this through assigning marked and unmarked[7] musical elements to narrative elements and plot conventions. For instance, Tarasti notes of Liszt's *Tasso* that the hero's struggle is scored in the minor (a "marked" element in Hatten's diagram of expressive genres and topical fields [*Musical Meaning in Beethoven*, 89] while the hero's triumph is scored in the major (an unmarked element). Similarly, in genres, especially those like historical romance and the Western or the sports film, we may find a composer underscoring (or we might say "marking") the struggle of the hero by employing minor harmonies in the "hero's" leitmotif that had earlier been stated in a major key (unmarked). The composer may weave the main motif and its variation throughout the score, but almost inevitably we will see the main motif in the major key returning as "The End" appears on the screen.

Second, music, quite naturally, will be used to highlight and then resolve narrative conflict. It is not unusual to find a motif for a historical romance hero scored in a major key while the villain's motif is scored in the minor. And it should come as no great surprise that in a majority of genre films, the triumph of the hero will be signified by a return to the main title or hero's motif (whichever is most appropriate) and, consequently, to a return to the dominant tonality in that selfsame music (i.e., if the main title is in A major, we can expect the closing title or end theme to also be in A major). The very return to tonality and the tonic is, then, a return to the unmarked, a return to the conventionally encoded musical element that audiences would expect at the film's end and to complement the achievement of the hero. This musical thematic development, moreover, is in keeping with the genre's mythmaking effort at "coercing" a resolution of conflicts and reconciling cultural contradictions embodied in the narrative conflict.

Third, music is instrumental in helping viewers, to quote Barthes, live "the myth as a story at once true and unreal" ("Myth Today" 115). Ernst Cassirer has stated: "The mythical form of conception is not something super-added to certain definite *elements* of empirical existence; instead, the primary 'experience' itself is steeped in the imagery of myth and saturated with its atmosphere" (10). Returning to our historical romance hero, let us say Captain Blood for instance: as he engages in a sword fight or love scene, the motifs employed to underscore his actions should not make us aware that this is a historical figure whose exploits are being reenacted by a movie star; instead, the music should be drawing us, to quote Barthes, into "the very *presence*" (115) of a specific heroic individual (and history be damned!), i.e., this *is* Peter Blood. Culturally encoded topics and expressive gestures emotionally inform the actions and image of the hero on the screen enabling the music to correlate to what Tarasti terms the "immanent narrative structure" (61) and dialogically contribute to a unity of signification and experience that will allow the viewer the live the myth as a story at once true and yet unreal.[8]

Fourth, music functions mythopoeically in film genres through the simple device of placement or, perhaps more accurately, through placement and repetition. Tarasti has observed: "The mythical universe is based on the simple division: before/after (*avant/après*).... Thus, using purely morphological criteria, one could deem mythical any sign in musical discourse which refers to some *preceding* sign" (68). As we shall see, this is where the idea of the leitmotif figures most strongly in the mythical subtext of genre films. To quote Tarasti again: "In this case, 'the mythical' would be an entirely syntagmatic phenomenon: the sign itself has no concrete characteristics, no special 'mythical' quality in the harmony, melody, rhythm, or timbre which would render it mythical. The mythicism results from the fact that we have heard it earlier and only now recall it" (68). In absolute music, a principal theme might be deemed mythic when repeated in the recapitulation; in popular music, the classic AABA formula could be seen as an instance of mythicism; and finally, we might even see the Schenkerian *Ursatz* "mi-re-do" descent and accompanying fundamental I-V-I harmonic structure as a form of mythopoesis. In the way that they are repeated in a score, motifs, topics and gestures resemble what one of my classics teachers referred to as "epic machinery," elements that are often characterized and deemed significant to the narrative by merit of their repetition or their *avant/après* placement in the text; this would include conventions such as epithets ("long-enduring Odysseus"), patronymics ("Penelope, Icarius' daughter"), catalogs, and epic similes.[9] These devices can function individually or in tandem as descriptors, which aid in memorization (for the poet/griot), as indexical signs signifying mythic values, and as mnemonic markers that ensure continuity and comprehension of the narrative — i.e., devices that contribute to the auditor's competency. Similarly, the repeated use of a topic or thematization of a gesture in a film score lends a mythic, *avant/après*, dimension to the music. Closely related to this, to paraphrase Tarasti, is the leitmotif's position in the narrative's syntagma[10]: a particular leitmotif (or gesture employed in a motif) stated to accompany the first appearance of the hero will be repeated, possibly modified, developed and varied within action scenes and the like; if it performs what Barthes might call a "cardinal function" ("Introduction to Structural Analysis of Narratives" 265) such as emphasizing that the hero is impelled to a specific act in response to a threat, the audience will be cued to expect heroic behavior in the ensuing action.

Finally, the contextual agents and interpretants the viewer brings to the theater will influence the mythical quality of the music. Of this last, Tarasti says that a musical sign can refer "to something beyond the work" but "knowledge of this larger paradigm is presupposed" (*Myth and Music* 71); later he adds, "A composer is therefore in many respects subordinated to the automatisms of the codes entailed in his cultural context" (71). The entire mythology of the West will inform musical mythopoesis in the Western film. In addition to previously viewed Westerns, filmgoers bring to their viewing experience values, attitudes, beliefs and feelings influenced by potential interpretants including paintings (a la Russell, Remington, Bierstadt), cowboy tunes (sung either by singing cowboys like Roy Rogers or the high school chorus doing "Cool Water"— if high school choruses do such things anymore), Marlboro ads, and family tales of westward expansion passed down through the generations. These interpretants will influence spectatorship and will become signifying agents depending upon the topic or gesture employed by the composer in underscoring the narrative conventions of the genre. With this in mind, let us turn our attention to the role of leitmotif, topics, and gestures in this musical mythopoesis with some prefatory comments on signs in music.

Leitmotif, Topic and Gesture

Following the lead of most new musicologists, I rely upon Charles Sanders Peirce's tripartite division of signs in my analysis of motifs, topics and gestures and their role in genre film music. Although many commentators discuss film music's expressivity and ability to communicate emotion, the discussions have had a tendency to generalize. The accuracy of the assessment, it should be noted, has seldom been in question, but the specifics have been shadowy as to how we arrive at conclusions like that of Royal Brown, who notes that "musical scores very often tell our emotions how to read a given filmic sequence" (*Overtones and Undertones* 54). Caryl Flinn echoes Brown's observation when she notes that "non-diegetic music, although never directly bound to human forms on the screen, is connected to film's characters by other means — most frequently through the use of leitmotiv — yielding a sense of 'human-ness' in this fashion. And, due to its widely understood connection — via late nineteenth-century romanticism — to emotional expression more generally, music has been associated all the more with the sense of human feeling" (*Strains of Utopia* 42). In short, most commentators are generally in agreement that the music provides an affective element to the film experience. What the new musicology and its focus on semiotics, topics and gestures can offer us is an avenue into exploring Flinn's "widely understood connection" and giving us some meaningful methods to more fully understand how music is expressive of emotion in the film context.

First, one of the major contributions of scholars such as Naomi Cumming, David Lidov and Robert Hatten is that their approach to musical semiotics offers compelling evidence that expressivity in music is more than an individual or idiosyncratic phenomenon.

Cumming, for instance, in discussing descriptive phrases attributed to major violin virtuosos, states:

> What is "heard in" the sounds, under these descriptions, has been heard according to a learned code of recognition. Judgment of what kind of sound is "neutral" will vary between the sub-tradition of performance, but despite this, the recognition of sounds as bearing qualities that marked them as "expressive" is not a matter of private feeling alone. If a "feeling" is involved, it is one whose interpretation has been culturally entrained [17].

This being "entrained" is the result of the factors alluded to earlier, including redundancy and contextual agency (the type of film in which a particular motif or gesture is heard). That we can read expressive elements in music is, for these scholars, located in music functioning as a sign system. Once again, Cumming notes, "I assume that it is a basic psychological proclivity *not* to hear sound as an uninterrupted quality, but to hear it as bearing information that is adaptively useful" (118), a description relevant to film scores where the utilitarian nature of the composition is a foregone conclusion. Cumming notes that "a sign is just a unit of meaning: something that brings to mind an idea, its 'object,' through the operation of an interpretive response, which may be manifested in a feeling, an action (or reaction), or reference to a conventionalized code" (69). Peirce's system works particularly well for music because of its complexity and flexibility, and for that reason I will be relying upon Peirce's categorization of signs by icon, index and symbol, and making only occasional references to his division of qualisigns, sinsigns, and legisigns. Here is a brief definition of these categories:

> A sign is an *icon* to the extent that its significance depends on the inner nature of the sign — typically, some sort of qualitative or structural resemblance between the sign and what it signifies. Paintings, diagrams, and color samples are predominantly icons. A sign is an *index* to the extent that its significance depends on a real connection between the sign and what it signifies. Proper names, demonstrative pronouns, evidence at the scene of a crime, and symptoms of a disease are predominantly indices. Finally, a sign is a *symbol*, Peirce's special sense of this term, to the extent that its significance depends on human convention or an arbitrary decision. Labels on diagrams, Chinese ideograms, and English words are predominantly symbols.... Most signs have more than one aspect [Harmon, "Semiotics and the Cinema: Metz and Wollen" 93–94].

Most new musicologists favor this approach because they find that in absolute music, as Robert Hatten notes (in an echo of Harmon's final statement above), "Signs may be multiply motivated, and the sign vehicle may in turn signify in more than one way" (*Musical Meaning in Beethoven* 258). Hatten then offers this non-musical example to illustrate this point: we see a footprint in the sand; in Peirce's system the footprint can function as an iconic sign, as an image of the foot; it can function as an index by signifying the dynamic action of a foot; and it can function as a symbol, signifying the presence of another human being (as in Robinson Crusoe) (*Musical Meaning in Beethoven* 258). Most of the work done in musical semiotics has dealt with absolute music (and to a lesser extent program music), and so we may find that all three classes are not necessarily present or at work within a particular film sequence and its musical motifs/leitmotifs. In fact, Naomi Cumming notes that "non-verbal indices (examples of indexical sinsigns) suggest a factual situation, and the sense of indexical words (indexical legisigns) depends upon the pragmatic context of their use" (89–90). She adds that "these requirements of indexicality do not look very promising for the exploration of non-textual instrumental music" (90). It is for this reason, however, that the index is all the more relevant to film, that is if we view the image and dialogue as equivalent to the musical text. David Lidov has noted that "the central distinction between the index and icon for Peirce is that the icon is *independent* of its object, whereas the index and its object are *dependent*" (*Semiotics* 148). This sounds like exactly the dynamic at work in film, as image and music work dialogically either as complementary or possibly competing sign systems. I contend that in large measure the sign systems are complementary, almost functioning in a synergistic manner. Caryl Flinn has suggested that the film score — "though less indexical a signifying system than its visual counter-part — secures much the same illusory plenitude to its auditor that theorists have been arguing the image grants for the spectator" (*Strains of Utopia* 46). This is not necessarily an either-or situation; we should perhaps grant the achievement of this plenitude to the synergy of the signs. As we shall see, a majority of motifs and leitmotifs, based on the gestures at play in the motifs, function indexically; but some motifs, those especially which we shall designate as topics, will function more symbolically. For instance, we will see examples of motifs used for suspense or motifs that incorporate particular harmonic or melodic styles (the best example being blues harmonies), or particular types of cadences that signify and express similar ideas or emotions both transhistorically and transgenerically. This is because the symbol, as Cumming notes, is a "rule-governed sign whose meaning is not context-dependent but freely able to be moved" (95). The slight differences we find in the meaning of a symbol will be attributable to codes, interpretants and contextual agents. For instance, a blues figure could turn up in a science-fiction film, a detective film, a sports film, a women's film, or even a historical romance (particularly one set in the 19th century South). The range of interpretations, however, will be circumscribed and actually coded as a result of repeated viewing and listening to scenes where the figure appeared almost exclusively when African Americans were on the screen or when a composer wished to evoke a feeling for an urban environment.[11]

In Peirce's system, according to Cumming, interpretants are "those ideas which allow a connection to be made between a sound and its particular inflection on 'vocality' within a given musical group" (75). Umberto Eco, as Robert Hatten notes, "views an interpretant as that which 'inferentially develop[s] all the logical possibilities suggested by the sign'— not merely the connotations of a denotation, but that which can 'explain, develop, [and] interpret a given sign,' beyond the rules provided by codes" (*Musical Meaning in Beethoven* 244). David Lidov states: "The interpretant is drawn out in time. Often a sign allows a range of interpretants. Several might come to mind. The response is like a quantum collapse; in responding we select one" (*Elements of Semiotics* 109).[12] An example of this drawn from opera but relevant to film music is this from Hatten's discussion of the use of "white-key clusters" in Alban Berg's *Lulu*:

> As a primitive or "crude" noise, it is opposed to more-sophisticated atonal sonorities, which offer a greater potential for significance than the relatively undifferentiated cluster. When by *association* with a character on stage we grasp the leitmotivic connection with the Animal trainer, it is easy enough to establish the proper *interpretant* for that conviction — namely, a crude, unsophisticated, blunt crass personality [*Musical Meaning in Beethoven* 262].

In the case of film music, one of the major interpretants is the image on the screen itself. Alan Ladd dressed in his golden buckskins, revolver strapped to his side, riding across the screen, with the magnificent mountains as a backdrop and lush green grazing fields in the foreground, functions dramatically in that "quantum collapse" of which Lidov speaks and plays a role in yoking what the film wishes to express on the screen to our emotional response to the strains of Victor Young's title music "The Call of Faraway Hills," playing under the action. To this we may add a host of other cultural codes and, as we shall see, the gestural qualities of the music itself; in the final analysis, to return to Naomi Cumming's point, what we feel "is not a matter of private feeling" but something that "has been culturally entrained" (17). Let us turn now to leitmotifs, topics and gestures.

There may be no more important element than the leitmotif in the scores of genre films. We have seen from some of the comments by scholars that there is an assumption that expressivity is embedded in the concept of the leitmotif. I am not here to argue that point but to confirm it with some musicological concepts. Basically, the leitmotif is a short musical motif that refers to a character or possibly a conventionalized action and that is repeated. The concept is most often and intimately associated with the music dramas of Richard Wagner. Caryl Flinn notes that the leitmotif for Wagner produced "meaning in two ways, first by anticipating them and second by retrospectively constructing them. The assumption here is that when the leitmotiv is first heard, the auditor experiences a vague emotional response that is only more fully understood later when the leitmotiv is repeated and readily associated with an object or theme" (*Strains of Utopia* 26). This, the reader may note, is very similar to Tarasti's description of myth in music. We will be addressing what causes that "vague emotional response" shortly.

Film music composers, it is generally held, borrowed the concept from Wagner but did not implement it in strict Wagnerian fashion. The reason is quite obvious: film is not opera, and to even think that a composer could fully develop the potential of the leitmotif in a filmic context is not logical. Adorno was one of the first to recognize this "shortcoming" in film music: "Just because the leitmotif as such is musically rudimentary, it requires a large musical canvas if it is to take on the structural meaning beyond that of a signpost" (5). James Buhler similarly notes that "the motifs are much more rigidly bound to the action in film, and they are consequently rarely granted the independence motifs have in Wagner's dramas, which is one reason the music in cinema rarely obtains the level of independence of music in Wagner's dramas" (*Star Wars,* Myth and Music" 42).[13] Justin London outlines what he sees as necessary elements in the leitmotif:

> In filmic contexts they must be quick enough to coordinate smoothly with the imagetrack and dialogue; it would not do to have a leitmotif/theme that takes five to ten seconds (or longer) to unfold. Leitmotifs must also be musically distinctive; a rhythmically undifferentiated scale or arpeggio is less readily grasped as a significant musical figure than one with a distinct melodic and rhythmic profile. Thus, stock musical gestures, from cadences and generic chord progressions to stingers and sequences that mickey-mouse the onscreen action, are to be avoided ["Leitmotifs and Musical Reference in the Classic Film Score" 88].

The leitmotif—even in its "imperfect" cinematic application—is a key element in both mythopoesis and expressivity in the film score. James Buhler in his discussion of the music of *Star Wars* and myth addresses the mythopoeic element when he states: "Just as Wagner's mythic impulse does not free the leitmotif of its linguistic element but actually leads back to it, so too the demythifying impulse of film music leads not away from myth but back toward it. This is the riddle of the leitmotif, which entwines myth and signification in a knot almost impossible to solve" (43). As you can see, Buhler's path to the mythical significance of (and signification in) the leitmotif is different than mine. This is attributable, as I have suggested above, to his notion of myth versus mine. He seems to be of the transcendental school while I'm from what we could term the temporal school: he sees myth in Wagnerian, pre-literate and spiritual terms[14]; I see it as an evolving contemporaneous phenomenon whose subject matter is readily located in the here and now—even when it is dealing with the past, as in the case of the Western and the historical romance. Myths may, as Cassirer notes, may deal with "ideal attitude[s]" (52) but the transcendental element of myth is not necessarily synonymous with spirituality or the evocation of classical mythology. Regardless of how we get there, one can see that the mythic impulse is inextricably linked to the leitmotif. As we shall see, motivic style and structure is correlated directly to the kernel structure (or Tarasti's "immanent narrative"): there will be clearly delineated leitmotivs for heroes and villains and other supporting characters, some of whom have dramatic significance as foils, catalysts and stereotypes. Tarasti would see in Buhler's and London's ideas the very heart of the musico-mythical experience: "In many cases wherein Western art music is reunited with myth, the same occurs as has already been seen in the area of primitive music and in connection with the semiotic model developed by Barthes: music is obliged to relinquish the complexities of its structure to allow for the emergence of mythical structure in musical discourse" (*Myth and Music* 51). Although he is referring largely to program music and opera, I believe the same applies to the use of the leitmotif in film music. For me — and reflecting back on London's thoughts about the brevity of the figures — we see in the leitmotif qualities similar to those epic conventions I mentioned earlier, such as epithets, patronymics and the like. They are shorthand markers (Adorno's "signposts") that help us identify character and perhaps give us some insight into their actions. But they are more as well, and this is where the element of expressivity comes in. Tarasti states: "The reconstruction of a myth is in many cases carried out in such a way that either a mythical story is expressed through music alone (as in vocal scenes in opera with a mythological subject) or the narration of the myth is at least intensified and colored with the expressive qualities of music — as occurs, for example, in ballet scenes of Italian or French opera seria" (*Myth and Music* 56). As has been suggested, to underscore a hero-villain conflict, the composers of serious music often rely upon expressive elements related to key (major for the hero; minor for the villain) or gestures ("lift" for the hero; "grief" for the villain) or harmony (resolution to tonic for hero; dissonance or no resolution or resolution to minor for the villain). Similarly, London notes that the leitmotif "also contain[s] an expressive content that is entwined with its musical structure.... Leitmotifs, as musical shapes embedded in larger musical contexts, are similarly expressive. They couple a capacity to refer with a sense of emotional expression" (89). As I hope to demonstrate, it is the presence of expressive elements (i.e., topics and gestures) in the leitmotifs that enable them to function as indices. When leitmotifs are then stated repeatedly (*avant/après*) in congruence with the visual images on the screen the affective quality of the music becomes more apparent.[15] The combination, or perhaps better alliance, of redundancy, narrative contextualization of the leitmotif, and the topical and gestural qualities of the motifs themselves, enable the viewer to relate the sign to the signified. And once that alliance is complete the viewer will, in Barthes's terms, be in the very presence of the myth.

Expressive elements are embedded in motifs in two significant ways: through topics, or as they are sometimes called, "style topics" (Neumeyer and Buhler 25), and gestures. Let us begin with gestures because, from the standpoint of expressivity, they are as David Lidov notes "the atomic level of signification in music" (*Is Language a Music?* 152). The growing interest in gesture is also allied to a renewed interest in exploring meaning and expressivity in music. Since the 19th century, the whole "esthetic of feeling" (Dahlhaus 71) has come under intense critical scrutiny, resulting in scholars' questioning of the efficacy and accuracy of concepts such as "painting genre," "empfindsamkeit" (the sensitive style of the 18th century), the "doctrine of affections" and those "literary or depictive programs" seen, especially by Hanslick, as "extramusical" or "esthetically 'irrelevant' additions to instrumental music" (Dahlhaus 131–132). The ideal was "absolute music," that is "independent instrumental music" (Dahlhaus 7). It wasn't just that music could not express the feelings of the composer or performer but that perhaps it was fanciful to think that it could be "expressive of" such emotional states. Over the last 30 years, musicologists have reopened the "expressivity" debate, and now there is an evolving body literature on emotional meaning in music. Semiotics has aided in this renaissance by addressing the question of *how* does music signify? Three areas have helped musicologists frame their enquiries: first, performance. Both Naomi Cumming and Robert Hatten refer to performance practices in their semiotic analyses of musical gesture and meaning. Anyone who has attended a recital or watched a conductor at work has a sense of how the body is involved in musical performance. The little dip and rising motion that brass or woodwind players (almost unconsciously) employ as they begin a period, or the trace of one's body or head as one plays a downward or upward figure, or the punching bodily movement that might accompany a fortissimo figure, or a sweeping motion of the conductor's body and baton as he leads the orchestra through a dramatic intervallic leap, all suggest somatic states and, as nonverbal gestures, they can be "read," and, as Naomi Cumming has shown, they are. Second, narratology has also been an illuminating adjunct study, prompting scholars to ask how (and often proposing that) music — even absolute music — tells stories. Mache notes that "narrativity in music implies that instead of starting from such static notions as form, symmetry or dissymmetry, proportion, or tone-hierarchies, one cares first for dynamic processes, either abstract, like energy distribution, or metaphorical, as scenarios and plots" (6). Finally, there is that body of musical literature, including opera and program music, where — whether the musicologist likes it or not — "extramusical" factors are crucial not only in the compositional decisions of the composer but in the audience's intellectual understanding and emotional response to the work. If a piece is entitled *Don Juan* it must be about something — otherwise why call it that?

Opera or program music is related to the above two factors in yet another way. On stage (or in the notation of the score) there are going to be gestural elements influencing what is communicated in the music. As we have seen, film music critics are almost universal in acknowledging the debt the classical film music composer owes to Wagner's music dramas and the work of post–Romantic composers, many of whom created very memorable tone poems. Regarding the gestural and endosomatic, Mary Ann Smart has written:

> Under this new aesthetic order [i.e., opera composition of the late 19th century], music might encircle the exhibited body, supplying a sensuous haze of sound to suggest erotic power; but its rhythms rarely traced or echoed the actual movements of a performer or duplicated the meaning of his or her words. Developments in composition abetted this change, as lush textures and greater density of both harmony and orchestration abstracted music from bodily motion: such "decadent" sonorities ideally represented the erotic potential of the staged body, but at the expense of marking its small-scale, real-time movements [4–5].

One might think she is talking about film music. But what I hope the reader drew from her ideas was the role of the music in complementing or augmenting the gestural (perhaps in even supplying the gestural).[16] It was these practices that might have led Adorno to recognize the importance of the gestural in film music. He states:

> The concrete factor of unity of music and pictures consists in the gestural element.... The function of music, however, is not to "express" this movement ... but to release, or more accurately, to justify movement.... The photographed picture as such lacks motivation for movement; only indirectly do we realize that the pictures are in motion, that the frozen replica of external reality has suddenly been endowed with the spontaneity that it was deprived of by its fixation, and that something petrified is manifesting a kind of life of its own. At this point music intervenes, supplying momentum, muscular energy, a sense of corporeality, as it were. Its aesthetic effect is that of a stimulus of motion, not a replication of motion [78].

In general, we can look to the concept of gesture as a potentially meaningful approach to analyzing the affective role of film music and film music's role in underscoring the conventions of film genres.

Let's begin with a definition; David Lidov states:

> The essence of a motor gesture is readily represented in music by a brief group of notes. The small gestalt of a few notes, motive or ornament or single figuration, is the atomic level of signification in music. Smaller units, notes, or even cells of two or three notes have syntactic and sensory values, but they do not usually constitute units of expression in the way slightly larger shapes easily do, as representations of gesture with a certain solidarity and wholeness and, at the same time, the capacity to possess individual character [*Is Language a Music?* 152].

To this we may add some modifiers from Hatten and Cumming. Cumming notes that "a melodic figure is 'gestural' insofar as it exemplifies the characteristics of direction, emphasis, and speed found in certain brief expressive motions" (88); Hatten often refers to gesture as "energetic shaping through time" and emphasizes that this is more than just a matter of notation: "Gesture presupposes the continuity of motion through a path for which tones provide the landmarks, analogous to the points outlining a smooth, curvilinear function on an X-Y coordinate graph" (*Interpreting Musical Gestures* 114). This "shaping" of energy within a motif, theme, or simple musical figure can then be "read" as a form of a sign with the ability to signify emotion (or some meaning beyond the physical reality of the notes). Naomi Cumming states: "A tonal motive heard as a 'gesture' embraces aspects of the indexical and iconic, as well as its 'symbolic' functions.... Musical 'gesture' is a perceived indexing of bodily motion, as carrying a definite direction, weight, and degree of impetus, to form a shape felt as 'iconic' of gesture in another domain of movement, which may be human and expressive" (152). What we will see, however, is that the iconic aspect of the gesture is less important to us than the indexical or symbolic. As Cumming notes, a gesture in music can be likened to an "Expressive 'gesture' occurring in verbal interchange, [in that it] may then be symptomatic of the physical changes accompanying an emotional state, but it is emotional information they present that is of most interest to an attentive observer" (92). Let's look briefly at how music gestures occur.

The ability of music to signify gesturally is located in the "rules" of music itself. Non-verbal gestures are played out in space: if I tell you a fish was "so big," I probably will use my hands and arms and extend them from a central point outward in opposite directions to signify the relative achievement of my catch. Or take the thumbs-up gesture; it has two spatial components: first, the thumb is pointed up, which we are in certain contexts "entrained" to read "symbolically" as a positive gesture; second, the remainder of the hand forms a fist — a contraction of space — to signify power or strength (imagine if you were to give the thumb's up with a flat hand: it could be read as the preface to the old magic trick: "now you see it; now you don't"); regardless, it will not communicate the same aggressive and positive feeling as the standard thumbs-up gesture. Musically, gesture unfolds within rhythmic and tonal spaces. Robert Hatten writes: "Gestural character and quality *emerge* for the listener from an interaction with tonality and meter as environmental fields with implied forces and orientations" (*Interpreting Musical Gestures* 117). In reference to tonality, Hatten, drawing upon Steve Larson's ideas about diatonic tonal space, notes that there are "three forces that constitute what I would characterize as *virtual environmental forces*: gravity (the tendency of tones to descend toward a pitch considered as a base, such as a tonic), magnetism (the attraction of tones toward more stable tones, which becomes stronger as the interval to the stable tone gets smaller), and inertia (the tendency of a pattern of motion to continue in the same way, even past a point of stability)" (*Interpreting Musical Gestures* 115). Victor Zuckerkandl nicely illustrates this phenomenon when he addresses the idea of movement — which he sees as not a matter of space but of "direction" (92) — when he notes that the motion from $\hat{1}$ to $\hat{5}$ is away from $\hat{1}$ and after $\hat{5}$ it is toward $\hat{8}$ (1); he adds that $\hat{5}$ points in both directions, a "knife-edge balance" in the realm of stability and instability (97).[17] He adds, "Thus the phenomenon of the octave reveals the structure of the world of tone: a rhythmical structure, we might call it, which stamps the form of back-and-forth, with-and-against, hither-and-thither, up-and-down, on all tonal motion — the form of a wave, then, of the pulse, of respiration" (104). It may seem a tad poetic and romantic but the theme has been suggested before (Deryck Cooke: "*What the actual notes of the scale are*—this is the basis of the expressive language of music: the subtle and intricate system of relationships which we know as tonality" [38]) and has picked up in recent musicology (with a bit more of an empirical stamp). Robert Hatten states: "One can easily imagine how 'yearning' might correlate with 'upward' motions, some upward motions are iconic with 'reaching' and 'reaching' relates to yearning through metaphors such as 'reaching for a higher existence.' 'Resignation' could then attach to 'descending' motions, through a similar derivation (as in 'lapsing' from an implied ascent) or simply by being considered oppositional to 'yearning'" (*Musical Meaning in Beethoven* 57). The gestural, then, is anchored within the tonal system and is a key feature in musical expressivity. Aaron Ridley states: "Tonality is the condition of the 'demanding' characteristic of music, so that within tonal music the satisfaction or frustration of such demands (of tones for each other) is what makes a melody coherent or incoherent" (52–53). This dichotomous or, perhaps better, dialogic relationship of coherence vs. incoherence within tonality is a central component in the mythopoeic power of music in genre films. If these gestures are moreover "attached" to an extramusical event we then begin to understand how operatic music, program music and film music can be expressive of emotional states. For instance, Veijo Murtomaki describes the hero of Sibelius's *En Saga*, who in process of the search, "becomes active, the virtuality of an action changes into a real action — [and] all this can be heard when the main theme is activated in a new Allegro tempo (bar 96ff) and the upward skips of a fifth repeated in a powerful manner" (489). We shall see that the same could be said about the leitmotifs created by Erich Wolfgang Korngold for his heroic figures Captain Blood and Robin Hood.

Similarly, meter and rhythm are subject to the same sort of influences in space. Again, earlier commentators like Victor Zuckerkandl saw meaningful correspondences between music and somatic states: "Meter is repetition of the identical; rhythm is return of the similar. The machines runs metrically; man walks rhythmically. Meter becomes the symbol of divisive, analyzing reason, rhythm the symbol of the creative and unifying force of life" (170). Robert Hatten, in relating meter to the concept of gesture, notes that "meter functions like a gravitational field that conditions our embodied sense of up versus down, the relative weighting of events, and the relative amount of energy needed to overcome 'gravitational' constraints (as in the ascending melody). Rhythm, as well as melody and harmony, plays with and against the metric field in a way that suggests human energy and flexibility" (*Interpreting Musical Gestures* 115). David Lidov echoes this in his analysis of force and momentum in "God Save the King":

> I believe the capacity of music to represent two contours derives from the independence of
> its rhythmic and pitch structures; acceleration and deceleration of rhythm play against rising
> and falling pitch. Acceleration after a highest pitch is quite different in feeling from accelera-
> tion before a highest pitch. The first often seems to release momentum, the second to accu-
> mulate effort. There is no acceleration at the climax in ["God Save the King"], but the
> repetitions of notes that commence there increase the emphasis on rhythm [*Semiotics* 221].

My guess is that when viewers (and auditors) think of an "energetic shaping through time"
they would naturally think in rhythmic or metrical terms. Lidov, for instance, notes: "The
variables of pulse are speed and intensity. Naively, speed is exciting. Intensity is involving"
(*Is Language a Music?* 154). Correspondingly, in films, music for chase scenes should by rights
contain gestures consisting of rapidly repeated notes or simple figures which signify heightened tension (a rapidly beating heart) and a body in motion; a love scene may employ gestures consisting of slowly repeated notes signifying intensity (this is especially effective if
tension is created through harmonic shifts under the repetition,[18] thus exacerbating the intensity of the forward movement of the tones).

Gestures then should be viewed as "atomic" units within motifs and leitmotifs and
essential to music's expressive role in the total film experience. Let's talk about how the gesture
works in concert with image. Gesture is not something separate from standard scoring practice;
in fact, it is part and parcel of what every composer has done since Max Steiner scored *King
Kong*. Although they are using the term somewhat differently from the way I am here, Adorno
and Eisler's thoughts on gesture are, in fact relevant to my argument: "The concrete factor of
unity of music and pictures consists in the gestural element.... The function of music, however,
is not to 'express' this movement ... but to release, or more accurately, to justify movement"
(77–78). It is not an isomorphic phenomenon where the music accompanies an action exactly
on the screen, a device termed "mickey-mousing" in the field (as a person makes a step a note
is sounded; if someone falls slowly we can expect a slow glissando to accompany the fall, and
so forth. It is a practice used sparingly in films today). This is not to say that music cannot be
isomorphic, but it is also just as liable to be contrapuntal. When we think of gestures in the
context of film scoring, however, we must factor in an element with which commentators like
Hatten, Cumming, and Lidov do not deal: the visual image and how it affects expressivity in
the gesture. Normally, as Cumming notes, "to be realized as 'gestural,' a pattern must be embodied in a specific act, but the inflected performance needs also to answer to the suggestions of
notated shaping, understood within a stylistic milieu" (138). As we hear a film score, our focus
is not on the performance *per se*, but on how it complements or underscores a scene. The fact
that we may not even know who is conducting is evidence of this. This then leads to us ask: is
the film image itself an agent in creating musical gestures in the soundtrack? Hatten has observed
that "deictic, or indexical, gestures are dynamically involved in the action upon their objects —
including various forms of rhetorical 'pointing' in which a composer or performer highlights a
particular musical event — as well as dialogical responses to other gestures" (*Interpreting Musical Gestures* 106). Ironically, Adorno and Eisler recognized the importance of the "gestural" in
their seminal work, *Composing for the Films*:

> The photographed picture as such lacks motivation for movement, only indirectly do we
> realize that the pictures are in motion, that the frozen replica of external reality has sud-
> denly been endowed with the spontaneity that it was deprived of by its fixation, and that
> something petrified is manifesting a kind of life of its own. At this point music intervenes,
> supplying momentum, muscular energy, a sense of corporeity, as it were. Its aesthetic effect
> is that of a stimulus of motion, not a replication of motion [78].

This echoes my contention that the film image and music are involved in a dialogical relationship resulting in a synergistic sign. It might be that the film image and music serve as complementary interpretants in creating that sense of movement, weight, and direction in the musical gesture. For example, let's take a look at a motif associated with the villain Calvera from Elmer Bernstein's score for *The Magnificent Seven*:

Figure 1.10. "Calvera" (Darby and Dubois, 445).

The striking feature of this motif is the forceful, abrupt gesture of the downward leap of a third at the closure of the motif. Its intensity is heightened by the relentless and narrowly circumscribed melodic range of the antecedent figure of measure 1 that extends into beats one and two of m.2; this antecedent phrase might be interpreted also as a gesture signifying a tightening grip, the tightening grip of Calvera on the villagers. The relentless regularity of the antecedent phrase intensifies the "gravitational" pull of the downward leap and makes the

Calvera and men from *The Magnificent Seven*. Gestural elements signify the tightening, violent grip of Calvera on the villagers.

motif's final statement all the more forceful and violent. Were we to add articulations to illustrate the force of the gesture one might hear this:

Figure 1.11.

And were we to diagram the movement and weight of the line of the figure it might look like this:

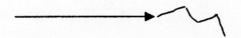

Figure 1.12.

Once can almost see a hand slashing rapidly downward to suggest a cutting off or closure. Manfred Clynes, in his study of eccentrics, has observed that anger is marked with just such a downward movement (35–36). And that is what the music signifies: Calvera as an unstoppable force, who through his violent pillaging is circumscribing the freedom (such as it is) of the villagers. Another important factor in the analysis of this motif is the dialogic relationship it shares with other motifs (and other gestures) in the score. In this particular case, this motif is the first "theme" (i.e., leitmotif) we hear after the main title. You may recall the famous main title from *The Magnificent Seven* with its vigorous rhythms and its dynamic melodic line that is much "freer" and more open than the Calvera motif:

Figure 1.13. Main title, *The Magnificent Seven*.

Where the "Calvera" motif is carefully constrained and tends downward, the main title features leaps of the fifth (what Hatten might see as "lift" gestures) that, if they are not marked with slurs, are conventionally associated with heroic and freedom (signified thus though the gesture's rhythmic flexibility). Stylistically, the main title would be unmarked, relying as it does on more conventional harmonies and topics associated with the heroic, while the villain's music would be marked by merit of its minor harmonies and unconventional (in contrast) melodic line. However, the foregrounding of the motifs in the main title, in a paraphrase of Robert Hatten, will yield them as marked at "the level of strategy" (*Musical Meaning in Beethoven* 117). This in turn means that the dialogic relationship between these opening motifs and their attendant gestures are our first aural introduction to the central conflict in the film (and in the genre) and are crucial in establishing the emotional subtext for the central conflict in the film.

The reader cannot have failed to notice that I used the term "conventionally" above to suggest that motivic and gestural signification is the result of cultural codes (which, in turn, may be seen to function as interpretants). One may see this almost as a compositional imperative owing to the fact that one of the composer's main tasks is to underscore the central conflict and other conventional narrative elements. One will observe as well that during periods of generic stability we find a corresponding motivic stability in scoring practice; for instance, if one surveys the historical romances of the '30s and '40s, one will find a number of gestural similarities in the scoring of hero figures and action sequences. These stable compositional practices are akin to the compositional practices of the classical era, where composers drew on "characteristic figures" to create works ranging from small-scale chamber works to symphonies and operas. Leonard Ratner refers to these "characteristic figures" employed by classical composers as *topics*; he states: "Some of these figures were associated with various feelings and affections; others had a picturesque flavor.... Topics appear as fully worked-out pieces, i.e., *types*, or as figures and progressions within a piece, i.e., *styles*. The distinction between types and styles is flexible; minuets and marches represent complete types of composition, but they also furnish styles for other pieces" (9). It is these signifiers that are essential to the study of the music of genre films. As conventionalized figures that "trigger clear associations with styles, genres, and expressive meanings" (Hatten, *Interpreting Musical Gestures* 1–2), topics drawn from the realms of classical, popular, and film music would seem to be a natural fit for leitmotifs; in fact, one might conclude that most motifs and leitmotifs in films are topics. This, however, is not necessarily true. Topics are, nonetheless, important tools in the composer's compositional toolbox. Neumeyer and Buhler note, "In the sound-film era, styles topics blur significantly with genre in the sense that certain collections of topics become closely associated with particular film genres, which can often be divined from the title music alone" (25). Because of their ability to convey emotion and their referential capacity they are also part of the musical sign system in film genres.

There are two elements that contribute to the signification capabilities of topics: gestures and contexts. Musicologists universally recognize the expressive element in the topic. Joseph Swain, for instance, writes: "Topics are lexical items, 'musical vocabulary,' 'configurations of notes and rhythms,' each of which identifies a 'particular expressive stance'" (49). Similarly, a cursory survey of the topics in Ratner's typology reveals that each is expressive of some emotional state: dances = "elegant," "pleasant and often lively," "buoyant" (9); march = "quicken the spirit," "reminded the listener of authority" (16); military and hunt music = "a favorite diversion of the nobility" (18); pastoral = "rustic" (21). From where does the expressive element generate? From a musical standpoint, the descriptive terms Ratner uses are largely attributable to the presence of some gesture or combination of gestures in the topics. For instance, Hatten notes of the pastoral that it is associated with "great consonance or diatonicism" and adds that "other 'simple' oppositions could be applied as well, highlighting such characteristic features as slow harmonic rhythm (pedal point and drone fifth), simple harmonization (parallel thirds), and rhythmic or textual suggestions of placed stasis" (*Musical Meaning in Beethoven* 79–80). The "energetic shaping" of the material will reinforce the "placid stasis" and thus be expressive of peaceful and soothing feelings. Moving to film music, there is an oft-used motif that I call the "suspense topic." The central gesture in the suspense topic is the trill or tremolo, a musical figure that alternates between stable and unstable tones but ultimately is expected to resolve to some stable harmony. In standard compositional practice, the trill is generally brief and the resolution is not "far in the offing"; in a suspenseful scene in a film, however, the trill is sustained beyond "normal" practice and the resolution is suspended or withheld like a fluttering pulse that will not be quelled. Consequently, the musical gesture signifies constant tension and the possibility that the action (be it threat, violence, etc.) will never be resolved. It is as though we have taken in a breath and experience a tightening in our chest and are waiting expectantly for the opportunity to exhale. If then this topic functions as a sign,[19] what category would it be in the Peircean system? A highly conventionalized sign or one that is less constrained or motivated is, in Peirce's system, a "symbol" or the legisign[20]; the symbol is an arbitrary sign that depends, as Robert Hatten notes of gestures that are categorized as symbols, upon "*conventions* or *habits* of interpretation" (*Interpreting Musical Gestures* 125). Naomi Cumming supplies this example of a legisign, which can also apply to the symbol: "a type becomes a 'legisign' when it is heard *as* conveying a content whose description is to some degree metaphorical. A root-position tonic chord might, for example be characterized generically as 'stable'" (84–85).[21] Thus a hymn form accentuating the classic IV-I ("Amen") cadence could conceivably become a topic.

A key element in both Agawu's and Hatten's work with topics is the element of conventions and cultural contexts. Kofi Agawu states: "Signs denoting topics are significant only within a cultural context that recognizes the conventional association of certain kinds of musical material" (16). These conventional associations, as Aaron Ridley points out, can be acquired by "stipulation" so that when we, for instance, hear the "Dies Irae" we automatically associate it with the text used in funeral services or the "martial exhilaration of brass band music" that comes from use by the army (16). Or, as he adds, "sometimes these devices acquire their conventional roles through simple overuse, so that what was once, in its earlier history, an original expressive feature, becomes later on something more like a signifier — as a certain kind of atonal doodling has become in many horror and suspense movies" (16–17). Thus, the hymn topic or the suspense topic mentioned earlier will only become a topic if the viewer-auditor has developed the competence to recognize what it signifies. As Agawu notes, a crucial facet of topic analysis is that "competence is assumed on the part of the listener, enabling the composer to enter into a contract with his audience. ... it is acquired by learning" (33). The viewer's competence and ability to read the sign is dependent upon the diversity of interpretants available to the viewer.

Moving to the film score, we find that composers actually employ topics from classical era music (especially fanfares, dances, pastorales, etc.), but because they are underscoring films that are so conventionalized there is also the possibility that new topics may emerge over time. In fact, Neumeyer and Buhler state, "Today, topics may well refer as much to earlier film-scoring practices as to specific topics" (25). A perfect example of this is the abovementioned "suspense topic" and one more intimately associated with the Western that could be termed the "Indian topic." Viewers of the Western have come to expect a particular musical style to underscore the presence of Native Americans on the screen. Claudia Gorbman has outlined some of the characteristics of the motif: "A 4/4 allegretto drumbeat (or pizzicato in bass viols), the first beat emphatically accented, with a simple minor-modal tune played by high woodwinds or strings, signified 'Indian territory'" ("Scoring the Indian" 83). "Musically, the following is typical of the gesture:

Figure 1.14.

Repeated hearings of this type of motif in Westerns enables the viewer to associate a particular emotional state — most often, in this case, it will be a threat or fear — as well as "a wealth of extra meaning beyond the directness of [the gesture's] qualitative and dynamic characteristics" (Hatten, *Interpreting Musical Gestures* 125). A perfect example of this occurs in *Western Union*. There is a scene in which a wounded man is brought into camp; the "Indian topic" is played underneath, clearly signifying the "Indian as threat" and suggesting that the dying man was killed by Indians — all of this even before a word of dialogue has been uttered about who attacked him. The use of the topic further suggests that the dream of running the telegraph line is in jeopardy. Ironically, we find out in time that the man was not killed by Indians but by a band of renegade Confederate rebels who are hell-bent on hindering progress and undermining the introduction of technology into the plains. However, the topic has done its work because for that brief moment we are convinced that indeed the Indians are the preeminent threat to the forces of civilization. Topics, then, can function indexically within genres if they are highly motivated, or they can function symbolically if they are less motivated, or they may have dual signifying capacities. In Westerns, the Indian topic may function symbolically, signifying the "Indian as threat," but in a contemporary comedy, the self-same topic will be generically constrained, thus providing the viewer with another interpretant and an entirely different reading: instead of the music signifying a threat, the conventional throbbing and tragic gestures of the topic "anchored" to comic images or incongruous behavior more than likely will render the topic humorous.

Contextual Agents: Music

We turn now to those agents that contribute to the tension between the conventional and inventional, the stable and the unstable; in short, those musical and extramusical elements that are responsible for the transformational nature of genre films. I have already discussed the role that leitmotifs (from a historical standpoint) and topics play in genres, and I have alluded to the role of the Western tonal system as well. There are a couple of other musical elements that are important to expressivity and the conventional or inventional in genre film music.

Harmony is an element of which the average viewer is really not aware; this is not because we do not hear the harmonies in the score but because, of all the musical elements, it is the one which we probably have the most difficulty describing. The average listener may say, "Oh, that was a lovely melody" or "That music was really exciting" or "That saxophone really captured a mood in that scene." But you probably won't hear, "Wasn't that an interesting harmonic change she used in that love scene" or "Didn't you think his use of major ninths was a bit precious?" Nonetheless, harmony is central to dramatic effectiveness and expressivity in music in the movies. The fact that we associate certain moods with certain sounds is often determined by the harmonies being employed within topics and motifs. For instance, as Deryck Cooke notes, "That the major third should be found to express pleasures should surprise no one" (51). He goes on to show how over the years the major third and, by extension, most major harmonies are often used in support of happier, lighter, or, if you will, more optimistic musical statements. Conversely, the minor third, as Cooke notes, has a "depressed" sound; he adds, "Western composers, expressing the 'rightness' of happiness by means of the major third, expressed the 'wrongness' of grief by means of the minor third" (57). On the surface this may strike one as over simplistic, but as one surveys the large body of concert works, theatre works, just plain old pop tunes, and, of course, film music, one will find confirmation for Cooke's statements. Similarly, as Bazelon notes, "Historically, dissonance — harsh, controversial, disconcerting sounds — " have been treated in films as a negative factor implying neurosis, evil, agony, and pain, the opposite of good and right, sweetness and light" (88). Leonard Rosenman, who chose to adopt a serial approach to scoring *The Cobweb* (1955), which is largely set in a mental institution, said that he wanted to show what was "'going on inside characters' heads" (quoted in Prendergast 123) and that he "wanted more neurosis" (119). This pattern will be quite evident in almost every genre where there is a villain, an alien, things out of the ordinary, or, generally speaking, any kind of danger.

Timbre and orchestral color are also key ingredients in expressivity in musical gestures and topics. Each instrument has a distinctive sound and, over the years and through repeated usage, composers have relied upon the timbres of those instruments to communicate ideas or even emotional states. For instance, we have come to associate the bugle or trumpet with battle and/or action sequences, this coding resulting from combined cultural influences: first, the bugle indeed was used in military actions, and, second, composers employed bugle call topics in serious and popular compositions (Tchaikovsky's *1812 Overture* being a prime example). Similarly, there is no reason that an organ will automatically suggest liturgical or religious ideas or feelings, except, of course, that for most people an organ probably has been part and parcel of their religious experiences from childhood. Once again, competence and context are key determinants in the musical instrument's ability to signify emotional states or culturally encoded meanings. Roy Prendergast, writing about Miklos Rosza's use of a musical instrument called a theremin in *The Lost Weekend* and *Spellbound*, notes the following: "At that time, the Theremin was highly effective device for expressing the warped psychological state of the film's main character" (69). Instrumental timbre and color are also extremely important in topics and gestures used to signify time periods and setting. The trumpet, because of its use in jazz and in films dealing with urban experiences, may be an automatic choice for the detective and gangster film set in an urban environment. Marimbas, as Irwin Bazelon notes, are used for "musical stereotypes for films set in Central America or Mexican locales ... [and] for other instances where ritualistic or symbolic association with the church is desired" (96). Roy Prendergast writes:

> There are a variety of ways of achieving an atmosphere of time and place, or, musically speaking, "color." In a broad sense, musical color may be taken to represent the exotic or sensuous aspects of music, as distinct from musical structure, or line, which might considered the intellectual side.... Color is associative — bagpipes recall images of Scotland, the oboe easily suggests a pastoral scene, muted brass connotes something sinister, rock music may imply a youthful theme, and so on. Also, color is not intrusive; it does not compete with the dramatic action.... The effect of color, moreover, is *immediate*, unlike musical thematic development, which takes time. In addition, color is highly flexible and can be brought in and out with relative ease by the experienced screen composer [213–214].

In this study I wish to examine what types of instruments composers select to underscore women's characters in different genres and what sort of orchestral colors are used in establishing conflicts between countries in the historical romance. One final item related to color. Irwin Bazelon has noted that "tone color (instrumental timbre) is especially significant at the beginning of a film, since opening music has the special associative impact of being there first" (97). Main themes and title music, in a sense, set the stage for not just the music, but for the entire mood, atmosphere, and drama about to unfold on the screen. Max Steiner's main theme for *Treasure of the Sierra Madre* (1948) quickly establishes locale with the trumpet flourishes which evoke Latin American musical rhythms and color (there is just a hint of the mariachi sound there); similarly, the protagonists' down-and-out quest is anticipated through the vigorous rhythms and slightly heroic sound that is woven into the theme.

Next, pitch and dynamics are important tools in the composer's musical vocabulary because they have the ability to affect the listener (viewer) on both a physiological and psychological level. Irwin Bazelon states:

> Pitch and dynamics also influence bodily reactions: they can disturb or calm and, in so doing, stimulate disagreeable or pleasant feelings.... High notes played forte (loudly) sound shrill and piercing. Although I doubt that they cause actual pain, they can produce considerable discomfort and, on occasion, intense fright. The same notes played piano (softly) are mysterious and ethereal, hanging suspended in midair. Low notes played forte, especially on brass or strings, sound rough and coarse and tend to growl when sharply attacked; performed on piano, they have an ominous, deep-dark coloration. High or low tones played staccato (short and clipped) have a different physiological effect than identical tones played legato (smoothly). Soft music can be restful and easy to listen to, or, by use of special musical devices involving accents or changes in embouchure (attack by the performer), it can become dramatic and cause apprehension [84].

Dynamics and articulations, as has been suggested, are important in the "energetic shaping" of musical gestures. Our sense of yearning, or of grief, or of slashing, pounding violent motions, or sweeping movements are partially the result of these factors. Whether or not these particular musical events indeed excite an affective reaction is open to question; that Bazelon's descriptions sound similar to the descriptions of musical gestures suggests that the music will be expressive of mystery, growling, the ominous, or the frightening. To see confirmation of these ideas one need only recall or go back and view the famous shower scene in Bernard Herrmann's *Psycho* (1960), where high-pitched slashing violin glissandos perfectly underscore the brutal murder of the Janet Leigh character.

In addition to tonality and harmony, one of the most important contextual factors in the music of genre films (and film scoring in general) is its reliance upon the sound and style of post–Romantic music. This is the music of the late nineteenth and early twentieth centuries, before the advent of atonality and the experiments in serial music of Arnold Schoenberg and the Viennese School. The composers of this tradition who most influenced genre film music are Richard Wagner, Sergei Rachmaninoff, Gustav Mahler, Richard Strauss, Peter Tchaikovsky, Modeste Mussorgsky and, later, Claude Debussy and early Igor Stravinsky. Recently, commentators such as Caryl Flinn (*Strains of Utopia*), Scott Paulin ("Richard Wagner and the Fantasy of Cinematic Unity: The Idea of the *Gesamtkunstwerk* in the History and Theory of Film Music") and Justin London ("Leitmotifs and Musical Reference in the Classical Film Score") have dealt with the large shadow post–Romantic music casts over the scoring practices of classical Hollywood composers. Let me summarize some of the major elements that these scholars and others before them have identified as key to film genre scoring.

The elements of post–Romantic music that had the greatest impact on scoring are its lush sound (derived from increased orchestra size), expanded harmonic language, chromaticism, use of program music, and use of leitmotifs in orchestral as well as opera music. Hollywood composers found the post–Romantic idiom compatible with their efforts in scoring films for a couple of reasons. First, Max Steiner and Erich Wolfgang Korngold, early music pioneers and trend setters in film scoring, came from eastern Europe, home to composers Wagner, Mahler, Bruckner, and Strauss; in short, post–Romanticism was a favored musical idiom in these regions, and young composers living in the shadows of these composers quite naturally were drawn to write in this style. The work of these composers, moreover, is characterized by a strong tendency to the programmatic and a belief in the narrative capabilities of music: Mahler's symphonies often have subtitles ("Tragic," "Resurrection"); Richard Strauss is known almost exclusively for his tone poems such as *Don Juan, Don Quixote, Also Sprach Zarathustra.* An audience's musical competency during the golden age of the studio system would have been influenced by the work of the post–Romantic composer, both the major composers and the minor light music composers whose works graced concert halls and other widely attended musical events. As Susan McClary notes, "Composers of music for movies and advertisements consistently stake their commercial success on the public's pragmatic knowledge of musical signification — the skill with which John Williams, for instance, manipulates the semiotic codes of the late nineteenth-century symphony in *E.T.* or *Star Wars* is breathtaking" (21).

Over and above this historico-biographical fact, however, are some more significant reasons. First, a dramatic one: Roy Prendergast states, "When confronted with the kind of dramatic problems films presented to them, Steiner, Korngold, and [Alfred] Newman merely looked (whether consciously or unconsciously is unimportant) to those composers who had, for the most part, solved almost identical problems in their operas. These three progenitors of film music simply looked to Wagner, Puccini, Verdi, and Strauss for the answer to some of their problems in dramatic film scoring" (39). On the surface, this idiom seems perfectly suited to film: one is using music to help tell a story, and in works like tone poems and operas a similar principle is at work. Tone poems normally attempt to tell a story through purely musical means by weaving themes and leitmotifs — associated with character and incident — into a symphonic whole. Second, one of post–Romantic music's most important contributions to film scoring was the use of the leitmotif because it afforded composers a shorthand method to develop character and to elicit emotion. Arnold Schoenberg's thoughts on the leitmotif are reflective of the post–Romantic approach to the concept: leitmotifs, he notes, "are intervals and rhythms, combined to produce a memorable shape or contour which usually implies an inherent harmony. ... everything depends on it use. Whether a motive is simple or complex, whether it consists of few or many features, its primary form does not determine the final impression of the piece. Everything depends upon its treatment and development" (qtd. in Simms 26). A film music composer, unlike the composer of serious concert works, does not have the luxury of composing an entire piece that largely adheres to classic rules of composition. And, as Buhler and Paulin (and Adorno before them) have noted, the Hollywood composer really does not develop the leitmotif in the classic way that Wagner, for instance, does in his operas. Instead, the composer's task is to establish a dialogic relationship between music and image (and even between motifs or topics) to capture a mood or augment the action in the pursuit of plenitude. Sometimes the composer may only have two minutes to work with, and that brief time frame does not lend itself to an extended musical event. A simple two to five measure statement may be, for the film composer, a more practical compositional form. A good example of this is Max Steiner's score for *Casablanca* (1942), in which he never really uses Herman Hupfield's "As Time Goes By" in its entirety (i.e., both the main theme and the bridge), but instead creates for all intents and purposes a leitmotif out of the first two measures of the song:

Figure 1.15. "As Time Goes By."

Then through chromatic, harmonic and rhythmic (at one point the theme is stated in 3/4 time) alterations he develops the theme to fit the image. This shorthand method of reference and expressiveness, as we have noted, derives its signifying power through culturally coded topics and motive-specific gestures. The use of a motif in a particular dramatic context narrows its meaning and focuses its affective power. Joseph Swain's comments on the leitmotif are very relevant to its use in film:

> The semantic principle of leitmotifs is the same as that of text matching. The dramatic context is the window that selects the meaning of a leitmotif out of that melody's entire semantic range, and, as before, that range ensures that the action on stage is appropriate for that motive.... Once the meaning of the motive is established — meaning that the semantic range of that melody has been narrowed down to something like that of a common word — it can be used for dramaturgy by elaborating or further specifying that meaning for more immediate contexts [60].

Film music composer Irwin Bazelon's comments — albeit jaded — about program music are relevant here: "Audiences," he states, have been preconditioned to accept program music

> at face value.... In this light certain primitive and naive programmatic responses are inevitable: rippling arpeggios suggest waterfalls, shimmering rays of light or wind rustling through trees; low, agitated tremolos portend danger or hint suspense; massive black chords imply religious connotations or invite comparisons with great epical events. Out of this preconditioned suggestivity evolved the adoption of puerile, musico-visual associations leading to stock clichés and standardized effects [77].

Consequently, the sound of a trumpet playing a blues figure in a hardboiled detective film or gangster film or played over an establishing shot of the darkened city will assume the status of a topic (the Gershwin blues topic) signifying the modern, morally ambiguous, and potentially tragic terrain of the city; some recent examples of this include the love theme from *Chinatown* (1974) and "The Victor" from *L.A. Confidential* (1997).

Finally, we come to the role popular musical styles, genres and topics play in scoring. Musical styles and genres, such as jazz, mariachi music, Baroque, medieval, and so forth, subsume all the elements I have discussed up to this point and in and of themselves can function as important musical topics. In most genre films, popular musical styles routinely rub up against non-diegetic music (underscore) newly composed for the film — sometimes much to the chagrin of the composer.[22] Consequently, the two cannot be like oil and water but must harmonize in a variety of ways. The presence of Richard Whiting's classic "Too Marvelous for Words" emanating from a record player in *Dark Passage* is as crucial to character and conflict as the rest of Max Steiner's score. The composer who immediately incorporates jazz into a score is attempting to communicate a specific set of ideas or values. For instance, Irwin Bazelon states: "Today [c. 1975], as a background for violence, and accompaniment for skull-duggery, murder, suspense, drug traffic, and means to convey emotional instability, jazz has been worked to death until it has become an audio trademark for neurotic drama" (109). I'm not sure a similar statement could be made today; composers might find another style more suitable for efficiently signifying those disturbed values he described above. Regardless, as a musical adjunct to color, musical styles and genres are essential to the composer working in historical subjects. Bazelon again: "An early liturgical chant puts one in the Middle Ages. A harp, recorder, viola d'amore, or lute in a score captures a Renaissance flavor. A French minuet playing softly in the background conjures up the seventeenth or eighteenth century. A Viennese waltz acts as a musical backdrop for a nineteenth-century soiree. The songs 'Dixie,' 'A Long, Long Way to Tipperary,' and 'Praise the Lord' identify the American Civil War, World War I, and World War II respectively" (110). In many cases, this type of music will be source music (diegetic music). Much of the musical score of Robert Altman's *Kansas City* generates out of the jam sessions taking place in the nightclub owned by Harry Belafonte's character. The music, moreover, achieves two things: first, by merit of it being performed in the style of early (late '20s and very early '30s) big band jazz it establishes a time and, by virtue of its being jazz (see Bazelon above), it underscores the "skullduggery" and violence that permeates Altman's narrative.

Contextual Agents: Extramusical Sources

The decisions that inform the selection and use of the abovementioned musical elements are conditioned by panoply of contextual agents that can be subsumed under two umbrellas: the movie industry itself and the musical community in attendance at the film. Figure 1.6 outlines some of the agents that influence the production and the reading of genre films. Composers find their work subject to industry politics (i.e., the power and influence of directors and producers), trends in music composition (both within the genre of film music and outside in the field of "serious" music composition), audience demographics, developments in technology, economic developments (sometimes the two work hand-in-hand — "We don't have a big budget; use electronic means to achieve your ends!"), current events, shifts in cultural ideologies (this could particularly affect the reliance upon certain topics, especially those that had traditionally been associated with underrepresented peoples), and industry discourse. It is beyond the scope of this book to look at these influences in depth but there are a couple of examples that I think may be more relevant to this study than others. Let's begin with industry politics.

   Books about film music are filled with stories, many of them horror stories, about the work environment of the film composer. These stories are peopled with villains (musically ignorant studio bosses, producers and directors), heroes (the composers) and exciting deadlines ("They don't want it good, they want it *Thursday*!").[23] These stories, however, are important in understanding the function and role of music in genre films. Industry discourse reveals that the films are indeed perceived as types that are expected to fulfill a certain artistic standard and also to ensure healthy bottom line figures; the reasoning goes like this: the *Titanic* was a blockbuster, let's make another *Titanic*-like film. These decisions, moreover (obviously), are not made by composers but by people who see film as a commodity, a product designed to make a profit. In order to ensure continued movie attendance (or consumption if we think in terms of a sales paradigm), quality and standardization are key elements: consumers expect the same quality every time they buy it, regardless of where they buy it. It is this philosophy which composers face most often. It is, moreover, a potential trap for the composer. If, let us say, composer X has garnered the approval of studio bosses and the director of a film and the film has done well at the box office, now, to quote Irwin Bazelon, "His track record is well known, and there is little guesswork about the outcome. 'Having done one,' especially a successful one, palliates fear and promotes film-company security" (45). However, composer X, as well as Y and Z, will pretty much be expected to produce something just as "good," something which will similarly put the film in the black. The quality issue centers not around "good" music but "effective" music: music that seems to work, even though what made it work is not clearly defined by the powers that be. However, the powers-that-be implicitly defined that which works: that which they can understand. Irwin Bazelon quotes Aaron Copland's famous line about his experience with producers in Hollywood during the studio era: "'The producers often claim, 'if I can't understand it, the public won't'" (Bazelon 17). This, of course, means we have to have some understanding of the producer and see the producer as part of a musical community — more of which in a second. Quite simply, the philosophy, as Bazelon states, is: "'what worked before can work again'" (17). This in turn leads to little risk taking in composition; as he states, the feeling is that "innovative music would call attention to itself, intrude into the film, and consciously upset people" (17). It is true that on occasion a good working relationship between a director and composer has developed and the composer's work can pass muster under the aegis of the director's reputation (or iron will). But more often than not the composer in the past and probably even today runs into the sentiment offered by producer Dore Shary: "'I think all music in pictures has to be cliché to be effective'" (qtd. in Bazelon 21). Composers, furthermore, brought in as they are at the tail end of the entire production process, find, as Roy Prendergast observes, that there is very little time or "opportunity" for the composers to "experiment with their art form" (41).

   A second and perhaps even more important contextual agent is the "musical community" in attendance at the film. This idea has been alluded to previously in discussions of the concept of competence. Joseph Swain uses the term community in his *Musical Languages* to refer to those who listen to music in a certain way. For instance, musicians themselves form one musical community, cognoscenti may form another musical community, and casual listeners form another. When we begin to think about a musical community in terms of moviegoers, obviously, the idea is complicated. In fact, it is probably safe to say that there really isn't a "musical community" *per se* at a film because the audience is not there first and foremost to listen to music. They do, however, hear the music and they also

Composer Max Steiner conducting original *King Kong* scoring sessions (Photofest).

purchase it — and in fairly large quantities, as is evidenced by the enormous sales of sound-tracks like *Breakfast at Tiffany's* (1961), *Saturday Night Fever* (1977), *Star Wars* (1977), and, most recently, *Titanic*. Consequently, from a purely aural standpoint and from an economic standpoint, certain compositional decisions are going to be made to satisfy this community as a musical community. Therefore, when that producer says to the composer, "If I don't like it, they won't," he, unfortunately, has a point. From a musical community standpoint, his taste in music and knowledge of music are closer to those of the majority of moviegoers, who have little or no knowledge of music, than they are to those of the minority, who have some musical knowledge and some understanding of the art of scoring a motion picture.

This, in turn, suggests that we should be compelled to examine this diverse, polyglot musical community in attendance at the movies. Now that may seem daunting, and indeed it needs more extensive investigation and research than I can provide here, but we can draw some conclusions about the moviegoing musical community based on the extramusical con-texts that have traditionally influenced their taste and, by extension, their musical compe-tence. First, during the studio era, the musical tastes of the audience would have been formed by their exposure to music in church, their (probably limited) exposure to music in concert halls, their exposure to the music of Tin Pan Alley, which was mediated by Broadway, radio, and finally Hollywood itself, and their exposure to movie music itself. I have addressed the elements of popular song styles and how they might have contributed to topics. As to the concert hall, the exposure of this community to classical music was probably not radically different than what is programmed by most community orchestras today: a preponderance of Romantic, post–Romantic era, and light classical works, like those of Ketleby or even Percy Grainger (extending up to Leroy Anderson), but very little of the musical avant-garde. Finally, the Hollywood context itself would have included what remnants were left of the silent film days where the repertoire, which came from sources like Erno Rapee, would have included music from the Romantic era (the Lento movement from Chopin's op. 35 Piano Sonata in B flat minor is recommended for funeral scenes [Rapee 160]) and light classical music from relatively unknown turn-of-the-century composers (E.T. Paull's marches, Ethelbert Nevin or even Gottschalk's "characteristic" pieces). The other Hollywood musical context would have been the Tin Pan Alley based tunes from movie musicals (remember that in 1933 Max Steiner's score for *King Kong* would have been in musical competition with Harry Warren and Al Dubin's hit tunes for *Forty Second Street* and *Golddiggers of 1933* — stiff competition).

Moving ahead to our own time, this scenario really has not changed a lot; the only substitution would be that the musical product of Tin Pan Alley has been replaced by the sound and the machinery of rock music, which from a purely musical standpoint has not strayed from the basics of the major-minor system which also dominated the music of the Tin Pan Alley years. If we look then at the implications of this context we can draw some conclusions:

- The music of this community is still largely characterized by reliance upon the major-minor tonal system that has dominated popular music for well over 200 years.
- The song forms have not changed radically in 100 years. There still is reliance upon a binary A-B contrasting thematic structure; in the music of Tin Pan Alley this form almost became a rigid formula of AABA. In the age of rock, the forms are not so pervasive, but they also have not altered the basic contrasting theme approach in any significant way.
- Broadway has evolved to more of a music-drama format — as opposed to the musical comedy — but the music is still cast, ironically, in forms that are closer to operetta than *Lulu*; occasionally one may hear strains of the avant-garde in Broadway scores but this is a rarity.
- Movies continue to have soundtracks replete with symphonically scaled forces in spite of the intrusions of the pastiche score (Kubrick's for *2001*) and the pop hit package (you name the movie today and it probably is an example of this one). The sound of those scores, moreover, owes more to Steiner and Korngold by way of John Williams than it does to the work of Schoenberg, Karlheinz Stockhausen, Elliot Carter, John Cage, Phillip Glass Steve Reich.

In short, it is a community whose very diversity and, ironically, corresponding musical conservatism has not obviated the need for genre and for effective musical topics and gestures to make their moviegoing experience a memorable one.

Final Thoughts

Before beginning the specific analyses of the genres I want to make a couple of closing comments about my approach and method here. My primary goal is to explore the relationship between myth, music, and how music functions in defining, shaping and communicating the conventions of the different genres. My approach is a decidedly formalistic one, focusing as I am on the narrative kernel of the genres and how music is used to augment and comment on the dramatic and narrative conventions of the individual genres. I will deal with contextual agents only as they are relevant to the discussion of the efficacy of the music in a particular genre in supporting the kernel structure of the films. Secondarily, I hope that these analyses will help audiences appreciate the skill and artistry that goes into creating a film score. One of my main concerns is not to suggest that film music composition is an exclusively formulaic activity. John Sloboda notes that "our appreciation of a 'great' melody rests partly on our appreciation that a composer has a great many options when generating a melody even if harmony and rhythm are determined" (52). The presence of ritual, conventions and musical topics and gestures in a genre may indeed earmark the film for widespread popularity, but we will also be celebrating those composers and artists who reviewed their options and then sought to diverge, alter, abolish or reinvent those conventions and gestures.

2

Alien Harmonies

The Science Fiction Film

One of the taglines in the promotional campaign for *Alien* (1979) ominously declared, "In space no one can hear you scream." That indeed might be the case, but we would not have been assaulted by silence, because that soundless scream would have been accompanied by music. In fact, we might expect that scream to be accompanied by some of the most avant-garde music one will ever hear in films. From the 1930s and through the 1990s, the science-fiction film has afforded composers an opportunity to flex their musical muscles in ways they were not able to in other genres. Lionel Stevenson, in his discussion of science fiction as romance, notes, "The new romantic novelists, who found their chief critical spokesman in Robert Louis Stevenson, were determined to employ themes and settings that could supply the excitement of danger, the glamour of unfamiliar surroundings, and the exaltation of heroic behavior" (100). Composers of the romantic era also responded to these same impulses, and film music composers working in the area of science fiction found similar inspiration. The genre has passed through the heroic to the paranoiac and back and is currently perched on a new wave of the paranoiac. Through all these changes science fiction has been the one area where composers could move away from the conventions of the post–Romantic idiom and embrace the innovations in 20th century music theory and practice. The key to why they were able to do this lies in the nature and the conventions of the genre. Let's begin with some basics.

For all the science, technology and intellectual speculation about the future that courses through science-fiction films, the films are still primarily concerned with the human condition and, in fact, with the affirmation of our humanity. Vivian Sobchak offers this definition of the genre: "The S[cience] F[iction] film is a film genre which emphasizes actual, extrapolative, or speculative science and the empirical method, interacting in a social context with the lesser emphasized, but still present, transcendentalism of magic and religion, in an attempt to reconcile man with the unknown" (63). The science fiction film, like other genres, is a site where cultural and ideological conflicts are acted out and resolved, and traditionally has also been a site where belief in progress (especially scientific or technological progress) has come up against distrust of the very same science and technology. Science has delivered a number of benefits to people living in the modern world (medicine, faster transportation, more efficient communication) but it also poses an ongoing threat to our very humanity (robots, automation, computer guided systems in all walks of life). J.P. Telotte states: "The genre seems to have at its core a concern with how we can 'be,' that is, with how we can maintain our human *being* within a context — as thoroughly constructed and technological as it is — that typically seems to condition, qualify, or challenge our traditional human identity" (7).

This affirmation of our humanity is played out in two dimensions: the personal and the social. Science-fiction films suggest that what makes us human and what we must fight to preserve are emotions, creativity, and intelligence, but this intelligence is grounded not in "high falutin'" scientific theory but in our ability to act resourcefully to solve a problem. In short, instinct may be a better guide to intelligence than logic. Consequently, as one reviews the past sixty years of science-fiction films one finds not only scientists as heroes by also hero figures drawn from the ranks of ordinary citizens or cultural agents who reside outside of the scientific world. Second, our humanity is reaffirmed in the preservation of our social institutions and the social order itself. Vivian Sobchak notes, "The horror film is primarily concerned with the individual in conflict with society or some extension of himself, the SF film with society and its institutions in conflict with each other or with some alien other ... with social chaos, the disruption of social order (man-made), and the threat to the harmony of civilized society going about its business" (30). In our encounter with the alien we find our humanity threatened and tested and we find out if we have the stuff to persevere and survive. J.P. Telotte, drawing on Foucault's *The Order of Things*, notes that science fiction "obviously has found the notion of 'alien systems' attractive and useful for comparing to and commenting upon our situation" (7). As we shall see, in the final encounter with the alien in science-fiction films, unlike in showdowns in the Western, the detective, the war film, or the historical romance, no one individual will necessarily stand out; instead the community will come together to save its collective hide.

The role of science enjoys a paradoxical status in the science-fiction film. Theodore Sturgeon has observed that "'a good science fiction story is a story with a human problem, and a human solution, which would not have happened at all without its science content'" (qtd. in Blish, "On Science Fiction Criticism" 167). Indeed, in many science-fiction films, one might say there is a conflict between scientific perspectives. There is the science of the alien, usually far advanced but oftentimes malevolent, and then there is the science of planet earth, that scientific knowledge we must draw on to defeat the alien. So in *Independence Day* (1996), for instance, the almost monolithic technological superiority of the aliens is finally defeated by the resourcefulness of a computer hacker who knows how to plant the virus and a cracker-jack fighter pilot whose native intelligence and resourcefulness enable him to master the technological nuances of the alien space ship. In a way, it gets down to a simple "Our computer beat yours! So there!" In the final analysis, science-fiction films reassure us that "good" science is that science which takes its rightful place in the social order and is always our servant and never our master. Over the last twenty years, in films ranging from *E.T.* (1982) to *Cocoon* (1985) to *Contact* (1997), we have observed in the alien "other" and their science a more benign aspect, but looking at the crop of films that began in the late 1990s, including the aforementioned *Independence Day*, *Starship Troopers* (1997), the continuing *Alien* series, as well as *Sphere* (1998) and *Deep Rising* (1998), it would also appear that some of the old paranoia is creeping back in. All in all, interesting times for the film music composer.

The music of the science-fiction film, as we shall see, effectively and evocatively underscores this human-versus-science conflict. The music is a blend of the conventional post–Romantic idiom and post–Viennese School experiments of the last eighty years. It is Strauss meets Subotnick, Wagner meets Webern, and Borodin meets Birtwhistle. The conventions of the genre place interesting — and I would imagine at times, welcome — demands upon the composer. Like a Romantic era composer, the film music composer faces a world where the rules are constantly changing: Want to write a rhapsody or a nocturne? Go ahead, even though such a musical form does not currently exist. Want to portray and communicate some ineffable sense of mystery about an alien landscape? Try using mixing bowls (as Jerry Goldsmith did in the original *Planet of the Apes*) or create new sounds with a computer. Vivian Sobchak has noted about the music of science-fiction films, "One might expect ... that in addition to functioning quietly in their crucial ways [standard film scoring], music in the SF film would function more overtly, more flamboyantly, less traditionally" (208). And she is right.

For the purposes of analysis I have identified seven major conventions within the genre: main title music, setting, science and technology, the alien, the hero or heroine, society, and the final encounter with the alien. Let us take an in-depth look at each one.

Main Title Music

More than just a convention of science-fiction films, main title music is a convention of all cinema. Its role in the total cinematic experience is very important; Fred Karlin explains: "Main-title music can say to the audience, 'The movie you are about to see is...' and then establish the overall tone and attitude of the film, or prime the audience's expectation as to what will follow" (*Listening to Movies* 128). And this is precisely the role it plays in science-fiction films. If we consider the types, or perhaps better sub-genres, of science fiction we will find a couple of different types of main title music. Michel Butor, in discussing science-fiction literature, identifies "three main types of spectacles: 'Life in the Future'; 'Unknown Worlds'; 'Unexpected Visitors'" (158). For the most part science-fiction films conform to this tripartite division with a good deal of boundary crossing as well; for instance, *Alien, Star Trek* and *Star Wars* (1977) all are about "Life in the Future" (even if they are "A long time ago in a galaxy...") but each has a secondary emphasis: *Alien* also has an "unexpected visitor," and the whole point of *Star Trek* was to explore "strange new worlds." If we look at the main-title music of science-fiction films, however, we find two dominant types which seem to encapsulate the tripartite division Butor outlines: one type of main title music enunciates the "quest" and the heroic, the other type enunciates the alien threat. The two types, moreover, draw on two different musical styles to create the proper mood and to tell us, "This film is about...." Let's take a look at each in a little more depth.

Main-title music which accentuates the quest or the heroic may be the earliest science-fiction main-title music; that is if we consider Sir Arthur Bliss's score for *Things to Come* (1936) to be one of the first, if not the first, science-fiction film in the sound era. The heroic in science fiction centers on a quest: it is the search for the new world, for new knowledge, for a solution to a problem afflicting earth, or to engage and defeat a force that might be threatening our social order. *Things to Come* depicted humankind on a quest to make a better society, grounded in science of course, and that quest was accompanied by a fairly classical score, with bits of Edward Elgar–like nobility mixed with some of the darker elements we find in Stravinsky and Debussy. If we are looking to understand the conventions of this type of main-title music we need to look at more recent films, especially *2001: A Space Odyssey* (1968) and, more significantly, John Williams's main title for *Star Wars*. *2001* used the opening theme of Richard Strauss's *Also Sprach Zarathustra* for its main title, and things really have not been the same since. The Strauss theme conforms to the conventions of scoring that draw on post–Romantic musical language, and its noble opening five-note motif perfectly captures a sense of yearning and reaching:

Figure 2.1. *Also Sprach Zarathustra.*

The motif's "lift" gesture exploiting perfect fifths and fourths and its final cadential stepwise movement toward resolution on the tonic is the perfect accompaniment for Kubrick's image of the mystical alignment of planets seemingly just sitting there for us to leapfrog over to reach some higher evolutionary state. The motif, moreover, is reminiscent of the topics we might find in classic Hollywood adventure and romance films with daring escapades and swashbuckling heroes. Similarly, John Williams exploits the same intervallic relationships in the opening bars of his main-title music for *Star Wars*; notice, however, that his use of the perfect fourth and perfect fifth relationship is reversed from the Strauss (e.g., the perfect fourth interval lies between the three pick-up notes at the beginning of the theme):

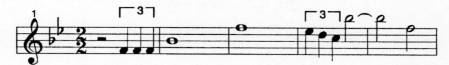

Figure 2.2. Star Wars, main title.

And like Strauss, Williams exploits a minor harmony (a minor seventh) to communicate that sense of yearning and the quest that is about to unfold "A long time ago, in a galaxy far, far away." Williams arguably set the standard for recent science-fiction quest films and as a result we will find a great deal of similarity in the main titles of films ranging from *Star Trek* and *The Black Hole* (1979) (the two that most immediately emulated the Williams model) to *Starship Troopers* (1997). In general, the main titles tend toward unmarkedness, featuring as they do foursquare, consonant harmonies and noble sounding melodies; they are scored, moreover, in classical tradition by utilizing the timbres of the brass instruments to emphasize the militaristic subtext of the films and to evoke in audiences associations with the march-like fanfare topics that are characteristic of brass instruments.

In marked — the pun may be taken as intended — contrast to the heroic quest main-title, is the main-title music for the alien threat film. Just as the heroic quest film relies heavily on gestures and topics characteristic of post–Romantic music, the alien threat film draws more of its musical inspiration from the Second Viennese school and other modernist movements. This is not to say that the scores are redolent with serial writing and aleatoric techniques, but there is a better chance of encountering elements from these musical schools in the alien threat film than there will be in the heroic quest film. If there is, however, an overriding musical characteristic in the main titles of these films it is dissonance. Recalling what we discussed in the introduction, the music that will be used must be of a nature to capture a sense of the extraordinary, the bizarre, the unknown, the abnormal, and the threatening. Nothing has worked better over the years to evoke these states than dissonance. So accustomed are we to the soothing and unmarked qualities of consonant harmonies in our pop music, the presence of predominantly dissonant music creates at best a sense of unease and at worst a totally unsettling and, well, alienating feeling.

The films that established the conventions for this type of main-title music were the science-fiction monster pictures of the 1950s. Beginning with *The Thing* (1951) and *The Day the Earth Stood Still* (1951) and then with *Them* (1954) the pattern was pretty much set. The main title for *Them*, for instance, begins with low rumbling notes played by two pianos[1]; next the strings enter with a swirling figure that moves downward, resolving in a dissonant chord. A theme begins to take shape but is never really developed as the strings state a descending chromatic four-note figure (all half steps) that one often hears in movies that stress suspense. This figure is intensified through sequential repetition on progressively higher scale tones so that it moves stepwise chromatically upward while concurrently getting louder. Finally, this motif reaches a climax and then a simple motif is introduced softly by piccolo, flute and vibe:

Figure 2.3. *Them*, main title.

Well, it is hardly *Star Wars*—in fact, it isn't even Buck Rogers from the 1930s—instead, it is an unsettling leitmotiv that gesturally suggests grief in its melodic descent and its failure to resolve consonantly. Typical of the themes of science-fiction films of the 1950s, this "ant" theme employs some very simple but effective devices to set the mood for the alien threat. Notable here, first, is the downward movement of the theme (as opposed to the upward movement of the Strauss and Williams themes mentioned earlier); second, the second intervallic leap (from E flat to A) is the dreaded tritone (or diminished fifth) described in music theory as *diabolus in musica* (the devil in music) because of its instability (not to mention the challenge it offers vocalists); third, the ending note in relationship to the beginning note is a minor second, an interval, to quote Deryck Cooke, which expresses a feeling of "hopeless anguish" (78); fourth, the leap upward is a minor seventh, another interval which does not connote pleasant feeling but, to quote Cooke again, is an "expression of painful feelings." (72). The resolution down a fourth is gesturally emphatic and ironic with the final note, in relationship once again to the beginning note of the motif, forming a tritone. It is hard to imagine one being able to pack so much unpleasantness, from a gestural, harmonic and melodic standpoint, into such few notes, but Bronislau Kaper has done it masterfully here. And, indeed, the main title sets the mood of terror, menace and mystery that await James Arness, Edmund Gwenn and Joan Weldon as they take on the giant mutant ants who threaten to reach out and destroy civilization with their spiky, atomically-mutated legs and beaks. Jumping ahead thirty years we find similar features in the main titles for films such as *Predator* (1987) and *Alien*. The main titles for both films begin with a very Ligeti-like tonal cluster that seems almost to emerge out of nowhere. *Predator*, like *Them*, introduces a strongly marked dissonant chord that leads to a repeated figure, played by a glockenspiel, that communicates a sense of

Them. **Bronislau Kaper's "Ant Theme" captures the terror, menace and mystery of these desert mutants.**

mystery and the unknown. This theme is punctuated by a more militaristic topic featuring a rhythmic pattern played by a snare drum in tandem with an ostinato pattern played by the piano. Finally, a heroic theme is picked up by the brass and plays in counterpoint to the largely discordant harmonies that continue to play throughout the theme. *Alien*, on the other hand, promises all of the mystery and terror of the unknown without the corresponding militaristic or heroic impulses. The Ligeti-like tonal cluster gives way to string playing that almost resembles white noise; the strings are played so that on occasion it sounds like bugs are flying about (the sound is very similar to that in Ligeti's *Adventures*, which was used in the final sequence of *2001*). The string motifs are complemented by Echoplex effects from the percussion and the final introduction of a simple motif that is the only real melody in the entire title:

Figure 2.4. *Alien*, main title.

Jerry Goldsmith, like Kaper, has chosen a simple but dissonant motif to communicate the mood of the film. Each title captures the film and the conventions of the films perfectly: they both use marked dissonances to establish our encounter with the abnormal; strings are used to build suspense through trilling and swirling figures; the brass suggest violence (especially when played forte and using flutter tonguing); and the winds offer a gentle counterpoint, suggesting perhaps our "innocent" or at least passive or pacifistic state, and the fact that these dissonant motives are oftentimes introduced by the winds also suggests that this passivity or pacifist nature is constantly open to threats from without and within.

There is a third category of main title theme which is more common today than it has been in the past, reflecting the transformational and progressive tendencies of the genre itself. Within the last twenty years science fiction has entertained the notion that "unexpected visitors" might not always be a threat, but, in fact, may be a boon to our social order. Films such as *E.T., Cocoon, Close Encounters of the Third Kind,* and, more recently, *Contact,* present us with more benign "Alien Others," who according to Vivian Sobchak "have become less other — be they extraterrestrial teddy bears, starmen, brothers from another planet, robots, androids, or replicants. They have become our familiars, our simulacra, embodied as literally alienated images of our alienated selves" (293). The main titles for films featuring these "alien others" are imbued with a warmer and, one might even say, more compassionate feeling. Dissonances are not to be found (or at least they are used in a more traditional sense), traditional harmonies and strong melodies with tinges of nostalgia and innocence are the order of the day. Look at the opening bars of Alan Silvestri's lovely theme for *Contact*:

Figure 2.5. *Contact,* main title.

The opening three note ascending motif features a lift gesture that outlines a minor third, which in turn gives the melody a sense of poignancy and longing, but the melody always resolves to the tonic or the dominant, which also communicates a sense of stability or at least fulfillment — and that is exactly what the film is about: our restless yearning for fulfillment and knowledge and our ability to achieve those goals. But this journey really is not about heroic voyages outward to strange new worlds but about finding ourselves in the stars. It is Henry David Thoreau meets John W. Campbell, or Arthur C. Clarke if you prefer.

Setting

There are three major settings for science-fiction films: earth, outer space and the spaceship (these could seem as two because the spaceship could be considered part of the outer space setting). In each case, however, the role of the setting is complex. Setting, be it outer space or earth, often establishes a mood for the film, and it is crucial for contextualizing the makeup and values of the society threatened by or learning to live with the alien other; also, it is the terrain for the conflict, the site for the introduction of the alien. Vivian Sobchak notes,

"The major visual impulse of all SF films is to pictorialize the unfamiliar, the nonexistent, the strange and the totally alien—and to do so with a verisimilitude which is, at times, documentary in flavor and style" (89). To complement this visual impulse we find composers drawing on a wide variety of musical topics and gestures to establish the mood and atmosphere of the settings. Let's take a look at the two major backdrops for the science-fiction film.

Beginning in the 1950s, many science-fiction films had earth as their primary setting, giving the lie to the notion that it was all space opera. Using earth as a primary setting heightens the alien threat, forcing us to band together to thwart this threat, preserve earth, and reaffirm our humanness. Thus, the composer's task is to create a musical landscape that simultaneously captures the normalcy of our lives and perhaps holding at bay the notion that such a setting could give birth to or be "visited" by mysterious and potentially dangerous forces. It is interesting that many films dealing with alien "invasion" begin in rural or even wilderness settings; *Them, The Beast from 20,000 Fathoms, It Came from Outer Space, E.T., Close Encounters,* and *Contact* all begin in non-urban environments. At some point, the forces of urban (or rural) society are threatened by and must deal with the alien, but in the initial stages of the narrative the threat lies outside the normal flow of our daily routine. In large part the establishing shots in a film will determine the nature of the music to be used. In general, composers will either write (use, as in the case of many of the Universal films of the 1950s) a specific cue (non-diegetic) or they will rely upon source (diegetic) music to establish the atmosphere.[2] A good example of the first is the cue "Sand Rock" from *It Came from Outer Space*. The cue features a lovely melody over an aerial tracking shot.

Figure 2.6. *It Came from Outer Space,* "Sand Rock."

This is very much the "pastoral" topic with its underlying steady and rolling rhythm, and its Western-tinged flowing melody carried by the winds; one might even go farther and say that the topic signifies the "American" pastoral. It is by all counts a conventional bit of scoring, relying heavily on stepwise melodic writing and conventional tonal harmonic language. It, in short, attempts to convey a picture of a typical small Western town, going about its business, oblivious to the threat that is about to come screaming into the picture frame.

Some composers, on the other hand, may rely upon marked gestures and motifs in underscoring a setting to intensify the suspense and foreground the coming conflict. Mysterious music and suspense topics, relying upon minor harmonies and unusual instrumentation, can convey this feeling. The "Desert" cue in *Terminator* uses a synthesizer, muted brass and a simple melodic motif that relies upon a simple two note theme that does not go much beyond a major and minor second. This theme is punctuated by echoing percussion to foreshadow the coming battle between human and cyborg. An example of how source music is used can be seen in *The Thing* when, after Dimitri Tiomkin has blown us away with the pounding "Thing" theme and the dissonances of the alien in the icy north, he returns us to the officers' club and some gentle dance band music playing in the background; the melody is relatively indistinguishable but it features a muted trumpet and a rather conventional fox trot rhythm — music that one might hear over any American radio station on any given day of the week in the 1950s. The "unmarked" popular music stands in stark contrast to the violence in the marked gestures of the cues that accompany the confrontation with the alien.

What is the sound of outer space? What a wonderful and, probably, slightly frightening prospect for a composer. When a composer underscores setting in most films there is, as I discussed in the introduction, some musical precedent that must be taken into consideration and which, in order to convey that sense of place to the viewer, must be quoted or at least suggested. Aside from Gustav Holst's *The Planets,* space is not often the subject of program music, opera, or even musical comedy. Popular music provides no topics, primarily because it borrows from film or the limited serious music examples cited above. Consequently, the composer and audience have limited referents (or interpretants) to influence both composition and listening expectations. It is in science-fiction films, then, that we observe some of the greatest innovations in film scoring. Early in the history of the genre composers quickly crafted specific topics and gestures that would serve them in good stead in their efforts to convey the pictorial images of what Vivian Sobchak calls the "immense and infinitesimal" (101). The composer, to communicate this sense of the immense, routinely summons forth two topics. The first is the use of strings scored in high registers oftentimes playing ostinato patterns or arpeggiated chords like this; the underlying gesture is that of the perpetually undulating wave:

Figure 2.7.

The one example that most immediately comes to mind, and one which the reader probably can recall with some ease, is the music that immediately follows the main-title of *Star Wars*; it is a simple motif, but it effectively conveys the space setting for the films. The reason for the reliance upon music that is scored in higher register might be found in an idea suggested by Carroll C. Pratt; Malcolm Budd in his analysis of Pratt's *The Meaning of Music* (1931) notes that "Pratt claims that *in addition* to hearing a difference in pitch between different notes we hear high notes as if they were coming from a higher position in space than lower notes and, in virtue of this fact, we describe the difference in pitch with spatial terms" (41). Not surprisingly, more recent scores attempt to capture the vastness and mysterious nature of outer space in musical gestures which recall the music of Ligeti which Stanley Kubrick used in *2001: A Space Odyssey*. Ligeti's music derives its ethereal and otherworldly quality from the way he constructs tonal clusters, especially for high voices and/or high strings. The mild (and sometimes harsh) dissonances that occur by having two voices singing a minor second as a sustained chord and then layering more voices on the chord is both eerie and uplifting. A good example of this is in Jerry Goldsmith's opening title music for *Alien*, discussed earlier, which retains the same qualities of the main title as it segues into the establishing shot of the *Nostromo* "steaming" through outer space.

The other sound of outer space is the twinkling of the stars. But, you may say, twinkling stars do not make a sound. Well, no, not as we sit here and view them from earth, but they do in a film soundtrack. Nine times out of ten a composer will use a celesta, a glockenspiel, chimes, or any instrument that has a chime-like timbre to replicate the twinkling of stars. Gesturally, the wave figure may also be heard in this topic, in this case signifying the twinkling light alternating between bright and dim states. The wonderful cue "Shooting Stars" from *This Island Earth* (1954) employs a glockenspiel to suggest the stars. The cue then states its "infinitesimal" and mysterious theme that features an interesting melodic pattern of a downward leap of a diminished fifth (the same as the tritone), then up a major sixth, followed by a descending chromatic stepwise pattern. This particular pattern can also be heard in scores for more recent films like *Star Wars* and the *Star Trek* series.

Finally, a special word here about a couple of "alien" landscapes which, from a musical standpoint, deserve some mention. The late 1960s witnessed the creation of three very innovative scores: the pastiche that Kubrick assembled for *2001*, Jerry Goldsmith's score for *Planet of the Apes*, and Leonard Rosenman's score for *Fantastic Voyage* (1966). What set each apart was their bold use of "modern" music. I have discussed the score for *2001* in more depth elsewhere,[3] but I want to briefly mention what the other two scores brought to the conventions of scoring science-fiction films over the last thirty years. In underscoring the alien landscape, each score went against type. For *2001*, in an incredibly flamboyant move, Kubrick used a

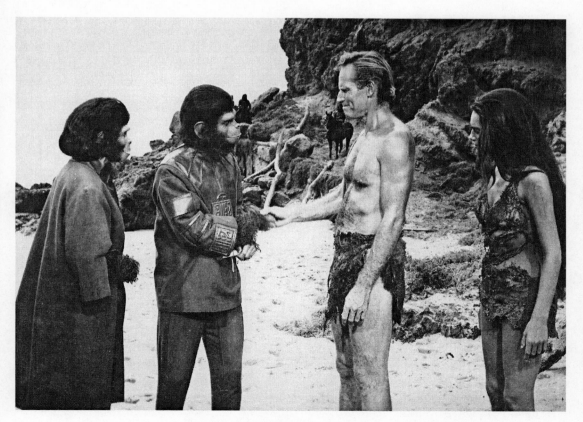

Planet of the Apes. Unusual meters and instruments transform the familiar landscape of the U.S.A. into a mysterious and potentially hostile environment.

Strauss waltz to depict the immensity of space and the technology that seeks to dominate the infinitesimal. The other two films, in marked contrast, relied upon brilliantly conceived atonal material to transform earthbound settings into alien landscapes. What makes *Planet of the Apes* so very stunning is how Goldsmith is able to "fool" us with his score. As we watch the three astronauts make their way across the alien terrain that looks suspiciously familiar, we forget that it is familiar because of the music. According to Irwin Bazelon, Goldsmith employs a serial (12 tone) theme in these sequences (86–87). This atonal theme is augmented then by the use of an Echoplex effect with plucked strings. Rhythmically the music, at one point, alternates between 12/8, 15/8, and 9/8 meters, which further contributes to the disorienting effect he is trying to achieve. Consequently, Goldsmith is able to transform the U.S.A. into a mysterious and potentially hostile environment. Rosenman's alien landscape, on the other hand, is the human body, and his music for the miniature ship's entry into this "alien" world is stunning. George Burt describes the effect of the music at this narrative juncture as follows: "the score's accumulating layers of musical sound both establish and sustain the feeling of suspension in space and time" (125). Rosenman achieves this effect with a musical gesture that is now commonplace in science fiction and is also one that Kubrick saw as efficacious in the music of Ligeti: a dissonant tonal cluster, a chord that is largely formed out of tones that are only a minor or major second apart, featuring a crescendo-decrescendo gesture. Furthermore, one will find that when a theme is stated in these films and in most outer space music these days, the interval of the second is most often used. Here is the major motif from Rosenman's *Fantastic Voyage*[4]:

Figure 2.8. *Fantastic Voyage.*

Not surprisingly, Goldsmith's cue for the establishing shot of the interior of the *Nostromo* in *Alien* utilizes most of the elements discussed above from his early *Apes* scores and Rosenman's *Fantastic Voyages* score.

Science and Technology

It could be said that science and technology are the *raison d'être* for all science fiction films; without it, they are just spooky stories or romances. They are also the central cultural issues or factors in the genre's kernel conflict. Science can be the cause of the central conflict and it can also be a partial savior in the resolution of the conflict: on the one hand, it is the major threat to our humanity and, on the other hand, it may be a boon. In general, however, the genre's basic impulse is to reflect a cultural skepticism about the role of science and technology in our lives. Dr. Carrington's admiration for the creature in *The Thing* brings into relief the danger posed by the scientific worldview: "Yes, a neat and unconfused reproductive technique of vegetation. No pain or pleasure as we know it. No emotions, no heart; our superior in every way." The score, working in tandem with other filmic conventions, tells us that yes, indeed, the thing may be superior to humans, but that will be to humankind's detriment. Richard Hodgens states that although science-fiction literature seems to reflect some awareness and appreciation for science, "in the sf film there is rarely any sane middle ground. Now and then, science is white magic. But far more often, it is black, and if these films have any general implications about science, they are that science and scientist are dangerous, raising problems and provoking widespread disaster for the innocent, ignorant good folks, and that curiosity is a deadly sin" (250).

As stated earlier, the threat lies in what science may do to our social institutions and, consequently, to our social order, and this threat retains a pretty strong grip on the imaginations of filmmakers and audiences in more recent films as Michael Ryan and Douglas Kellner note: "Perhaps this is why technology is such an object of fear in conservative science fiction films of the current era [e.g., 1970s, 1980s]. It is a metaphor for a possibility of reconstruction that would put the stability of conservative social institutions in question" (253). What is interesting about the music that underscores the scientific in the films is that it reflects our conflicting ideas about science itself. Some films, like *Things to Come* and the *Star Trek* series, have cast technology and science in an almost heroic mode. For instance, in *Things to Come*, the end of war and the beginning of the rebuilding of society based on scientific progress is heralded by the "Happy March."[5] The actual music for the "Building a New World" continues the march-like feel and the dissonances are used to capture mechanistic sounds of building — of metal meeting metal and of human energy being marshaled — Virgin- and Dynamo-like — to build a better world. The melody that finally emerges is not ominous but more lighthearted, and when the brass makes its entrance it is as a preface to a final triumphant chord. Similarly, in *Star Trek* (both the first film and *The Wrath of Khan*) the music that underscores shots of the *Enterprise* sound as though they should be played under a love scene between Paul Henreid and Bette Davis in *Now, Voyager*. In *Star Trek: The Motion Picture*, when Kirk is being shuttled out to the *Enterprise*, after having been away from her for a long while, Jerry Goldsmith transforms the main theme from a heroic anthem into a warmer, almost romantic paean to the captain's ship. String writing dominates the sound early in the cue, the tempo is slowed down, and as Robert Wise alternates shots of the ship slowly coming into view with Kirk's misty-eyed absorption with the ship, the music communicates a sense of reverence, veneration and, well, love. The music transforms this technological object into something that is human, something that is an extension of the good that underlies our quest to seek new worlds and to understand and learn. The music offers the premise that technology is indeed the servant of humanity and not its master.

Most science-fiction films, however, suggest that making science our servant is not easy and, in fact, is fraught with danger. Perhaps the greatest irony here is that in science fiction, the music that we normally associate with the irrational is associated with enterprises that are grounded almost entirely in the rational. Musical gestures associated with science and technology in science-fiction films are represented by dissonant and atonal music suggesting the futuristic, otherworldly, and dangerous aura that science assumes in the films. A perfect example of this is from the 1955 film *Tarantula*. The musical cue "Radioactive Research" is used to underscore a scene where the well-meaning but misguided Dr. Stevenson returns to his work in his lab. As the camera tracks Dr. Stevenson entering his lab, the music introduces a high-pitched ostinato pattern consisting of a minor second scored for strings. There is a shift to an overhead shot of the doctor's isolation tank with black gloves and a vial. As the doctor places his hands in the gloves and prepares to fill a hypodermic needle, the woodwinds and low strings introduce the following motif:

Figure 2.9. *Tarantula,* "Radioactive Research."

As with previous examples, you will note that Stein has relied upon the minor second as well as a rather angular intervallic leap to convey a sense of mystery and suspense to the scene. Lift gestures in such cases are neutralized and nearly rendered null and void because of the subsequent tragic (or sighing) gestures as in the second measure above. Without the music the actions of the doctor would be fairly innocuous; with the music they portend doom. Similarly, in *Independence Day*, the music that accompanies the arrival at Area 51 and the descent into the bowels of the secret UFO experimental installation is in marked contrast to the otherwise "unmarked" heroic and militaristic score that David Arnold crafted for the film. More atonal and haunting in effect, the music thrusts us into a world removed from the normal: the inchoate danger of its scrubbed clean, sterile and high-tech, scientific iconology becomes obvious as we realize that the scientific secrets being explored in this out of the way, secret place by the whacked-out scientist (Brent Spiner) and his egghead companions have brought us to the brink of extermination — a situation that will be corrected by a man who cares more for the environment than technology and a fighter pilot who cares more about duty than technology.

In addition to using atonal musical gestures, some composers rely upon the sound of synthesized music to highlight the threat of science. The rather cold and odd sounds that a synthesizer can produce seem to offer an effective correlative to the excesses of science. Jerry Goldsmith very effectively mixes cues using a standard orchestra and the synthesizer in his score for *Logan's Run* (1976). Most significantly, the synthesized cues usually signify that science has indeed gone too far (or we have let it go to far and now it is our master). In one such scene, the musical cue entitled "Flameout," a "select" band of people are brought together in a ritual where their bodies are literally taken up in a pseudo-transcendent moment until they are finally vaporized at the apex of their trip. Below, audiences watch in rapt and unwitting wonder and cheer as the bodies spark and disappear. In short, we no longer question the routine extinction of human life, but merely accept the ritual as necessary (shades of Shirley Jackson's "The Lottery") and trust totally in the "benefits" that scientific progress has bestowed upon us. The dissonances and textures produced by the synthesized music are the perfect aural complement for this dehumanized and, from our standpoint, irrational ritual.

Finally, a word about the use of music to underscore the scientific in *2001*: it is, to say the least, ironic. The three sequences where the trappings of science and technology are most on display are the space docking sequence, which uses the Johann Strauss waltz, the trip to the moon from the space station (Strauss again) and the opening scene in part three ("Jupiter Mission: 18 Months Later"), where we are introduced to *Discovery* and astronauts Dave

Bowman and Frank Poole (Gary Lockwood) and which uses the *Gayaneh Ballet* music by Khatchaturian; these pieces of music are, from a musical standpoint, closest to the classic Hollywood score, replete with conventional romantic and post–Romantic harmonies and soaring or at least contemplative and easily recognizable melodies (the *Gayaneh* selection is ironically pastoral in feeling). In short, dissonance is limited to its most conventional usage and is not a privileged harmonic language. In a sense, however, the film foreshadows our ambivalence about science and the alien over the last thirty years. Less and less do we make automatic associations with science as evil but see the misapplication of it in human terms. The scientific prowess of E.T. is never presented in aurally threatening terms, but the music accompanying the team of scientists and medical people pursuing his trail is fraught with the old dissonant and threatening musical topics and gestures of the 1950s.

The Alien

Aliens are physical embodiments of the Other, that which is separate from our earthbound humanity. In many films prior to the 1970s they symbolized the negative aspects of science: one group of aliens was so advanced scientifically as to be devoid of humanity (*Forbidden Planet, War of the Worlds*, etc.); another group represented scientific experiments gone bad or the result of questionable (read nuclear) experiments (*Them*); there were, of course, creatures from other planets; there also were those creatures who had mutated because of science gone awry (*Tarantula, The Deadly Mantis*, etc.); and, finally, there were alien objects like the monolith in *2001*. There are also those aliens who are byproducts of either the folly or evil of certain social institutions. Ryan and Kellner, in writing about *Alien*, state, "The film thus depicts corporate capitalism as a predatory, survivalist machine; self-interest takes precedence over community. The alien is a projection of the principles of the capitalist system" (184). Vivian Sobchak, moreover, has noted that "SF Creatures" are "less personalized" and that they "lack a psyche" and seem to be engaged mostly in "external activity" (32). One may recall here why Dr. Carrington (*The Thing*) and Ashe (*Alien*) admire their respective alien nemeses and what the good citizens of the small town in *Invasion of the Body Snatchers* (1956) try to sell Kevin McCarthy: the belief that the alien state is wonderful because it is pure, devoted only to survival and freed from the things that encumber humans, such as emotions. But it is this last point that makes the aliens such a threat: if they do dominate they will destroy those very things that affirm our humanity, namely the ability to love, to create, and to appreciate beauty.

It is not surprising then that composers rely upon those musical devices that are "marked" to reflect the abnormality of the alien state. Dissonance, atonality, polychords, chromaticism, tritones and other avant-garde harmonic and melodic devices (electronic music especially) as well as irregular meters and polyrhythms are the preferred devices used to signify the alien threat. J.P. Telotte suggests that our fear of robots (and by extension any alien being) centers on our fears of being replaced by them and "how we often seem controlled by a kind of program not so very different from the sort that drives the artificial beings which abound in our films..." (*Replications* 4). It is this undercurrent of fear that the music of the alien exploits. In the 1950s, composers generally wedded dissonance to dynamics in portraying their aliens. This correlation reflected, in large measure, the larger-than-life-size figures of the giant ant, or a praying mantis, or beasts from the age of dinosaurs. Typical of the sound is Henry Mancini's

cue from *Creature from the Black Lagoon* (1954), which was used often in Universal science
fiction in the '50s. The cue features a plodding bass line, dissonant chords played by the brass
(often using a flutter tongue — tremolo — effect to heighten the tension), and strings outlining minor seconds or a similar dissonant ostinato pattern.

Figure 2.10. *Creature from the Black Lagoon,* "The Thing Strikes."

The following motif from *It Came from Outer Space* is typical of the kind of motif a composer would ascribe to the alien in 1950s science fiction:

Figure 2.11. *It Came from Outer Space.*

Typical of alien music there is not a lot of stepwise melody writing, but instead Stein relies
upon dramatic octave leaps, especially the octave leap up followed by a minor second down.
Thus even though the leap is upward, the marked interval (tritone) foregrounds the gesture
and negates the conventional "yearning" signification and substitutes disequilibrium. Ever
since Miklos Rosza used a similar pattern in *The Lost Weekend* (1945) the use of leaps of an
octave or minor seventh and then the "sigh" gesture which resolves downward a minor second (or combination of the minor second and minor third or the augmented fourth) have
been associated with tragic, abnormal or disturbed states. And so we see the use of the tritone in the motif associated with the Deadly Mantis and, as we have already seen, Bronislau
Kaper used the tritone in his "ant theme" for *Them*. These harmonic and melodic consider-
ations are then wedded to unusual instrumental timbres to paint an image of something relentless, dominating and lying beyond the pale of common humanity. Since the debut of *Planet*

of the Apes and *2001* in 1968 composers have come to favor tonal clusters to suggest the alien as well; usually scored for very high voice or strings, the tonal cluster sounds otherworldly (almost heavenly) but the dissonances are calculated to put the listener on edge and create a sense of suspense and uneasiness.

Recent science-fiction films featuring more benign aliens generally downplay discordance, but one will probably find a mixture of musical topics and gestures, some of which fall outside the strict parameters of the melodic and harmonic vocabulary of the post–Romantic tradition and some of which employ that very vocabulary, to tell us something about the "new" alien. The five note motif that the scientists use to communicate with the aliens in *Close Encounters of the Third Kind* is not a model of voice leading, but it does not grate on the ear because it does not exploit minor or altered harmonies and dissonant intervallic relationships. However, Williams's music for *E.T.* really goes against the old type and suggests that this little visitor from outer space has not only the capacity for human love and understanding but also the potential to achieve something heroic:

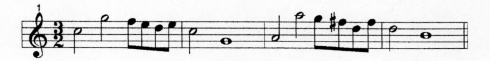

Figure 2.12. *ET,* main title.

Consonant intervallic leaps of the fifth, the fourth, the octave and the third are generally part of heroic topics employed in other genres. Just like good science, the good alien is one whose alien identity and whose alien powers are subordinate to human concerns and will be brought in to serve the best parts of our common humanity. Vivian Sobchak's thoughts about the "new" aliens may provide some insight into why the musical gestures are as they are:

> From *Close Encounters* on, then, special effects in mainstream SF have been transformed from signs of a rational and objective science and technology to representations of a joyous, and "sublime," intensity — thematically linking postmodern culture's new "detached," "free-floating," and "liberated" sense of emotional transcendence with the transcendental. Alienated emotional transcendence becomes objectified in the transcendental and loving alien, and the alien-ated experience of "rapture" or "religious transport" is narrativized literally — as human beings are ecstatically "carried away" in body and spirit, as "religious transport" is effected by "alien transportation" [287–88].

As we look to future chapters that deal with romance and religious experience in films, we will find these same ideas and musical topics and gestures cropping up again. One, in short, should not be surprised to find a great similarity between what Alfred Newman did in *The Song of Bernadette* (1943) to underscore Bernadette's visions of "the lady" and what composers do today to underscore their characters' encounters with the alien.

Society

Much like the Western genre, the society depicted in the science-fiction film is a cross section of the society at large. Generally speaking, all or some of the major social institutions will be represented as countervailing forces to the alien. Thus we find ministers who deal with the alien by seeking religious guidance; the family is often the most threatened but at times calls forth the most heroic behavior as Dad or Mom sacrifices to save the family, reminding us that human bonds are stronger than technological ones; the government will rely upon power and or political negotiation; finally, the scientific community can be counted upon to offer solutions to the threat or to extend olive branches (recall the feeble attempts of the scientists in *The Thing* to establish communication, while the military guys torch the walking vegetable played by Jim Arness). As is the case in many genre films, the community often finds itself in a position where it needs to make sacrifices to preserve our all too human but wonderfully humane and diversified society. But the key element is that the society must work together as a unified whole. There are, moreover, two related societal themes that sometimes complement the cooperation theme: either no one institution should emerge as the dominant power, or, as in the case of *The War of the Worlds*, the institutions are basically powerless and it is only with God's help — ironically through germs — that we can deal with this alien threat. The music representing the society will be, like the society, very diversified, relying upon a mixture of conventional topics common to most domestic dramas and varying types of source (diegetic) music. Source music is most revealing in creating an impression of the society and what kind of threat the alien may be. In the case of some films, the source music will be recognizable, reflecting mainstream musical trends, which, in turn, communicates a sense of normalcy or, as in the case of the square dance in *War of the Worlds*, our human capacity for fun and enjoyment of life — two things which are about to be threatened by invaders from Mars. The source music in *THX-1138* (1971), which we hear as Robert Duvall walks through the public part of the underground complex, is very much like Muzak, soft orchestral music featuring lushly orchestrated strings playing pleasant tonal melodies, the perfect music, as George Lucas seems to be suggesting, for a narcotized society whose emotions and sexuality are constantly kept in check. The source music also might be ironic as is the case in *Independence Day*, where one of the opening sequences features R.E.M.'s "It's the End of the World as We Know It (And I Feel Fine)," underscoring the irony that it is indeed the end of the world but people are just blithely going about their business as if everything is fine — although it won't be for long.

In terms of conventional musical cues, there is not a lot of consistency. I really could not find, as I did with the alien, a stable body of scoring conventions and musical topics that signify society in the science-fiction films. The filmmaker's vision of society is communicated through the selfsame music that is used to underscore establishing shots for the setting, such as the pastoral topic "Sand Rock" from *It Came from Outer Space*. However, not every film, even those with rural settings, will rely upon a pastoral topic; it is just as likely that a popular song may be playing in the background during the film's opening and throughout the exposition. Music, however, is central to the delineation of the kernel conflict in all the films. In *Logan's Run*, for instance, we have already seen that the evils of scientific progress are communicated through the use of synthesized electronic music. In the same film, Jerry Goldsmith portrays the "natural world" that lies above the underground world by relying on a classical pastoral topic: the music features a lovely flowing melody, which, in addition to the lushly orchestrated strings, employs the oboe to convey a sense of the bucolic and the pastoral. There is more than just scene setting going on here; Goldsmith is telling us something about a society that's been lost, a society that, through the efforts of Logan and his female companion, must be reclaimed and brought back to those dwelling in a technologically advanced but humanly (humanely!) ignorant state below the earth. Similarly, in *E.T.*, the music that underscores the appearance of the "stranger" in the opening sequence after E.T. has been abandoned is similar to the musical gestures we associated with the alien in earlier films, the point being that the real threat is not the little critter trying to make his getaway through the forest but the man with the keys looking for him. The dissonant music features swirling figures and glissandos in the strings and a rhythmic gesture that we often find in militaristic topics or accompanying violent actions:

Figure 2.13 *E.T.*, rhythmic pattern.

The *Star Wars* series, of course, offers ample opportunity to study the conventions of scoring the social order, but let me just mention a couple of small examples. Ironically, because the aliens are the social order Williams relies upon marked musical elements and the conventions for scoring we normally associate with the historical romance or action adventure film at work. The forces of good are identified by heroic topics or, as in the case of the love theme for Han and Leia, classic melodic writing featuring soaring melodies and interesting harmonic (and slightly exotic) shifts — which are there to remind us that this is not a present day, earthbound relationship here. The forces of evil, as in the music for the Death Star or in the "Imperial March," are characterized by dissonances, tragic or violent gestures, and minor (or modal) harmonies. The final images of the films celebrate the heroic and triumph of good, and, as in the case of the *Return of the Jedi*, the celebration of the natural world. Similarly, the older films, especially *War of the Worlds* and *Them*, feature closing themes which use bells to suggest the triumph of higher powers or at least some sort of religiously based moral system and an accompanying heroic theme scored for brass and strings. Thus, the films' final musical statements reaffirm the social order: tonal music dominates, things are back to normal and it is not "the end of the world as we know it."

The Hero/Heroine

As one views the large corpus of science-fiction films, one will be hard pressed to find a lot of distinctive music that underscores the specific activities of the hero figures. Unlike aliens, it is hard to nail down a circumscribed body of musical topics that immediately suggest the hero in science fiction. The reason for this is that in science-fiction films the real hero is society itself. The act of heroism is the defeat of or reconciliation with the alien. So, in *Tarantula*, although John Agar is instrumental in discovering the identity of the monster and rallying the townsfolk to take on the monster, in the final frame it is the air force (in the person of Clint Eastwood) and napalm (ironic, isn't it?) that deliver the final blow. The myth equates social order with cooperation.

Science-fiction films, however, do feature main characters, heroes and heroines if you will, and they can be drawn from any sector of society. In some cases they may be members of the military (*The Thing*), representatives of the government (*Them*), scientists (*The War of the*

Worlds), or just "ordinary guys" (both the Richard Dreyfuss and Melinda Dillon characters in *Close Encounters of the Third Kind*). The hero or heroine will generally be seen to embody some characteristic that reaffirms human uniqueness or even a particular cultural value (he or she may be particularly resourceful, possessed of common sense and patriotism, a champions of progress or democracy, etc.). The music of the hero or heroine is similar to that of the hero figures in the action adventure or historical adventure films, depending upon their role in society. Consequently, the accompanying music may be characterized by martial or even pastoral topics, or by uplifting and assertive gestures, and even romantic melodic writing (if there is a love angle). A good example of this is a musical cue entitled "Agar to the Rescue" from *Tarantula*, which accompanies the young doctor as he hurries to help the female lab assistant of Dr. Stevenson. The music features some trademark heroic "yearning" gestures: it is conventionally and markedly tonal with swirling bass strings to suggest activity while the violins and violas play a simple but effective chromatic motif that builds on gradually ascending scale tones (i.e., the motif starts on C and then repeats but on D or D flat and so forth up the scale). Under the action the music conveys a sense of urgency and confidence and resolve on the part of the doctor. Another good example of the heroic theme is the "Presidential Theme" from *Independence Day*. The piece is marked "Maestoso"; here are the opening two measures:

Figure 2.14 *Independence Day,* "Presidential Theme."

The melody is simple, outlining a major third in the first measure and a perfect fourth in the second; the melody derives its nobility and power from the descending bass line, which makes that simple melody seem as though it is reaching for some goal; the antecedent sighing gestures (beats 3 and 4 in m.1, all of ms.2 and 3) heighten the expressive power of the lift gesture in m.4, creating a heroic trope.[6] The harmonic structure in the two measures, moreover, is rock solid tonic-dominant-subdominant- dominant chords (regardless of the inversions used). Once the complete theme is stated, Arnold effectively modulates from a V^7 chord in second inversion up to E flat major and restates the theme again; the modulation by means of the chromatic mediant adds a sense of dramatic movement upward and forward. The motif for Will Smith's character, "Hiller's Theme," has similar nobility. As is the case with so many genre films, these themes come together in a coda-like finale in the film's final sequence when the combined forces of government (the president), science (Jeff Goldblum), the military (Will Smith), and ordinary citizens (Randy Quaid's drunken fighter pilot) join forces to bring down the seemingly indestructible alien force hovering over earth.

Reflective of the shift in the genre over the years is the music that accompanies heroic activity in *E.T.*, most notably, the use of E.T.'s theme (quoted earlier) to underscore the boys' flight from the authorities. Once again, this is pretty standard heroic stuff: a dramatic leap of a fifth, followed by a graceful eighth-note figure which returns to the root and then down a fourth. The melody is put through different permutations in the film (scored slowly and lovingly, scored in a minor key, etc.), but in this sequence it really takes on a swashbuckling feel as the kids do dramatic leaps with their bikes, make narrow escapes, and, finally, through the powers of E.T., rise above earth and the (ironically for science-fiction!) hostile forces of society down below with the theme ringing out forte over the action. As I stated above, the transformational nature of the genre has brought us to a point where the myth of the hero is subject to generic improvisation: heroes no longer need be agents of social institutions but can be kids, forces of innocence and tolerance, and the too-curious alien whose only wish, like Dorothy in the *Wizard of Oz*, is just to get back home. The heroic behavior on the part of kids and E.T., however, is conducted in support of a pretty standard value and one that Americans have related to since the writing of "Home Sweet Home" back in the nineteenth century: there's no place like home — even for an alien.

The Final Encounter with the Alien

This is the culminating point in the films, that moment when earthlings show their mettle and must defeat or reconcile themselves to the alien in order to preserve their humanity. Depending upon the nature of the science-fiction film (i.e., heroic quest vs. alien threat) the music used in this sequence will vary somewhat from film to film. The heroic quest music will bear strong resemblances to what we might encounter in historical romances. If, for instance, when you listen to the music for the famous charge of the light brigade from the 1936 film *The Charge of the Light Brigade*, you will notice that Max Steiner has scored the sequence in quasi–*1812 Overture* style by weaving themes and motifs associated with the three combatants into an aural tapestry, or, actually, an aural narrative style.[7] Similarly, in the final confrontation between the rebel forces and the empire in *Return of the Jedi* (1983), John Williams weaves Luke's motif, the "Imperial March," his war music (reminiscent of Holst's "Mars, the Bringer of War" from *The Planets*) and so forth to symbolize and add emotional depth to the battle scenes. *Independence Day* achieves a very similar effect as the alien theme, with its ominous minor second motif, is finally drowned out by variations on "The Presidential Theme" and "Hiller's Theme."

The music for the alien threat differs slightly. Although in some of the films a military theme or at least musical topics we associate with the military (particular drum patterns, brass fanfares, march-like rhythms, etc.) might be woven into the confrontation cue, one most often finds the music associated with alien itself dominating the scene. If, indeed, the composer has not written particular motifs for the society, then there is a good chance that there will be no corresponding music for this cue. For instance, in *The Thing*, the Thing's motif (characterized by a plodding rhythm) dominates the music with standard suspense topics (tremolos played by strings in a high register, rapidly tongued brass figures, dissonant chords, etc.) filling out the cue. In *It Came from Beneath the Sea* an ostinato pattern sets the tone for the relentless attack by the giant octopus; this is then augmented by a simple minor second motif scored for the brass, which is occasionally punctuated by a bugle call motif (using the interval of the fifth) that is sounded by flutes. Finally, the composer uses sharply attacked chords against the ever-present tremolo pattern in the strings to heighten the tension of the sequence and to underscore the impending violent end of the beast, which is, indeed, underscored by a final crashing tutti chord. What is perhaps most interesting is that these cues actually conflate the conflict and the narrative thrust of the films: our curiosity about the alien is generally underscored by suspense music, but this curiosity must inevitably give way to violence or at least the threat of violence. Finally, the end title music will signify what the outcome has been: a triumphal march plays over the credits at the end of *The Thing*, chiming bells and a hymn topic underscore the concluding images of *The War of the Worlds*, bells are part of the closing moments of *Them*, and so forth. The music at the end should tell us if the social order is preserved, and the music will signify that stability by evoking recognizable topics, unmarked tonalities, and triumphant gestures. If the final music is redolent with dissonance and unresolved melodic lines and harmonic progressions, then the message of the film is that threat to the order still exists and we have not been reconciled to the alien and, consequently, to the best parts of our own humanity.

In-Depth: The Day the Earth Stood Still *and* Close Encounters of the Third Kind

For this analysis I have selected two science-fiction films from the "unexpected visitors" category, *The Day the Earth Stood Still* (1951) and *Close Encounters of the Third Kind* (1977). The films are two good examples of the transformational genre and, consequently, will provide us some insight into changes and transformations in scoring and musical topics and gestures in the science-fiction genre. Let's first look at *The Day the Earth Stood Still*.

A relatively early entry in the science-fiction movie phenomenon of the 1950s, *The Day the Earth Stood Still* embodies many of the qualities we associate with the genre during that era. An alien being from a more scientifically advanced civilization threatens earth, and the people of earth must rise to meet this threat. Unlike many of the unexpected visitor films of the era, the alien (Klaatu) in *Day* is not a monster or a bug-eyed villain or jelly-like glob (*It Came from Outer Space*) but, instead, is humanoid and espouses pacifistic ideas and demonstrates quite human values (even better than some humans in the film!); for instance, he connects immediately and genuinely with Bobby (Billy Gray), son of Helen Benson (Patricia Neal) and he is able to win her confidence as the plot thickens. Reflective of the Cold War era, moreover, the movie raises issues about global politics (and hostilities) and peace. Paul Haspel notes that in the boardinghouse scene where Klaatu first interacts with "ordinary" people on earth, "The ensuing conversation emphasizes ... the prevailing climate of cold war paranoia.... Mrs. Barley's words make clear her belief, in the absence of any evidence, that the spaceship's arrival represents some sort of communist plot — an underhanded Soviet attempt to subvert capitalist democracy in the United States" (67). In fact, if one were to state the basic theme of the film, one might say that it is a film about peace and living cooperatively. One of the reasons (a la *Things to Come*) for the superiority of Klaatu's civilization is that they have been able to progress scientifically, and they have been able to do that because they have eliminated aggression by relying upon a police force made up of robots like Gort. So, in essence, the message of the movie is basically a positive one: live in peace, do not threaten anyone (in any corner of your world or in any galaxy) and you will be better off. The tone of the film is not one, however, of uplift and its conclusion (regardless of Herrmann's final triumphant sounding major chord) is fraught with ambiguity. Some of that ambiguity can be understood by looking at the score of the film. What I will try to show here is that, message notwithstanding, this film is about a threat, and the film's emotional spine (and consequently the musical spine) centers on fear. In this way, in spite of how it stands outside the pale of many unexpected visitor films, it really conforms to the general paranoiac feel of much science fiction of the fifties.

Bernard Herrmann's score is typical Herrmann: it is imaginative, innovative, and brilliantly illuminates the emotional core of the film. As has been noted, one of the striking features of the score are the colors he achieves. Christopher Palmer states: "Herrmann attempted to give the film a feeling of otherworldliness, and dispensed with traditional strings and woodwind. He substituted an array of electronic instruments — two Theremins, electric violin, electric bass, electric guitar — and balanced them against three organs (one pipe and two Hammond), two pianos, two harps, timpani and percussion and brass (no horns) with four tubas for Gort, the robot" (267).[8] The score, indeed, does succeed in communicating an otherworldly quality; in fact, it is that quality which dominates the film — much as it does in much science fiction of this era — and it is in the predominance of that quality where we find the threat located. The main-title music establishes the tone of the film effectively by featuring the harps and percussion playing an arpeggiated figure in the high registers which, as we discussed above, simulates the twinkling of stars and the infinite mystery of outer space; it communicates, to quote Christopher Palmer, a "feeling of weightlessness" (268) (see figure 2.16).

Underneath this ostinato-like figure the main theme is sounded by the theremins first and then the brass. The first part of the main theme is a simple descending three-note motif that is given its eerie and foreboding character by initially outlining a tritone (D to G flat) and following this up with four variations of this pattern, all beginning insistently and ominously on the same note (D).

Allegro maestoso

Figure 2.15.

The second motif (see figure 2.16) is interesting because it blends the outer space "weightless" gesture with one we often associate with the heroic quest category; in this motif the brass announce a simple four note motif of D-A-A-D$_1$).

Figure 2.16. *The Day the Earth Stood Still,* main title.

It is basically the same intervallic structure that Strauss uses in *Also Sprach Zarathustra*. The chordal accompaniment underneath the held D strongly suggests a movement toward some positive resolution, the kind of music one might hear as someone undertakes a quest. It also, however, conveys a sense of mystery (Palmer calls it "mystical overtones"). In this particular context, the quest would seem to be Klaatu's, for it is his journey which lies at the heart of the film, but the mystery would be ours: what does this alien's presence mean for us? It is interesting to note that the score for the *Star Trek* TV series employs a very similar musical motif to preface Captain Kirk's words about "Space, the final frontier..." The main title for *The Day the Earth Stood Still* then establishes two moods or ideas for the viewer as the narrative progresses: the plot will be concerned with a mystery from the beyond, and, via the minor second motif, there is something ominous about what lies in the beyond. Unlike other films, there is no suggestion of violence and no overt threat (i.e., in crashing dissonances and loud dynamics mixed with the dissonances or atonal qualities of the music), but the threat is there in subtler form. Let's turn our attention to a couple of sequences now to see how Herrmann brings this threat to life through his music.[9]

There is no music to establish setting in the film, nothing to give us a sense of the community that is about to be visited. Instead, we are thrust immediately into the arrival of the alien into our community. Musically, Herrmann focuses immediately on the alien with a short cue called "Radar" followed by one called "Danger." The first, with its sprightly rhythms, emulates radar signals being bounced all over the planet (notice the similarity to the rhythmic elements in the main title to *Vertigo* here), and the second, which, in its use of a descending bass pattern, echoes the ominous character of the main title. The cue that follows immediately underscores the landing of the ship and the docking of its two crew members, Klaatu and Gort. The opening of the ship is accompanied by a similar structure as in the main title. In the higher registers there is a two note motif that never goes beyond a major second, and most often sounds the minor, lending an eerie feeling to the scene. This is the motif we will hear most often in conjunction with Klaatu's actions. The motif is played against rumbling low notes in the bass register, which, when played in tandem with the chord structures in the mid-registers, really highlights that ominous or threatening feeling. It is the combination of the high notes, which suggest mystery, and the darker tones in the lower ranges that suggest two contrary and oppositional impulses. The next part of the cue involves the appearance of Gort. Initially, the theremin dominates as Gort appears. Gort's motif, as noted above, is scored for the tubas and, in almost a mirror of Klaatu's motif, never really strays much beyond a ½ step (or bent notes) melodically. Gort's motif, however, is augmented by a plodding, relentless rhythm, which, like the similar rhythmic pattern in *The Thing*, contributes a darker and more threatening tone to the motif. Although the general threatening tone of the film is not one of violence, we are reminded often enough of the awful power of these visitors. In this particular cue we are shown one of these moments as Gort destroys the weapons of the military personnel who shoot Klaatu. The vaporizing of the weapons is accompanied by, appropriately, a crashing rhythmic pattern, which offers an interesting counterpoint to the somewhat static but, nonetheless, relentless quality of the opening measures of the cue. Rebecca Leydon notes, "Herrmann's electronic musical resources, then, serve several narrative goals in the film. First, they perform an alienising function — including the alienese invoked by xenophobia and anti-communist hysteria; second, they epitomize the sounds of science — including science gone horribly wrong; and finally, they mark off a space of numinosity, associated with Klaatu's 'sacred' mission and that of the 'priestly' scientists" (34). Thus within this first scene Herrmann has, first, brought the musical elements from the main title into the action proper and, second, provided a sort of emotional overture to the coming action by announcing the general themes in the action: Klaatu comes to us a mystery, and with him he brings a potentially destructive power. What does he want? And what can we do about it?

The Day the Earth Stood Still. Bernard Herrmann chose the theremin as the instrument that we would associate with Gort's presence on the screen.

The next cue I wish to discuss is important because it is, musically, the only real glimpse we get into our societal backdrop of the narrative. The human factor (i.e., love, creativity, etc.) is not explored in this film score. There is no tender music to underscore the relationship between Helen and Tom Stevens (Hugh Marlowe) or even Helen and her son. The only emotions we find explored musically are fear and terror. There is, however, one "human" moment in the film that gives us some insight into the theme of the film. It is the scene where

Bobby has taken Klaatu to Arlington and the Lincoln Monument. As we might expect, these are the only moments in the film where the music conforms to conventional melodic and harmonic topics. As Klaatu and Bobby survey the masses of white crosses at Arlington an elegiac and reverential melody, part hymn topic and part pastoral topic, is played by a single brass instrument and then is picked up by a choir of muted brass.

Figure 2.17. *The Day the Earth Stood Still*, "Arlington."

The melody is a simple motif outlining a major triad and beginning on the third. It at once captures the nobility of the sacrifice and the sadness underlying the magnitude of the loss of so many lives. This, of course, complements the thematic thrust by reminding the viewer of the wages of our aggressive behavior and providing an emotional grounding for our need to accept the warning that Klaatu brings. As the characters move to the Lincoln Monument the trumpet motif heard earlier in "Arlington" is sounded again. This time Herrmann alters the theme, and with each variation it seems to ascend, simultaneously communicating an elegiac tone (sighing gestures) with a feeling of nobility (lift gestures).

Figure 2.18. *The Day the Earth Stood Still*, "Lincoln Memorial."

This complements the action perfectly as Klaatu finds in the words of Lincoln inscribed on the statue something worthwhile in the human spirit and sees in Lincoln someone, were he alive, he feels he could talk to and who would understand his message. When he asks Bobby about powerful or influential people to whom he could talk, an eminent professor's name is mentioned as being one such person; notice that the power is intellectual and not political. An interesting message is delivered and musically underscored here: our humanity is best displayed in the pursuit of peace and justice and this pursuit should not be left to our present day politicians who, unlike Lincoln, will merely distort the purity of those concepts in the pursuit of the here-and-now of the real-politik. The trope-like fusion of the elegiac and noble gestures that pervade the music in the sequence suggests that the ideals are worth preserving but our aggressive methods may undermine that quest.

The only other musical glimpse we get of society occurs just before the final confrontation, and that is during the search for Klaatu when Herrmann merely uses the main-title music to underscore the "Panic" that is being felt. This also is the preface for his shooting — once again our overly aggressive tendencies are emphasized — and his rescue by Gort. The music in the final sequence, ranging from Gort's easily unlocking himself from one of our most sophisticated materials to the rebirth of Klaatu to his final speech to the assembled scientists, is constructed from the basic motifs announced early in the film. The themes built on the minor second and played by the theremin sustain the element of mystery and suspense in the sequence, and the more threatening timbres underscoring Gort's actions serve to intensify the threat, especially in light of the fact that we now know that Gort's policing powers are unlimited (he could destroy the planet — draconian, but effective as a peacekeeper!). The one final threat of violence, when Gort stalks Helen as she has come to deliver that most famous of all science-fiction lines, "Klaatu barada nikto," varies the basic motif slightly by having the motif repeat sequentially on a different ascending scale tone. Musically speaking, however, the minor second is the dominant interval in the development of themes throughout the sequence, which is quite in keeping with the conventions of scoring the alien-vs.-human confrontation in science-fiction films. The only respite we get from the dissonances associated with Gort and the main-title quotations comes when Gort is reviving Klaatu. The cue, entitled "Rebirth," is a strangely sweet little theme, turning ever so slightly from the disjointed feel of the alien motifs and sounding a more tonal melody with more movement (down a half step — down a major fourth — up a minor third); it retains, with that final minor third, the somewhat mysterious quality but there is a less "alien" feel to the motif. This, of course, makes sense dramatically, because it is at this moment that the future of earth stands in the balance: if Klaatu dies, Gort may well destroy earth; if he lives, there is hope. Quite naturally, when a human concern is presented, especially one divorced from pure fear, the music will reflect those softer emotions.

The music preceding Klaatu's warning to the scientists reprises the main themes, with particular emphasis on the contrast between the high mysterious theme and Gort's darker plodding rhythmic gesture. The concluding music has a touch of the heroic topic as the brass carry the motifs which coloristically seem to echo the themes from Arlington and the Lincoln Memorial and there is an echo of the second theme (D-A-D1) from the main title. These serve to reinforce the hope that earth can begin to police its aggressive tendencies and find real freedom and progress in peace. The fact that the entire cue also reiterates the main-title music suggests that there is some doubt and that the future is not assured. The current social order has been preserved largely through the graces of Bobby, who Klaatu admires for being "warm, friendly, intelligent," Helen, who has faith enough to believe that he wishes to help the people of earth and in turn helps him, and Professor Barnhardt (Sam Jaffe), whose respect for science and his belief in its ability to improve our lives would make him a natural ally of Klaatu. In short, the film reaffirms the need to preserve the human values of warmth, friendliness, intelligence, and concern for something other than self (see Helen in contrast to Tom, who will sell out Klaatu and her, so he can be "a big man"), and supports the idea that we need to employ science to progress and to improve our lot. In the end, however, the music reminds us that the alien threat is not entirely lifted. It is not the music of the Lincoln Memorial that leads to that final cadence and the tonal stability of the major final chord played over "The End," but a reiteration of the motifs of the main title. The threat remains, and if we do not seek to change part of the social order (i.e., eliminate aggression, which implies altering politics as we know it) we have not learned anything and other Gorts may visit us. The theme is clear: by becoming a threat to the universe, we in actuality threaten ourselves. The final message delivered by the music of *The Day the Earth Stood Still* is same as those ominous words uttered in the last lines of *The Thing*: "Keep watching the skies!"

Close Encounters of the Third Kind also deals with "unexpected visitors" and it also has a pacifistic message; however, that is where the similarity ends. Although the message of *The Day the Earth Stood Still* does indeed center on pacifism and controlling aggression, the confrontation with the alien is from beginning to end colored by the threat of annihilation. The encounter with the alien in *Close Encounters*, on the other hand, is far more benign and more rewarding in a spiritual and psychological sense: this encounter leads to discovery, discovery of artistic expression, discovery of self, discovery of love, and, finally, discovery of an opportunity for rebirth and, apparently, transcendence. The theme of the film suggests that if we open ourselves up to and embrace the mystery of the other, we will be rewarded. *The Day the Earth Stood Still* suggests that our encounter with the alien *had better* result in our progressing beyond our current aggressive and "primitive" state, or else; *Close Encounters of the Third Kind* suggests that our encounter with the alien *will* result in a some sort of rebirth of wonder. John Williams's music underscores this theme perfectly.

The main title is one of the more interesting ones in the history of science-fiction films. Under white titles against a black background a chord begins to take shape until one steadily becomes aware of a high pitched tonal cluster forming as the titles draw to a close; this chord sounds very much like an aleatoric cluster, with the strings basically just selecting a note and playing, but it could also be a closely voiced chord made up primarily of minor seconds and diminished fifths (tritones). Regardless, it is reminiscent of the tonal clusters in *2001* and it pretty much communicates the same message: one of mystery and uncertainty. The chord builds and resolves to a crashing major chord as the screen fills with the light of a wind blown desert. Williams's musical gesture (the surging crescendo and slashing decrescendo) here is simple and sets the tone for the narrative: mystery and drama; the unknown and the shock of the real come together in this one gesture. In spite of its originality, it is similar to our previous films in its use of the minor second and highly pitched strings to communicate a sense of mystery and the feel for outer space.

There are five motifs that dominate Williams's score for *Close Encounters*. These motifs are intended primarily to underscore human activity and to give us insight into the emotions and motives of the principal characters, Roy (Richard Dreyfuss), Lacombe (Francois Truffaut), and Jillian (Melinda Dillon). The first is a simple two note motif that outlines a tritone and is often sung by a choir and usually precedes moments of revelation, especially when Spielberg introduces the Devil's Tower iconography in the film; the second is a simple dissonant cluster that anticipates or underscores the appearance of the alien "threat"; the third is a sixteenth note motif that is associated with pursuing the aliens:

Figure 2.19. *Close Encounters of the Third Kind.*

The fourth is a whole-note pattern (C^m-D^m-G^m) that sometimes extends over an octave. Notice that the motif combines an element of mystery in the stepwise movement to the second with a more dramatic lift gesture in the leap of the fourth:

Figure 2.20. *Close Encounters of the Third Kind,* "The Mountain."

The fifth motif is a simple descending four note pattern (G-F-G-E); and the sixth motif is the famous five note motif that becomes the basis for communication between humans and aliens.[10]

Figure 2.21. *Close Encounters of the Third Kind,* "The Conversation."

Let's look at a couple of sequences to see how Williams uses the motifs to underscore the conventions of the formula.

First, there is not a lot of music to establish setting in the film; in fact, unlike most science-fiction films and Spielberg films in particular, the filmmaker does not rely on source music to encode setting and create the atmosphere of human "normality." The only music we have to establish setting or evoke the social milieu occurs anytime the scientists and military are mobilizing to investigate an unusual phenomenon (World War II airplanes in the desert, a tanker in a desert region of Asia, etc.) and when the final encounter is being planned and put into operation. Usually, the tonal cluster, either scored for strings or sung by the choir, precedes the sighting of the object. Generally speaking, however, the music that predominates these scenes is aggressive and is dominated by military topics, featuring the use of minor harmonies and brass, oftentimes scored in lower registers to lend an ominous tone to the activities of the scientists and military personnel. Overall, the tone is one of determination and resolve as these members of society prepare to meet the unknown. Williams's scoring lends just the right amount of suspense to these scenes: the music simultaneously suggests that these alien visitors are not here to threaten us but that they are nonetheless an unknown and, therefore, *may* still be a threat to us.

Where the music from *Close Encounters* most differs from that of *The Day the Earth Stood Still* is in the underscoring of the alien and the "hero(es)." Neil Lerner has noted of the score that it contains "among other things, a familiar rendering of a certain kind of musical modernism that encodes that which is meant to be perceived as 'alien'" (102). This modernism, however, is not exactly the same kind of modernism we encounter in a couple of great Jerry Goldsmith scores, *Alien* and *Planet of the Apes*. The reason for this is that the underlying tone, the emotional spine if you will, of the film is not fear of the threat but the quest to find out, to answer the question Roy asks: "What is it?" Consequently, aside from the ubiquitous (and very modernistic) tonal cluster and the tritone (which quite frankly in this context does not sound harsh at all, but instead sounds more like an interval seeking resolution), the score downplays harsh dissonances (made possible by dynamics or instrumental technique, etc.) in the major motifs. The motifs outlined above are, in fact, most often associated with the main figures. We hear the tritone when little Barry is molding a miniature Devil's Tower as the residents of Muncie await a second encounter with the aliens on the hilltop road (only to be fooled and foiled by helicopters) and later when Roy sees the film of Devil's Tower on TV (the point at which it sinks in that what he has been seeing in his mind and trying to capture in sculpture in his living room does in fact really exist). The three-note, whole-note motif performs a similar function but it is usually sounded when a revelation or contact is close at hand, as in the scene mentioned above where it swells up when the selected band of residents delightedly awaits the second encounter with the approaching lights of the alien vessel. It also is employed when Roy and Jillian (Melinda Dillon) approach Devil's Tower and when they mount the hill guarded by barbed wire. A variation of it even occurs later as Roy and Jillian make their way to the encounter site on "the dark side of the moon" at Devil's Tower, when Roy slips and falls and almost cannot make it up the hill. As in *2001*, moments of anticipation, moments portending this encounter and our spiritual growth, are accompanied by a similar motif which ascends the scale in a lift gesture meant to capture the feeling of yearning and reaching.

The alien, on the other hand, is represented by dissonance and atonality but not in the same degree as in previous films. In addition to the previously mentioned tonal cluster and the tritone motif, the alien is also represented by the five note "Conversation" motif that has come to be associated with the film. The stereotype of the alien threat is communicated clearly in one scene, however, where the aliens abduct Jillian's son, Barry. The music in the scene

Close Encounters of the Third Kind. John Williams's music for Roy, Jillian, and Barry's experience with Devil's Tower is both mysterious and epiphanaic.

owes a lot to the influence of Ligeti (and by extension *2001*).[11] Williams employs a pattern of clusters, crescendos, and glissandos to capture the fear and the threat that may be posed by this alien encounter. The music is reminiscent, or should I say seems to conflate elements, of Ligeti's *Atmospheres, Adventures* and his *Requiem for Soprano, Mezzo-Soprano, Two Mixed Choirs and Orchestra.* The scene opens with the choir sounding a tone cluster and then the orchestra enters with an *Atmospheres*-like chord. The remainder of the scene, like many science-fiction films before it, relies upon a contrast of rhythms and motifs scored in the lower registers against string motifs (tremolos or rapidly bowed) and clusters in the higher registers. The rhythms, oftentimes carried or announced boldly by the brass, are jagged gestures and suggest the threat of violence. In short, the tension and uncertainty signified in the marked atonal elements help heighten the expressive qualities of the more tonal and unmarked musical motifs associated with human efforts to confront the alien visit.

These motifs all come together in the final encounter on the "dark side of the moon" at Devil's Tower. Williams sustains the suspense and sense of mystery in this scene through the interplay of the motifs outlined above. The approach of the mother ship is signaled by the arrival of some "scout" vessels accompanied by the chorus and a tone cluster, which is then followed by a rather delicate melody played by a flute. Once the ships have positioned themselves over the landing area Williams weaves repeated chords stated by the brass, with some orchestral touches reminiscent of the chords in *Atmospheres*, and the five note motif. As the mother ship itself approaches in a roiling cloudbank filled with thunder, the music takes an ominous turn. Reminiscent of past science-fiction films, low notes are sounded in the double basses and cellos and are answered by glissandos in the strings and chords sounded in the brass. As in the films of the fifties, the dramatic contrast in timbres and pitches heightens the tension and the sense of an imminent threat. However, in the midst of the rather atonal orchestral textures, a heroic note is sounded in the brass. And, as the ship hovers over the landing zone, one hears the five note motif. Because this motif had been used in the prior scene where the scientists made "friendly" contact, it signifies a more optimistic feeling, a sense that an opportunity for communication is possible and the prospect of a friendly encounter has assumed at least equal footing with the threat of a deadly encounter. The opening of the door of the mother ship is underscored by the orchestra's playing a chord reminiscent of those heard in Ligeti's *Atmospheres,* especially, if one can recall *2001,* the chord that underscores the supernova sort of explosion that occurs in the climactic scene when Bowman is hurtling toward Jupiter in the space pod. This is especially evident in the second opening when the long-limbed leader of the aliens makes its appearance. But throughout this scene the predominant motif is the five note "communication" motif that suggests that in the midst of the unknown there is hope for understanding and communication. As the threat diminishes steadily throughout the scene, the motif dominates until we reach the point that "When You Wish Upon a Star" is quoted and we have almost a complete triumph of not only tonality but also popularity! It is easy to be cynical about Williams's use of this popular standard, except that lyrically the song quite accurately sums what has happened in the encounter: "When you wish upon a star, makes no difference who you are / Anything your heart desires will come to you." The song goes on to talk about "sweet fulfillment" and something coming like "a bolt out of the blue." And, indeed there is sweet fulfillment as the space ship takes off with Roy aboard and as the five note motif, now forming the basis for a longer end-title theme, swells as the closing credits come up. We see not just order restored but life made better by the encounter: Jillian has her son back and has been touched in a special way by the experience; Lacombe has realized his dream by being able to communicate via the Kodaly musical sign language with the aliens; and Roy has been taken up literally and figuratively, he is freed from his wife (perhaps the scariest scene in the whole film is Ronnie's unwillingness to hug Roy as he feels he is on the verge of a nervous breakdown) and stands, as the music tells us, on the brink of a transcendental and fulfilling experience.

In conclusion, the contrast between the two films and their music is dramatic. There is a genuine sense of triumph at the end of *Close Encounters*; human beings have met the challenge of the alien and have responded in the best human fashion: they have used their intelligence and art (music) to reach out to the alien other and their reward is to be struck by wonder and a sense of a common bond that unites all living things (in this case the desire to communicate). Using a simple melody to forge that communication link suggests a sort of innocence and openness and tolerance. Interestingly enough, the aliens have also called forth an important "human" quality in us: the creative. All those "called," as Lacombe notes, have some creative ability and in that act that very human quality is reaffirmed in the film, with, once again, music (an art) forming the basis of communication. *Close Encounters*, then, replaces the alien threat with alien communication, suggesting that perhaps we have become more tolerant, more open, more accepting of that which we do not immediately understand and holding out the promise that by being more tolerant, open, and accepting we will discover the best parts of our humanity and transcend difference and aggression, and that we can do this without fear. John Williams's score illuminates this theme by aurally presenting a world where the tonal and the atonal not only co-exist but commingle in, well, perfect harmony.[12]

Close Encounters of the Third Kind. The blending of the five note Kodaly motif and "When You Wish Upon a Star" confirms the benign nature of the aliens. Photofest.

Conclusion

The history of science-fiction movies has always dealt with the tension that exists between our quest for scientific progress and knowledge and the preservation of our humanity. Vivian Sobchak says of some of the films of the last twenty-five years, "Inherent in the big-budget SF film which moves toward the neutralization of its many alien images is a visual aura of confidence and optimism" (110). As we have seen from the above, the music of this particular sub-genre would seem to support that perspective. It is interesting to note, however, that for over fifty years the musical gestures that gave emotion and meaning to the films of the fifties still play a vital role in recent films. Composers still rely upon tritones and minor seconds to capture a sense of mystery and menace that attends the encounter with the alien. The popular music (either from sources or the score) and the tonal music associated with the hero and the society remind us of our desire for order and stability. The ultimate triumph of tonality in the scores of science-fiction films serves as a reminder of our desire for order and for a language that speaks to our all too human emotions and dreams.

3

Music for the Mean Streets

The Hardboiled-Detective Film

"I don't know which side anybody is on; I don't even know who's playing today."
— Dick Powell as Philip Marlowe in *Murder My Sweet*

The sounds of mystery and mean streets. Welcome to the world of the hardboiled detective, where corruption and greed are pervasive and where the detective, like a modern day Adam in a decaying Eden, continues to be tempted and risks damnation. Beginning in the thirties, but really coming into its own in the 1940s, the hardboiled detective film took its lead from the *Black Mask* pulp fiction of the 1920s and Depression era and took the detective formula, as Raymond Chandler noted, and plopped it down in the streets where it really belonged. In contrast to the puzzle plot or British style detective story, the hardboiled school featured urban settings, professional "dicks," and violence; no more "spillikins in the parlor" (Chandler, "The Simple Art of Murder" 19). During the 1940s, *film noir* proved to be a fertile seedbed to transplant the detectives of the earlier crime fiction, and not surprisingly the earliest film detectives were drawn from the works of two of the best of the *Black Mask* school: Dashiell Hammett and Raymond Chandler. In fact, the basic conventions of the genre were pretty much outlined in a series of films made in the forties, the most notable of which were Hammett's *The Maltese Falcon* (John Huston, 1941); *Murder, My Sweet* (Edward Dmytryk, 1944), which was based on Chandler's *Farewell, My Lovely*; and Raymond Chandler's *The Big Sleep* (Howard Hawks, 1946). In the 1950s, partially in reaction to HUAC hearings, the genre experienced a bit of a shift in emphasis as the private investigator (PI) gave way to what Thomas Schatz calls the "hard-nosed cop on the beat" (*Genres* 140) such as Glenn Ford in *The Big Heat* (1953). Since that time we have seen continuing redefinitions of the PI to reflect the changes in American culture, with the most notable shifts occurring with the introduction of African-American detectives (Richard Roundtree's Shaft in the '70s, Eddie Murphy's Axel Foley in the '80s and Denzel Washington's Easy Rawlins in the '90s) and women detectives in the hardboiled mold (Kathleen Turner's V.I. Warshawski). Reflective of these changes and other cultural shifts, the genre has undergone transformations, and the music of the mean streets has similarly undergone transformations as well.

The detective film, like the science-fiction film and the Western, is about finding order in a contested space; in this case, the space is an urban setting. Thomas Leitch notes that "like all popular genres, crime films work primarily by invoking and reinforcing a cherished, but not entirely convincing, series of social bromides: The road to hell is paved with good intentions, the law is above individuals, crime does not pay" (14). Like the science fiction and horror genres the emotional spine of the films foregrounds some fairly unpleasant emotions and motives: fear, greed, revenge, violence, and other forms of pathological behavior that deviate from conventional middle class values and norms. R. Barton Palmer describes the overall effect of *film noir*, and by extension many of the detective films, as "that of a nightmare" (19). The dominant conventions of this nightmare setting include the society (composed of the agencies of justice like police and lawyers, the rich, the famous and the infamous), the city itself and its environs, the detective, who is but a glimmer of light in an otherwise very dark worldview, a dangerous woman (Schatz calls her the "*femme noire*"), suspense — as the detective picks through clues and dead bodies — and violence. From this very brief survey, the reader may already be anticipating the sounds that will emanate from the film soundtrack to underscore the narrative of these films. Let's take a look at each convention in some depth and then look more closely at the scores from a couple of classic films.

Theme

Quite simply, the detective narrative, be it puzzle-plot or hardboiled, is about right and wrong and the pursuit of justice. The social order is disrupted by an act of violence or greed; the agent of that disorder must be pursued and captured (or killed — preferably shot in the navel if you're Mickey Spillane), and the order must be restored to the community. The *Black Mask* school, however, changed the dynamic of the detective narrative a bit; as Russel Nye notes, "the tough-guy detective story concentrated, as [Joseph] Shaw [*Black Mask* editor] said it should, on scene and situation rather than plot. The answer to 'who dun it' was less important than the atmosphere, tone, and dramatic surrounding, how it was done and for what reasons" (256). Thus motive and emotion became more important in the hardboiled school and by extension in the detective film. In these films, as Barton Palmer notes, "crime results from the pathological pursuit of gain; it is the preeminent and inalterable fact of life, not a social and moral problem" (73). The films, moreover, imply that this greed is pervasive and, as Palmer notes, "In this dark world of crime, violence and annihilation, nothing is certain" (19). Consequently, when the detective begins his or her quest it is, as Stanley Solomon suggests, a "trip through an underworld or hell, not necessarily criminal but essentially decadent, perilous, and depraved" (213). The detective enters the fray likewise for gain (25 dollars a day and expenses) but eventually makes an emotional commitment to the case (to protect an innocent victim, revenge a personal wrong, help a friend, or just do something right in the face of so much evil), but as Palmer states, in the process he or she "discovers darkness everywhere, finds it to be life's ruling principle, and learns that even the rich and the privileged are usually no better than the poor and deprived. In the battle between good and evil, the greater strength is wielded by the latter" (73) and at the end there really is no hope for "restoration of order and justice" (73).

The mythology of the genre, however, is that in spite of these overwhelming odds, the detective, the man who, as Chandler stated, must walk these mean streets but cannot himself be mean, makes his best effort to right the wrongs he encounters. There is, moreover, always some measure of success: the killer is apprehended or at least found out; bad things do happen to bad people along the way; and, in the majority of cases, the detective walks away with his own integrity and personal code of justice intact. He may have been tempted but his overwhelming sense of right, as opposed to his own personal acquisitiveness, prevails. So Sam Spade tells Brigid he must send her over even though he feels deeply for her. Two seminal films, *The Maltese Falcon* and *Double Indemnity* (even though it is not technically a hard-boiled detective film) lay out the basic message of the films: in the former, the falcon, the object of murder and mayhem, is a phony and all the parties walk away empty handed, and in the latter, Walter Neff has to admit that he killed Barbara Stanwyck's husband for the money and for her and he ends up with neither. In short, the pursuit of material possessions, the ruling passion of greed, comes to naught, and only the detective's solitary and lonely adherence to a code of justice triumphs; it may be a minor victory but, to quote Barton Palmer, in the face of this "dark world of crime, violence, annihilation [where] nothing is certain" (19), it stands as an affirmation of individual integrity and right.

The composer then faces an interesting challenge in scoring these films. He or she must find musical correlatives for the pervasive evil and greed in the world and for the detective's quest. In one sense, the task appears quite simple and straightforward for there are two dominant emotional states communicated in the films. First, we are confronted with the abnormal. The crime, the motives, and even the detective him or herself lie outside the norms of conventional society and behavior. The abnormality here is not the same as that of the science fiction and horror films (it is not so overtly "other" or "out there" and flamboyant), but it is subtler and more ambiguous. The other emotional state is one of suspense, which derives from the threat to society and the detective posed by the abovementioned forces. The suspense is heightened, moreover, because the integrity of the detective is bound to be tested as the narrative unfolds. The detective, like the cowboy, is possessed of the skills and some of the mentality of the best and worst parts of the social order: he can be as ruthless and violent as any criminal if he needs to, and he will not be above bending the law to crack the case. Consequently, unlike the Western and the historical romance, composers may not be able to paint the hero in broadly heroic strokes. The music that underscores the detective's actions will be a slightly schizoid mixture of classic heroic gestures and those we associate with the *femme noire* or his adversaries at times. In most films, moreover, one will not find clearly developed leitmotifs for the villains, for to do that would tip the mystery. In short, as one watches the films, one should be prepared for a certain aura of musical ambiguity to match the moral ambiguity being played out in the narrative.

Main Title Music

As with main-title music for other genres, the main-title music for the detective film largely is responsible for setting the mood and the emotional context for the films. Consequently, the titles for early detective films in the late forties and early fifties will be a mixture of suspense and heroic topics, occasionally blended with violent musical gestures and tropes, including trilling strings in the high registers, rhythmic brass figures, and melodic writing that exploits blues topics and intervallic leaps of the perfect fourth and fifth (these last being classic lift gestures we associate with hero figures). These three gestures largely correspond to the three dominant elements in the films: suspense, the city setting, and the character of the detective hero. In *Murder My Sweet*, for instance, the main-title music begins with trilling strings and an angular motif that suggests violence, and then, as the credits finish rolling, the "detective's theme" is announced:

Figure 3.1. *Murder My Sweet,* main title.

Similarly, Alfred Newman's main title for *Call Northside 777* (1948) opens with a descending figure, portending possible tragedy or fate, and then breaks into a more heroic theme stated by the brass. There is an aura of melodrama that hangs over these themes with their use of minor harmonies and their lack of smooth melody lines.

There were not a lot of changes in the main-title music for the cop films of the fifties and, in fact, we do not see much change until we get into the 1960s and 1970s. The '60s gave us the wry, almost world-weary PI, and title music like Johnny Mandel's for *Harper* (1966) reflects this new worldview. There is an almost comic feel to the theme as it begins with a series of disconnected two note gestures stated by the brass and answered by a similarly disconnected figure in the drums. Finally, the two note gesture is shaped into a four note motif, a trope in fact, played by muted brass fusing a blues topic with a slightly comic figure; the bridge is an antiphonal motif with a three note figure being answered by a four note figure. Running as it does over the opening sequence with Harper rising and making his way on the L.A. freeway system (in his beat-up sports car) to meet a client, the theme tells us more about the PI in this case, cynical but somewhat easygoing, and little about the darker aspects of the case.

The 1970s introduced elements from the rock revolution of the previous two decades into main-title music. Of course, the most ostensible bow made to rock came in Isaac Hayes's soul-funk inspired theme for *Shaft* (1971), but other films borrowed elements from rock to revitalize the genre. Lalo Schifrin relied upon timbral diversification in his use of electric piano and electric bass for his music for *Dirty Harry* and *Sudden Impact,* while Michael Small employed electric bass and piano to enunciate a slightly funky line to his theme for *Night Moves* (1975); however, the remainder of the title draws upon past models with its descending two note sighing (tragic) gesture followed by three note pattern with a small intervallic leap. There is, however, nothing particularly heroic about these themes. In fact, these scores, like those of *Chinatown* (1974) and *Klute* (1971), point more toward subtler orchestral colors and less melodramatic writing, which goes well with their emphases upon the darker psychological evil that drives the crime: greed and lust are more sexual and pathological than in the old days.

Finally, there is what I would call the nostalgia main titles. Main titles for films such as *Farewell, My Lovely* (1975) and *Hammett* (1982) feature a solo instrument (reminiscent of the trumpet in Jerry Goldsmith's *Chinatown*) playing a languorous minor key melody employing blues harmonies throughout; a good example of this is David Shire's main title for *Farewell, My Lovely,* which features a trombone as the lead solo instrument:

Figure 3.2. *Farewell, My Lovely,* main title.

Of course, one would be hard-pressed to find a lot of themes like these in the past; they merely recall the past in their sound. The solo clarinet (*Hammett*) and trombone *(Farewell, My Lovely)* do, however, draw attention to the detective and his solitary quest to right wrongs in a corrupt world: world-weary, their markedness foregrounds them against the ensemble in the background, battered and tired but not defeated.

Setting and Society

As was suggested above, the city and the people inhabiting it are key conventions in the detective film. In *Black Mask* detective fiction, as Russel Nye notes, "danger was everywhere, nor was it rational" (257), and filmmakers found in the city setting the perfect visual correlative for this irrational danger. The films suggest that our lust for wealth and our greed have created the urban environment, making it at once the symbol of opportunity and those material rewards promised us in the mythology of success and the American Dream, and a threat to those selfsame values; as Ralph Willett states:

> Their ominous power renders the canyons of concrete and steel overwhelming at street level. The juxtaposition of great buildings and dwarfed, anonymous individuals became a standard visual device in both film and photography, and was used in the post war decades to depict, through modernist architecture, the oppressive power of corporate capitalism [88].

The opposing forces of striving and oppression ultimately render the city, to quote Willett, as a site of "instability" (7). Similarly, Barton Palmer says in his discussion of the *noir* crime melodrama, "In such films, a frightening but alluring urban landscape functions as the locus of unfulfilled desire, as the place where urges that cannot be satisfied within the confines of respectability can (if only perilously) be acted upon" [71]. Consequently, in underscoring the scenes of the city, composers need to capture this longing mixed with the portending tragedy that attends this longing. One will not find a lot of establishing shots of the city in detective films; we are instead usually thrust immediately into a crime scene, and the musical gestures that accompany suspense and violence will predominate. This, however, is revealing from a musical standpoint because we are not supposed to dissociate the crime from the setting: they are, in fact, one and the same, inextricably linked visually and musically. The other inextricable link is that between the city and the people of the city.

The society of the detective film is largely made up of political institutions (police, legal, and governmental), social institutions (family, church), and entertainment institutions (night clubs, bars, etc.). There are two filmic elements, one visual and one auditory, which are crucial to this society, especially as it is part of the city setting. First, visually, the city and the institutions are cloaked in darkness or are subject to what Ralph Willett calls "stylistic distortions": "The city in *film noir* becomes the site of paranoia and despair, conveyed by hysterical acting and by visual style, especially stylistic distortions.... Non-materialistic lighting and framing establishes an unsteady world of moral relativism in which all characters are subject to stylistic disruptions. Identities and values are constantly shifting" (89). This visual world of shifting values is complemented by the dialogue and the narrative which relies heavily upon lying, which as Stanley Solomon notes, seems to be the norm in Marlowe's world in *The Big Sleep*, where even he resorts to it "as a matter of convenience" at times (221). Indeed, what drives the drama, what sends the detective deeper into the sludge of society, is the lie. The reason for this is simple: the society itself is corrupt and the corruption, especially in films since the fifties, is pervasive. Ralph Willett has stated that in the films of the 1960s and 1970s, "crime now becomes coexistent with the status quo; all institutions adopt the structure of the amoral underworld" (96). The motivating force of greed and the corruption that accompanies it, in turn, leads to what J.P. Telotte sees in *Kiss Me Deadly* as a failure of communication: "we might recognize, in both this film world and the one we inhabit, a level on which our common discourse frequently and all too easily becomes transformed from a form of communion to a tool of appropriation and self-satisfaction — a tool that promises to appropriate and perhaps eventually destroy us" ("Talk and Trouble" 79). Consequently, as the detective encounters representatives of our different social institutions, his quest to uncover clues is also a quest to determine the truth, which becomes virtually impossible and, consequently, becomes a factor in building suspense and paranoia in the films.

Musically, this greedy, corrupt and lying social order is made manifest in two ways: through the actual film score and through source music. In classic hardboiled detective films, composers usually supplied appropriate "city music" or "crime music" for establishing shots and for the detective's pursuit of clues and the criminal. Generally, the music for establishing shots or opening scenes and pursuit sequences share some common elements. The dominant one will be aggressive rhythms, marked by syncopations or aggressively repeated notes (either eighths or quarters) like this passage from the opening of Robert Aldrich's *Kiss Me Deadly*:

Figure 3.3. *Kiss Me Deadly*, opening sequence.

Second, melodically, the underlying violence and tension in the setting will be conveyed through a combination of elements. Melodic and harmonic elements associated with popular jazz or the type of blues topics and jazz topics (simple blues harmonies and "swing" rhythms — where two beats are not felt strictly but as part of a triplet — typical of jazz performance) we find in concert pieces like Gershwin's *Rhapsody in Blue* or, even more appropriately, his *Second Rhapsody*, are part of the film composer's language for the mean streets. I have previously referred to this specific usage of blues harmonies as the Gershwin blues topic. We also find reliance upon dramatic and angular intervallic leaps such as the ones used by Henry Mancini in the following cue from *Touch of Evil* (1958), which, as William Darby and Jack DuBois point out, "is more surly and jazzy in keeping with the urban decadence/*film noir* qualities of the story. It becomes more insistent and more syncopated as the doomed car moves through the streets on the Mexican side of the border, pauses to pass the immigration inspection, and then blows up" (466–467).

Figure 3.4. *Touch of Evil*, "Evil."

Third, setting is also captured in the music that accompanies the quest for clues. Music that often features regular eighth note or sixteenth note broken chords or arpeggiated patterns suggest a sense of movement and restlessness and, as in Western films, pursuit. Typical of this cue type is the following one entitled "The Conspiracy" from *Double Indemnity* that is used to underscore Walter Neff's narration (Brown, *Overtones and Undertones* 125):

Figure 3.5. *Double Indemnity*, "The Conspiracy."

Finally, the tension and violence in the setting is conveyed through sharply contrasted orchestral timbres. A wonderful example of this is the cue "Rollo Tomasi" from Jerry Goldsmith's score for *L.A. Confidential*, where Goldsmith alternates driving, syncopated rhythmic patterns in the percussion with rapidly paced and somewhat disjointed melodic patterns played largely in the lower registers of the piano and with the brass and strings playing sustained notes featuring tremolos (a suspense gesture) and rapid crescendos.

We also get a glimpse into the nature of the society through source (diegetic) music. Source music will, of course, vary, from time period to time period. In the films of the forties and fifties, one will most commonly hear jazz or popular tunes in nightclubs or in the homes of the villains. In *The Blue Dahlia* (1946), Gus's bar is constantly filled with the sounds of big band jazz, or, as the William Bendix character calls it, "monkey music" (which may or may not be a nasty and not too subtly coded reference to the music's African American roots). Similarly, in *The Big Heat*, when Bannion goes to talk to Lucy Chapman at the night club where she hangs out, there is jazz playing in the background; later we hear "Put the Blame on Mame" at the Retreat Club; and, finally, gang moll Gloria Grahame dances to a jazzy mambo in the apartment of her brutal mobster sugar daddy, played by Lee Marvin. *The Blue Dahlia* uses the then popular "Accentuate the Positive" by Johnny Mercer to somewhat ironically underscore the party scene that greets war hero Johnny (Alan Ladd) when he returns home to his "loving" wife. The use of jazz in these films is interesting because, in spite of the popularity of big bands through the 1930s and 1940s, the association with the gangster element suggests that this may still be marginalized music, not totally acceptable and, drawing on the mythology of it origins, still associated with those outside the mainstream, those bordering on the edges of respectability and those in quest of illegal gain in the corporate culture.

Jazz can still be found in the films of the '60s and '70s, but more often than not rock music will be used as a backdrop to the moral decay of the city. *Madigan* (1968), for instance, has a scene with Sheree North, Madigan's ex-mistress, singing the great Don Raye and Gene DePaul standard "You Don't Know What Love Is." The segue to her apartment is accompanied by a slow and languorous blues tune as she puts him to bed *sans* sex. Similarly, cocktail piano jazz and mild bossa nova fill the Bel Air Motel in *Harper* as Lew tries to find the missing husband of Lauren Bacall. In the same film, however, the dominant sound as Lew hits the town looking for clues is that kind of rock music made by people who really didn't know it or like it: in short, it's rock music with trumpets or with an organ (however, because the organ was a popular instrument in mid-sixties bands like the Rascals, it is slightly more viable and believable). Of course, the music's function is, first, to give one a sense of place and time and also to make Lew look a little bit like a fish out of water. He's swimming in a world that he doesn't quite understand and which, for all its youthful exuberance, hides secrets and threats.

Two films that do not technically fit the detective mold but have elements of the genre and which use rock music effectively are *Mean Streets* and *Point Blank*. Ralph Willett's analysis of the music used in *Mean Streets* could also be applied to the use of the music in many detective films:

> The active centre of Tony's bar is a jukebox which pumps pop music into the atmosphere turning it into the medium for the guys' everyday experience. Like the music, their street language is staccato, brusque and intense....
>   The music is mainly urban soul, interspersed with Motown, Rolling Stones, R and B, and doo wop, an eclectic mix ranging from lyrical anthems to rabble rousers like Johnny's entrance number, "Jumpin' Jack Flash." It is the sound of a discontinuous culture in which satisfactions are short-lived [93].

Notice here, first, the reiteration of the lack of fulfillment or disappointed hopes theme that has been alluded to throughout this section, and second, the correlation of rock with a brusque, intense, and discontinuous culture. It would seem that rock music is the perfect soundtrack for the postmodern condition. *Point Blank* similarly uses rock music to signify the violent "landscape." In an especially brutal fight scene that takes place in a back room of a discotheque, rock music and flashes from the accompanying light show provide an aural context and, interestingly enough, a cover for Lee Marvin's rage as he takes on a couple of adversaries in his quest to find heist money that is rightly his. Once again, the use of the music in this context signifies meaningful correlations: it is theme music for urban violence, at once a mask and an aural emblem for the brutal underside of our culture.

Finally, viewers should also be on the lookout for how "real" classical music is used in detective films. When classical music is used it provides a kind of wholeness or brings a sense of completeness to the portrait of the society in a film by giving voice to another taste culture. Traditionally associated with the wealthy and the arbiters of taste in a community, classical music in a detective film provides a counterpoint to the rawer or at least more common musical strains that underscore the actions of people in entertainment venues. One interesting item here is that both *Double Indemnity* and *Kiss Me Deadly* utilize Schubert's "Unfinished Symphony"; in *Double Indemnity* the opening measures of the first movement complement Miklos Rozsa's use of a similar string passage in his score. In the case of both films, the music's energetic and swirling passages capture nicely the underlying tensions that reside below the surface respectability and everyday activity and that will inevitably lead to violence and death. *Kiss Me Deadly* for all its brutal cynicism employs a great deal of classical music; in addition to the abovementioned Schubert work, it features a Strauss waltz, used to underscore Velda's work at the barre, and the aria "Ach, so fromm" from *Martha*, which is sung by a down-and-out opera singer. Once again, the music stands in dramatic counterpoint to the non-diegetic score and the pop tune "Rather Have the Blues," which underscore the generally cynical mood of the movie: everybody is reaching for a little bit more but seemingly getting burned in the process — pun intended!

The Detective Hero

Raymond Chandler's assessment of the hardboiled detective is as relevant to the hero of the detective film today as it was back in 1950 when he wrote in "The Simple Art of Murder" "But down these mean streets a man must go who is not himself mean, who is neither tarnished nor afraid. He is the hero; he is everything. He must be a complete man and a common man and yet an unusual man" (20). Thomas Schatz sees similarities between the detective hero and the cowboy hero: "Like the classic Westerner, the hardboiled detective is a cultural middleman. His individual talents and street-wise savvy enable him to survive within a sordid, crime-infested city, but his moral sensibilities and deep rooted idealism align him with the forces of social order and the promise of a utopian urban community" (123). In another generic parallel, the detective, as Barton Palmer notes, bears some resemblance to the heroes of chivalric romance (81) in his quest to find the truth in the face of insurmountable odds and in his ability to maintain his moral bearings in a morally ambiguous world. In short, we should look at the hardboiled dick as the kind of man or woman we would like to have on our side in the fight against the forces of crime and disorder.

With that in mind, we could assume on the one hand that all this archetypal heroic behavior would lend itself to the heroic topics and gestures we might find in Strauss's *Ein Heldenleben* or *Don Juan* or, from the film music world, in the style of Korngold's music for *Captain Blood, Robin Hood,* or *The Sea Hawk.* On the other hand, the kernel conflict in the detective film, unlike some other genres, is not set against a clearly delineated moral backdrop (King John is evil, greedy land barons are evil) but again one that is morally ambiguous. Detectives, like the cowboy, walk a moral tightrope: on the one hand, they are champions of justice, but, on the other, they will resort to almost criminal-like violence to keep the investigation going. They are, moreover, constantly tempted and often succumb, if ever so tentatively, to embrace the meaner aspects of the mean streets only to pull themselves back in the nick of time. We don't really know if Sam Spade will cut himself in on the take from the sale of the falcon; Dick Powell's Marlowe seems somewhat taken with Helen Grayle (Claire Trevor) and could potentially become an accomplice in murder; Al Pacino's character in *Sea of Love* (1989) allows his passion for Helen (Ellen Barkin) to keep him from turning in a glass that might have incriminating fingerprints, and so it goes throughout the history of the genre. In the final analysis, they do remain (Don Quixote–like) true to their quest but their victory is always tentative: sometimes they don't get the girl, sometimes the source of corruption remains untouched and viable at the end, sometimes they themselves are agents in murder with disastrous consequences. And like the cowboy, they often remain outside the norms of social institutions like marriage; Thomas Schatz states: "The hero's inability either to effect real change or to find solace in the ideal of romantic love reaffirms his isolation and his commitment to apparently outmoded values" (130).

Consequently, the music that composers write to capture the character of the detective is often a surrealistic blend of streetwise, jazzy sophistication with world-weary bluesy ambivalence about the city mixed with an occasional old-fashioned heroic gesture plus some stark dissonances thrown in for good measure to remind us of the almost monolithic corruption and violence lying in wait for the detective. We find that the idioms of jazz and the blues most often figure in the musical topics and gestures associated with the detective, functioning as musical correlatives to the language of the detective, which consists, according to Ralph Willett, of "Wisecracks, slang and general verbal toughness" (8). The idioms, moreover, are often (but not always) stated by solo instruments. Roy Webb relied upon saxophones to capture the chromatic sinuousness and bluesy feel in the Marlowe motif in *Murder My Sweet* (see figure 3.1). John Barry's theme for the character of Dashiell Hammett is played by a clarinet and is particularly effective in one shot where the camera tracks Hammett walking up a hillside sidewalk until he emerges out into an intersection with the city of San Francisco as a backdrop. The bluesy quality and the mournful sound of the clarinet captures perfectly Hammett's isolation and lonely quest in the midst of a city of millions. Similarly, Peter Matz's music for James Garner's take on Phillip Marlowe in the 1969 film *Marlowe*, prominently features a flute, bongo, and electric guitar stating a theme with blues harmonies and the feel of L.A. "cool jazz." At times the music, as in the abovementioned cases, has a sinuous melody line without a lot of wide leaps, but at other times, we find some themes that do have more dramatic writing and more angular melodies. A good example of this is the theme for Gene Hackman's character, Harry Moseby, in Arthur Penn's *Night Moves* (1975), which features a solo oboe and, although graceful in its general outline, has a certain angular and unstable quality because of the types of intervallic leaps that Michael Small employs. Similarly, the motif associated with the Mike Hammer character in *Kiss Me Deadly* also employs wider leaps and more aggressive rhythms, the perfect complement to his more violent and cynical personality.

This last point is a key one in analyzing the music for the detective hero. One must be sensitive to the nuances of character in the detective. Some of them are cool and sophisticated and sexually charged, like the Michael Douglas character in *Basic Instinct* (1992), and the music is correspondingly chromatic, dramatic and neurotic. Some are world-weary like Hammett in *Hammett* and Marlowe in the '70s version of *Farewell, My Lovely*; their music bespeaks loneliness and alienation. Other themes may throb with a violent undercurrent, featuring musical gestures that stress subtle and slightly arrhythmic bass lines, and high strings sounding dissonant chords or cluster-like chords. A good example of this is Lalo Schifrin's theme for Dirty Harry in *Sudden Impact*, which features a solo trumpet and a contrapuntal melody line in the high strings and a driving shuffle-like rhythm in the bass line. The music will underscore the particular temptation and weakness of the detective and his particular strengths, which is why we find what some might term love themes being associated with the detective in *The Big Sleep* and *Chinatown*.

The "Femme noire"

"*Femme noire*" is name Thomas Schatz gave to the lead women characters in the hardboiled detective film. This character, according to Schatz, is a "sultry seductress who preys upon the hero and whose motives and allegiances generally are in doubt until the film's closing moments" (114). In actuality, there are at least two distinct types of *femme noires*. The first is the woman who is at the heart of the crimes, like Brigid O'Shaughnessy in *The Maltese Falcon*, of whom Schatz writes: "Brigid is the archetypal hardboiled heroine: beautiful, apparently helpless and victimized, drawing the detective into the intrigue and then exploiting his particular talents — and his naive romanticism — in her perverse quest for wealth and power" (129). Around this type of character spin the violence and the mystery in the films. The other character type is the woman whose motives are suspect until the end, when she is ultimately redeemed either through helping the PI solve the case or just through clarification of a misunderstanding. Ellen Barkin's Helen in *Sea of Love* and the Kim Basinger character in *L.A. Confidential* pretty much fit this profile. The films may also use, like the Western, dual female leads representing the dark and light ladies. In *Murder, My Sweet,* for instance, Velma (aka Helen Grayle) assumes the role of the dark temptress, who, according to Barton Palmer, is blamed for all the evil, "an Eve, a whore who does not know her proper place and wants to pose an as an honest woman, disrupting family relationships and breaking the circuit of normal desire" (83). Anne Shirley, on the other hand, is the young innocent whom Marlowe saves and who rewards him with a closing-title clutch — of course, we don't know if the relationship will go anywhere beyond the final scene in the taxi, but the point is made: Marlowe has remained true to his quest, and that final kiss is symbolic of the minor triumph of a return to (temporary?) normalcy. As Barton Palmer has noted, "In the ordinary studio film, feminist theory has demonstrated, women can be constructed as either object of the male gaze (and thus elements of a male fantasy that can be acted on and fulfilled) or barriers in the way of masculine self-assertion" (141).

The music of the *femme noire* narratively has the responsibility of conveying passion, seduction, mystery and danger; in essence, the music complements the spectatorial male gaze by inscribing the woman's character through some powerful, culturally conditioned topics and gestures. First, just as solo instruments are used to identify the character of the detective, so they are also used to identify the *femme noire*. In *Sudden Impact*, for instance, Lalo Schifrin uses a solo saxophone over a suspense topic (which, in this context, also signifies a disturbed state) in a scene featuring Sondra Locke after she has committed a murder. The music, with its reliance upon marked minor (tragic) melodic gestures and blues topics, suggests her alienation and her own personal torment upon being driven to employ violent means in seeking personal justice for a crime committed earlier in her life. Second, the seductive character of the *femme noire* is signified by sighing gestures and chromatic melodies. Classical composers, such as Saint-Saens in Delilah's aria, "Mon coeur s'ouvre a ta voix" from *Samson et Delilah*, and much of the score for Wagner's *Tristan und Isolde*, rely upon chromatic writing to communicate the idea of seduction and passion. This excerpt from "Mon coeur s'ouvre a ta voix" is a good example of this type of chromatic writing for the seductress:

Figure 3.6.

Roy Webb, in *Murder, My Sweet*, creates an effective theme to accompany the scenes between Helen Grayle and Marlowe. There is just a touch of Wagner's "Liebestod" in it, with its chromatic sinuousness and its ascending melodic pattern, to suggest that Marlowe is indeed succumbing to this woman. The underlying marked minor harmonies (very reminiscent of Cole Porter's in "So in Love") are, however, a reminder that to be seduced by her is to be corrupted:

Figure 3.7. "Velma Is Seductive."

Similarly, in *Kiss Me Deadly*, although she is not a major *femme noire* character, Carl's sister — a woman of dubious morals and even less constancy (Carl's sister: "I have lots of friends." Hammer: "I *bet* you have.") is given a seductive little prefatory theme played by a clarinet that slides up the scale and then descends a minor second (sigh gesture) leading to a blues topic played by a muted trumpet. Third, the actions of the *femme noire* are often underscored using dissonant harmonies. A good example of this, once again, is in Miklos Rosza's score for *Double Indemnity*, where, as Christopher Palmer notes, "when Phyllis assures Walter over the phone that she has been able to arrange the murder in accordance with their plans, this [main] theme is given so rancid a harmonization as to impress upon us the full force of her evil" (197). Finally, one will find, as we did with the detective hero, that minor harmonies seem to communicate most effectively the darkness of the world that the *femme noire* inhabits. There are two good reasons for this. First, as Robert Hatten, Deryck Cook and Eero Tarasti have all noted, the minor is correlated with the tragic. In no other genre, with the possible exception of the women's film, is the tragic so intimately associated with the feminine as in this genre: she can spell doom for the detective. Second, the minor harmonies, the reliance upon minor seconds, dissonances and solo jazz instruments, by merit of their marginalized status in the realm of popular and serious music, signify that the woman in the detective film is one who lies outside the norm, who is not a "traditional" woman and whose lusts could spell doom to the hero.

Suspense

Suspense is just another way of talking about clues. Clues are the glue in the detective's quest, those bits of information that keep the narrative moving forward. In the hardboiled school, the clues add a further interesting element to the narrative because, unlike the puzzle plot, they are not just little facts that will be pieced together to form a coherent mosaic of the crime, but are attended by the threat of violence and may not just be misread but may be out and out lies. In short, when the detective enters a room to investigate a crime we should expect not only mystery but danger. Consequently, the scoring for these filmic moments is fairly straightforward, the character of each largely determined by the nature of the crime. The search for clues in a mystery about murder and robbery, for instance, may employ different musical topics and gestures than a mystery about murder and sex. The most common type of musical motif used to create suspense is one that I call the suspense topic which employs three musical ideas working simultaneously. The suspense topic is created by using high trilling strings; lower trilling strings, which we sometimes hear but are more common to science fiction and horror, seem to connote portentousness as much as suspense. The high strings, as we discussed in the introduction, have a more neurotic and, well, high strung feeling and an edgier quality. While the strings are trilling, there will be a rhythmic pattern established in the lower registers. One option might have a piano plucking out a single-note asymmetrical pattern (reminiscent of an irregular jabbing gesture like one might see in a knife fight), or an electric bass doing something similar; another options would be closely voiced brass instruments stating a rhythmic motif. Meanwhile, in the middle registers a marked melody, usually with a disjunctive quality, or sustained chords played by the woodwinds or muted brass and emphasizing minor or dissonant harmonies will fill out the texture of suspense. One scene in *Kiss Me Deadly* that uses a variation on this occurs when Mike is talking to Eddie, an African American boxing manager, and, as Eddie tells Mike of a threat that he lives under, the brass begin a descending pattern that is then answered by a mysterious melody played by the strings. In the same film, as Mike looks for clues in an apartment, we hear an ostinato pattern taken up by the strings while vibes and a harp state a simple two note ascending motif which leads to some interplay between the winds and the muted brass as the scene builds. The ascending motif, usually slurred, shares a similar gestural movement with the lift gesture, but the effect, it being a narrower leap, carries with it a sense of suspension as opposed to resolution. We could term this a suspension lift. By not developing a clearly stated melody or extended motif, the scene has a sense of incompleteness and, consequently, irresolution — or maybe we should say it is oxymoronic: a resolution to a state of tension as the prevailing mood of the scene. In *Marlowe*, the search for clues in one scene is underscored by a dissonant pattern stated by high strings accompanied by fragmentary and angular gestures in the brass and winds in the middle registers; the sense of danger communicated by the piano in the lower registers fills out the scene. As Marlowe discovers a dead body, the piano and brass become more agitated, a snare drum is added to the mix, and the strings build tension into the scene by playing an ascending figure (suspension lift) in the higher registers.

In contrast to these gestures and topics, one finds, especially in films since the 1970s, more reliance upon disjunctive rhythms, dissonance, and tonal clusters to create suspense. *Chinatown*, as we shall see, was an important film in establishing this approach to scoring suspense. In that film, Jake's trips to crime scenes and sources of possible clues are handled with simple close-voiced chords that suggest a disturbed state as much as suspense. Films since the 1970s have dealt more with conspiracy and darker kinds of crimes, and the marked dissonance and alternating meters we associate with neurotic tendencies seemingly fit the mood of these films better than the classical gestures and topics I discussed above. For example, in Jerry Goldsmith's score for *L.A. Confidential*, we see him employing and varying the following rhythmic pattern in scenes of pursuit and suspense (*see* Figure 3.8).

The variations on this pattern, particularly the eighth-sixteenth figure, is most effective as the three detectives in the film burrow deeper into the corrupt alliances of law enforcement, city government and prostitution. Similarly, *Sudden Impact*, which mixes violence,

Figure 3.8. *L.A. Confidential,* "The Victor."

revenge, and sex in equal doses, has a scene where Harry is being pursued by the small town thugs who were responsible for the rape of Locke's character and her sister (and who, ironically, Locke is now simultaneously pursuing herself); to underscore the scene, Lalo Schifrin relies upon cluster-like chords scored for strings, brass, and gongs to contribute a disturbed mood to the impending violence in the scene. What is interesting about the use of clusters and dissonance is that they almost seem to work contrapuntally with the visual rhythms in the scenes: a single chord may hang over a series of quick cuts or over a pan of a scene. The effect is that the actions are almost secondary to the dark and disturbed motives signified by the music and the music's ability to communicate that this darkness and corruption in the characters is where the real danger lies.

I should perhaps mention here that the abovementioned musical topics and gestures are not the only ones the viewer would encounter in the detective film. Occasionally, a director and/or composer will take a completely different tack in scoring a film. One case in point is *Shaft* (1971) where, during one of Shaft's expeditions through the city, in search of clues to help him find a missing person, Isaac Hayes and Gordon Douglas opted for a heavily tinged gospel tune in three-quarter time sung by a chorus and soloist. It did little to build suspense, but it nicely underscored Shaft's commitment to tracking down the bad guys and it provided a nice aural tapestry for Shaft's walk down "those mean streets."

Violence and the Final Showdown

These two conventions exist separately within the genre but they also function together in the climax of the film. It is altogether possible that one will not hear a lot of violent music in the detective film, although there may be numerous violent sequences. The reasons for this are attributable to a couple of factors. First, violence is really the province of the criminal; the detective will only be forced to use it as a means of last resort. In short, Sam Spade, Philip Marlowe, Shaft, Harry Moseby, or even Moses Wine will have to be provoked or be in an untenable situation before they will rely upon violence as a means to solve the crime. In most detective films, there are many suspects but the identity of the master criminal is usually concealed until the end. Consequently, aside from an occasional short burst, the most sustained violent sequences will largely be confined to the film's climax — and that is not necessarily a given when we think of films such as *The Maltese Falcon.* Music for violent scenes will be correspondingly short, consisting most often of rhythmic gestures and dissonant chords. If the sequence is more protracted, a second injunction against music comes into play: violent sequences contain a lot of diegetic sound, such as furniture crashing, glass breaking, guns being fired, knuckles meeting flesh and bone, etc.; consequently, music can very easily get lost or, worse, detract from the dramatic impact of the violence of the diegetic sounds. Although violent scenes would seem a natural for musical accompaniment, especially with what we have seen in the science fiction film, in reality, the composer's efforts might get lost or actually detract from the point the filmmaker is trying to make.

This is not to say, however, that detective films are devoid of musical gestures to underscore violent sequences. The type of music will depend upon the nature of the violence. For instance, in classic violent scenes, especially like those in the final showdown, one might encounter a structure similar to that of the suspense topic or danger topic where the composer will employ three layers of musical ideas such as high strings either trilling or sustaining a dissonant chord while the brass and winds toss musical and/or rhythmic phrases back and forth. The following is an example of this modeled on the music from the torture sequence that occurs early in *Kiss Me Deadly* and an off-screen violent episode in *Harper.*

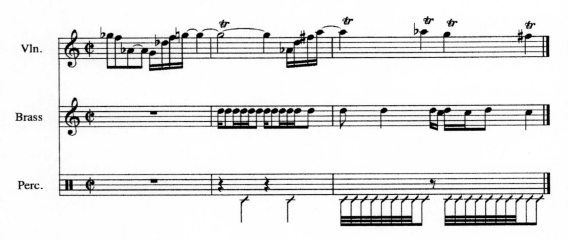

Figure 3.9.

There is another variation on violent musical gestures and topics that is used to underscore the psychopathology of the violent person. Instead of underscoring the action, the composer provides an aural backdrop or glimpse into the emotional state of the violent men. A good example of this is Roy Webb's cue in *Murder, My Sweet* when Moose takes Marlowe to Amthor's apartment in the hopes of finding out where "his Velma" is. After being told to cool his heels outside while Amthor pumps Marlowe about the jade, Moose bursts back in the room, at which point Webb begins the cue with the "Moose Molloy" motif first used early in the film when Moose mysteriously turned up in Marlowe's darkened office. This motif is a classic villain gesture: it is generally scored in the lower registers (i.e., the bass clef); it has a regular but plodding rhythm; and the interval between the second and third notes is a tritone, an interval we associate with aliens and monsters. Here is the motif as it is stated upon Moose's first appearance on the screen and as it used in the scene described here; notice that Webb increases the tempo in the scene at Amthor's and as result heightens the potential threat posed by Moose:

Moose's Entrance

At Amthor's

Figure 3.10. *Murder, My Sweet*, "Moose Molloy."

Next he brings in a simple, two-note brass motif underneath tremolo strings in the lower registers. After Moose pushes the chauffeur, who is trying to calm him down, Webb introduces a more quickly paced variation of Moose's motif in anticipation of Moose's choking of Marlowe. As Moose actually chokes Marlowe, Webb's cue conforms to the formula for violent cues discussed earlier by accentuating different timbres in the orchestra; for instance, he begins with a simple sustained and dissonant chord played by the brass that gradually crescendos; this segues into a tremolo string figure (suspense topic); he then returns to the crescendo brass figure. Aside from the stinger when Amthor finally slugs Marlowe with brass knuckles, the music of the entire scene is rather understated, accentuating the threat of violence and the pent-up rages and potential for violence in the odd couple of

Understatement in the musical cue from *Murder, My Sweet* belies the overt violence on the screen.

Amthor and Moose. The dissonances and angularity of the entire cue, like those in science fiction and horror, are intended to convey a subliminal neurotic and disturbed quality that augments and intensifies the overt action. Lalo Schifrin's cue for the brutal beating of Harry by the small town thugs in *Sudden Impact* is similar in many regards: the cue begins with a glissando played by chimes that settles into a dissonant chord stated in the low registers that steadily builds into a cluster dominated by high strings. The beating itself, like Moose's action, has little rhythmic dynamism but, instead, relies upon the more neurotic approach accentuating high strings playing slurs (sighing gestures), glissandos, and jagged rhythms that slow down as the strings build toward a climax and a trilling figure at the end. Unlike the overt violence we find in the confrontations in science fiction films, the violence in detective films, especially the post–'60s films, is more psychological, scored more, if you will, to human scale — not normal, but human. What is interesting in all of the examples is that the composers seem to be trying to bring to the forefront psychological motive for the violence rather than just score the action. The message of the violence is that the detective, in making the journey into the dark recesses of American society, will not only encounter the readily understandable forces of greed and desire but will also have to deal with the unpredictability of the psychopathic personality, an even darker recess in the darkest of terrains.

Analysis: The Big Sleep *and* Chinatown

Beginning with the opening title music of these two films, a great deal can be deduced about the evolution of the hardboiled genre over a thirty year time period. Steiner's score for *The Big Sleep* utilizes the orchestral conventions of the classical Hollywood score of the 1930s and 1940s, keeping heroism and action in the forefront, and avoiding privileging topics and gestures that might signify the seamy, corrupt milieu of L.A. Jerry Goldsmith's score for *Chinatown*, on the other hand, is a subtler affair, employing innovative orchestrations and more avant-garde compositional techniques to underscore the more disturbed psycho-sexual-political web of corruption that informs the film's narrative. Goldsmith's score, in fact, eschews heroism in favor of a theme (and leitmotif) that captures a doomed love in the face of moral and political corruption.

As was discussed earlier, composers often provide musical codes for the different strata of society involved in the crimes. In these two films we have three clearly defined strata: the world of the wealthy (in both films they are also clients or victims); the world of the detectives, Marlowe (Humphrey Bogart) in *The Big Sleep* and J.J. Gittes (Jack Nicholson) in *Chinatown*; and the world of the criminal. The world of the wealthy in both films is signified through source music and the iconography of setting (opulent mansions, etc.). In *The Big Sleep*, the famous scene between Marlowe and Vivian (Lauren Bacall) where they discuss gambling and horses (an exchange redolent with double entendre) is underscored by a solo piano playing some of the great songs of the 1920s and 1930s: the famous "blue pajama song," "I Guess I'll Have to Change My Plan" (1929; Howard Dietz — Arthur Schwartz), Rodgers and Hart's urbane paean to wedded love, "The Blue Room" (1926), and, finally, Haven Gillespie and J. Fred Coots's "You Go to My Head" (1938), a harmonically lush torcher that was and continues to be a jazz standard. These songs provide a sense of plenitude by providing an aural layer of Tin Pan Alley sophistication to the visually iconographic upwardly mobile veneer for these "civilized" people having drinks in well-mannered public places. Similarly, the music coming from sources in *Chinatown* is also comprised of great pop tunes and performances: on a stakeout, Jake listens to Bunny Berrigan's incomparable version of the Vernon Duke and Ira Gershwin standard "I Can't Get Started" (1936) on the car radio, and later when he and Mrs. Mulwray (Faye Dunaway) are having a drink at a posh hotel a piano plays "Easy Living" (1937; Leo Robin — Ralph Rainger) and the great Dorothy Fields and Jerome Kern Academy Award winning song, "The Way You Look Tonight" (1936). Once again, the music is classic period stuff, providing a sense of plenitude by capturing perfectly the veneer of the sophisticated society: their languorous melodic lines and stunning harmonic changes provide a smooth, cool, romantic, sophisticated, elegant and charming background for the tapestry of lies that is being woven for the detective to unravel.

The musical coding for the world of the criminal differs in each film. In classic hard-boiled fashion, *The Big Sleep* uses small combo jazz to underscore the criminal element in the scene where Marlowe goes to visit Eddie Mars (John Ridgley). In one segment, Vivian sings a morally ambiguous ditty backed by the combo, and, later, as Marlowe leaves the club we hear Gershwin's "Liza" (1929) in a hot jazz rendition featuring a clarinet solo. It is interesting to see how during this time period when big band jazz was still dominant, the filmmaker used the small combo jazz, a style which from its inception in the late teens and into the 1920s was associated with marginalized elements in society, including irresponsible youth, bootleggers, and African Americans. Here it is a perfect backdrop for Mars's marginalized quest for the Myth of Success. *Chinatown*, on the other hand, needs no specific musical cues to represent the criminal element because the previously mentioned pop songs have already represented them. No raucous jazz intrudes into the world that Polanski and Goldsmith create, for to do so would be, in detective novel terms, a red herring. Marlowe is facing off against the marginalized element represented by Eddie Mars; Jake is facing off against a society not corrupted by the marginalized element (preying upon the wealthy), but a society corrupted by individuals who should be the very exemplars and guardians of community values and mores. Ralph Willett writes: "[Noah] Cross, a creature of immense malevolence whose daughter Evelyn is married to Mulwray, is the centre of this narrative of public and private perversity. In the blunt words of Robert Towne who wrote the screenplay, he is a 'man who raped the land and his own daughter'" (98). Marlowe's heroic themes, however, stand in dramatic counterpoint to the music of Mars's club: there is no ambiguity about who the bad guy is or his faith in basic goodness of Vivian. The music Jake hears, on the other hand, is part of a seamless social fabric — on the surface — and he must be wary not to be seduced by "Easy Living" and "The Way You Look Tonight," and he must discover, as the score suggests, that the evil is enveloping him.

The hero's quest for justice in the face of this corrupt society is where the composer supplies the music of suspense and action. In general, both composers effectively communicate a sense of danger in the scenes where the detectives are pursuing leads and clues, but their approaches are different and that difference is emblematic of shifts that have occurred in the genre since the forties. Steiner's score reveals Marlowe to be a man of action, an urban knight-errant seeking justice in a corrupt world. The film's main title announces the dark terrain that Marlowe will be traversing with its marked dark tones and minor harmonies; these are echoed in one form or another throughout the film generally in descending melodic gestures like this:

Figure 3.11. *The Big Sleep,* **main title.**

We hear this motif as Marlowe is driving to Realito and later just before the big showdown with Mars. However, the dominant musical gestures and topics in the film correspond to the way in which Hawks deals with the conflict. Marlowe is really lined up against underworld types, with Mars at the head; Mars's corruption, unlike Noah Cross's, is seemingly more overt: his assault on social mores is motivated by greed and possessiveness but it lacks Cross's psycho-sexual pathology. He preys on the wealthy but consorts with those on a lower socioeconomic strata. It is interesting that the penultimate provocation that leads Marlowe to really confront Mars is when Mars's heartless thug Canino (Bob Steele) kills "Jonesy" (Elisha Cook, Jr.). Marlowe's quest then is scored in a fairly straightforward fashion. He is given his own motif, which is usually sounded when he is about to go into action or when he has an insight about a clue. Part swashbuckling topic and part whimsical comment, the motif seems to be an amalgam of musical ideas from post–Romantic music, most notably the opening of Strauss's *Ein Heldenleben* and his *Till Eulenspiegel,* and evocations of Mahler's symphonies (especially the final movement of his Symphony no. 6, often called the *Tragic*). Steiner's motif for Marlowe is this:

Figure 3.12. *The Big Sleep,* **"Marlowe."**

The initial phrase that outlines a minor third gives the motif a somber tone but that gives way to the striking lift gestures preceding the downbeats and an ascending melodic line that recalls the great swashbuckler themes from Korngold's scores for Errol Flynn films of the 1930s. There is also just a touch of a bugle call topic in the theme to suggest the call to action. This particular gesture is usually used, in typical Steiner fashion, with others in any given scene, especially when he is searching for a clue and when suspense is being built into the scene. A good example of this is the first encounter with the villains. After a short romantic interlude in a bookstore with Dorothy Malone, Marlowe follows Geiger's car to the little house outside the city. The pursuit begins with a repeated minor third figure that suggests action and something ominous. As Marlowe gets into his car, the Marlowe motif is sounded. When he arrives at the stakeout Steiner evokes the classic suspense topic: the strings begin a trilling figure while the brass and woodwinds play the following "stalking" topic.

This is again countered by the Marlowe motif, which, in turn, gives way to an ominous figure in the low strings with the brass playing isolated chords above. The scene uses the trilling strings and the Marlowe motif one final time before Marlowe settles into his car and waits out the rain and the villains in the house. Throughout the film this is Steiner's approach

Figure 3.13. *The Big Sleep.*

to the conflict; he keeps Marlowe's quest in the forefront with the swashbuckler motif and relies upon the tried-and-true topics and gestures outlined earlier in the chapter to convey the forces that are arrayed against the hero.

Jerry Goldsmith's approach to Gittes's quest is quite different. Other than the love theme, there really is not a motif or particular musical gesture that we associate with Gittes. Instead, Jake's quest is always accompanied by motifs that meld suspense and corruption. The thing that struck me the most when watching *Chinatown* was how close to horror and science-fiction music Goldsmith's score was in the suspense scenes. The pursuit-of-the-first-clue scene in *Chinatown* has an entirely different feeling from the one in *The Big Sleep*. There are no aggressive rhythms, nothing to tell us that a knight errant has set out on a quest to right a wrong. Instead, as Jake surveys one of L.A.'s waterway canals, all we hear is a tonal cluster followed by delicate little descending sighing gestures played by a piano — a gesture often associated with the tragic; a harp is next brought in and the suspense is built by relying upon an interplay between high and low strings. There appears to be no clearly defined melodic line or harmonic progressions in most of the cues, just what appears to be an undifferentiated use of musical timbres and dissonant musical ideas. The use of the dissonant cluster and the largely unmelodic and angular melodic motifs seems intended to put one on edge, to give one the creeps if you will, as much as they are to suggest danger for Jake. The markedness of the dissonance here is striking because we so often associate it with, as we have seen, the abnormal and the psychologically twisted. If, as Michael Eaton suggests, *Chinatown* does not subscribe to detective genre's "faith in the eventual victory of human rationality" but instead is about, in Robert Towne's words, "'the futility of good intentions'" (40), about the victory of the irrational and corrupt, then Goldsmith's musical decisions are dead-on perfect. Throughout the score Goldsmith does not vary this approach to the quest for clues very much. The initial tonal cluster is the one consistent motif he employs, and this is always balanced with orchestral textures that rely upon lighter sounds: prepared pianos, harps, and strings. Even in the scene of greatest tension and danger, when Jake enters Ida Session's apartment, Goldsmith relies upon the piano, harp, and percussion and not brass to convey an atmosphere of danger — even when he uses a stinger upon discovering the body. The overall effect is of being placed in an unbalanced, abnormal environment, much like what we expect in the horror film when the threat of mysterious and malevolent forces is pervasive and imminent. Thomas Leitch has observed that "nature itself is against Gittes" (212) in his hunt for the murderer, and Goldsmith's music perfectly captures that idea by providing a disturbing and dissonant aural backdrop to the exterior scenes on the fringes of L.A. Goldsmith's score makes the pervasive corruption of L.A. almost overwhelming; there is no heroic music to counterbalance the dissonant and astringent sounds of the lean orchestral ensemble that he relied upon in the score.[1] Ryan and Kellner note that

> *Chinatown,* in an anti-heroic gesture consistent with the sixties sensibility [that] lies behind it, recodes the figure of the detective hero by portraying Gittes as a flawed man who cannot control events. Throughout much of the film he wears a bandage on his nose, signifying his weakness and vulnerability. The tough guy detective of Hammett, Chandler, and others,

by contrast, is a paragon of individualism who is courageous, resourceful, and usually successful. He stands outside of the corrupt universe that he inhabits, subscribes to his own code of honor, and usually succeeds in exposing and defeating evil. Such a figure, *Chinatown* suggests, is an anachronism [82].

Correspondingly, where Steiner's music underscores the corruption by employing classic suspense and violence gestures, Goldsmith's underscores it in more deeply disturbing, modernistic, and psychological "language." Polanski and Goldsmith dialogically create a cognitive dissonance between visuals and music: the visuals tell us Jake is the sharply dressed, wholly competent, and courageous detective, while the music tells us that his quest will be anything but a linear path to truth and justice; instead, he will be overwhelmed by forces that give the lie to the honest, the decent, and the rational.

Finally, we turn our attention to the *femme noire* in each film. With the *femme noire* comes romance as well — or at least lust; and, once again, reflecting the time periods and the nature of the evolution of the genre, the approaches to romance and the *femme noire* are markedly different in the two scores. Generally speaking, in many detective films, the private eye is able to salvage a relationship out of the chaos and corruption in which he has been embroiled. From a narrative standpoint — and also an audience expectation standpoint — the "girl" symbolizes the small triumph of the detective: he doesn't get the big bucks for cracking the case but he gets something more meaningful: the love or at least affection of a good woman. Implicit in this is the restoration of some order in society with a "normal" relationship, as opposed to seductive and deceptive one, being signified in the final *mise-en-*

Chinatown. Jake Gittes's quest leads him to cross paths with the very heart of corruption: Noah Cross.

scène during the end titles and the music playing under them. There is, in short, a suggestion of a new, more ordered beginning and a cleaning of the moral slate; love is redemptive and there is still hope for society. However, to get to this point at the end titles makes for interesting music in the films. In *The Big Sleep* there are a number of *femmes noires*: Vivian, Carmen, and Agnes all could qualify in one way or another. The only woman, however, who is given the classical *femme noire* topic is Carmen. In the opening scene of the film when Marlowe enters the Sternwood estate he is greeted by the child-like and seductive Carmen, whose entrance is accompanied by a similarly seductive, descending and chromatic motif excerpt played by the strings which is reminiscent of the Saint-Saens aria discussed earlier.

Figure 3.14. *The Big Sleep*, "Carmen."

The main character, Vivian, has no particular theme except for the love theme. The love theme for *The Big Sleep* may strike one as being somewhat odd for a hardboiled *film noir* thriller because of its triple-time meter and its sweeping, swashbuckling theme. In fact, if one removed the slightly dissonant and darker brass figures which punctuate the musical phrases of the theme, one could easily place the piece in any costume drama between 1935 and 1955. It is not a soaring melody a la *Gone with the Wind*, but its long, elegant melodic line strongly suggests the classically romantic.

Figure 3.15. *The Big Sleep,* "Love" (Darby and DuBois, 56).

This, however, is in keeping with Steiner's vision in the film: Marlowe genuinely believes she is the "good" sister and he genuinely falls for her (which of course contributes nicely to the duplicity he must deal with from all concerned, including Vivian herself), and, in a sense, when he solves the crime he "rescues" her much like the knight-errant of old. The music is used in the bookstore sequence with Dorothy Malone first and then after that it is only in the Bogart and Bacall scenes. It really is a great theme because it is not overly bright sounding to begin with and Steiner does something interesting things with counterpoint and accompanying figures in his scoring of the theme. For instance, in the scene where Marlowe and Vivian are driving away from Mars's club, Steiner introduces the theme with a trilling figure in the low strings to suggest suspense, but as the dialogue builds and Marlowe reveals his feelings, the theme takes on all the characteristics of the classic love theme. On the other hand, later in the film when Marlowe and Vivian are escaping from Mars's house in Realito the love theme is darker: he maintains a swirling string figure in the background as the theme plays, and it is once again punctuated — it almost seems interrupted — by a darker and more dissonant motif in the brass. In the end, however, it is the love theme brought up over the final image of Marlowe and Vivian, which initiates the end titles, which in turn are capped off with a final flourish of the Marlowe motif, suggesting that something may come of the relationship and that in the end the good guy wins out and justice has prevailed after all.

Chinatown's love theme, on the other hand, is an entirely different matter. In a sense it is mythological: it is the kind of music you would expect to hear in a mystery set in an urban environment and taking place in the 1930s. It has the feel of a jazz tinged torch song com-

The Big Sleep. The classic detective film score holds out the promise that the good guy can indeed win the heart of the girl at film's end.

plete with marked minor harmonies, a blues topic, and a mournful solo trumpet carrying the melody. The love theme also serves as the main-title music for the film, contributing a sense of somber reflection fused with just a tinge of romance to overall atmosphere of the film. The primary theme is in a minor key and conveys the archetypal urban-jazz topic by emphasizing minor seventh and sixth harmonies with an occasional diminished fifth and ninth thrown in for more color and harmonic interest. A delicate tension is established from the very outset by using the ninth scale degree for the first note of the theme and having the bass line almost function as a pedal point by alternating I6 and I7 chords.

Figure 3.16. *Chinatown*, "Love Theme."

Each phrase initially conveys a sense of upward movement as it moves into the major harmony, but the resolution is always back to the minor key preceded by a descending leap of a fourth or a fifth — which could be read as an overtly dramatic sighing or tragic gesture. The third theme, which precedes the final cadence, comes about as close as you're going to get to capturing that classic romantic love theme feeling in the song. There is a subtle shift emphasizing major harmonies, and the melody is sustained in the higher registers until it finally returns to a minor harmony after a half note triplet (over a C major chord), which in actuality seems to be functioning as the fifth for the F#m7, which is preparation for the B7-9 chord leading to the final cadence, which effectively alternates between E maj.9 and F#m7 chords. It is a melody laden with sadness and not just a little tragedy, much like Jake's affair with Evelyn and her demise in Chinatown. Unlike Steiner's theme, which signals the triumph of romantic love, Goldsmith's theme, especially his third theme, reminds us that romantic love cannot redeem those touched by corruption; Jake and Evelyn's attempt at finding some normalcy in their relationship is doomed by the large shadow of the incestuous Noah Cross, who has raped his daughter and is now raping the land and by extension the innocent people of the city. The fact that the music serves as end-title music is a further reminder of both Jake's and Evelyn's separate quests (Evelyn's being to protect her daughter), both noble in their own right and both doomed.

Conclusion

We can look to the respective love themes from these two films to find a musical emblem for the shift in the transformational genre of the hardboiled detective film. In his analysis of *Chinatown*, Michael Eaton notes that the detective story "is an optimistic genre with a touching faith in the eventual victory of human rationality" (40). Steiner's use of the love theme throughout and especially at *The Big Sleep*'s end bears this out. The music is basically optimistic and romantic, and played so grandly as it is at the film's end, it signals a victory for both Marlowe and Vivian over those threatening her family, a return to normalcy, and perhaps even love triumphant. It is even more significant and appropriate that, in keeping with Chandler's vision of Marlowe as the knight-errant, Steiner makes the final musical statement in Hawks's film the Marlowe motif, a gesture that reaffirms Marlowe's classic heroic status. This motif, in tandem with the love theme, reminds us that the hero is indeed "everything," a common man but an unusual one. He is a man, moreover, who can make a difference in a world threatened by corruption; he may, in fact, be able ever so tentatively to stem the tide of that corruption. Goldsmith's achingly somber love theme, on the other hand, reminds us of an underlying sadness in romance, that there may be a glimmer of hope for some refuge from a corrupt world. But it is not to be. Just as the theme never moves out of the minor (tragic) mode, so their love is doomed. The bad guys win. Jake isn't Raymond Chandler's hero; he isn't everything and he may in fact be tarnished and afraid at the film's end. Thomas Leitch writes: "Despite his pertinacity, his detective skills, and his unexpected idealism, Gittes does not realize the monstrous nature of the crime he is investigating until it is too late to stop its corruption from spreading still further. He can neither persuade the police to arrest the killer he unmasks nor can he save the life of the heroine he has come to love" (202). The evil men and institutions emerge triumphant and one man isn't enough to stem the tide of corruption.

4

Swashbuckling Symphonies
The Historical Romance Film

Introduction

Watching films such as *Captain Blood* (1935), *The Sea Hawk* (1940), or *Gone with the Wind* (1939), one might be convinced that it was this genre that inspired Jack Warner's dictum about films as fantasy and fantasy needing music. The films are rich with music, the kind of music we associate with the archetypal classical Hollywood film score. Not surprisingly, Kathryn Kalinak and Royal Brown both hold up *Captain Blood* as the epitome of the classical Hollywood film score. There are some minor ironies in this situation: on the one hand, it makes perfect sense that the films should be so richly scored; they are after all romance, and the conventions of post–Romantic music are a perfect fit for the emotional subtexts of the films; on the other hand, they are films about history and, consequently, should be grounded in the realities of historical and musical fact and data — after all, there really was an American Civil War, a conflict between Spain and England, an El Cid, and a Richard the Lionheart. Of course, this historical perspective, to paraphrase Robert Frost, with all its matters of fact is all well and fine but, obviously, we are dealing here with history being filtered through a very special prism. Marcia Landy states: "Historical representations may often seem to reiterate dominant cultural ideas and values, but a closer scrutiny reveals that popular history represented through the cinema is a pastiche of conceptions about the world: a fusion of current and practical strategies of survival couched in clichéd, proverbial language characteristic of commonsensical approaches to knowledge" (1). In short, it is not the job of the historical film to be a textbook or dissertation on history. Its job is to be a narrative retelling of the exploits of some efficacious individual in a historical context. Brian Taves notes, "Adventure's history is based on facts that have been mythologized to reveal a pattern purpose and progress in mankind's endeavors — a movement along the road toward freedom for all people" (96). We, in fact, may learn less about history *per se* than about our own cultural values as we reflect on the historical film. The genre's progression and evolution bears this out. Reflective of our belief in democratic ideals during the pre–World War II years, films like those about Robin Hood, to quote Taves, "deal with the valiant fight for freedom and a just form of government, set in exotic locales and the historical past. This is the central theme of adventure, a motif that is unique to the genre" (4). In contrast, the films of the post–World War II era reveal something else: "In what was clearly a reflection of the experience of World War II and disillusionment with the Old World, Europe was now often portrayed as a near-barbaric cesspool of depravity and corruption in such films as *The Black Book/Reign of Terror* (1949); *Captain from Castile* [1947]; *Prince of Foxes* (1949); and the *Flame and the Arrow* [1950]." (Taves 74). Add to this our reappraisal of non–Western cultures in the context of Western expansion and one finds a problematized historical film, as is evidenced by movies ranging from *The Wind and the Lion* (1975) up to the remake of *The Four Feathers* (2002), where both the old certitudes that inspired westward expansion and democratic ideals themselves are brought into question.

Before examining the conventions of scoring in the genre let's take a look at the genre as a whole and the type of historical film I will be concerned with in this chapter. There are thousands of films that use history as a backdrop for some individual drama. Jeffrey Richards identifies the following: the epic, the historical biography, the romantic melodrama, and the costume drama (1). I am not sure that any categorization of the historical film will hold up even to minor scrutiny and analysis; for instance, couldn't the epic also be a melodrama, and couldn't the costume drama also be a melodrama? I think, however, Richards's basic categorization is about as good as it might get, and it is not my job here to cavil with his research. Brian Taves's categorization of historical adventure is very useful; it allows him to analyze films as disparate as *The Prisoner of Zenda* (1937) and *Lawrence of Arabia* (1962) to reveal an underlying monomyth, if you will. However, when we turn to an analysis of the films from a purely musical standpoint, a different sort of categorization seems to emerge. The musical scores for the two abovementioned films are markedly different: both have their heroic fanfares, but the *Prisoner of Zenda*'s darker musical moments are confined to underscoring the evil deeds of the king's evil brother (Raymond Massey) and not to under-scoring the darker psychological recesses of a politically and sexually conflicted British army officer. There are no swelling romantic themes and pledges of eternal love in *Lawrence* and no ambiguous political solutions in *Prisoner* for the composer to worry about. What I have done then is chosen a body of films that I call historical romance. These films focus on a relationship between a man and woman occurring at a moment in time when, accord-ing to Taves, history is "at a crossroads" (96). As we shall see presently, the drama centers on issues of love and honor, individualism and community (state), and freedom versus oppres-sion. This allows me to cover a fairly diverse body of films ranging from the naturals such as *Captain Blood* and *Gone with the Wind* to *El Cid* and *Rob Roy* (1995) and the most recent remake of *The Man in the Iron Mask* (1998). My reason for going with the romance is that, from a purely musical standpoint, it is the species of the genre that established the conven-tions of scoring for most historical films. Consequently, *Ben-Hur* (1959) — which would not qualify here — contains many of the elements that are part of the score for *The Sea Hawk*, such as a dramatic and moving main title, a beautiful love theme, and marches and action music to accompany the spectacle. However, *Ben-Hur* is not first and foremost about love and freedom, unless you consider the hero's relationship to God a kind of love story and the underlying struggles of the Jews and Romans the dominant narrative impulse of the film; it is, instead, a film about faith. In my analysis of the music of the historical romance, I will be focusing on the following conventions: the main title, the hero, the love relationship with the heroine, spectacle, the villain (or blocking force if a collective villain), and a final duel or con-frontation. Let's begin, however, with a look at the dominant themes and values contained in the historical romance.

Themes and Values

As I suggested above, the historical romance is as much about contemporary attitudes and values as it is about the values of a society at a given time in history. Developing as they did during the Great Depression and the years between the wars when issues of democratic forms of government versus dictatorships and individualism versus the ideals of the communist collective were a preoccupation of many moviegoers, the films articulated a mythology about personal (and predominantly male) efficacy and the quest for freedom that resonated with Western viewers. Thus at the heart of the historical romance stands "the Individual," the central hero figure, who faces a variety of conflicts: he must at times choose between love and honor; he must at times choose between his own code of behavior and that of the court, state or community; he may have to exist outside the law to validate the law; and so forth. Nonetheless, in the end, the community will be reconstituted and reaffirmed pretty much in accordance with the dominant mythology of the culture. As Leger Grindon notes, "The relationship of the individual to society is the central theme — the animating conflict — of the historical fiction film. A tension exists between the personal needs of the individual and the needs of the community for cooperative action and mutual responsibility; at the same time, the individual and society are bound in permanent union" (9). The films, then, like many of our American film genres, validate the efficacy of the individual, perpetuating the myth that the individual can make a difference and that a society that is dedicated to freedom and justice must be predicated on the values and actions of such efficacious individuals.

The second major theme of the historical romance is freedom and, at times and more specifically, democracy. Brian Taves notes that "adventure in the cinema deals primarily with liberty and overcoming oppression as a historical phenomenon" (13). Historical romances from *Captain Blood* through *El Cid* and *Robin and Marian* (1976) up to the recent *Man in the Iron Mask* weave this theme of fighting corruption and oppression into the love stories that stand as the emotional core of the films. Often the films deal with the struggle between love and honor, with those two ideals or values needing to be reconciled for the new and better society to be established at film's end. In the majority of cases, the heroine must see the wisdom of the *hero's* choice and capitulate to his quest for freedom and his need to validate his own personal code of honor. From a musical standpoint, love themes and main titles or the hero's motifs will be very similar, and they will be used interchangeably or in tandem to score different scenes (e.g., the hero's motif will form part of the underscoring for a love scene). An interesting musical issue that arises in this analysis is: what kind of musical topics and gestures signify freedom? Historical context figures significantly in the types of topics and gestures that constitute musical codes for heroism and freedom; these codes, moreover, will likely be derived from what Jeffrey Richards calls the "Code." He states:

> The Code is, of course, the Code of the ruling class and its prominence strongly implies an Establishment mentality behind the films. The metaphor of the Establishment is most frequently the monarchy.... The Crown functions as an object of devotion, the sanction of the action, the symbol of all that is true and good and worth fighting for.... The monarch, on the other hand, is seen as embodying fair-minded and disinterested central government, opposed to the anarchic, centrifugal tendencies of these individual power groups [unscrupulous aristocrats]. The interests of the monarch are thus identical with the interests of the people. The monarch by being monarch is *ipso facto* defender and protector of the people's rights. He embodies the soul and traditions of the nation [5].

It is important to point out here, as Richards notes, that this monarchy is "of the constitutional rather than the absolute variety" (5) — a neat trick in the Musketeer films when we know full well that the monarchy is indeed of the absolute variety. Consequently, what emerges in the scores is a kind of musical tapestry that reconciles the efficacy of the individual with the values of the dominant class. Marcia Landy notes:

> In the music of the films and in operas, especially Verdian opera, one hears brilliant fanfares of trumpets and trombones. Orchestras, like choruses, function in both literal and metaphoric fashion to provide the necessary musical accompaniment and to generate the proper solemn, ritual, or ceremonial affect. Orchestral and choral music also functions as a means of distinguishing between the individual and the collectivity, especially of distinguishing the great individual from the masses. The use of many instruments contributes further to this sense of the vastness and greatness of the individuals and the events. Orchestration also contributes to the illusion of transcendence, or surpassing both individual and collective struggles, where the interests of the state is visible as a major producer of monumental national images consumed through visual and aural modes [111].

From a democratic standpoint, the paradox of these films is resolved in the music: a strong individual can be just that, an individual, and be a defender of democratic values in a caste system. Kevin Costner's Robin Hood states, "Nobility is not a birthright, it is defined by one's actions," as fine a piece of Jeffersonian ideology as you'll ever hear uttered by a member of the ruling class in medieval Britain. And the music of the films mythopoeically affirms and reconciles this paradoxical theme through the use of neoromantic idioms favoring heroic musical topics, echoing works ranging from Beethoven to Richard Strauss to Wagner. The universality of the topics and gestures (that is, from a Western standpoint) pretty much adumbrates the class issues by sweeping us along with soaring melodies and stirring rhythms that underscore the efficacy of the individual so that we feel that his triumph is a triumph for all of society.

Knowing that Western expansion from the 16th through the early 20th centuries informs these films should prepare us for some major shifts in the values and attitudes conveyed in more recent films. It is more difficult to paint the Moor in a starkly evil light; the Spanish cannot in all honesty be portrayed as less concerned with freedom than Britain or France; and it certainly is harder for us to buy into the idea that a monarchy, constitutional or otherwise, is the proper vehicle for promoting democratic ideals and maximizing the freedom of its citizens. In short, many of the myths that have driven the narratives in historical romance are suspect and are being demythologized and reevaluated these days. Consequently, we see that Sean Connery's Robin Hood in *Robin and Marian* is less of a freedom fighter and more of a Peter Pan figure that just can't give up seeking out adventure. Sean Connery's Muli in *The Wind and the Lion* (1975) is every bit as heroic (maybe even more so) than his adversary Teddy Roosevelt (Brian Keith), even though he is a Muslim. There is, in short, a recognition of the prevailing attitude that imperialism is an evil and those powers who were the linchpins in that imperialistic expansion are not to be viewed as benignly as before. Brian Taves notes of adventure films since the 1960s:

> In adventure, plot is nearly always foremost, with character secondary and growing out of incidents.... Adventurers were presented as idealized role models or as figures who moved toward such a status, not as thoroughly flawed antiheroes. This tradition goes against postclassical filmmaking, which during the 1960s saw a change from reliance on stories to movies principally about characters, with only a background consideration of plot [89–90].

This, of course, means changes in the music. Those musical topics associated with "other" cultures, and which previously connoted evil, will either give way to new topics or gestures or, because of other contextual issues, will no longer carry negative connotations. Even the music of the hero may have to be altered to account for those deeper and more troubling psychological currents that inform the actions of our heroes nowadays. A good example of this can be seen in two screen treatments of the mutiny on the *Bounty*. In the 1963 version of the film, Bronislau Kaper handles the departure of the *Bounty* from the port of Plymouth in "classical" fashion. There are swirling strings to accompany the unfurling of the sails and brass figures to underscore the frenetic activity of the crew, and the entire sequence closes out with a majestically scored chorus of "Rule Britannia" as the ship moves out of the frame but holding briefly on the image of the Union Jack waving proudly off the stern of the ship. In the 1984 version, *The Bounty*, synthesizer wizard Vangelis underscores the departure in much darker tones. The bold confidence gives way to dissonance and decidedly unheroic melodic lines, sounds reminiscent of the gestures we associate with the neurotic and darker elements in other genre films; here the music aurally portends the disaster that awaits all concerned on the ship. It is not that heroism is dead or that adventure no longer has an appeal, it is just that we are more skeptical of these things and the music reflects this skepticism.

Main-Title Music

The main title for a historical romance, like that for other genres, establishes mood, gives one a sense of place and, in many cases, outlines the major conflict in the film. Brian Taves's comments on music in adventure films in general are applicable to the main title: "The music accompanying adventure is martial in nature, with a stirring, patriotic quality setting the stage for battles, underlining the hero's feats of courage, daring, and physical agility. There are contrasting themes, of quiet love to accompany the heroine, another to emphasize the solidarity of the group of good comrades, often constructed into a semi operatic whole" (71). The main-title theme may contain up to three major topics: one, containing gestures to signify the heroic tenor of the film; a second that helps establish setting and mood; and a third, that signifies the love relationship. Let's look at each in a little more depth.

First, the heroic element is the predominant one in the main title and it reinforces the centrality of the hero's quest. The heroic dimension is most often signaled by musical motifs based on the types of fanfare topics we have heard in classical and light classical repertoire; traditionally, these types of motifs exploit lift gestures, usually either of a fifth or outlining an octave. Deryck Cooke notes, for instance, that an ascending figure employing the intervals of 1-3-5 suggests "an outgoing, active, assertive emotion of joy" (115). And that is exactly the feeling that is communicated in the opening fanfare of most historical adventure films. The rhythms underlying the intervallic leaps are also usually martial in nature or at least aggressively enthusiastic; for instance, the following example from *The Adventures of Robin Hood* by Korngold is typical of this rhythmic gesture:

Figure 4.1. Opening from *The Adventures of Robin Hood*.

Once the fanfare is stated, the main theme will be taken up, often by the strings, or by the brass with the strings providing an exciting contrapuntal theme featuring swirling or ascending figures. Royal Brown notes of Korngold's main-title theme for *Captain Blood*: "Quite characteristic of the Korngold sound here is the way the theme is beefed up with parallel thirds (a harmonic coloration one hears often in Puccini) which along with the instrumentation and the pace, draw the listener into an overall aura of pomp and excitement" (*Overtones* 99). Anyone who has listened to any of Richard Strauss's tone poems, such as *Don Juan* (especially *Don Juan!*), *Ein Heldenleben*, or *Also Sprach Zarathustra*, will immediately recognize the sound. Alfred Newman's wonderful main title for *The Prisoner of Zenda* (1937) bears the stamp of Strauss as it begins with a fairly standard trumpet fanfare that leads into the stirring main title played by the brass; this is followed immediately by a melody in the strings that bears a strong resemblance to the opening of Strauss's *Don Juan* as the strings and brass combine in a statement of the theme. These thematic materials are developed and lead into a statement

Figure 4.2. Main title, Prisoner of Zenda.

of the film's love theme, which, in the second repeat, uses the main theme in counterpoint. This blending of the heroic and romantic, as we shall, see is a central musical gesture in the historical romance. Similarly, Franz Waxman's main title for *Prince Valiant* (1958) features an opening brass fanfare with the brass then announcing a vigorous rhythmic pattern featuring a repeated triplet figure similar to the one in Wagner's overture to *Rienzi*. The main theme itself features a four note ascending figure also reminiscent of that from *Don Juan* (the overtly Straussian elements of this particular main title are almost dismaying in their intensity). Most often the heroic theme that is used will appear again in the film to accompany the actions of the hero, particularly in action sequences. Occasionally, the music signifying the community — I am thinking here of the opening themes of Korngold's *The Adventures of Robin Hood* (1938) and *The Sea Hawk*— that is, music which accompanies the hero as he leads his followers on their adventures or into battle, will be introduced first. This, of course, gets the audience prepared to accept and conflate the exploits of the individual with the good of the group.

A variation on the main title is one that employs minor or modal harmonies. The themes, for instance, for *Mutiny on the Bounty* (1962; Bronislau Kaper) and the most recent *Man in the Iron Mask* (1998; Nick Glennie-Smith), stress the minor mode, as both films have tragic overtones; however, they utilize the same melodic materials as the themes in the major mode, i.e., sweeping melodies, and intervallic leaps exploiting fifths and octaves. The minor lends a different tone to the main title and hence the emotional subtext of the film. Once again, Deryck Cooke's analysis of larger structures is useful here in helping to understand the effect (or is that affect?) of the minor mode. He notes that in a pattern which features an ascending 1-3-5 minor pattern, "we shall expect to find the resulting phrase expressive of an outgoing feeling of pain — as assertion of sorrow, a complaint, a protest against misfortune — and we shall not be disappointed" (122). He also notes that the ascending 5-1-3 minor "gives a strong feeling of courage, in that it boldly acknowledges the existence of tragedy and springs onward (upward) into the thick of it" (125). Themes like those mentioned above do indeed capture the underlying tragedy or the protest against misfortune and the courage that is summoned as the hero or heroine acknowledges and confront their fate.

Main titles may also play a role in creating atmosphere and suggesting a sense of place. The trumpet fanfare and martial rhythms of Max Steiner's main title for *The Charge of the Light Brigade* are augmented by familiar British tunes; while Miklos Rosza's theme for *The Four Feathers* (1939), on the other hand, relies almost exclusively upon Middle Eastern musical figures with only a brief nod to a heroic theme later in the title music. Similarly, Elmer Bernstein's main title for *The Buccaneer* (1958) introduces a suitable "Yankee"-inspired topic over the credit for Charlton Heston as Andrew Jackson, and the main titles for films such as *Ivanhoe* (1952; Miklos Rosza), *Knights of the Round Table* (1953; Miklos Rosza), and *The War Lord* (1965; Jerome Moross) employ a medieval sound — largely conveyed through modal harmonies and a quasi-organum style in parallel motion — to convey a feeling for these ancient times.

Finally, main titles of historical romances since the late 1960s reflect the trends we have and will see in other examples of the transformational genre. The old faith in the classic hero is not always present in more recent films. The dark brooding theme of *Robin and Marian* that underscores the establishing shot of a desolate tract of land and a nearly abandoned castle conveys the fact that King Richard's quest is little more than a waste and has brought him to a hellish place to die a hellish death. The theme also establishes the elegiac sadness of the film as a whole. On the other hand, a new convention that one will observe more and more often in the new historical films is the use of indigenous music and instruments in the main titles. We do not necessarily have quotations and borrowings of indigenous styles cast in the symphonic mode, but titles which could be actual tunes from the time period, played by period instruments with modern instruments merely providing harmonic support. Carter Burwell's main title for *Rob Roy* (1995) does all of the above by employing authentic Scotch instruments and an elegiac initial theme featuring a melody with an appropriately narrow range and characterized by the Scottish snap.

Later on it opens up a bit in deference to the heroic character of Rob with some dramatic leaps, but even these are not out of character within an authentic Scotch melody. The use of indigenous music is an interesting phenomenon because it, like the earlier themes, conflates the hero with the community of which he or she is a part, but unlike those themes this conflation of values is not achieved through a "universal" sound but by means of evoking a specific setting and, consequently, that setting's or culture's role in the drama is heightened. In short, the main title has met the challenge of multiculturalism and in a number of cases succeeds in conveying a strong sense of cultural as well as heroic identity.

Figure 4.3. Scottish *Snap*.

Historical Backdrop: Setting and Society

The music in the historical romance is crucial in delineating the place, the time, and the social strata of the characters of the drama, and it must do these things in terms understandable to the moviegoer, whose knowledge of these things may be very great or very limited.

Consequently, most composers rely upon the "universal" sound of the classical Hollywood movie score with minor borrowings — or, perhaps better, filtered borrowings — of period topics and indigenous musical topics to communicate a specific sense of time and place. That the post–Romantic impulses of the classical score should work in this context is not altogether surprising. Brian Taves notes that the historical context, first, "underlines the importance of the film's subject" (93) and the classical score, derived as it is from the world of serious music, immediately communicates a feeling of importance and seriousness to the subject matter. Secondly, the historical backdrop, at least in most pre-'60s films, is reflective of tried and true notions of romanticism in the fine arts; once again, Brian Taves states: "Adventure luxuriates in appealing, romantic locales: faraway or isolated places, distant both spatially and temporally, unexplored or belonging to a time long past. The range of iconic possibilities and the genre's vast terrain, taking place in almost any corner of the globe, is one of adventure's enticements to the viewer" (174). This romantic iconography, as we shall see, is a perfect inspiration for the composers as they attempt to give us a feeling for time and place. I will look first at the kind of musical topics and gestures composers draw on to establish a feeling for setting and then discuss how the social context (i.e., social stratification, social ritual, etc.) is scored.

Obviously, Hollywood composers had adequate models and inspiration for how to communicate an exotic feeling from the repertoire of serious music since the 18th century. From pieces such as Mozart's "Rondo alla Turca" through Mendelssohn's *Italian* Symphony up to the Spanish inflected compositions of French composers such as Ravel and Ibert, the serious composer has drawn upon elements of indigenous music to convey not just a sense of place but a romantic sense of place. Consequently, when Korngold and Steiner had to do the same thing, they cast the indigenous music in light of the popular post–Romantic style of their classical forebears. This historical backdrop can be achieved through musical topics and gestures (set pieces, melodic motifs and harmonic elements) and through instrumentation. A good example of where purely musical elements, specifically harmonic ones, are key in establishing the historical backdrop is in *El Cid*. Derek Elley writes: "*El Cid* derives some of its [musical] material from the earlier *Knights of the Round Table* score (notably the essence of the Cid's theme), but the prevailing use of the Phrygian mode as a harmonic basis for the score establishes the Spanish flavour of *El Cid* clearly enough, along with the free use of mordents and grace notes" (159). The following is a good example of what Elley is talking about:

Figure 4.4. "El Cid Theme."

The eighth-sixteenth-eighth figure is a very "Spanish sounding" gesture, especially when placed in the context of the harmonic movement in this passage. Similarly, composers draw upon stock musical topics to convey a Middle Eastern atmosphere. Although some might not consider it a classic historical *romance*, Jerry Goldsmith's *The Wind and the Lion* provides us with a good example of such a Middle Eastern topic with its chromatically beguiling alterations:

Figure 4.5. *The Wind and the Lion* (Prendergast 164).

On the other hand, to capture a sea setting composers often seemed to borrow from Debussy's *La Mer* or give symphonic treatment to sea shanty type melodies. The seafaring theme from *Captain Horatio Hornblower* (1951) features the same three note lead motif that Alexander Courage used in his theme for the *Star Trek* TV series, a simple melodic idea that suggests moving out and up (as in lofty goals) and which is often used to underscore the actions of hero figures because it uses some form of a 1-3-5 or 1-5-1 intervallic structure (as in Strauss's *Also Sprach Zarathustra*). Finally, medieval settings will generally employ either folk melodies (depending upon the culture) or the "church" modes and parallel movement (organum topics) in the instrumental voicing to convey that time period. In *Ivanhoe*, for instance, Miklos Rosza establishes the British setting with a melody that draws upon a common rhythmic pattern that one finds in both folk melodies and those generating from dances at court:

Figure 4.6. *Ivanhoe*, rhythm.

Modes are used in establishing shots early in the films or may be used the underscore the actions of the hero — primarily because they convey a sense of dignity and solemnity. Miklos Rosza effectively used medieval gestures to underscore the love relationship in both *Ben-Hur* and *El Cid*. Derek Elley notes the following about Jerome Moross's score for *The War Lord*: "The authentic period setting, full of the paraphernalia of the age (from chickens to war machines), certainly provides a firm foundation for the script's designs; so, too, does Jerome Moross's glowing score, its modal *Thomas Tallis*–like love theme tinged with the same autumnal melancholy as Russell Metty's Technicolor images — images of hard, grey stone, inhospitable shorescapes, and faces bathed in amber tones" (156).

Finally, a sense of place can be established through instrumentation. Instruments native to a culture will be incorporated into the standard symphonic orchestra to provide color and a "feel" for the place. Kathryn Kalinak notes that "Korngold's Port Royal cue [in *Captain Blood*] ... uses unusual instrumentation to define the exotic nature of the port (triangle, celesta, harp, and muted trumpets), and assigns percussive instruments the job of carrying the melody" (91). *King Solomon's Mines*, on the other hand, completely dispensed with the standard classical score in favor of indigenous vocal music of Africa. However, most often the composer will fold the indigenous instruments into the context of the orchestra so one will hear a sitar against the backdrop of the orchestra to suggest India, drums and flutes will convey the Middle East, banjos the frontier, and harps will be substituted for lutes in courts of England.

Speaking of lutes, source (diegetic) music is often used to communicate a sense of time and place as well as to encode social norms and social stratification. The elegance of court life in 19th century Ruritania is often communicated through the use of a Strauss waltz topic at an elegant ball, as in *The Prisoner of Zenda*. Military processions and parades or entrances of royalty will be introduced with trumpet fanfare topics — seemingly coming from unvalved trumpets (the best examples of this are when we hear what are obviously the warm tones of the French horn dubbed over those unvalved, single piece, and circular horns blown by Roman legionaries). Songs interpolated into scenes are also important for coding social norms. *The Knights of the Round Table*, for instance, features a scene around a campfire at Christmas time where a courtly song extolling the merits of the king is sung by a troubadour accompanying himself with a lute. Similarly, *The Sea Hawk* features an interesting Korngold song ("Dona Maria's Song") with words by Howard Koch that is sung at the courts of Queen Elizabeth. It is a love tune that mixes some interesting chanson-like rhythms with some decidedly twentieth century harmonic twists on medieval harmonies. In each case, the elegance and *dignitas* of the tunes suggests the civilized values of the upper classes, and they are scored in musical terms (melodically, lyrically, harmonically) that are familiar to the average listener and that further suggest that the values of the court and those of the moviegoer are indeed one and the same. The music associated with the villain or the "other" will punctuate the decidedly non–Western musical elements and instruments, those that particularly grate on the ear, e.g., Middle Eastern vocal styles, reed instruments with harsher timbres, and more rhythmically complex or just alien percussive gestures.

The Hero

The hero of historical romance is something of an ironic figure: he is a man of action who is also, according to Brian Taves, "fundamentally peaceful" (105). He is, according to Taves,

> usually attractive, endowed with personal magnetism, ardent romance, a natural leader with worthy goals and a sense of duty to a country or cause.... The hero is politically motivated and patriotic, selfishly dedicated to justice. Epitomizing altruism, the hero is pure of purpose, brave in war, honorable, fair, and chivalrous, behaving as a gentleman and recognizing a code of conduct. Peace loving at heart, the adventurer only kills the most dangerous of villains, often in highly stylized duels [111–112].

Jeffrey Richards echoes these ideas and adds a couple of points: "The typical swashbuckling hero is the gentleman hero, well born, comfortably off, a man of breeding and polish, daring and humour, gallantry and charm. He maintains a decent standard of behaviour, fights for King and Country, believes in truth and justice, defends the honour of a lady" (4–5). Like the epic hero, the hero of historical romance is the embodiment of the highest ideals and values of the dominant culture, which in the majority of cases means a white, male dominated, Christian culture of Anglo Saxon lineage. Leger Grindon has observed that "the historical film strives to expand its characters into a portrait of a people, to synthesize the individual and collective causes operating in history" (6), and the hero stands at the center of the experience by embodying diverse cultural ideals in a code of action that, as Brian Taves notes, "has many different aspects — a code of honor, of behavior, of chivalry, of comradeship, of faith, of patriotism, of politics, all ultimately interrelated" (136).

The musical gestures and topics used to accompany and communicate this code have stood the test of time in concert halls and even in popular music. Most of what I have discussed in regard to main-title music applies to the music for the hero. Strong vigorous melodies featuring intervallic leaps (especially fifths and octaves) with sweeping, ascending melodic lines predominate in the musical gestures for hero figures. The archetypes clearly are the scores for *Captain Blood* and *The Sea Hawk*, where Korngold skillfully created themes for his heroes that captured and communicated the dual nature of the hero: the peace loving man of action. Kathryn Kalinak notes that the leitmotif for Peter Blood is "an extended theme consisting of two shorter motifs: the heroic brass fanfare ... and a second, contrasting, lyrical string melody. Throughout the film Korngold separates and recombines these motifs, the A motif underscoring moments of Blood's heroism and the B motif emphasizing his more human and vulnerable side" (105–106):

Figure 4.7. *Captain Blood,* "A" motif.

Figure 4.8. *Captain Blood,* "B" motif.

Similarly, in *Captain Horatio Hornblower*, we find a vigorous fanfare topic serving as the kernel theme for the captain, but later in the film when he is at his writing desk and then later as he walks among the wounded after sinking the enemy ship *Natividad*, the composer introduces a motif in the style of Edward Elgar that is noble, contemplative, and gentle. The music reveals that there is a sensitive and feeling *man* under the hard exterior and business-like demeanor of the *captain*. One final example of the hero's theme is in *El Cid* where Miklos Rosza, in gestures similar to Korngold's, features a bold intervallic leap, in this case a leap of the fifth on the first two notes, which, after a short almost appoggiatura-like figure, makes a leap of a sixth followed by an ascending melodic figure (see figure 4.3). We see then that the hero's music connotes aspiration and action, and these qualities will be blended with a softer or more sweeping theme (usually as a love theme) to reveal his two sides.

Transformations and revisionism in the genre have also meant revisionism in the music for contemporary heroes. The music of *Robin and Marian* eschews martial topics in favor of pastoral and elegiac ones. The music in some films, as we shall see with *Robin Hood: Prince of Thieves*, oftentimes adds a comic element—this, interestingly enough, often proves to be the humanizing element in the films rather than the more conventional love theme. It is also is an interesting means whereby the excesses and stereotypes of heroism are kept in check; on the one hand, we still need our heroes, but, on the other, we seem intent upon deconstructing the archetype of the superhero and the swashbuckling dash of the Errol Flynn–inspired hero. There is, however, no consistent model for heroic music in newer films. Perhaps because of the popularity and effectiveness of the music for *Star Wars* we seem willing to accept old-fashioned heroes and the music that accompanies their actions. Consequently, more recent films reveal a fairly even split between those which visually and musically either debunk or deconstruct the hero and those which seem to want to resurrect the old archetype. Films like *Troy* (2004) mine much the same musical turf that Korngold and Steiner did back in the '30s and '40s, and even scores like that of Carter Burwell for the somewhat iconoclastic *A Knight's Tale* (2001) do not completely abandon the topics and gestures we have come to associate with the heroes of romance.

The Heroine and Love

For all the battles and action and swashbuckling panache and adventure, the real central preoccupation of the historical romance is the romantic relationship between the hero and the heroine. It is the love theme, moreover, which supplies a large measure of the narrative tension to the hero's struggle between love and honor. He may love a woman who is from the enemy camp or who wants him just for herself and resents any risks he may take which might jeopardize their happiness; or she may be, as in the case of *El Cid*, a woman who, at least for a short time, wishes him dead as a matter of family honor. Whatever the situation, the relationship must be as storm-tossed as the political events swirling around the lovers. As I hinted at earlier, the films use the romance to conflate the political and personal. As Leger Grindon notes: "The chief archetypes of the historical romance are the lovers and the great leader, and marriage is its chief goal. The fate of the lovers points to the historical attitude of the film, happy marriage signifying the alliance of conflicting forces" (11). Let me first make a few comments about the role of women in the films and how that might affect compositional practices, and then let us look at conventions of the love theme in historical romance.

Women's roles in historical romance films made before the sixties conform to the stereotypes and conventions associated with heroines in fictional romance. Brian Taves rightly notes that the women in the films are usually "a support or at best a partner, assisting or measuring the hero's progress" (123). However, as I suggested above, the woman's presence in the film is meant to build tension and so she may not conform to the qualities of the "Cult of True Womanhood," which, as E. Ann Kaplan notes, are "piety, purity, domesticity, and submissiveness" (116). And indeed, as Taves notes, "Despite remaining comparatively inactive, such women may govern the hero's actions, expecting to be pursued with determination by a hero who will courageously overcome any obstacle, dare to perform any mission, to secure her approval and respect" (124). Consequently, two musical impulses or perhaps better gestures accompany the actions of the heroine. First, what could be termed "the feminine," the soft, elegant, and beautiful aspect of the heroine, leads the composer to rely upon gently flowing melodies with occasional lift gestures (almost as a reminder that these women are linked to the hero's quest) and, second, harmonies that suggest yearning (suspensions, chromatic changes, etc.). Rebecca's theme from *Ivanhoe* is a good example. The theme is a trope which fuses a liturgical topic (complete with modal parallel movement in the harmony as a means of encoding her Jewishness) with the gentle melodic contours and lift gestures that simultaneously suggest love, honor, dignity and yearning.

Adagio ♩ = 48

Figure 4.9. Rebecca's theme."

In actuality, one may not often find a theme just devoted to the heroine because of her role in the film, and for that reason the theme that most often is used to underscore her first appearance will be either a distinctive love theme or a variation of the hero's theme. By doing this, composers establish the emotional underpinning of the love vs. honor conflict and also suggest that the two conflicts will be reconciled in the marriage of the principals. Royal Brown writes of the music for the final scene of *Captain Blood:*

> Yet the music in particular raises the reunion of the couple to the level of the film's heavier political matters. Indeed, the use of the romantic theme both to introduce the couple's exchange of love vows and to back the Queen's promise of a fleet to fight the Spanish says a lot about the way in which the film manipulates its narrative themes. It is as if the saving of England from the clutches of the evil King Phillip of Spain were totally bound up in the romantic involvement of a Spanish noblewoman for an English nobleman ("It's strong, but it never occurs to me anymore that I'm Spanish and you're English," says Dona Maria in the coach to Thorpe, who is wearing Spanish garb) [*Overtones* 11–116].

Similarly, the *Prisoner of Zenda* ends with the heroic theme moving into the love theme as the closing titles appear on the screen.[1] In short, if we want to get insight into the women in the film from listening to the score, it is to the love theme that we must look because that is where the heroine's character is musically most fully developed.

The archetypes for the classical historical romance love theme can easily be found in the literature of post–Romantic composers such as Wagner and Richard Strauss. Listening to Strauss's *Don Juan* and Wagner's *Tristan und Isolde* will provide one with the primary building blocks for what Korngold in *The Sea Hawk* and *Captain Blood,* Alfred Newman in *The Prisoner of Zenda,* Franz Waxman in *Prince Valiant* and Trevor Jones in *Excalibur* (which borrows from the Prelude and the "Liebestod" of *Tristan*) all do in the love theme in their films. Kathryn Kalinak nicely describes the general outlines of the love theme in her description of Korngold's theme for Peter Blood and Arabella Bishop in *Captain Blood:* "It depends upon several standard devices for emotional expression: dramatic upward leaps in the melodic line; sustained melodic expression in the form of long phrases; lush harmonies; and reliance upon the expressivity of the strings to carry the melody" (88). The theme from *The Sea Hawk* similarly exploits a sequence featuring leaps mainly of the fourth and sixth with a contrasting stepwise descending pattern, thereby bringing the more heroic element (represented by the leaps) into more dramatic relief.

Piu Cantabile

Figure 4.10. *Sea Hawk* (Brown, *Overtones* 102).

Captain Blood. **The music for heroes like Captain Blood often figures prominently in love scenes as well.**

Alfred Newman's very Richard Strauss–like love theme for *The Prisoner of Zenda* similarly begins with a descending movement in the melody only to dramatically sweep up an octave (dominated by a sixteenth note run) in a heady admixture of passion and heroic sweep.

Figure 4.11. *Prisoner of Zenda* (Darby and DuBois 83).

These last two examples are also good illustrations of how love themes oftentimes also echo the heroic themes announced in the main titles. In some cases, like that of *The Sea Hawk, Captain Blood,* and *The Adventures of Robin Hood,* the love theme can be a reworking and variation on that heroic theme or will be used in tandem with the heroic themes. Royal Brown writes of the love theme and heroic theme: "On a deeper level, however, the similarity of the two themes also brings together the narrative themes of heroism and love, not only because of the more romantic nature of Thorpe's theme, but, more importantly, because it almost never appears except in sequences where Dona Maria and Thorpe are together" (*Overtones* 103). In other cases, like that of *El Cid*, the composer may write a new theme but with strong echoes of the heroic theme. The love theme from *El Cid*, for instance, like the Cid's theme, begins with a leap (of a fourth as opposed to a fifth) to a half note which is immediately followed by another half note which is held over to the next measure to be followed by two eighth notes and a quarter note triplet before it resolves to the home key and then begins an ascending pattern made up of two measures of triplet figures. The Cid's theme also begins with a leap to a sustained note that is immediately followed by two sixteenths, which aurally have almost the same feel as the triplet. The love theme echoes the Cid's heroic theme in its initial leap of a fourth and its use of the triplet (echoing the eighth, sixteenth, eighth pattern in the Cid's theme); melodically the feeling is more sustained but there is also a dignified air that pervades the melody. Here are both:

Figure 4.12. *El Cid* theme.

Figure 4.13. *El Cid*, "Love Theme."

Finally, the transformational tendencies of the formula also reveal corresponding changes in the scoring of the love theme, mostly in composers breaking away from traditional love themes rooted in post–Romantic conventions. Love themes may incorporate musical topics that more strongly suggest geographic locale. The "love theme" from *The Wind and the Lion*, for instance, employs Middle Eastern orientalisms, while Elmer Bernstein's love theme from *The Buccaneer* (1958) has more of a folk-like quality (a pastoral-like and narrower melodic range and a more "foursquare" harmonic structure) befitting its American setting. And, finally an interesting contrast is offered in two films dealing with the mutiny on H.M.S. *Bounty*. Bronislau Kaper's love theme from the 1963 version loosely borrows melodic elements from traditional Tahitian music and, in very Western fashion, harmonically delights the ear by shifting between progressions built around tonal centers of A minor and A major. It begins in A minor with an interesting downward figure, starting on the second and ending on the fifth. That, in turn, is answered by a figure of narrow melodic range; this sequence is repeated but in A major, nicely preparing the listener for a lovely leap of a fourth supported by an $II^{\flat 7}$ chord. Thus, some of the elements of the classic love theme are retained but there is decidedly geographic feel to the theme as well. In stark contrast to this theme is the music that underscores the relationship of Fletcher and Maiamiti in *Bounty*, where there really is no theme music developed but only an ominous chord sounding under the first passionate kiss between the two lovers. The message is quite clear: there is no romance here, only impending tragedy and misery.

The Villain

The villains of historical romance can be either native born (like King John or the Sheriff of Nottingham) or foreign born (Ben Yuseff in *El Cid* or Menelaus in Robert Wise's *Helen of Troy*). In either case, they are categorized as the "other," someone who, as Brian Taves notes, represents not the ideals and strengths of the culture but its "failings" (121) or qualities that are inimical to the progress and continuation of the culture's destiny. If the central theme of the film centers on the pursuit of liberty and freedom and the efficacy of the individual, the villain will embody values diametrically opposed to those ideals. Jeffrey Richards outlines the qualities of the swashbuckling villain: "[He] is the reverse side of the coin, the dark side of the mirror. The villains are often gentlemen themselves and embody some of the same qualities as the hero: courage, resourcefulness, and swordsmanship. But they are fatally flawed by ambition, greed, or simply *hubris*" (5). It is, in fact, "excessive pride, avarice, and ambition ... that bring about his downfall" (Taves 121). Similarly, the foreign villain "follows the unscrupulous pattern evident throughout the genre of presenting adventure villains as the enemies of liberty and justice. Eastern villains are established as predators, indigenous destructive forces who willingly cause civil war and are even more dangerous to their own race than the forces of occupation" (Taves 193). Whatever the villain type, the viewer will long to see his demise; so odious is he, so alien are his values, and so much a threat is he that his elimination is the only safeguard to our virtue. Geoffrey Vickers in *The Charge of the Light Brigade*, when he takes it upon himself to countermand orders in order for his regiment to engage Surat Khan on the plains of Balaclava, asks his men to "prove to the world that no man can kill women and children and live to boast of it." That, in a nutshell, is the villain and that is the conflict.

In my analysis of the science-fiction film, I discussed the musical treatment of one form of the alien "other." It is interesting to note that there are some similarities between the music that underscores the actions of the monsters and aliens in science fiction and the music for villains of historical romance (not surprisingly, these will also hold true for the monsters in horror films and the "bad guys" in Westerns). In keeping with music's mythopoeic role in developing and resolving conflicts, the villain's music provides an aural counterpoint to that of the hero and the lovers, exploiting two key musical elements: melodic or harmonic variations and instrumentation. Let us look at each in a little depth.

The melodic and harmonic elements in the villain's motifs will be marked, and, in their rejection of conventionally unmarked elements we traditionally associate with the consonant and beautiful in Western music and the classical Hollywood score, they signify values diametrically opposed to those of the hero and heroine. The villain's music is colored by minor harmonies, melodic dissonance, and rhythmic topics and gestures that can be characterized as aggressive or "primitive." A perfect example of this is in Alfred Newman's score for *The Prisoner of Zenda* when the king's evil brother, Michael (Raymond Massey), is introduced. The melody, which is first stated by low brass, sounds almost like a variation on the heroic motif but the intervallic leap is downward and the harmonies that support the melody are minor in character, a gesture and marked musical event that generally signify the tragic. Similarly, Michael Kamen uses a narrow melodic line that seems to conflate Verdi and Gregorian chant and György Ligeti (like "Dies Irae" but with more sinister overtones) in his music for the cave of Cardinal Richelieu in *The Three Musketeers* (1993); the melody must compete with darker harmonies and dissonances, which in the final analysis give the melody a sense of incompleteness.

Instrumentation is also important in the coding of villainy in historical romance. Just as the hero will be given bright and heraldic or militaristic topics, the lovers lush strings and even lusher harmonies (even if they are chromatically tinged), the villain's music by contrast will feature strings and brass scored in lower registers (which signify a more ominous character). In general, topics intended to communicate villainy will also be more percussive. Kathryn Kalinak, in her discussion of the music for Darth Vader in *Star Wars*, nicely captures the major conventions of instrumental scoring for the villain in historical romance as well: "The instrumentation also carries connotations of darkness as well as militarism, especially in the choice of trumpets, horns, trombones, and basses for the melody and low percussion instruments such as a bass drum and timpani in the accompaniment (denoted '*marcato*')" (195). Thus we find, as in *Captain Horatio Hornblower*, muted brass playing in the lower registers when the villain El Supremo is introduced. The music is also marked by a more aggressive rhythm than we associate with Hornblower. The following example from the assassination scene in Alex North's score for *Cleopatra* illustrates perfectly how aggressive rhythms — we could perhaps designate them as hammering gestures — commonly signify villainy.

Figure 4.14. *Cleopatra,* "Assassination" (Bazelon 342).

Similarly, the villains in *Baghdad*, the "Black Robes," are introduced with a plodding march-like bass line and a slightly dissonant (read more Middle Eastern) theme stated in the low brass; the motif is further developed by adding a swirling figure in the low strings with an occasional suspense topic tremolo thrown in to heighten the tension. Finally, the contrast between the heroism of the Cid and Ben Yuseff in *El Cid* is very telling, as Miklos Rosza uses percussion almost exclusively every time Ben Yuseff makes an appearance on the screen. The music for the Muslim leader is very polyrhythmic, with deeper resonating drums predominating in the motif. A great example of how a villainous topic — we could term it the Arab War Topic — is created occurs in the scene where he speaks about *jihad*: the first part of the speech is underscored with the drum figures, and as he moves on to talk of world domination Rosza introduces brass to accentuate the militaristic quest of the villain. In all three of these examples — and I would venture to say in most gestures for the villain — rhythm is an important element, an element which enables us to identify where the villain stands in relationship to standards of "civilized" behavior, social norms, and the code of the hero. Just as the topics and gestures that accompany the hero and the lovers are meant to get our hearts to swell and to stir our blood to noble action, so the gestures for the villain are meant to remind us of untrammeled violence and fill us with uneasiness.

Spectacle

Whatever drawbacks there may be in scoring the historical romance, one thing is certain: it is a genre which affords the composer ample opportunity to utilize his or her skills because of the sheer amount of music that is needed. This greater need for music is largely due to the presence of so much spectacle in the films. The elements of spectacle include

> period setting — architecture, as in the temple of Moloch in *Cabiria* (1914) and the gladiator school in *Spartacus* (1960), mass action (conquering armies, coronations, striking workers), and the broad visual landscape of "nature," represented by the plague in *Monsieur Vincent* (1947), the sea and the shore in *The Vikings* (1958), and the desert in *Lawrence of Arabia*, and representing the protagonist's adversary in *Suez* (1938) or his ally in *Alexander Nevsky*" [Grindon 15–16].

Most of the abovementioned examples of spectacle are perfect for music because, as Kathyrn Kalinak notes, "'Naturalistic' sound drops out, and the music, turned up to full volume, provides the only sonority on the sound track" (*Settling the Score* 97). Not only is music foregrounded in such sequences but it, first, saves the scene from being utterly boring and, second, provides an emotional subtext for the action. Long shots of warriors preparing for battle with occasional intercutting of close-ups and medium shots without accompanying dialogue reveals little about the warriors' state of mind and their emotions; music provides the emotional grounding for the coming action. I think we only *think* it is exciting observing armies preparing for and marching into battle; in actuality, if one were to turn off the sound and just watch, the spectacle would be considerably less involving without the music.

Spectacle is also important as a backdrop for the actions of the hero. Composers generally create a sort of musical tapestry consisting of motifs and topics that convey atmosphere, geography, action and psychological states. Because of the wide range of actions in spectacle sequences, many of the topics and tropes we have discussed in relationship to other genres will play important roles in such sequences; for instance, in *Captain Blood*, as Kathyrn Kalinak is in essence describing the use of the suspense topic when she observes: "Korngold's music intensifies the suspenseful potential of the scene through the use of *tremolo* strings, cymbal rolls, horn flutters, an exceptionally high flute part, and crescendo" (*Settling the Score* 93). Spectacle often demands that we hear bits of the hero's theme folded in with the villain's music as well as themes that identify place and time. Franz Waxman's music for the oxen raid in *Taras Bulba* (1962), for instance, reinforces both the character of the Cossacks and the setting of the steppe by using a rhythmic motif similar to Khatchaturian's "Sabre Dance," with kettledrums and percussion predominating. An even more stunning example of this is the scene in *Gone with the Wind* where Scarlett goes through the train station yard looking for Ashley. The music emphasizes a somber throbbing gesture as she winds her way amongst the dying and the wounded. The intensity of the music is heightened as the camera tracks and pulls back to reveal the awful extent of the horror of war, finally stopping with a close-up of a tattered Confederate flag flapping in the wind to the accompaniment of a sad bugle call topic and statement of "Dixie." Similarly, in court romances, stately march-like topics accompany ritualistic actions at court and, depending upon who the participants are, the music either convey a sense of pomp and dignity to the occasion, or, if we encounter marked motifs incorporating dissonances and unconventional elements, we may be cued that villainy may be afoot at court. We will see some of this in the analysis of the Robin Hood films.

Perhaps the best example of scoring spectacle occurs in battle sequences. These sequences can be but are not necessarily confined to the final confrontation, which we will look at presently, and are often peppered throughout the narrative. A good example of how music amplifies the emotional subtext for a battle scene is in *The Four Feathers*. The first battle scene begins with a simple and insistent drumming pattern, which, as we have noted above, aurally identifies the native forces and provides a sense of foreboding if not impending doom — even though the hero's forces may win the battle, the presence of marked motifs associated with the villain contribute greatly to a sense of unease and suspense. As the battle unfolds and develops to a fevered pitch, musical gestures and themes featuring brass instruments begin to predominate, but the underlying rhythm established early in the sequence is maintained as though to remind the viewer of the tenacity of the hero's adversary. Similarly, in the Battle of Valencia sequence in *El Cid*, the brass carry the melody as the troops march on the city and the theme is restated in an ascending sequence (that is the theme is repeated but on gradually ascending scale tones). The underlying fury of the upcoming battle is communicated by a rapidly arpeggiated figure in the strings. A common device in this battle and many action sequences in historical romance is the ostinato. Ostinato patterns, although superficially suggestive of stasis, gesturally convey a relentlessly rhythmic pounding sense of movement. Kathyrn Kalinak, in writing about the action sequences in *Captain Blood*, notes the following: "In *Captain Blood* Korngold uses the standard musical device of the ostinato, a repeated melodic or rhythmic figure, to propel scenes which lack dynamic and compelling visual action" (*Settling the Score* 85). In general, historical romance feature large amounts music, including fully developed musical moments (e.g., a complete march or processional or symphonically scaled compositions).

Finally, a brief word about how composers have accommodated generic transformations in scoring spectacle in more recent films. Just as our attitudes about war, heroism, and the roles of women in society have changed over the years, so composers have had to find musical correlatives to signify these ideological and attitudinal changes in their scores. Great heroic flourishes in battle sequences give way to more dissonances so as to remind us that war is now viewed as equal parts heroic enterprise and tragic waste. The action of the heroes may evoke heroic topics but composers may also fold in comic topics and gestures to remind us of the all too human frailties of our hero figures (a device used by Richard Lester in his musketeer series scored by Michel Legrand). In Terence Malick's recent *The New World* (2005) there is little lyrical in the score to underscore the romance of Captain John Smith and Pocahontas.

The Final Conflict

Finally, the elements of spectacle, character and conflict all come together in the final battle or final individual confrontation (showdown!) with the villain. Musically, there appears to be no set formula here, as the following three examples will illustrate. For instance, in *Scaramouche* (1952), the final duel between Scaramouche (Stewart Granger) and DeMaynes (Mel Ferrer) uses no music at all, following a dictum subscribed to by Henry Mancini that sometimes less or even nothing is better. The lack of music, however, makes the restatement of the love theme at the end and over the end titles more dynamic. Second, there is the final duel in *Prince Valiant*, where we hear no music until toward the end when Waxman introduces slow sustained ringing notes; the effect here is contrapuntal: manic action is underscored by almost static countervailing tendencies in the music. The effect, however, is subtle, because this visual-aural disjuncture creates a tension, allowing the scene to build to an effective conclusion. The less-is-better philosophy works here in that the action unfolds naturally, with the music anticipating the climax. Finally, the most conventional use of music is probably Max Steiner's music for the charge at Battle of Balaclava in *The Charge of the Light Brigade,* which bears a strong resemblance to Tchaikovsky's manipulation of themes in his *1812 Overture.* Steiner begins with a steady march rhythm as the light brigade begins its foray into the "valley of death," and then as the order to charge is issued he brings in a swirling string figure to heighten the intensity and to preface a quickening of the tempo. The remainder of the scene is underscored in almost Mickey-Mousing fashion as he weaves a tapestry of sound with snatches of "oriental topics," Russian anthems, and British patriotic tunes, underscoring the heroics and villainy of the different combatants; the "suite" reaches its dramatic conclusion with fortissimo chords announcing the death of Surat Khan and triumphal fanfares heralding the British breakthrough in the lines and their glorious sacrifice. Just listening to the music one can visualize and figure out what is happening on the screen at any given moment. It really is reminiscent of the great Tchaikovsky overture and, on its own, is equally as thrilling to listen to. As I suggested earlier, this structuring of motifs and topics into a coda to underscore the final confrontation is the most conventional and most often employed means of scoring this type of sequence.

Conclusion

Although the historical romance, like other genres, is subject to many conventions, it is also a genre where composers have been able to be quite flexible in underscoring the action. This is due to the diversity of the types within the genre: the British historical romance will call for different types of music than will the Spanish epic; seafaring yarns will differ from crusader yarns; and so forth. But, transgenerically, there are some fairly stable conventions and, interestingly enough, many of these have remained stable over the years. Heroic musical gestures have not altered much from the *Three Musketeers* of 1935 to those underscoring the musketeers in the 1990s. Villainy still employs marked musical topics, gestures and motifs that run counter to unmarked (tonally and rhythmically acceptable) musical events that audiences have come to expect and love in the genre (and in other forms of serious and popular music); one slight difference we may observe is in contemporary villains' music, which might employ more dissonances suggesting an underlying psychological pathology as opposed to motifs which might suggest more of a social pathology: in other words, the villain is psychologically disturbed, not just a social outcast or misfit.

Perhaps the biggest transformation in the genre centers around the scoring of setting, society and spectacle. Recent soundtracks reveal a breakdown in the Eurocentric outlook that has dominated the genre since the thirties. More indigenous music, music placed in positive settings and reinforced through positive images, is more common in the films so we cannot so readily associate villainy with the mere sound of "Middle Eastern" melodies, leaps, rhythmic patterns, or other musics that are perceived to lie outside the pale of civilized society. Similarly, we can expect to find conventional scenes scored in unconventional ways in more recent films; for instance, a filmmaker may choose to suggest that heroic gestures (like those of the cowboys in the final gunfight in Sam Peckinpah's *The Wild Bunch*) are indeed perhaps are only marginally heroic, with equal parts bloody waste and nihilism — Captain Blood is just Peter Pan but there is no Never-Never Land here, only a Waste Land of confused human motives and evil political ones.

In Depth: The Sounds of Sherwood

Although separated by more than fifty years, *The Adventures of Robin Hood* (1938) and *Robin Hood: Prince of Thieves* (1991) illustrate the durability of film genres and the efficacy of the transformational genre. The central theme of both films is the quest for freedom, the struggle of the oppressed common folk to throw off the yoke of tyranny and oppression. Both films present King Richard the Lionheart as a fair and able king who loves his subjects and would do nothing to harm them, but because he is being held hostage as a result of the Crusades, lower level nobles and administrators who exploit and abuse Richard's subjects are usurping his power. Both films deal with the efficacy of the individual (a decidedly American value) and the mobilization of the oppressed classes to gain their freedom and natural rights. And finally, both films feature a classic romance between Robin and Maid Marian.

Where the films differ is in the details. The personalities of the hero and heroine are slightly different. The films have different major villains and their motives and quest for power are different. The 1938 film seldom questions the class structure and, in fact, paints the upper classes as defenders of democratic values. Robin is himself a knight and earns a title at the film's end. The 1990 film is more critical, albeit in a subtle way, of the class structure:

Mastrantonio's Marian is every bit the equal of Robin in Costner's *Robin Hood: Prince of Thieves.*

Robin is referred to as spoiled child; Will Scarlet, the product of one of the Earl of Locksley's extramarital affairs, becomes emblematic of the carelessness and abusive nature of the upper classes; the sheriff will resort to rape to make his way into the upper class; there is, in general, more corruption within the institutions of the culture (government, religion, etc.); through the character of Azeem the moor, whose scientific knowledge and poetic soul reflect a more cosmopolitan and civilized outlook on life, we perceive the society to be backward and almost barbaric; finally, Robin's recanting of the abuses of his class stand in marked contrast to the final images of the Flynn version where he willingly embraces the title conferred upon him and whisks away the symbol of his new status: Maid Marian. In Costner's film, medieval politics are a metaphor for our contemporary political scene: the film reaffirms our belief in the basic soundness and goodness of our democratic institutions by portraying the sheriff's forces as a radical fringe whose will to power is driven by a perverted ideology (i.e., instead of radical fundamentalist Christianity we have witchcraft) and a reliance upon violence to achieve their ends. This could be any political scenario of the last 35 years: the Weathermen, the Posse Comitatus, the Michigan Militia, the Branch Davidians or even al-Qaeda. Finally, Mastrantonio's Marian is fully Robin's equal and she is something more than Robin's reward for fidelity to Richard. We will see that the scores of the two films provide us with some interesting insights into how the films attempt to articulate the myths of freedom and democratic virtues while simultaneously either abandoning or revising the myths and values that inform the conventions of the genre.

Main Title Music

Korngold's main title music for *The Adventures of Robin Hood* begins with a bright march-like intro featuring a triplet rhythm on the second beat (see figure 4.1); then Korngold introduces the main theme, characterized by a jaunty lift gesture and very economical melody line which is supported throughout by that second beat triplet rhythm. The harmonic alterations and slightly chromatic feel to the motif at once fixes it within the post–Romantic idiom and also suggest a modal basis in the harmony, which would be in keeping with the period setting of the film.

Figure 4.15. *The Adventures of Robin Hood,* main title.

This is the dominant leitmotif we will come to associate with Robin and his merry men and it captures the adventurous and fun-loving spirit of the film.[2] There are two secondary themes that are introduced in the main title of a more dramatic nature, each of which will figure significantly throughout the film. They reinforce the more serious dramatic intent of the film. As the director's name fades the music gives way to a more noble and soaring theme as the written preface describing Richard's quest to "drive the infidel from the Holy Land" and identified by Fred Karlin as "King Richard's Theme" (*Listening to Movies* 98):

Figure 4.16. *The Adventures of Robin Hood,* "King Richard's Theme."

This theme, as we shall see, will be elided with the love theme to form a trope expressive of the genre's heady admixture of romance and heroism. "King Richard's Theme" leads to a fanfare built on a triplet rhythm that accompanies the reading of the news about Richard being held hostage. This music will be quoted with some regularity throughout the film to suggest nobility and the status of the ruling class.

Michael Kamen's main-title music is strikingly different. Gone is the swaggering jauntiness (a quality we associate quite naturally with Flynn's Robin) and in its place we have a more intense, driving and darker theme, but one that still communicates the positive outlook of the hero. Kamen, like Korngold, relies upon a triplet rhythm in the accompaniment, but his use of it strikes one as more gesturally thematized as it seems to impel the melody line forward and to suggest an overall tempo for the film itself; contextually, it owes more to Danny Elfman, via *Batman*, than to Gustav Mahler. Kamen effectively creates tension with a melody that fuses a simple three note motif, employing a classic leaping gesture — that also recalls fanfare topics from classical music — against sustained tones that seem to be seeking resolution back to the tonic; it is the key motif associated with Robin's character.

Figure 4.17. *Robin Hood: Prince of Thieves,* main title.

It creates wonderful tension and drama by beginning as a pick-up on the last beat of a measure and then resolving on the first beat as a suspension with a C being held over seven beats against a B♭ in the bass. The next statement has a similar harmonic ambiguity, as it resolves to an E♭ chord in the treble against a B♭ in the bass and an open fifth B♭ chord in the accompaniment. The third statement foregoes the two note pick-up in favor of a quarter note pick-up, and the melody resolves to a strict B♭ chord. The second section moves the triplet figure to the melody line and places a dark, very modal (Dorian) four note counter melody in the bass. This is stated twice and then the other major "heroic" theme that will be featured in the film is introduced: like a trumpet call to arms, the melody begins with a simple two note motif of a fourth followed by an echoing motif which uses the interval of the fifth (see figure 4.23). This theme is restated a step higher and eventually gives way to a broader restatement of the opening theme minus the driving triplet rhythm. The main title closes with the opening motif and the two note figure in a seeming competition to dominate the title music. The final bars leading to the opening scene in the Muslim prison bring the main title to a somber and dark close as the modal harmonies dominate in place of the more lively fanfare topic used previously. Kamen's theme seems to throw more emphasis on the dramatic import and darker elements of the film and it emphasizes the character of the hero in the drama, where Korngold's theme seems to feature the music of the merry men and the swaggering adventure that awaits the viewer.

The Villain

Traditionally, the primary nemesis in the Robin Hood legend has been the sheriff of Nottingham with King John standing in the background as a shadowy figure of political expediency, a usurper of the worst sort. The sheriff's villainy is predicated on the disparity between his role of sheriff and what he actually does: he is supposedly a protector of the people but he is actually an oppressor. The legend also suggests that the rivalry between Robin and the sheriff is a personal matter, almost like personal competition. In either case, the villains represent the danger of entrusting power to men who do not recognize the rights of the individual and, from an American viewer's perspective, democratic principles. The films and their scores only differ in their presentation of the villains' motives.

The Adventures of Robin Hood features dual villains: King John (Claude Rains) and the Sir Guy of Gisbourne (Basil Rathbone). That fact that King John is the villain in the 1938 film underscores the more political bent of the film. This is not a local official who is squeezing the populace for personal gain, but the brother of good King Richard, who, with foreign assistance (i.e., Sir Guy), is seeking to usurp the throne of King Richard, who has been away on the Crusades. In short, a weasel is undermining the just rule of the people of England while the legitimate king is on a noble quest to keep the country and the world safe for Christendom and, by extension, democracy. Korngold, unlike Kamen, does not really give John or Sir Guy a distinctive motif. Court life in general is underscored with topics that suggest power and class but not necessarily evil. The motif "Old England" provides the segue to the first scene at court, and a fairly routine fanfare topic played by the brass is used in other scenes and, in particular, the archery tournament. The villainy of the two men is musically underscored in their actions, most notably any action which shows them taking from the poor or trying to thwart the efforts to obtain King Richard's release from captivity. The first evidence of this is observed in the sequence where soldiers are seen terrorizing the inhabitants of the shire to get money. The theme, which Fred Karlin calls the "poor people theme" (*Listening to Movies* 98), that accompanies the action is built upon a simple motif that draws on classic villainous musical gestures:

Figure 4.18. *The Adventures of Robin Hood,* "Poor People."

The downward chromatic melody line (featuring tragic sighing gestures), the scoring of the motif in the lower instrumental registers, the use of jagged rhythms (the cue actually begins with the downbeat scored for low strings), the initial downward leap of a minor second, the use of minor harmonies, and the rising tension conveyed through the upward stepwise movement are gestures we associate with villains and with an atmosphere of tension and oppression. The motif, in fact, is almost a distorted mirror image of the opening merry men motif (i.e., "Robin Hood's Theme"): it is not a jaunty celebration of freedom; it grinds on, creating dramatic tension in the scene by being repeated on ascending scale tones, an aural metaphor for people being lashed by oppressive overseers. Robin's interventions in the sequence are usually signaled by a trumpet figure echoing the rhythm accompanying his heroic motif. There is one other example of "villain's music" in the film and that is in the scene when Robin is sentenced to hang. Korngold scores this sequence by having Robin's heroic motif played in a minor key. The message is clear: Robin's heroic quest to free the people is in jeopardy; when he is freed, however, the same music is scored in its proper major key. In the final analysis, we do not get any insight into the characters *per se* but only into their actions, which, in keeping with the film, is what is really important: their evil seems grounded in a pure demonstration of power and their motives are nakedly aggressive.

Robin Hood: Prince of Thieves presents us with a somewhat different villain. First of all, King John makes nary an appearance in the film. Instead, it is the local thug, the sheriff, who

Adventures of Robin Hood. Robin takes his stand against the king's and sheriff's men.

is the primary nemesis. Alan Rickman's sheriff of Nottingham is more darkly drawn than either Claude Rains's King John or Basil Rathbone's sheriff. There are cultish and frankly Klanish overtones to his lust for power, and his reliance upon a witch-like "advisor" (Geraldine McEwan) in his quest for power is emblematic of the satanic subtext in his desires: He is wanton in his use of women; when he seeks to coerce Locksley into joining him, his armed minions wear white robes and hoods and he is masked; he seeks the auguries of the witch in plotting his moves; he kills his own cousin; he nearly desecrates the church in his attempt to forcibly take Marian — this last act a perverted attempt to ally himself with royal blood. He will, it is clear, however, never achieve nobility of either the artificial sort or of the "natural" sort of which Robin speaks (which is reminiscent of Jefferson's notions of a natural aristocracy), where a man's nobility is judged by his deeds and not just by a title. He is a minor administrative official who has overweening ambitions and grand designs and he willingly tromps on any one who gets in the way of his selfish desires. And herein lies the difference: where the villains of the 1938 film are power-hungry and slightly ineffectual, Rickman's sheriff is genuinely evil, driven by naked self-interest and lust. He represents individualism run amok with no regard for community, class, family, or institutions or morality. Consequently, the music underscoring his actions seldom reflects class; it suggests the darker psychological and pathological recesses of the individual rather than communal politics.

The best example of music for the sheriff comes after he has attacked Locksley's castle and has returned to Nottingham Castle. The sequence begins with tonal cluster-like chords that swell in counterpoint to a combination of percussive motifs and a solo flute playing a dissonant melody set against low strings, as he makes his way into the bowels of the castle to plot his next move with the witch who resides in his keep. The melody takes us into the mind of the sheriff: it is fragmentary, dominated by a two note motif of a minor third that leads to exotic trills and downward portamentos, classic tragic gestures all. We have seen these gestures in both the detective and science-fiction film, and they are ones we associate with the disturbed, the other, the abnormal. Unlike the music we associate with the verdant green of Sherwood and the natural beauty and bounty of the countryside outside the castle, this motif illuminates the dark motives of the sheriff and his unnatural desires and his unnatural means of satisfying them. These same musical gestures will be quoted later when he attempts to stir up the local citizenry against Robin. Like the Flynn film, this film also features a sequence where the villain's men terrorize the poor folk. For this scene, Kamen relies upon a similar two note motif, tremolo strings (in an echo of the trilling flute of the earlier sequence), and a descending, jagged melody line that suggest what happens when sheriff's private unnatural desires are brought out into the public arena. I suppose, in a way, the music captures a favorite post-sixties nostrum: the personal is political; the perversion of the common good or the commonweal is rooted in the evils of an unchecked, avaricious, and self-aggrandizing individualism. *The Adventures of Robin Hood* seems to suggest that the threat to our individualism and democratic values comes largely from the outside (even though John is Richard's brother — remember, there is a lot of Norman vs. Saxon rhetoric that gets tossed around in the film) or comes from the attempt of one class to oppress another. *Robin Hood: Prince of Thieves* suggests that the threat is internal: ironically, it is the individual lust for power and greed that stands as the greatest threat to individual freedom because it demands communal conformity to the will of that individual. In both films, evil derives from the misapplication of power, whatever the motive.

The Hero

The mere mention of the names of the stars of these two films tells us that we will be looking at two distinctive approaches to the role: Flynn's Robin Hood is a bold, brash, swashbuckling (if you will), sincere, and dashing figure cut from the same cloth as the storied heroes of popular romantic literature and films. Kevin Costner's Robin Hood, on the other hand, is more reserved, more calculating than cocky, more determined than dashing, and more steady than swashbuckling; even his skills with sword and bow strike one as exceptional competence. He is, in short, the kind of Robin Hood we might have expected Gary Cooper to play in another era. Both men are, however, "to the manor born" and are committed to the same virtues and values: freedom, the cause of the oppressed, and a devotion to Maid or Lady Marian. Consequently, the musical motifs that accompany their actions are not markedly different, and the composers employ topics and gestures that signify their status as men of action and men of romantic passion.

First, both composers rely upon common heroic rhythmic gestures and melodic topics in their motifs for the heroes. Korngold actually utilizes two different motifs at different times in the film. The first is, of course, the central theme from the main title, and the other, which often underscores Robin's entrance into the action, is almost an ur-gesture, a classic fanfare topic played by the brass:

Figure 4.19. *The Adventures of Robin Hood.*

This lift gesture, the hallmark of which is either a leap of a fourth or fifth, is a common element in more fully developed motifs that Korngold uses to underscore Robin's heroic actions. For instance, the following motif echoes the hero's fanfare but it is to be played simply and with nobility. It is rooted in the language of romantic and post–Romantic musical literature, sonorous, vigorous, and exploiting the lift gesture that signifies aspiration or quest-like qualities. The motif's sense of nobility and heroic spirit is enunciated by a downward movement and then followed by a lift gesture of a fourth — a common gesture for hero figures — that leads into a stately melody that ascends stepwise over an octave.

Figure 4.20. *The Adventures of Robin Hood*, "Epilogue."

Notice that the first four notes echo the heroic fanfare discussed above (see figure 4.19). Korngold's most notable use of the motif is in scenes between Marian and Robin, when he wishes to conflate the heroic and romantic, the political and personal, in an elegant package.

Another motif associated with Robin as hero and lover is entitled "Victory" in the piano score. Like figure 4.20, it is a phrase made up of an initial sustained note followed by eighth or quarter notes. And like the previously mentioned motif, it is created out of standard heroic topics and gestures (fanfare-like dramatic leaps and ascending stepwise melodic lines or sweeping gestures). He varies this motif depending upon the dramatic context (it will either be as we see it in figure 4.21 or he may begin with either a quarter or dotted quarter and follow that with some combination of quarter notes and eighths). Regardless of its rhythmic structure, it is often associated with both Robin and Marian and will play an important role in the big love scene.

Figure 4.21. *The Adventures of Robin Hood,* "Victory."

Both these motifs, like those in post–Romantic music literature that employ sustained tones and ascending melodic lines, are effective in conveying notions of vigor and male efficacy. And in this film both are meant to underscore Robin the man of action and Robin the gentle lover.

Michael Kamen's rhythmic motif for Costner's Robin initially seems to owe more to Danny Elfman's inspired main title for *Batman* than to the language of conventional historical romances. Like Korngold's themes, the motif features the sustained note fused with an ascending lift gesture. Kamen's motif, however, built upon the repeated triplet figure as it is, provides a more dynamic sense of drive and movement:

Figure 4.22. *Robin Hood, Prince of Thieves,* main title.

The darker shadings of this Robin Hood are underscored by Kamen's use of modal harmonies and his use of basses and other darker instruments, suggesting not only the hero's strength but also foreshadowing the hero's struggle against darker forces with more pathologically sinister motives. Michael Kamen's other motif for Robin is built upon the self-same triplet rhythm described above. Like Korngold's "Robin fanfare," the motif is a simple figure, reminiscent of a horn-call or hunting topic and utilizing a repeated quarter-eighth rhythm that is built on the interval of the fourth. This is followed by a stricter quarter note leap exploiting that most common heroic gesture the open fifth; this in turn is followed by a figure that exploits leaps of the fifth and has about it the sound of the bugle call.

Figure 4.23. *Robin Hood, Prince of Thieves.*

The pattern is given some intensity by repeating it at the interval of a second higher (i.e., it begins on C). As with Korngold's motif, the topics and gestures emotionally elide heroism with nobility, reminding us that Costner's Robin possessed of an innate nobility, or, if you will, the nobility of deed as opposed to the lesser nobility of birth.

Finally, the heroes are both given lyrical motifs that are meant to reconcile the man of action with the man of romance or the tender lover. I will be saying more about the love scenes later, so for now let me just outline the basic motifs. In *The Adventures of Robin Hood,* Korngold uses the "King Richard Theme" to conflate the man of action with the lover. The motif (see figure 4.16) appears in altered form and serves as a preface to a variation on the love theme. The passage below is played as Marian says to Robin, "Every minute you're here you're in danger." The music is expressive of her love for him while simultaneously reminding us of his bravery in coming to see her to declare his love.

Figure 4.24. *Adventures of Robin Hood,* "King Richard" theme variation.

Kamen's lyrical motif is also the main motif from the main-title music. By changing the accompaniment from the driving triplet figure to a slower arpeggiated pattern or some other type of accompaniment, the motif can be augmented or scored differently to accentuate its lyrical or singing quality. Whether played rapidly or slowly, the lift gesture combined with the scale-wise progression of the theme clearly is intended to signify the heroic and to also communicate a sense of time and place by highlighting intervals common to medieval music.

Figure 4.25. Main title, *Robin Hood: Prince of Thieves.*

Kamen theme, like Korngold's "King Richard's Theme," is used to foreground the emotional subtext of action sequences and, more subtly and trope-like, function contrapuntally in the love scenes.

The Men (and Women!) of Sherwood

With issues of class and power being central to the Robin Hood film mythology and to historical romances in general, one would expect our two composers under consideration here to find good musical analogs to cue the audience's reactions to and emotions about the conflict between the classes, and indeed they did. However, because it is the hero's job to resolve or at least reconcile the conflict between the classes and because the hero in these films is partially responsible for "mobilizing" the folk, we find that heroic topics and gestures dominate the motifs for the group as much as they do the exploits of the hero himself. Like the cowboy hero, Robin's skills are a blend of what he has learned as a knight, as a member of the aristocracy, and what he has learned during his sojourn in the forest, and these skills are brought to bear in defending the values of the oppressed class while simultaneously affirming the best values of the ruling class. As both films progress, the synergistic fusion of motifs suggests an important narrative fact in the films: Robin's fate and that of his followers are intertwined.

Both composers are able to communicate a vigorous and free-spirited feeling in their respective motifs. Korngold employs two themes to underscore the actions of the men of Sherwood. The first is actually the opening theme of the movie. Although labeled by Fred Karlin the "Robin Hood Theme," it is impossible to see it only applying to Robin because it is used in scenes with both himself and his men: in a scene with Robin and Little John (Alan Hale) at the stream, in a slightly altered and humorous form in the scene with Friar Tuck (Eugene Pallette), in the scene when Robin has captured Marian and the Sir Guy, and, most interestingly, in the prelude to the final battle scene, where the theme is scored in a minor key as the men make their way to the castle for the final showdown with the forces of King John and the Sir Guy. Scored as it is in a minor key, its markedness foregrounds the tension and imminent threat and, at this point, uncertain outcome by signifying that evil King John could conceivably triumph over the men of Sherwood. The other is a theme that Fred Karlin calls "Little John's Theme," which is used in almost every scene where the men of Sherwood are involved in battle:

Figure 4.26. *The Adventures of Robin Hood*, "Little John's Theme."

It notably echoes the opening notes of Robin's themes (see figures 4.20 and 4.21) but in a much more vigorous and foursquare fashion, conveying the bravery and determination of the men of Sherwood in their quest to gain their freedom.

Kamen's theme, on the other hand, is marked "Jig tempo" and is in 12/8 time, thus giving it a more dance-like and folkish quality.

Figure 4.27. *Robin Hood, Prince of Thieves,* "Little John and the Band in the Forest."

Unlike Korngold's theme, which relies upon typical neo-romantic chromaticism in its development, Kamen's theme never strays far from a basic folk tune inspired tonic-dominant, tonic-subdominant harmonic structure. Kamen's theme is also not as pervasive in the film as Korngold's. In their reliance upon gestures that employ vigorous rhythms and dance topics that stress fundamental harmonic progressions (even Korngold's changes for this theme are not as chromatically serpentine as those for the love scene music), the music for the men and women of Sherwood in both films is intended to remind us of their free spirits, their lower class roots, but also of their understated heroism.

Robin and Marian

Yes, the films are about freedom and democracy, but they are also love stories, and a major component in the scores of historical romance films is the music for the lovers. Korngold's music for his lovers is clearly in the classical Hollywood tradition, owing a great deal to post–Romantic music literature; Kamen's music, on the other hand, has a slightly more contemporary feeling because of the generally narrow melodic range and the folk-like elements he employs.

In scoring the romantic scenes and shaping the development of the relationship between the hero and heroine, both composers allude to and suggest the heroic themes used in other parts of the films. This practice, as I discussed earlier, is common to both Korngold and Max Steiner.[3] In both Robin Hood films, the blossoming of the relationship is developed in a fashion similar to that of *The Sea Hawk*: there is a "conversion" of one party to the political cause of the other that goes hand in hand with expressions of love and devotion. For instance, Korngold develops the concurrent romantic relationship and heroic triumph at the end by weaving together Marian's courtly theme with Robin's heroic themes and adding a separate love theme that draws on elements of both. In order for Robin to win her love he must convince her of his "political purity," i.e., that his motive for robbing from King John is to help King Richard (and the poor as well). To this end he generally blends the motifs into a kind of romantic-political suite. For example, in the scene in the camp when Robin and his men have waylaid Sir Guy, Marian, the sheriff and their train, Korngold quotes the central motifs to develop the lovers' commitment to one another and, by extension, the cause. At the feast, she sees the riches he has amassed through his exploits and she is skeptical of his motives; as the scene unfolds, however, the music lets us know that she now begins to see him in a different light.

He asks her to accompany him to an area of the camp where the poor who have been driven from their homes are taking up temporary residence. As they walk through this area, the "villain's motif" (or "poor people's theme") heard earlier is stated softly. Next they enter a natural surrounding and, as Marian asks why he is involved in the outlaw's life, we hear "King Richard's theme" (figure 4.16). Before he utters a word, the simple nobility of the motif anticipates his response and, as the scene progresses, the music further validates the idealism of his actions, revealing him to be more than just a thief but a man of integrity and dignity. Furthermore, the combined elements of the *mise-en-scene* (a two shot of Robin and Marian isolated from any political contexts and Marian's gentle gesture in reaching out to him) and the dialogue function dialogically with the score to transform the musical theme from being a mere aural analog for Robin's devotion to King Richard to a romantic gesture that underscores their romantic bond to one another. As the theme plays she states, "I'm beginning to see." Finally, he takes her hand and kisses it and says, "That's reward enough," and as he does Korngold introduces Marian's theme, a gentle and lilting courtly topic in 6/4 time.

Figure 4.28. *The Adventures of Robin Hood,* "Marian's Theme."

The first time we heard this was at a banquet earlier in the film when King John is seemingly trying to get Marian interested in Sir Guy; stated as it is here it becomes emblematic of her commitment to Robin. The conversion has been accomplished.

The big love scene incorporates five motifs, each with a slightly different character but unified by the romantic-heroic gestures embedded in prior stated motifs. The opening music is the love theme and begins while Marian is talking to her lady in waiting about Robin, telling her about how he is "brave and reckless and yet he is gentle and kind." The theme features prominent upward leaps that function as a gestural accompaniment to the words "brave" and "reckless" and then resolves to "kind"; the overall effect of the gestures is to express a heart filled with love and admiration.

Figure 4.29. *The Adventures of Robin Hood,* "Love Theme."

Note how measures three and four are an echo of the opening measures of "King Richard's Theme" (figure 4.16), thus musically cueing us to the political-romantic nature of their relationship. The next motif, played when Robin enters her chambers, is a restatement of the heroic music cited in figure 4.22; Korngold develops the theme as Robin feigns leaving and leaps onto the vines outside Marian's chambers. Because strings carry the weight in the scene, the theme has a decidedly romantic, as opposed to heroic, feel to it. Korngold then restates the love theme as Robin comes back into her chambers and kisses her. As he prepares to leave, Korngold introduces another variation on the "King Richard Theme" (see figures 4.16 and 4.24); using material from the first two measures alone, the theme builds in intensity and passion until it resolves into the love theme. Robin declares yet again his love, leading to a kiss on the highest note of the motif. A few moments later, as Marian warns him of the

The Adventures of Robin Hood. Robin and Marian's commitment to one another is also a commitment to Robin's cause.

danger he faces by being with her, Korngold once again introduces "King Richard's Theme" *sotto voce* to underscore Robin's speech about England being bigger than Normans and Saxons fighting. Marian responds by telling him that she wishes she could help more, and as she speaks these words, Korngold brings in the high strings and the melody soars, magically blending the heroic and romantic as the lovers kiss. This is followed, as in the scene at Robin's camp, with a restatement of Marian's theme as Robin prepares to leave. Korngold's wonderful handling of the themes clarifies and intensifies the complex nature of the lovers' political-romantic relationship and their commitment to one another and the cause of the disenfranchised and their struggle for freedom. The message in the music is clear: Marian (and by extension the audience) loves this man for his heroic character.

Costner's version of the love relationship bears some similarities to Michael Curtiz's, but there are a couple of transformations that Michael Kamen had to accommodate when he wrote his score: Robin and Marian are also from same class, but she sees him as the worst example of their class, a "spoiled boy" totally lacking in a commitment to protect "his" people. This explains Marian's concern for "her" people and her irritation at Robin when he angers the sheriff, resulting in a threatening visit from Sir Guy to her estate. She also distrusts him because — and this is really interesting — he ran off to play soldier and have adventures in the Crusades; never mind the trauma and suffering he has gone through. In short, he seems to her little more than a Peter Pan type who just won't grow up. Like her counterpart in the 1938 film, she is also skeptical when she visits his camp, but in the end he wins her over and the music once again provides some excellent emotional cues for us to assess the relationship. Kamen's theme is more folk-like, the accompaniment resembling the plucking of a stringed instrument, and the melody sounds as though it was meant to be played on a recorder or some other traditional wind instrument.

"The Scene at Waterfall" (the name of the cue) and the scene in Robin's camp feature a nice point-counterpoint exposition of the themes as they are woven throughout the scene. As Marian happens upon Robin bathing by a waterfall, the musical cue begins with Robin's three note heroic fanfare stated in the bass line while the love theme (or what the printed music and soundtrack call "Maid Marian") is suggested in the melody line. Later, as they approach the camp, the three note heroic theme from the main title is used, but the triplet bass of arpeggiated chords suggests a pastoral topic and a more bucolic feeling than the aggressively repeated triplet figure on the same note in the main title. Then in the arrow-shooting contest, where Robin is about to display his prowess with the bow, Kamen's cue takes the edge off the competition by the introducing the love theme played by an oboe. As the love theme plays in the background with the strings swelling, Robin draws the bow, but Marian distracts him by blowing in his ear forcing him to miss his mark; the music conveys effectively that the power of love is equally as strong as the power of the bow.

Later, in the scene when he shows her the booty they have collected, an entirely new theme is introduced as he talks about admiringly about King Richard. At this point, she sees that he is not keeping the booty for himself (maybe he isn't a spoiled boy!); in almost rhetorical fashion he asks her, "You thought I was keeping it all, didn't you?" and her embarrassed response is to offer to throw her dagger in with the booty. At this point, the love theme is brought in to let us know she has had a change of heart and is committed to him romantically and to his cause.

The love theme itself gets its fullest expression in the scene following the feast when Marian is taking her leave. Kamen begins the scene with quotations — or maybe it would be

Figure 4.30. *Robin Hood, Prince of Thieves,* "Maid Marian."

better to call them allusions — to the heroic fanfare: one is a direct quote in the accompaniment, and then to introduce the theme he features a minor key variation of the three note motif — its markedness serves as a nice tension building preface for the unmarked theme itself. The theme's folk-like simplicity seems to emerge out of the dark and deep forest surroundings, with the main theme (figure 4.22) being carried by a harp and eventually an oboe. The warmth of the orchestration envelops the lovers in this moment as they pledge their love, honor and fidelity. He asks her to get word to Richard of Nottingham's plan, and she expresses fear that she will lose all. When he asks if she will do it for her king, she says "No, I'll do it for you"; at this point Kamen brings in the strings and the cue swells to its climax as the lovers kiss. Like Korngold's structuring of the scene in the forest, Kamen allows the music to inexorably gather intensity as the lovers commit to England and one another. Kamen eschews Korngold's chromaticism and transformational development of musical ideas in favor of simplicity. The simplicity of the music, moreover, combined with the setting also suggests that their commitment is a commitment to the people who have sought the refuge of the forest and have placed their hopes for freedom in the hands of Robin Hood.

Conclusion

In comparison to other genres, the historical romance has largely retained its optimistic outlook on adventure, politics and love. Why? Perhaps it is the perennial appeal of *amor vincit omnia* as a theme in our popular culture, or perhaps it is the nostalgia factor, the fact that we can willingly suspend our disbelief and accept this utopian view because it is in the past. Whatever the reason, the genre has proved resilient and, as we have seen, the composer's task hasn't changed much over the years. Audiences still expect to see heroes of great daring and resourcefulness who are also sensitive lovers. Composers in turn respond by writing themes that capture the grand sweep of heroic action and passion, hearkening as they have done since the 18th century to the dependable musical topics and gestures for love and heroism. Audiences still want to see the average person resist tyranny and ultimately triumph in the face of overwhelming odds. Composers continue to reaffirm those beliefs through music that suggests that the extraordinary man and woman are committed to the collective good and that their triumph is not just an individual victory but a victory for us all. Secondarily (or maybe it is primarily), the films also perpetuate a mythology about the connection between love and politics, that romantic commitment is a necessary element in the struggle for freedom. To this end, both versions of Robin Hood include a grand restatement of the love theme at the end of the film; the composers both recast the theme in more heroic terms, either by having the brass predominate or by altering the tempo so it sounds more like a march or courtly fanfare topic. Used as it is in tandem with a restatement of the hero's theme, the music reminds us that heroism is not dead and indeed "love conquers all."

5

The Rhythm of the Range

The Western Film Score

Introduction

Thanks to Elmer Bernstein and the Marlboro Man one could make the claim that we have the rigorous rhythms and classic foursquare "Western" harmonies of the theme for *The Magnificent Seven* (1960) "hot-wired" into our collective consciousness as the quintessential music for the classic Western. The burden it imposed on composers working in the genre must have been almost daunting, much like the burden placed on post–Korngold and Steiner composers working in any genre during the 1930s and 1940s. The ubiquitous nature and perennial appeal of the theme is evident in main titles ranging from *The Cowboys* (1972) by John Williams to *Silverado* (1985) by Bruce Boughton, all of which hearken in some way to the Bernstein archetype. As we survey the entire corpus of Western main titles, however, we find that *The Magnificent Seven* is less a pioneering score and more of an apotheosis for the scoring in the genre. Without wishing to deny the score its due as an innovative contribution to the literature of film music, one can also see it as the culmination of gestures and motifs firmly established in the studio era. In this chapter we will look at how composers from Max Steiner to Bruce Boughton have musically imagined the Myth of the West.

My approach to the Western owes much to John Cawelti's pioneering analysis of the genre in his classic *Six-Gun Mystique*. Much has been written about the Western since Cawelti's book was published in the late sixties, but little has altered the basic soundness of his analysis of the conventions of the genre, especially as those conventions relate to the mythology of the West. The music in the majority of Westerns from *The Big Trail* (1930) to *Dances with Wolves* (1990) underscores the conflict between the forces of the wilderness and the forces of civilization. The motifs, topics and gestures that we most often hear, moreover, are used to underscore the conventions that Cawelti identifies as central to the genre: the cowboy, the women, the townspeople, and the topography of the land itself.

Main Title Music

Surveying main-title music for the Western yields a messier landscape than that which we observe in other genres, and some of this is attributable to John Ford and the nature of scoring Westerns early in the sound era. Unlike the historical romance, where we might have a classic studio system craftsman like Michael Curtiz working with classic studio system composers like Steiner or Korngold, in the Western we have the imposing presence of John Ford, an auteur calling (all!) the shots in production. So, unlike in a film such as *Captain Blood*, where there is one composer, in *Stagecoach* (1939) we have five composers getting screen credit for the score. The main titles (and scores for that matter) of Ford's films are, moreover, often pastiche scores or what Roy Prendergast calls "paste-pot-and-scissors" scores, which, according to him, were fairly common practice in the 1930s (29). The main titles of Ford's films, moreover, sound at times more like folk song medleys than main-title music, mixing as they do classic film composition and American folk music. To communicate a sense of place and time, the director relies upon the moviegoers' musical competence and their ability to connect standard folk tunes like "She Wore a Yellow Ribbon," "Drill Ye Tarriers," "My Darling Clementine," and "The Girl I Left Behind Me" to the topography and the narrative contexts of the Western. The music that Ford used is clearly part of the 19th century and, in the case of some of the tunes, it is associated with the military or at least with westward expansion, i.e., the kind of tunes one might have heard in a 49er camp or in saloons on the edge of the wilderness and civilization. In the main titles to Ford's Westerns and some others in the first two decades of the talkies, composers underscored the basic ideological conflict about to be played out on the screen with a variety of musical materials. For instance, in both *Fort Apache* (1948) and *The Searchers* (1956), the opening musical motif is an "Indian" theme, combining a pounding, strict 4/4 tom-tom–like rhythm with a slightly discordant harmony that supports a stereotypical Indian melodic topic. After that, the music shifts to theme(s) associated with the forces of civilization. In *Fort Apache*, it is a collection of folk and popular tunes of the 19th century, which in effect function here as musical topics. In *The Searchers*, it is the main-title theme sung by the Sons of the Pioneers and its opening musical question, "What makes a man to wander?" This would become a pattern until the rise of the "adult Western" in the mid and late 1950s.

Of course, Ford was not the only director making Westerns in the golden days of the studio system (it only just seems like that sometimes!) and, consequently, we do find other approaches to the main title. One variant to Ford's approach is that taken by composers scoring the "Empire Builder" Western. One of the best examples is Max Steiner's main title for *Dodge City* (1939). One of the most prominent features of the theme is the driving march rhythm that underpins the stately melody that consists of an initial single sustained note against which we hear a countermelody.

Figure 5.1. *Dodge City*, main title (Darby and DuBois 32).

The syncopated downward dropping gestures and mirroring syncopated lift gestures that strive to resolve upward to the tonic are countered by a severe regularity in the rhythm which suggests struggle and the mythical march of progress, of men and women making their manifestly destined journey to carve out thriving cities in the midst of the wilderness. There is little here to suggest the homey folksiness in Ford's main titles, this being classic composition translated into a language for manifest destiny. The basic elements of the theme, however, which never stray far from simple progressions and heroic leaps, are strong enough to suggest the kind of "Americanness" that composers such as Aaron Copland and Roy Harris were exploring in their more serious compositions during this same time period.

In the 1950s, reflecting changes in the genre as a whole, the main titles take on a complexity to match the subject matter of the films. Edward Buscombe has observed, "The later 50s, the Eisenhower years, were times of peace and plenty in America. But Hollywood, its nose to the wind, sensed the tensions that seethed beneath the tranquil surface" (24). Consequently, as Michael Coyne has noted, after *A Duel in the Sun* (1946) Westerns became "increasingly adult in theme and sophisticated in style" (48). If Ford's Westerns helped define the musical style of the studio era Western, Anthony Mann's Westerns helped define or at least are emblematic of the shift in the genre in the 1950s. The discordancy that characterizes the main-title music of his Westerns has less to do with the role the denizens of the savage wilderness play in his dramas and more to do with the existential plight of his protagonists. What *A Duel in the Sun* and Mann's Westerns served up to audiences was a somewhat disturbing psychological subtext that informed the classic ideological conflict in the narratives. Bronislau Kaper's score for *The Naked Spur* (1953), for instance, employs some of the same gestures and motifs that he used in his score for *Them* (1954): dissonance, jagged rhythms and a seeming lack of a logically developed theme. Muted brass state a simple three-note motif that rises and falls while low strings state a meandering counter-melody. As the title comes up on the screen, a dissonant chord is sounded and then we hear an aggressive and, quite frankly, violent motif scored for brass. It is hard to discern a theme in the classic sense of the word; we instead get a sort of free interplay between the brass, strings and snare drums. The entire effect is unsettling, signifying nothing of the expansive nature of the West and its limitless possibilities but only the driven nature of the protagonist, whose moral center is ambiguous if not outright absent at times.[1] Much the same is true for the main title for *Warlock* (1959) where composer Leigh Harline begins with a classic fanfare opening but quickly moves the music into more unsettling territory. Harline's dominant theme is an angular melody, exploiting repetitive and rhythmic elements in contrast to the folk-like and pastoral topics or expansively melodic and harmonic language of his predecessors. The reason for this lies in the fact that the music not only introduces the film but underscores the opening action on the screen: the camera tracking the outlaws as they ride into Warlock. In short, the main titles of the TV generation Western do indeed sound deep and often disturbing psychological currents.

In the 1960s, we are confronted with irony of *The Magnificent Seven*: in this decade, which would witness a precipitous decline and reevaluation of the Western, filmgoers would finally be given a musical theme that metonymically and archetypally signified the American West for many Americans. The groundwork for the revolutionary impact of this theme was in actuality laid in 1959 with Jerome Moross's powerful theme for *The Big Country* (1958). His masterful blending of simple but dramatic melodic themes and rugged rhythmic energy strongly suggested the feeling of the West encountered in cowboy songs and the work of serious composers like Copland. Tony Bremner, in his liner notes for *The Big Country*, attributes the Western sound of Moross's score to his use of the pentatonic scale and the "simplicity of his harmonies." These simple (Bremner might say direct and honest) elements are given dynamic vitality by merit of the marvelous syncopated interplay between basses and tympani, the horns and bassoons, and the strings and high brass, which carry the melody:

Figure 5.2. *The Big Country*, main title.[2]

It is a stunning contrast to the plodding and/or disjunctive rhythms of the psycho–Western, made all the more stunning because of the bold, four-square harmonies that underline the rhythms, the use of open fourths in the horn accompaniment, and the dramatic leaps in the melody line. The basses, tympani and horns dominate the first half of the measure while the melody line is more active in the second half of the measure. As a result, the theme combines a feeling of restless energy with some classic heroic gestures and topics. Similarly, Bernstein's theme also communicates this feeling of restless energy, especially in the accompanying pattern, which is probably the part of the theme most people associate with the title as opposed to the melody line itself:

Moderately with vigor

Figure 5.3. *The Magnificent Seven*, main title.

And like Moross, he relies upon a similar pattern of lift gestures that we have come to associate with classic adventure heroes. Moross's and Bernstein's themes and those of the imitators who would follow in their wake through the next four decades, moreover, resurrected many of the same musical ideas that had inspired serious composers of the American music renaissance in the 1930s and the war years, ideas rooted in American folk music and cowboy tunes. The remarkable thing about Bernstein's theme is that for all his reliance upon ideas developed by Copland, Harris and others, he really seemed to create something quite revolutionary and authentic with the theme. It is has about it a "rightness" for the genre; today, one merely need hear that opening two measure rhythmic motif and one is immediately transported into the West of myth and legend.

As I mentioned earlier, the popularity of Bernstein's theme seems anomalous in light of the paroxysms the genre would experience in the 1960s. A quick scan of Jack Nachbar's filmography of '60s films reveals words such as "feeling of loss for the vanishing West" (*Lonely Are the Brave, The Man Who Shot Liberty Valance*), "antihero" (*Hud*), "mockery of the idealistic quest" (*The Professionals*), "calling into question the idealism of John Ford's *Stagecoach*" (*Hombre*), "cynical three-hour Western epic" (*The Good, the Bad, the Ugly*), "serious statement about the relationships between blacks, whites, and Indians" (*The Scalphunters*), "literate discussion of capital punishment" (*Hang 'Em High*), and finally, and maybe most dramatically, "John Wayne parodies himself" (*True Grit*) (pp. 135–136).[3] Not surprisingly, the same year that Wayne parodied himself in *True Grit*, popular songwriter Burt Bacharach, who was one of the great Brill Building craftsmen of the 1960s, scored *Butch Cassidy and the Sundance Kid*. The score was, by Western standards, unconventional — but then again so was the film, mixing comic moments with meditative ones in its depiction of the closing of the frontier and the flight of two American anti heroes to new frontiers and death on foreign soil. The sound of the West was no longer the rugged rhythms of *The Magnificent Seven* but instead the urbane rhythms and rhymes of "Raindrops Keep Falling on My Head" crooned by B.J. Thomas. The Western entered a second "golden" tyranny-of-the-theme-song era (the first ushered in by Tex Ritter singing Dimitri Tiomkin's evocative theme for *High Noon* in 1952). In late '60s and early '70s, no one style dominated. Instead, main titles were produced by a mixed bag of writers consisting largely of classic composers (John Barry's faux folk theme for *Monte Walsh* and his more traditional one for *Dances with Wolves*) and popular or folk artists (Bob Dylan's for *Pat Garrett and Billy the Kid*; Leonard Cohen's music for *McCabe and Mrs. Miller*), and reveal a genre in search of itself. This in turn led to the quasi–New Age contributions to the genre in the 1980s. Oddly enough, it seemed that the genre had come full circle and happened upon a variation of the John Ford type of score with "songs" written by folk or rock musicians dominating the overall character of the film's music. Instead of the music being collections of well-known folk and pop tunes of the previous century, the scores sound like collections of material from the folk revival of the 1960s, ranging from Dylan for *Pat Garrett and Billy the Kid* to musicians like Ry Cooder (*Geronimo* [1993], *The Long Riders* [1980]) or others associated with Windham Hill–Narada–type labels up to Jon Bon Jovi for *Young Guns* (1988). One can read counterculture, politically correct or revisionist, in these choices, but the point is that the old certainties had been replaced by a more pluralistic vision of the West and the music is reflective of this pluralism.

Setting

One of the first tasks of the Western musical score is to establish a sense of place or, perhaps better, a *feeling* for the sense of place. What is most problematic about music's role in signifying an emotional element in the topographic conventions of the genre is that for all its preoccupation with space, the *mise-en-scène* is usually filled with people as well. So to say that a composer is using this gesture or that topic to provide an aural analogue for the topography might be misleading, especially if the hero is part of that shot. It is not surprising, then, to find that main-title music is often used when the landscape is featured. A good example of this is the journey of the magnificent seven to the Mexican village: Bernstein uses the main title throughout the sequence, especially where the director uses long shots to track the progress of riders. In cases like this we can easily conclude that we are to conflate the main character(s) with the environment. The topography and "the man" are one. That, in turn, would support most commentators' interpretations of the role and place of the cowboy hero in the films: he will ultimately be called upon to defend the values of civilization, but he is at heart a denizen of the wilderness and, in fact, may not be able to reconcile that part of his character with the demands of civilization (consequently, both Shane and Ethan Edwards in *The Searchers* must walk or ride away from the "blessings" of home and family and toward the very same setting from which they emerged at the film's beginning — the desert for Wayne in *The Searchers*, the "faraway hills" for Ladd's Shane). John Cawelti has written, "The moral character of the hero also appears symbolically in the Western setting. In its rocky aridity and climatic extremes the Great Plains landscape embodies the hostile savagery of Indians and outlaws, while its vast openness, its vistas of snow-covered peaks in the distance, and its great sunrises and sunsets ... suggest the epic courage and regenerative power of the hero" (*Six-Gun Mystique* 40). And so it should be.

With the exception of some more recent Westerns, filmmakers have traditionally relied upon underscoring to signify values and emotions inherent in the topography of the West. The topography of the land in the Western, as a backdrop to the kernel conflict in the genre, asks us, on the one hand, to stand in awe of its grandeur and beauty and, on the other, to look upon it as a challenge to be conquered on the road to a "greater" goal — the establishment of civilization. It is a beautiful obstacle. Jane Tompkins notes, "Nature is the one transcendent thing, the one thing larger than man (and it is constantly portrayed as immense), the ideal toward which human nature strives.... The landscape's final invitation — merger — promises complete materialization. Meanwhile, the qualities that nature implicitly possesses — power, endurance, rugged majesty — are the ones that men desire while they live" (72). The dialogic relationship of music and topography should, moreover, signify the values in our American monomyth, i.e., freedom, opportunity and equality, all of which are hallmarks of the mythology of the American experience. Thomas Schatz has written: "As America's foundation ritual, the Western projects a formalized version of the nation's infinite possibilities and limitless vistas, thus serving to 'naturalize' the policies of westward expansion and Manifest Destiny" (*Hollywood Genres* 47). Jane Tompkins echoes this perspective when she states that the "openness ... provides infinite access. There is nothing to stop the horseman's free movement across the terrain.... The possibilities are infinite" (74–75). The topography in a sense does not really dwarf the human element but, instead, asks us to see the two as inseparable. Through that elision we see *our* infinite possibilities and *our* role as avatars of Manifest Destiny and the American Dream. As I noted earlier, there is hardly a time when we just have music underscoring shots of the Western landscape; like a Frost poem, there is always a person present, and like Frost's poems the Western is, ultimately, about people and not nature. One film where we actually hear music underscoring a visual traversal of a terrain devoid of any humans is in the opening of *How the West Was Won* (1963). Alfred Newman's music beautifully conveys the "infinite possibilities" of the topography: a simple but moving melody line and an orchestral timbre that is reminiscent of Alan Hovhaness's Symphony no. 2 (subtitled "Mysterious Mountains"). The strings cast an aura of mystery over the cloud-covered plains, and then the melody, largely carried by the woodwinds, exploits gentle leaps of the fifth and fourth while underneath we hear a sporadic tom-tom–like rhythm; then Newman brings in a gentler version of his main-title music played by the strings. The cue subtly suggests the kernel conflict by initially suggesting the forces of the wilderness but finally emphasizing the forces of civilization, as if to say: here is this beautiful but untamed territory that soon will come under the sway of the white man and his ways.

The Searchers. **The music for the cowboy hero is indistinguishable from the music for the frontier setting.**

In the majority of cases, however, musical gestures and topics associated with the topography of the land underscore establishing shots or transitional moments in the film. These topics and gestures in the Western are, moreover, dominated by distinctive rhythmic and/or melodic motifs. Claudia Gorbman seems to be speaking of musical topics when she notes that "certain melodic types characterize Westerns: either based on Western ballads, or the typical calls of bugles in the case of the cavalry film, or 'Western frontier' melodies in major keys with skips of perfect fourths and fifths, connoting the grandeur of the frontier landscape" ("Scoring the Indian" 86). A good example of the type of "Western frontier" melody that inspired film music composers over the years is "I Ride an Old Paint":

Figure 5.4. "I Ride an Old Paint."

One can see some melodic (and harmonic) similarities in the gestural qualities of this traditional song in many main titles, including the following by Victor Young for *Rio Grande* (1950):

Figure 5.5. *Rio Grande.*

We can also see similar rhythmic characteristics in the following figure, which for all intents and purposes has become a topic and which I call the "rolling prairie topic":

Figure 5.6. Rolling prairie topic.

In terms of topographical scoring, we can look to Ford's *Stagecoach* (1939) as an archetype for the use of musical analogues to convey the wide-open spaces as sites for adventure as opposed to more personal conflicts. Whenever the stagecoach is moving across the landscape the galloping main-title music is sounded; it is a variation on the classic cowboy song "Oh Bury Me Not on the Lone Prairie" with its simple harmonic language, jaunty rhythms, and a vigorous melodic line with a narrow range. A galloping rhythm with just a hint of syncopation underlies the melodic line with the straight four or two rhythm punctuated by an accent off the beat:

Figure 5.7. Galloping rhythm.

In the process, the song loses its elegiac and "lonesome" feeling and instead becomes a galloping topic, an archetype for passage across the hostile, arid land.

A more recent example would be the journey of the Magnificent Seven to the Mexican village they have been asked to defend. Bernstein musically conflates the landscape with the heroes as he relies almost exclusively upon the main title to underscore the long shots and tracking shots of the riders making their way over the rugged terrain. Once again, that distinctive rhythmic figure, stressing irregularity, the rugged and the restless, is combined with the dynamic main-title melody (*see* Figure 5.8) to convey a strong feeling of the heroic and the expansive.

Next, we have John Barry's cue, "Journey to Fort Sedgewick," which like so many traveling or journeying topics begins with a distinctive rhythmic motif, in this case a gently rolling and syncopated accompaniment pattern to underscore the topography of the Black Hills

Moderately with vigor

Figure 5.8. *The Magnificent Seven*, main title.

setting; against this he has set a rhythmically inventive melody line that hearkens to the types of melodies Copland created for his ballets *Rodeo* and *Billy the Kid*.

Figure 5.9. *Dances with Wolves*, "Journey to Fort Sedgewick."

Victor Young's main title for *Shane*, on the other hand, is a good example of yet another vision of the Western topography that could be described as romantic and elegiac, and which relies heavily upon the conventions of the pastoral topic. Unlike the previous examples, Young's theme, reflecting his own compositional strengths, stresses melody over atmospheric rhythms. As the camera tracks Shane's journey toward the Starrett farm with the lush green of the range and the grandeur of the snow-capped mountains in the background, the orchestral sound emphasizes the strings, a slower tempo and a melodic line that has a more soaring quality by merit of its expansive melodic range. There is that hint of the cowboy tune in the middle section, but overall it is the type of theme that reaffirms Tompkins' comments about nature being the "one transcendent thing" in the Western (72).

Figure 5.10. *Shane*, Main Title: "Faraway Hills" (Darby and Dubois, 289).

The empire builder Western relies upon similar musical gestures. Two of the best examples are Steiner's music for *Dodge City* (discussed earlier) and Dimitri Tiomkin's score for Howard Hawk's *Red River* (1948). Tiomkin's score foregrounds the cattle drive and by extension the topography of the land that must be traversed to get the cattle to market. His "Get Along Little Dogies" theme masterfully elides the basic elements of the cowboy song with the pentatonic harmonies common to many Westerns and heroic gestures associated with post–Romantic tone poems. He opens up the melodic range of the main theme and smoothes out the rhythms so it sounds less as though it would be strummed on a guitar by a cowboy around the campfire. This melody is reworked throughout the drive and takes on a definite heroic cast when they cross the Red River. In this sequence, brass dominate the scoring and the cue is marked by multiple crescendos and vigorous melodic leaps (lift gestures). Typical of the empire builder Western, the musical gestures signify an expansive and transcendent

Figure 5.11. *Red River* (Darby and Dubois 245).

setting by superimposing the heroic on the topographic. We simultaneously *feel* this expansive quality of the topography because the heroics in the score correlate to the action of the hero in the environment. But then, you may say, the composer really isn't really communicating a feeling for place but for the people. To address that issue we only have to imagine — sticking with Tiomkin's music here — taking the "Red River Crossing" music or his prelude from *Duel in the Sun* or even Young's main title from *Shane* and using these themes to underscore Gary Cooper walking through the town in *High Noon*. The heroic sweep and grandeur of the melodies and rhythms would render Cooper's walk incongruous. In the case of the themes mentioned, there is no such incongruity but instead a sense of rightness about the music underscoring the visuals on the screen.

If we can consider the town, farm, or fort setting part of the topography, we encounter an entirely different set of musical motifs, topics, and gestures than we would have for shots or action on the plains. In the same way that the music of the plains is also the music of the cowboy hero, the music of the town or fort may be the same as that associated with people (i.e., the community). In many cases, diegetic music is used to create a feeling for the particular character of a city or town. So, as the cowboy approaches the town, the first music we hear might be "modern" musical sounds emanating from a saloon. In another instance, we might hear someone strumming a Jew's harp or plucking on a banjo, or it could be a hymn emanating from the church. The music selected will depend upon factors ranging from simple logistics (the saloon happens to be the hero's first stop) to more complex (the town is the site of villainy and values diametrically opposed to those of the hero or the "good people" of the community). For instance, in *Silverado* (1985), after a dazzling shootout and rescue at a farm, the protagonists head toward Silverado for a final showdown. Kasdan tracks the heroes riding past a cemetery and underneath we hear classic brass fanfare topics. The camera continues to track them until the town of Silverado comes into the frame, at which point we hear the main title again. Broughton then restates the main title as the men ride into town. As the camera cuts to a wounded Rae (Lynn Whitfield) being attended to by Stella (Linda Hunt) in the city itself, the composer introduces somber sounding motifs that gradually become more agitated, culminating in a dissonant gesture as Slick (Jeff Goldblum) stalks Rae. The music reminds us that dysfunctional, "lawless" elements hold sway in the town. A similar situation exists in Dimitri Tiomkin's music for *High Noon*, where the shift in locale from plains to the town occasions a shift in compositional strategies. Gone are the pastoral topics, the ruggedly gestural rhythms, the grand soaring melodies. In their place is a simple, melancholic, repeated song that almost restricts our vision and emotions and focuses us claustrophobically on Cooper's preparations for the arrival of Frank Miller. The music clearly underscores the dubious nature of his quest: unlike the Magnificent Seven, who transcend their outlaw backgrounds to become heroes, Cooper accepts the responsibility of preserving civilization for a group of people who hardly seem deserving of his sacrifice, and the marked harmonies and elegiac tone of "Do Not Forsake Me Oh My Darling" complement the sheriff's problematic quest for justice.

Finally, we come to the relationship between music and topography and Native Americans in the Western. Kathryn Kalinak has astutely observed that because we always hear the main title when the stagecoach is traveling across the landscape, "it is the Indian music, ironically, that seems out of place in Monument Valley, and Native Americans who seem outside the natural order of things in *Stagecoach*. Thus music positions Native Americans not only as Other, but as intrusive, as not belonging" ("The Sound of Many Voices" 182). That sense of otherness, from a musical standpoint, is the result of the marked musical elements used to underscore the presence of the Native American in the Western. As we have seen, the rugged rhythms, pastoral topics, heroic lift gestures, and rolling melodies of the musical score situate the hero and/or the positive forces of civilization early in the topography. Consequently, when we then hear the gestures and topics associated with the forces of savage wilderness, they will seem out of place, alien and threatening. But through the contrasting nature of unmarked and marked elements and culturally encoded musical topics the composer is able to establish an emotional subtext for the basic conflict in the Western and to show that the land is the contested site in that struggle.

The Cowboy Hero

Critical commentary over the last forty years has revealed that the cowboy hero is one of the more complex figures in American movies. On the surface, the hero seems an uncomplicated figure: a man of bravery, adequate intelligence (though this is never really an issue), considerable skill with a gun, and a seemingly simple code of conduct. That perhaps is how we viewed the man as kids sitting in darkened theatres on a Saturday afternoon but, as critics and adults, we find ourselves pondering the complexities of this hero (both male and female). On the one hand, the Western hero fulfills those simpler attributes listed above in the way that any hero does. John Cawelti writes, for instance, "The hero's primary moral concern is to preserve himself with individual dignity and honor in a savage and violent environment" (49). Stanley Solomon adds, "Yet the truth seems to be that the Westerner deliberately patterns his life as a solitary romantic, a wanderer, an isolated human being ultimately beyond the understanding of everyone else. ... he is not commonplace, and is not about to settle for an average existence when the romantic call to adventure prompts him to move on" (24–25). On the other hand, the hero is also part of the larger struggle of civilization vs. the wilderness, a struggle that is of necessity a paradox: he must use skills largely cultivated through contact with the forces of the savage wilderness to help eliminate the threat posed by those selfsame forces in an effort to establish civilized values. Ironically, as Thomas Schatz notes, "it is these actions that finally enforce social order but necessitate his departure from the community he has saved" (57).

Turning to the music for the cowboy, it would seem logical to look for themes, topics, and gestures that will capture a sense of individualism, heroism, a sense of oneness with the environment and, perhaps, a sense of violence. As is the case with so many genre films, main-title music in the Western is also used to underscore the actions of the hero. Let's review some of the dominant topics and gestures associated with the hero. First, we have lyrical and/or stirring melodies that emphasize the romantic (e.g., daring, brave, dashing, etc.) qualities of the hero. *Lonesome Dove* (1992), *Wyatt Earp* (1994), the scoring of the "Get Along Little Dogies" theme in *Red River* (1948), and *Shane* provide good examples of this type. In *Lonesome Dove*, Basil Poledouris begins with a striking hymn-like trumpet theme outlining an octave through leaps of the fifth:

Figure 5.12. *Lonesome Dove*, main title.

This leads to a sweeping 3/4 time main title that inexorably moves upward via sweeping gestures countered by easy stepwise movement. Victor Young's theme for *Shane* also fits into the romantic category. It is cast very much in the pastoral topic mode with its gently rolling melody that emphasizes leaps of a fifth and sixth, which, as we have seen in previous genres, are often associated with heroic behavior, and its use of the prairie topic in the accompaniment. The melody has an elegiac cast to it as well as it wavers between the fifth and sixth scale tones in the fourth and fifth measures, suggesting the passing of a way of life, a theme that is driven home to the viewer when Shane tells Riker that *their* days are through on the frontier. We have also noted earlier that this theme is also used to establish the frontier setting, but it is never used unless Shane is present in the *mise-en-scène*, suggesting that we connect him with the wilderness. There is one other theme used to underscore Shane's actions in the film and that is the music used to accompany his ride into town for the final showdown, but I will discuss that in more detail later; for the present, let me just say that this second motif underscores the violent strain that is part of the hero's character. Similarly, Max Steiner, in *The Searchers*, at times scores the gentle strains of "Lorena" in a minor key to suggest the darker side of Ethan's personality.

Some Westerns stress the hero's ruggedness and privilege gestures that signify the hero as a man of action. Elmer Bernstein's themes for *The Magnificent Seven* and *The Sons of Katie Elder* (1965) are two prime examples as is John Williams's theme for *The Cowboys* (1972) and Bruce Broughton's for *Silverado*. Rhythmic gestures are most important in these types of themes. In the example below from *Silverado*, the slightly syncopated accompaniment, juxtaposed with the classic heroic leaps, suggests that these are men of action.

Martial and Majestic

Figure 5.13. *Silverado*, main title.

Turning our attention to those more recent films sometimes described as adult Westerns, we find a different hero and, not surprisingly, different music. Phil Loy notes of the post–1955 Western, "They began to shift foci, as the hero became more frequently a loner, an alienated individual more akin to the contemporary anti-hero than the cowboy hero of the 1930s and 1940s" (11). Later he suggests that the heroes in early 1950s Westerns could be classified as Northrop Frye's Type 4 hero, that is, a person "superior to neither other people nor his environment" (36) while post–1955 heroes fall into the Type 5 category, being individuals "with *inferior* moral qualities; he is someone others look down on and hold in contempt or fear" (36) (italics mine). Similarly, Thomas Schatz suggests that the new Western hero may have "cynical, self-conscious, and even 'incorporated,'" traits, which "render him increasingly unheroic, more like one of us" (59). We have already discussed the main-title music for Anthony Mann's Westerns, and, like the classic Western before, he relied upon this same music to underscore scenes with his heroes. A growing reliance upon marked elements in scoring the hero suggests to viewers that they must expect unconventional (if not heroically ambiguous) behavior on the part of the hero. In *The Naked Spur,* the only unmarked, conventional music associated with hero is the "I Dream of Jeannie" theme that Kaper uses to underscore the scenes with Stewart (Howard Kemp) and Janet Leigh (Lina Patch). There is, I should add, an almost disorienting feeling to these scenes because there has been nothing musically prior to these scenes to suggest any kindness or civility in Kemp's character. He is a hard, driven man who, like his counterparts in the hardboiled detective formula, would be a criminal if he weren't an agent of the law. The thematization of the marked characteristics in the hero's music reminds the viewer that civilized values may be tenuous at best and that the hero walks a razor thin edge between the pull of the wilderness and the demands of civilization. The biggest contrast in the musical analogues to accompany the heroes is in the orchestral timbres employed to underscore each. In the pastoral and heroic topics in classic Westerns there is a greater reliance upon strings or mellow horns, conventional harmonies, and gently rolling accompaniment patterns (the prairie topic); in action and contemporary Westerns there is more reliance upon brass, dissonant harmonies, and angular, if not asymmetrical, rhythmic patterns.

Town and Community

Critical perspective on the idea of town or community in the Western is quite wide ranging and diverse. To Jane Tompkins, "the town represents a simpler, more benign social order, a place for everyone and everyone in her place" (85); while Thomas Schatz sees in *Stagecoach* a set of "complex, contradictory values" in the community (*Hollywood Genres* 50). Similarly, John Cawelti, specifically addressing women's roles in the Western, notes of the community, "The town offers love, domesticity, and order as well as the opportunity for personal achievement and the creation of family, but it requires the repression of spontaneous passion and the curtailment of the masculine honor and camaraderie of the older wilderness life" (49). Finally, Stanley Solomon states, "Although the Westerner is commonly an isolated figure, a man apart from society, much is made in the genre of various forms of community. Other genres may take communal relationships for granted, but the Western evokes a genuine feeling for whatever fleeting moment of communal relationship there may be" (22). What we have then is a challenge for the composer to find musical motifs, topics and gestures that signify this drive for order, as well as the diversity, affection, and dysfunction that attends the forces of civilization. Most Westerns have a tendency to blend source (diegetic) and non-diegetic music, with filmmakers privileging source music over the non-diegetic and with good reason. Nothing communicates a sense of place, especially the enclosed places that are central to the community, than the music that would actually emanate from those buildings or settings. Consequently, source music used to signify the conflict between civilization and the savage wilderness will include music played or sung in Indian camps, in saloons, within households (informally such as Charlie singing for Laurie in *The Searchers* or formally, as in the grand march played for the party at Sergeant Major O'Rourke's house in *Fort Apache*), and at ritual celebrations ranging from weddings to funerals. As one can see, filmmakers and composers draw upon a range of musical styles to communicate the rather complex set of values suggested by the encroachment of civilization on the wilderness. In fact, some of the source music is as emblematic of the struggle to establish civilization as the iconography of the little farm sitting on the edge of the wilderness, like the Starrett's farm in *Shane*. At one end of the spectrum will be music that embodies the values of European culture, including classical music such as waltzes, piano or orchestral works written by European composers. As a group these could be labeled "high culture topics." At the other end of the spectrum will be music that has a decidedly urban sound (that is, urban for the late 19th century), music that one might hear in saloons and dance halls. It is not uncommon to have a pianist (and sometimes banjoist) playing vintage songs from the turn of the century or playing ragtime versions of older 19th century tunes ("Oh, Dem Golden Slippers," etc.). In this same area of the spectrum we find the occasional production number like Frenchy's number "See What the Boys in the Back Room Will Have" in *Destry Rides Again* (1939); these types of numbers oftentimes are newly composed for a film and will have a bit of an anachronistic ring as they are clearly Tin Pan Alley products introduced into a pre–Alley environment, reflecting compositional styles more appropriate for the 1940s rather than the 1870s. That bit of subtlety, however, is not important, because, after all, it is just the sound and general style that is important for signifying the corrupt side of the march of progress and civilization. And that is exactly what we are supposed to infer from this music. This is marginalized music of the time period, the late 19th century equivalent of ragtime, jazz, swing, rock and rap. We find then that blues topics, ragtime topics, and popular tunes (with harmonic language that stretches the conventional I-IV-V folk topic harmonies) come to signify oppositional values, oppositional not only to the values of the wilderness but to the more salutary virtues of civilization (home, family, religion, good business, etc.). Consequently, the piano will not be the vehicle for the musical virtues of Bach, Chopin or Beethoven (or even hymns) and even the humble banjo will not be a vehicle for the homespun virtues of folk tunes picked or strummed within the context of a frontier home; instead each will be featured playing musical styles that are culturally coded as marginalized, reflecting a degeneration of the instrument and by extension the music and the values of civilization.

In the middle of the spectrum, we have the music signifying the positive elements of civilization, music that seems to reconcile the virtues of those elements of high culture and folk culture that are attempting to take root on the frontier. This section of the musical spectrum features its own topical and gestural range, extending from the hymn topics that might be sung at weddings and funerals to simple dance topics (jigs and reels) played by guitar, fiddle, and banjos at country dances and parties (the little community dance in *Shane* is a good example here) to the middle class popular tunes such as those of Stephen Foster, which will be found in a variety of settings ranging from home to city. These are musical topics that validate socially accepted rituals and, consequently, that affirm the efficacy of civilizing influences on the frontier. Once again, John Ford's films offer us a perfect crucible (and a model) for the integration of source music into the narrative. He employed a wide range of "acceptable" tunes symbolizing the positive side of the march of civilization, as Kathryn Kalinak notes, including hymns like "Shall We Gather at the River," folk tunes like "The Girl I Left Behind Me," "cowboy" tunes (*faux* and genuine) like "Ten Thousand Cattle" ("The Sound of Many Voices" 169–171), and, finally, actual popular songs like "I'll Take You Home Again, Kathleen" (1876) in *Rio Grande* (1950). This last example is a particularly effective musical moment in a Western because of how convincingly it establishes the virtues of civilization: it is a song which extols the merits of love, romance and marriage; it is sung serenade style (using a very folk topic) by four soldiers to a lady who has come from the East; finally, it prefigures a reconciliation between her (and her values) and her husband (John Wayne as Captain York) and his values. In the final analysis, the use of source music here and in other genres is a shorthand method of coercing us to correlate culturally coded associations with values embedded in the conventions of the genre.

Non-diegetic music is rarer to find in these settings and even if it is used, it will often be orchestral settings of familiar tunes, ranging from folk tunes to Stephen Foster. The one instance of a body of non-diegetic music to underscore the role of the community is in the material written for women in the films. John Cawelti has stated that "women are the primary symbols of civilization in the Western" (47), and indeed in the division of female characters they serve as appropriate symbols for the diversity, the complexity, the success and drawbacks of civilization. Cawelti states that "the blonde ... represents genteel, pure femininity, while the brunette ... symbolizes a more full-blooded, passionate and spontaneous nature, often slightly tainted by a mixture of blood or a dubious past.... The dark girl is a feminine embodiment of the hero's savage, spontaneous side" (48). On the one hand, we have the music for the "blonde" in *Shane*; on the other, that which is used for the scenes between Howard Kemp (James Stewart) and Lina Patch (Janet Leigh) in Anthony Mann's *The Naked Spur* (1953). In each case, the composers (Victor Young and Bronislau Kaper, respectively) had to score either a familiar 19th century tune or something evocative of the 19th century to suggest qualities about the women. Be it original tune or borrowed, gentle strings, sentimentality, and grace inform the scoring decisions, and in the process the benign side of domesticating the wilderness is accented. Young's lovely and highly evocative folk-like theme for Marian simultaneously conveys the role of the woman as symbol of the hearth and as a symbol of that something ineffable that the hero will never be able to embrace within the confines of civilization. Scored simply for strings, the melody transcends its folk roots and becomes emblematic of the decorum, grace and order that accompanies the establishment of homesteads in the midst of the wilderness.

Figure 5.14. Marian's theme from *Shane* (Darby and DuBois 290).

Dimitri Tiomkin achieves something similar in *Red River* with his motifs for Fen (Coleen Gray) and Tess (Joanne Dru). If ever there was a case where music reaffirmed the role of women as a civilizing influence it is in the love scene between Matt (Montgomery Clift) and Tess. Tess joins Matt on his watch and, in her usual fashion, begins talking nonstop until a rider interrupts her. Then Tiomkin brings up the main-title music ("Get Along Little Dogies"). This time, however, it is introduced softly with a solo string predominating, and it sounds less like a "cowboy song" and more like a love theme. As they continue to talk and touch one another, the music builds up until the moment of the kiss when the full orchestra takes up the theme in a lavish and lushly romantic setting. This is very reminiscent of Korngold's scoring in films such as *Captain Blood, The Sea Hawk,* and *The Adventures of Robin Hood*, where he would take the heroic main title and rescore it for love scenes and in the process, as we have noted, fuse the heroic and romantic. In this case, the scoring forecasts the new civilized order where the cowboy tune (signifying the cattle drive and a male work ethic) is elided with the romantic yearning of Tess, which, in turn, will lead to marriage (Matt will not, like Dunson, let this opportunity to share his material success and future with a woman elude him). Similarly, Bronislau Kaper's scoring for Lina Patch in *The Naked Spur* is particularly effective (acute!). His reworking of Stephen Foster's "I Dream of Jeannie" in the scenes between Kemp and Patch is in marked contrast to the more dissonant (read disturbed) music that underscores the relentless quest and mission of the film's hero. The music leads us to believe that Lina will be able to break through Kemp's hatred and almost monomaniacal commitment to

The Naked Spur. The unmarked music of the heroine highlights the marked music associated with the hero in the "new Western."

bring in Vandergroat (Robert Ryan) and touch some human core in him, some spot where forgiveness and reconciliation reside.

The "dark" woman is intimately associated with the dysfunctional side of civilization. However, unlike the Indian or the greedy landowner (cattleman or otherwise), her role is more emblematic than dramatic, i.e., she is seldom an antagonist in the main conflict. Musical topics and gestures for the "dark" woman will be the same ones described above for the darker aspects of civilization because she often is a saloon singer, dancer or a denizen of these worlds. Consequently, her actions will most often be underscored by source music, as is the case with Frenchy in *Destry Rides Again* or Chihuahua in John Ford's *My Darling Clementine* (1946). If non-diegetic music is written for the dark woman, it will feature marked elements, darker, more psychological (or perhaps pathological) motifs, often stressing modern (read dissonant) harmonies and angular and less romantic melodic materials.

Forces of the Savage Wilderness

John Cawelti has very aptly captured the paradoxical nature of this particular convention in his book, *The Six-Gun Mystique:* "The savage symbolizes the violence, brutality, and ignorance which civilized society seeks to control and eliminate, but he also commonly stands for certain positive values which are restricted or destroyed by advancing civilization: the freedom and spontaneity of wilderness life, the sense of personal honor and individual mastery, and the deep camaraderie of men untrammeled by domestic ties" (52–53). Cawelti notes that civilized values include things like home and family and enterprises such as the establishment of farms and businesses, which, in turn, reinforce the values of "hard work, mutual loyalty, and achievement" (49). The forces of the savage wilderness are those whose values stand in direct opposition to those listed above. We commonly think of Indians or white free-range ranchers who are intent upon thwarting the efforts of farmers, businessmen, clergymen, and teachers who seek to bring civilized values and institutions to the frontier. The music associated with these forces will, similarly, stress marked elements that signify those abovementioned oppositional values. In place of the four-square harmonies associated with the hero we can expect to hear more dissonance. Instead of sweeping melodic gestures, like those in the themes for *Shane* or *Lonesome Dove*, we will have angular, edgy melodies that seem to lack fixed tonal centers or line. The only element the two contrasting musical styles (for heroes and villains, that is) might have in common would be rhythmic ones. As we have seen, rigorous and syncopated rhythms are a key gestural feature of all music in the genre. The intimate connection of the forces of savagery with the wilderness demands that marked but similar gestures be used to communicate this connection to the topography. From a dramatic standpoint it makes sense as well, as in the hard-boiled formula where the music for the hero will almost seem to echo or even replicate that of the villain, the rhythmical gestures for cowboy and denizen of the savage wild *must* be consistent: the hero's commitment to civilization is always tempered by his methods, which may ultimately lead to his alienation from the very community he has defended. Let's look at couple of examples of how composers underscore the forces of the savage wilderness.

As we shall see, Indians are the stereotypical exemplars of the values of the savage wilderness, but they are not the only ones. The greedy land baron (*Shane*) and the marauding bandit (*The Magnificent Seven*) generally are accorded their own motifs and gestures to heighten the conflict. As suggested above, rhythmic elements predominate and harmonic and melodic materials will be marked, featuring aggressively repeated notes, dissonance (or at least tonal ambiguity), and narrow melodic ranges. The following example of music for Calvera from *The Magnificent Seven* is a good example:

Figure 5.15. "Calvera," *The Magnificent Seven* (Darby and DuBois 445).

Of course, cowboys-and-Indians is pretty much how we have simplistically reduced the formula at times. From the standpoint of the kernel conflict in the genre, it does make some sense. If there is a force which clearly spells oppositional values to those of the forces of civilization, it is the Native American. In current critical terminology, according to Richard Maltby, "The Hollywood Indian represents an Other defined in relation to White American experience" (Cameron and Pye 35). Reflecting on the music for the "other" in science fiction and horror, it is interesting to observe that the music for the Native American shares some similarities with these other genres. Stanley Solomon has noted that "Indians are still not well understood, nor have they totally lost their movie roles as a mysterious if not exotic, people ... and not surprisingly, the function of the Indian community has been limited to incidents of violence, with a few major exceptions such as Ford's *Cheyenne Autumn* (1964)" (23). Turning then to the music we should, as I suggested above, be hearing sounds that are not associated with the conventional elements of film music or even Western music (i.e., serious or classical music). Musical topics and gestures for the Native American generally fall into two camps, rhythmic and melodic or harmonic.

One of the most common rhythmic signifiers for Indians is the strict 4/4 tom-tom beat we so often hear in films. In fact, the rhythm probably would be written as it is in this figure:

Figure 5.16. Indian drum rhythm.

This in and of itself is not particularly "alien" to Western ears, seeing as how the downbeat is stressed as it is in much Western music. Normally, this strictly regulated beat is the foundation and is heard in counterpoint with a more rhythmically irregular beat pattern in the melody line as in m.2 of this variation on this topic.

What is "alien" and helps signify "other" in these rhythmic gestures is that rhythmic pattern in measure two where we oftentimes find either an initial sixteenth, eighth or dotted eighth-sixteenth pattern or thirty-second-dotted sixteenth pattern leading to a more regular eighth note pattern or even quarter note rhythm.

Looking at melodic motifs that help signify the Native American, we find a couple of different examples. First, some Indian topics feature fairly narrow melodic ranges. Although

Figure 5.17. Indian motif.

a passage may begin with an octave leap, the melody will eventually settle into something that seldom exceeds the range of a fifth. The following example from David P. McAllester's "North American Native Music" in *Musics of Many Cultures* is a good example:

Figure 5.18. "Sioux Rabbit Dance" (310).

Beyond this one finds the intervals of the third, the fourth and fifth to form the most common patterns in what composers borrow to signify Native Americans in films. Those intervallic leaps in many cases also tend downward. The following is a example from *Cheyenne Autumn* of scoring for the Native American in classic Hollywood films; one will notice, moreover, how closely North has tried to emulate actual Native American musical styles like the one shown above, especially in the initial sixteenth-eighth lift gesture and mirrored sixteenth-dotted eighth downward leap in m.2:

Figure 5.19. *Cheyenne Autumn* (Darby and DuBois 415).

Hearing this music in contrast to source music drawn from folk or popular tunes or an unmarked classic Hollywood theme points up the otherness of the music. Irregular rhythms, melodies that emphasize repetition and rhythm and harmonic structures built off what may be largely modal progressions all contribute to the alien nature of the music for the Native American. In action sequences with settlers being chased by Indians or cowboys fighting them, these elements are yoked with conventional elements of scoring in action scenes. One of the most interesting tropes used to signify the threat of the other is the one we hear in the Indian fight in *Red River* where Tiomkin fuses Indian topics with the suspense topic to signify the Indian threat and villainy. A similar trope is used in the scene in *Winchester 73* (1950) when Lola (Shelley Winters) and Steve (Charles Drake) are being chased by the Indians.

The Final Showdown

The final showdown in the Western produces a musical "mixed bag," and that is because the final showdown has evolved and metamorphosed from the days of Owen Wister's *The Virginian*, with its classic fast-draw showdown between hero and villain. In fact, in the case of the classic two-man fast-draw showdown on Main Street, directors and composers often opt for silence, letting ambient noise (wind, creaking doors, etc.) aurally contribute to the tension as the adversaries silently march toward that moment when they will be forced to draw. In many films, however, the final showdown provides a perfect opportunity to employ motifs, topics, and gestures classically associated with climactic scenes in other genres. Both *Shane* and *Red River* employ similar musical elements to heighten tension between adversaries. Dimitri Tiomkin relies upon a simple, strict, four-beat stalking gesture, featuring basses and percussion, as Dunson (John Wayne) dismounts and resolutely makes his way through cattle and past a threatening Jerry (John Ireland) to confront Matt (Montgomery Clift). Above the relentless rhythm we hear the brass announce a short motif, a leaping and falling gesture, that is likewise relentlessly repeated and which further propels the action. Tiomkin accompanies Jerry's "pulling" on Dunson with a stinger and then returns to the stalking gesture as Dunson bears down on Matt. As Dunson challenges Matt, "Go on, draw," Tiomkin drops the music out but brings it back in after Dunson slaps Matt. From this point on, he relies upon strings, stating brief, disjointed chromatic ascending and descending figures. Perhaps the most striking moment comes, however, when Tess (Joanne Dru) stops the fight and begins to dress the men down for the fools they are. As she lectures the two, Tiomkin brings the main title back in, which he has previously used in a love scene with Matt and Tess; this time, however, he scores it first in a minor key and then, as she softens her rebuke (asking Dunson if he's hurt), he shifts to major. This leads to the immediate reconciliation between the two men as the woman has been able to negotiate the triumph of cooperation and a new beginning for the cattle ranch. Tiomkin's scoring of the scene musically brings closure to the elemental conflict between the three characters, and Tess's dominating presence clearly signifies the triumph of the forces of civilization.

Similarly, Victor Young's score for *Shane* weaves snatches of the main title ("The Call of the Faraway Hills") with Marian's theme and classic showdown and climactic motifs and gestures. The climax in actuality begins with the fight between Shane (Alan Ladd) and Starrett (Van Heflin), leading to a poignant farewell to Marion (Jean Arthur) in which she asks Shane why he is going to fight Wilson (Jack Palance). He responds that he is doing it for her and all her family. Young employs the main title to underscore this scene, stressing mid-range strings and giving the music a feeling of the minor by accentuating a counter-melody in the basses. It is a wonderful moment, as the music for the hero becomes the accompaniment and the aural symbol for his commitment to the preservation of the values of the farm and family. As Shane rides to town with Joey scrambling after him, Young also relies upon a strict four-beat ascending melodic motif featuring basses and timpani. Occasionally, we hear a fragment of "The Call of Faraway Hills" but, in keeping with action sequences (with the exception of Steiner maybe), there is no single theme development; instead, short figures are tossed between sections of the orchestra creating a sense of restlessness and ambiguity. When the camera pans to reveal the town the strings are brought to the forefront, sounding a stepwise chromatic motif. A cut to the interior of Ryker's reveals the men getting ready for action. As Ryker (Emile Myer) crosses the frame, tremolo strings give way to a brass stinger and, finally, a shift to a sixteenth and dotted eighth combination as Wilson dominates the frame. As Brother Morgan Ryker (John Dierkes) mounts the stairs, Young alters the motif sounded earlier for Wilson:

Figure 5.20. *Shane*, "Villains" (Darby and DuBois 290).

As Shane enters the saloon and spots Wilson, we hear a slashing gesture consisting of a dotted eighth and two thirty-seconds, which Young will thematize as part of the showdown sequence. Next, Shane walks to the bar and we hear a sustained low note. Then, in quick succession, there is brief descending pattern followed by a quietly stated regular 4/4 pulse as he leans against the bar framed by a classic Stevens low angle shot. During the actual fight itself, Young drops the music out much as Tiomkin had done in *Red River*, but brings it back in when Rufe appears in the floor above. Shane shoots and Rufe pitches forward through the rail to the floor below, accompanied by a stinger played by the brass. The short eighth-quarter figure is stated, which then gives way to a gentle oboe theme as Shane makes his way out of the bar to a waiting Joey. The oboe provides the transition to the final scene where Shane's speech reaffirms for Joey the incompatibility of the ways of the gunfighter and the ways of the farmer, encouraging him to grow tall and good and to take care of his parents. In both films, the lack of thematic development reminds us that the outcome is not assured, and the ways of civilization will be tested one more time; but in both, the final musical analogue confirms the inevitable progress of civilization.

In stark contrast to this method, some films may demand a more symphonic approach, like that in *They Died with Their Boots On* (1941), where director and composer opt for a musical coda not unlike the final movement of Beethoven's 9th or Dvorak's *Symphony from the New World*, or even Steiner's own climactic music for *The Charge of the Light Brigade*. In these cases, all the themes are restated — we might say in *avant-après* fashion — and they are restructured in almost symphonic fashion (and scope!) to underscore the triumph of civilization over the forces of the savage wilderness.

In-depth: The Searchers *(1956) and* Dances with Wolves *(1990)*

One could subtitle this in-depth analysis "The Only Good Indian..." because these two films exemplify the nature of the transformational genre and its relationship to changes in our mythology of the West, especially in regard to the treatment of Native Americans on screen. The John Ford–John Wayne film hearkens to the classic myth of the West, with farmers and cowboys pitted against the forces of the savage wilderness (i.e., the Indian), who must be subdued to make way for progress. The film perpetuates a particularly horrible late 19th century sentiment: The only good Indian is a dead one. Costner's film, on the other hand, almost

Shane. **A wounded Shane entrusts the care of his parents and the preservation of civilization to young Joey.**

completely subverts this myth by instead suggesting that in the tale of the settling of the West, the Indian is the true hero of the myth and the forces of civilization are the villainous savages. In Costner's vision of the West we have a new dictum: Only the Indian is good. In this analysis, I will focus on how composers Max Steiner and John Barry underscore the basic conflict in the myth of the West, focusing on the music for the hero, the Native American (and by extension the wilderness setting), and the underscoring of the resolution of this fundamental conflict.

The Searchers is in many ways a representative late Max Steiner score. Working with Ford he had to accede to the great director's love for period music or at least period popular tunes that aurally contextualized his unique vision of the West. Steiner's preference was to score everything himself and, if necessary, write original songs in period styles, but, being a realist and long time Warner's employee, he knew that he would have to answer to the combined forces of the front office and the director. He never failed, however, to make any borrowed material his own, and that is very much the case with *The Searchers*. There are three dominant themes that he weaves throughout the film, tying them together with classic Western and adventure movie topics and gestures. The three themes correspond with the central conflicts in the film: the main title "The Searchers," written by Stan Jones, is a musical commentary on Ethan; the 19th century popular tune "Lorena" is used to signify home and love (for my analysis, I will call this theme the "Homecoming Theme") and provides an emotional subtext for Ethan's relationship to both Martha (Dorothy Jordan) and Debbie; and, finally, Steiner employs and varies standard Native American musical topics to underscore the villainous side of the kernel conflict. Other themes, like the one for Marty (Jeffrey Hunter) as he first rides up to Aaron's ranch shortly after Ethan arrives, are brief and may be heard but once.

The main title begins with a classic Indian topic, with a throbbing, strict, four beat pulse, to announce the Indian threat that pervades the entire film. There is then a transition to the vocal main theme, which will only make occasional appearances in the film, but which significantly tells us something about the troubled quest of Ethan Edwards (John Wayne). The lyrics refer to a man who is searching for something and, even though he may cook his meals, he finds his heart won't warm; in the second verse, he wonders if he will ever find peace of mind in his quest; the final verse emphasizes the theme of love, expressing the hope that the man may find a place where there is no hate and where he many find "a tender love" (Buscombe 71).

Oddly enough, this particular theme is not used that much in the film, a fact that is surprising on one count because it seems to be so much about Ethan and Marty's quest and about Ethan's character in particular; it is not surprising, on the other hand, because Max Steiner often bristled at having to graft other people's tunes into his own scores, the most notorious example of which was his experience working on the score for *Casablanca*, where he was forced to use Herman Hupfield's "As Time Goes By" as core material for that score.[4] Nonetheless, as Darby and DuBois's analysis of the score for *The Searchers* points out, Steiner found ways to integrate this theme as well as some other traditional melodies into his score (53–55).

In the opening scene of Ethan approaching the home of his brother, Steiner introduces some of the dominant motifs that will be woven throughout the film. The most important is the one I call the "Homecoming Theme." In actuality, it is a popular song from 1857 entitled "Lorena" (music by J.P. Webster and lyrics by the Reverend H.D.L. Webster).

Figure 5.21. "Lorena."

Steiner's initial scoring of the theme begins with a simple strumming pattern on a guitar, suggesting the pastoral with just a hint of the elegiac. Significantly, it plays under a shot of Martha silhouetted in the doorway and walking out onto the porch, where she stands leaning on a post as she watches Ethan approach on horseback (the post actually acts as a divider: she is on one side and his figure is on the other). The music and shot state simply the nature of their relationship: she has accepted home and domesticity and he has wandered and has lived outside the pale of civilized ways. Consequently, the music suggests a dual referent: on the one hand, the theme signifies the unspoken love between Ethan and Martha and it also signifies home, especially the homecoming, where it seems that he hopes to be reconciled to the life his brother has staked out. On the other hand, the visual iconography of the post in the shot suggests that there is a great divide that may never be breached. Significantly, the lyrics speak of a love unrequited:

> We loved each other then Lorena,
> More than we ever dared to tell;
> And what might have been, Lorena,
> Had but our lovings prosper'd well.

The lyric seems to have been written with Ethan and Martha in mind. Steiner varies this theme in different scenes to underscore both Ethan's feelings during his quest and the two men's efforts to effect another homecoming, that of Debbie (Natalie Wood) back to what remains of her "civilized" community. To this narrative end, it is given its sweetest treatment when it plays underneath a scene early in the film when Ethan gives Debbie his medal for a locket, thus reinforcing its role as an aural signifier for the values of home and Martha's presence in his life. Later, when Ethan realizes the Indian raiding party has drawn the militia out so they can attack a farm, Steiner varies the theme in a marked fashion. As he rubs his horse down, Ford uses a close-up to capture the pain and hopelessness of his situation; under the close-up, Steiner re-scores the theme in a minor key, suggesting the portending tragedy: Ethan has lost Martha to Aaron (Walter Coy) and now he may be losing her forever to the Indian threat.

Figure 5.22. "Lorena" in minor key.

The "Homecoming Theme," however, is restated in its original form at the end of the film when Laurie and Marty are reunited and when Ethan returns Debbie to her new home. It may be the ultimate musical statement for the triumph of civilization in that it suggests a reconciliation of polarities that exist in the genre. Martha and Ethan are separated by Ethan's status as an outsider: he is a borderline outlaw, a soldier in the Confederacy, an intimate with the ways of the Indian, which suggests a life outside that of his farmer brother's circumscribed world. Martha, as we see, has accepted the life of the rancher's wife and all that implies: home, child rearing, and marital fidelity. The appearance of the theme at the end as Ethan returns Debbie to her home brings the triumph of civilization and a reconciliation of differing ways of life to resolution: Marty, who is one-eighth Cherokee and a bunch of other nationalities, is united with a woman who is tough-minded like her mother but is also reminiscent of Martha in her love for the outsider. As all the family files into the house, we are left with a final image of Ethan standing in a swirl of dust with the arid landscape in the background. A this point, "The Searchers" is restated, with the "Homecoming" motif functioning on two levels: it is a reminder of the love he has lost but it is also a reminder that home is paramount and that he has remained true to his love by bringing her daughter home and preparing the West for a new order. Related to this is the fact that the theme is stated in two earlier scenes featuring Debbie in the Indian camp; the first is when Debbie seeks out Marty after they find her in Scar's camp and the seconds is when Marty rescues her. As Edward Buscombe notes, "all Ford's films are about home: finding it, building it, losing it" (64). Associating the theme with Debbie in the midst of the search keeps the theme in the forefront of the viewer's mind.

The second theme used in the opening sequence is the Celtic folk tune "The Wearing of the Green," which underscores Aaron's entrance into the scene but seems to be more of an aural commentary on Ethan's military background. Next, as Aaron goes out to greet him, the main title theme written by Stan Jones is played, but in 3/4 time, and it is brought to an abrupt end when Martha says, "Welcome home, Ethan," signaling the restatement of the homecoming theme but with more dramatic texture and just a slightly ominous tone underneath.

"The Wearing of the Green," with its kinship to military music, is set in opposition to all the music used to underscore the actions and signify the threat of "the Other" in the film. Typical of the composers of the classical age of Hollywood, Steiner relies upon stock topics when underscoring scenes with Native Americans. Claudia Gorbmann notes that "Hollywood developed a specific vocabulary for representing Native Americans: "a rhythmic figure of four equal beats with the accent falling on the first, often played by drums or low bass instruments; the use of perfect fifths and fourths in the harmonic design; and the use of modal melody" (qtd. in Kalinak, "The Sound of Many Voices" 181). Steiner's gestures fall neatly into these two related camps. First, he employs the four-beat rhythmic figure mentioned by Gorbmann to announce the Indian threat (see figure 5.16). Second, he employs standard melodic and harmonic gestures that "fill out" the portrait of the Indian. One such gesture employs simple stepwise movement with a narrow melodic range and what might be described as an asymmetrical harmonic progression, i.e., going from A minor to A flat minor. Taken in tandem with the throbbing rhythm, the two elements provide music that is markedly "alien" in contrast to the more conventional (unmarked) motifs developed for the whites in the drama. Their markedness, moreover, contributes a darker and more menacing layer to the Indian threat. In the first encounter, for instance, the half step movement (so close to the gesture employed in stalking and suspense topics) adds an ominous element to the introduction of the Indian into the scene. Two small gestures are employed to underscore Scar's (Henry Brandon) actions; one is a three note ascending pattern that outlines a minor third and the other is a pattern that begins with a descending minor second (B to B flat) that then resolves a fourth lower (on F) — a gesture conventionally associated with grief or tragedy. In both, the presence of the minor second adds an ominous and forbidding dimension to Scar's threatening presence. As we have seen in science fiction (and as we shall see in horror), the minor second and the tritone are commonly used to underscore the alien threat. That they would be used to emphasize the "alien" threat of the Native American in this context should not be surprising.

A second, more fully developed Indian theme in the score is the one for Look (Beulah Archuletta), or as Ethan so gleefully refers to her, Mrs. Paulie. Lifted out of the context of the film, it is a charming little melody which exploits the intervals of the fifth and the second; it is like a Native American version of Debussy's "Golliwog's Cakewalk" in its humorous effect, gained largely by constructing a trope fusing the throbbing quarter rhythm of the Indian menace motif with some lively rhythmic variations reminiscent of the Scottish snap or ragtime topic — that is, ragtime in classical post–Romantic sense and not genuine ragtime as pioneered by Scott Joplin. Darby and DuBois note that this motif has the ability to, at one turn, capture the comic quality of the scenes with Marty and Look, and, at the other, become a menacing figure when the name "Scar" is mentioned:

The Searches. The Indian threat is made apparent as young Debbie is forced to show scalps to Ethan and Marty.

Figure 5.23. "Indians" (Darby and DuBois 54).

The bottom line is that the Indians are caught on the horns of a musical dilemma: they are a menace but with strong strains of buffoonery. It is the menace, however, which carries the day and dominates the scoring in *The Searchers.*

When it comes to the final showdown Steiner is allowed to flex his compositional muscles. In his score for *They Died with Their Boots On,* he demonstrated his capacity to construct tone poem-like climaxes for his films; the final battle sequence in that film, in fact, has echoes of the *1812 Overture* in its intensity and juxtaposition of motifs. One can perceive the arch of the battle and visualize the outcome from merely listening to the score. Similarly, in *The Searchers,* he underscores the action by incorporating the motifs that he has previously stated and varied throughout the film. The mythical dimensions of the showdown are achieved through motivic *avant/après* linkages and his reliance upon topics whose referential capabilities extend beyond the film itself and out to the genre as a whole. The sequence begins with the comic exchange between the Reverend Clayton and Lt. Greenfield, but the music first makes a notable entrance as the men mount up and begin their slow march to the Indian village. Steiner relies upon a steady, slow, march-like tempo under a variation of the main title played by low woodwinds. There is a cut to the village where we hear the familiar Indian rhythm cited earlier (figure 5.16). And then, as Marty steals into Debbie's tent and wakes her, we hear the "Homecoming Theme" briefly stated. Scar's entrance and the sound of Marty's gunshot lead to a cut to the militia and the order to charge. Steiner relies upon a fairly conventional rhythmic gesture of an eighth-note triplet and quarter played very rapidly to accompany the charge through the Indian camp. There is a cut to Ethan as he enters Debbie's tent and scalps Scar. It is an interesting and musically ambiguous moment as the three-note descending gesture is stated. We might assume that it underscores Ethan's hatred for Scar, but it could also be read as an aural correlative for the "savage" action Ethan is about to perform: he is now one with the savage. It also intensifies the drama of the scene when he finally spots Debbie. As he emerges from the tent after scalping Scar, Steiner uses a single note played *sforzando*—stridently might be more accurate—by the brass to complement the look of hatred on Ethan's face; as he spots Debbie we hear an ominous three-note rhythmic figure and the chase is on. As Ethan pursues her, Steiner employs a conventional galloping topic; then he very briefly states the main title as we see Debbie and Ethan through the opening of the cave to which she is running for safety. When he finally reaches her and picks her up and raises her above his head, just as he had done early in the film when she was a little girl, we hear the "Homecoming Theme." The showdown ends on a note of reconciliation: Scar is defeated, so is Ethan's hatred and Martha's love, once again, triumphs in his heart through her daughter.

The homecoming brings together the main themes starting with a fragmentary restatement of the main title as the riders come into the frame and then building to a lovely statement of the "Homecoming Theme" notably as Laurie (Vera Miles) runs to Marty. The underlying rhythm in the accompaniment is different, accentuating a classic Western dotted eighth-sixteenth pattern. The melody continues as the families file in through the door to the house and, as the last person goes in, the men's chorus enters, singing a verse from the main title where the song assures us that the man will find peace of mind but where he will find it remains a question mark. It ends with the "ride away" tag line.

Through the open door we see Ethan stoically viewing the scene, his right hand grabbing his left elbow in a classic blocking gesture, and then he turns from the open door and walks away into the swirling dust, heat, and aridity of the landscape. The door shuts and the screen goes to black. Steiner clearly validates the mythology of the Western in the denouement: the "Homecoming Theme" reminds the viewer of the centrality of the home in the triumph of civilization; the restatement of the main title reminds us, moreover, that the cowboy will always be a marginalized figure by virtue of his connection to the ways of the wilderness and of his solitary and problematic quest for peace; he may find it, as the song says, "But where, Oh Lord, where?"

Dances with Wolves

Just when fans thought the Western was truly dead, along came Kevin Costner's *Dances with Wolves* (1990). Part old-fashioned Western and part frontier epic, the film proved enormously successful at the box office, garnering seven Academy Awards. If Ford's film reaffirmed the old notion that "the only good Indian is a dead one," *Dances with Wolves* stands emblematic of the transformational and progressive genre by proclaiming quite the opposite: "Only

Indians are good!" Since the 1960s, there has been a marked transformation of the myth of the West in film, with the suggestion being, quite bluntly, that civilization stinks. Michael Ryan and Douglas Kellner note in their analysis of 1970s Westerns that "during this period, the western undergoes a process whereby its conventions are made visible, it increasingly assumes the form of a tradition that is reflected on and referred to in film. That process takes several forms — elegy, historical realism, and genre subversion and satire" (79–80). Instead of cavalry and cowboy heroics, films such as *The Outlaw Josey Wales* (1976), *Tom Horn* (1980), and *The Long Riders* (1980) asked audiences to view the outlaw or the marginalized as exemplars of the spirit of the West. Their vitality and resistance to the forces of greed, corruption, dominance, and racism suggested a new myth of the West: civilization stinks and the wilderness is our salvation. Those films, however, were not blockbusters, and the genre slipped into oblivion for almost ten years. Some, I think, hoped *Silverado* (1985) would revive the old-fashioned Western, but it really didn't. It took Costner's hybrid to infuse some life into the genre again. *Dances* has some of the old-fashioned virtues of the Western: camera work that embraces and celebrates the topography of the West, four square heroes in both the white man's camp (i.e., civilization) and in the Indian's camp (this in fact may be the secret to the film's great success), a moving love story, just the right mixture of action and violence, and, finally, a genuinely villainous adversary, the military, who, ironically, in the history of the genre were once viewed in a more positive light and seen as protectors of the highest ideals and values of civilization.

John Barry's score perfectly underscores the classic elements of the Western but also makes a nod to the progressive genre in its scoring for Native Americans. For some — and actually, I am one of them — Barry's selection as the composer for this film was rather surprising. When one thinks of composers who might have been tabbed to score a frontier epic, the obvious choices would have included Bernstein, Goldsmith, Williams, James Newton Howard, and James Horner. All have bona fide Western scores to their credit and have tapped the great store of Western topics and gestures in their work. Barry's one notable Western was *Monte Walsh* (1970), a somewhat offbeat example of the genre and one which ranks as an early example of the "civilization stinks" trend in the Western. And this may be why his score works so well in *Dances*: he is an Englishman steeped in the conventions of scoring for "hip" subjects and spy thrillers, and it seems he approached the project determined to not ape the conventions of the classic Western. In the final analysis, as we shall see, the score works and in fact may be just right for this reification of the myth of the West.

In keeping with the conventions of the genre, at the center of the film stands the hero, and Barry keeps the heroic tenor of the film front and center in his use of the "John Dunbar Theme," which predominates throughout the film. Like the "Homecoming" theme in *The Searchers*, Barry varies it to underscore and comment upon Dunbar's steady progress towards oneness with the Sioux and his revulsion at the encroachment of civilization on the lives of his adopted community. One way in which the Dunbar theme differs from themes or motifs associated with other cowboy heroes is that it is exclusively associated with Costner's protagonist and, unlike for pieces such as "The Call of Faraway Hills" from *Shane*, we are not asked to identify the theme with topography and the man. However, like other classic Western themes, it combines the elegiac with the heroic, featuring intervallic leaps of the fourth and fifth. It begins by emphasizing the fourth (because it begins with a downward leap that seems to exploit a I-V melodic pattern, i.e. F-C-F) and only rises to a third above the tonic. Thus it has a very narrow melodic range while still retaining the heroic cast of the leap of the fifth. Then the melody makes a dramatic octave leap and resolves back down to the fifth scale tone.

Very slowly

Figure 5.24. "John Dunbar Theme."

Rhythmically, Barry insinuates a touch of syncopation as the melody often falls off the beat, especially after sustained notes. He, moreover, achieves a nice rolling, folk-like effect by employing a variation on the prairie topic in the accompaniment so the bass line and the melody almost mirror one another. Against the half notes and dotted quarter in the opening two measures he has a two eighth-note, quarter and half note pattern in the bass; so the melody and accompaniment almost act in an antiphonal manner with the melody line countering the bass with more movement in the last two beats of the measure. It is interesting that he uses the same bass line in Kicking Bird's theme. The Dunbar theme then, in its reliance upon unmarked tonal and heroic elements, conventionally signifies values we associate with civilization while at the same time functioning as a quest theme: underscoring the journey of a man who wants to see the West before it is gone but who at heart is a loyal soldier.

Barry, however, also uses the theme to comment upon the evils of civilization. This is most evident in the Death of Two Socks sequence. First, it is important to note that although Barry gives the wolf its own motif early in the film, when the animal is killed by the soldiers late in the film Barry underscores part of the scene with a marked, minor key variation on the Dunbar theme. From this I think we can read that, unlike previous cowboy heroes, Dunbar is not just an intermediary between the forces of the savage wilderness and civilization; in fact, his quest is to be one with the wilderness. He is more concerned with sketching in his notebook what he sees than he is with discovering how he can exploit it for materialistic ends or for personal fame and fortune. So when Two Socks is killed the music suggests that Dunbar and the wolf are one but that his quest for oneness with the savage wilderness is threatened by the agents of civilization. One may have noted that this is almost diametrically opposite to Steiner's use of his "civilization" theme ("The Homecoming Theme"), where key shifts to the minor to suggest a threat to Martha and the home and, by extension, civilization.

This, of course, then demands the question: what is the filmmaker's and, by extension, composer's view of the savage wilderness? It would seem that if Dunbar is to become one with his surroundings and the Lakota, those surroundings should have some positive values — that is, if we want to believe the quest is a positive one. It is here where Barry most dramatically departs from the conventions of scoring for the Western. Let's look at two elements of the savage wilderness to see how he achieves this and attempts to forge new topics to reflect the transformational genre.

Barry's approach to capturing what Cawelti calls "the fresh and open grandeur of the Western landscape" (41) and the "special openess" (42) of the topographic panorama differs slightly from the work of composers such as Elmer Bernstein or Bruce Broughton, who seem to favor dynamic rhythmic patterns cast in the mold of Copland's ballet scores. To suggest a feeling of the rolling and fertile plains, for instance, his theme "Journey to Fort Sedgwick" instead hearkens to pastoral and prairie topics in its rhythmic use of the I-IV in the opening of the theme and a nicely syncopated bass line that uses an initial eighth-note and quarter-note ascending pattern, followed by five eighth notes in a descending pattern.

Figure 5.25. "Journey to Fort Sedgewick."

The melody itself does not begin on the downbeat but on the second half of the first beat (i.e., an eighth note), replicating the bass pattern. The entire effect is gently rolling and rhythmical, and the harmonic shifts employing I-IV progressions (C-F; F-B♭) provide a nice sense of rest-lessness and movement. This subtle modulation anticipates what he will do with the theme he wrote for Kicking Bird (Graham Greene) and to the basic harmonies in the "Buffalo Hunt" sequence, where we find the following progression: V(G)-Vmaj; I(C)-Imaj.^{7}; IV(F)-IVmaj^7; VII(B♭)-VIImaj^7; III(E♭)-IIImaj^7. The entire musical movement is built on a cycle of fourths. This reliance upon quartal harmony seems to be Barry's nod to the exotic element of the American wilderness and is reminiscent of the scoring for setting in the elegiac Westerns of previous decades.

It is in his music for the Native Americans — and especially in contrast to the music for the forces of civilization — where we see a real departure from previous musical gestures and topics associated with Native Americans. Ironically, for all its attempts at communicating a more positive image of the Lakota, the film may in fact actually rob the Native American of a distinctive voice by having Barry substitute unmarked musical elements in place of the cliché-ridden but marked Indian motifs and gestures. We end up with music that retains some interesting rhythmic ideas, but melodically and harmonically the themes are undifferen-tiated from the music for the white leads. A prime example is the theme titled "Kicking Bird's Gift." The music's marking is "Serenely" and the melody is just that. In 4/4 time, it is a gen-tle melody supported initially by a common I-IV (F-B♭) chord progression that shifts abruptly to a major III-VI chord progression.

Figure 5.26. "Kicking Bird's Gift."

The underlying rhythm completely ignores the classic strict four beat Indian topic, and the melody avoids the usual intervallic leaps of the fourth and the more insidious half-step movement (a common figure in suspense topics) that Steiner relied upon in most of his underscoring of the Native American. The rhythms here are closer to those in the John Dunbar theme, and the melody could almost be seen as a variation of that theme by virtue of its upward movement. The only "exotic" element which might signify the Other is the abrupt tonal shift, which is not present in any of the other motifs in the score.

A second example of Barry drawing upon conventionally unmarked topics and gestures to signify the Native American's kinship with Dunbar is in the cue entitled "The Buffalo Hunt." This actually may be Barry's most "Western" music in the entire score. The entire first part of the cue is thematized upon a simple triadic lift gesture:

Figure 5.27. "The Buffalo Hunt."

The gesture will be familiar to auditors as one associated with hero figures — if it weren't such a common gesture, one might think it was borrowed from Korngold's score for *The Adventures of Robin Hood*— and although it differs from Victor's Young's "Call of Faraway Hills" from *Shane*, it is eerily reminiscent of that theme. The point here is that as Dunbar and the Lakota begin their quest for buffalo, the music used to underscore their journey is reminiscent of classic Western topics we generally associate with the forces of civilization. This then raises a question: are we to correlate the music with the actions of the Lakota or is this music for Dunbar's involvement in the hunt? The answer is probably "yes!" At this point, the music is signifying an alliance, a bond if you will, between the white man and the Indian. The cue eventually evolves into a jaunty variation of the Dunbar theme, which confirms Dunbar's integration into the Lakota community. The music is an aural exclamation point for the — possibly prescient — act of heroism that serves as the climax of the sequence, when Dunbar shoots a charging buffalo to save the young Lakota boy. In this scene, Costner and Barry have subtly established Dunbar as a hero in the Lakota camp by making him a defender of their values and by having him draw upon his heroic strengths to save a member of the community.

An interesting dilemma for Barry is that he actually had to write music for two different types of Indians in the film. One of the subplots in the film is the ongoing tension between the Lakota and the Pawnee. In a nice bit of narrative misdirection, we are introduced to Indians in the film in the form of the savage Pawnee as they attack Timmons, the mule team driver. As the scene unfolds, we almost settle back and say, "Well, by golly it will be a good old fashioned Western," as the Pawnee behave much like their cinematic forebears in previous portrayals of Indians on film. The music that underscores the scenes with the Pawnee utilizes more conventional Native American topics and gestures. There is the bow to the throbbing drumbeat, but even here Barry chooses to vary it with rolls and cascading timbres of a more irregular nature. He alludes to the suspense topic by employing high strings and tremolos to suggest the threat and a half-step

In *Dances with Wolves*, the hero joins forces with the Indian to preserve their way of life.

descending pattern to suggest menace. On the whole, he seems committed to finding different aural analogues to flesh out the Pawnee threat. In the scene mentioned above, Barry develops the threat by beginning with a pedal point in the basses and then introducing an angular and very unmelodic motif in the high strings, which is then countered by a jagged theme underneath. Throughout, he, like Steiner, emphasizes the half-note descending gesture supported by unusual, asymmetrical harmonic shifts. As they ride off, with the arrow-ridden body of Timmons in the foreground, we hear something approaching the classic Native American topics employed by Steiner and others, ending with the classic ominous half-step gesture.

Where this film may most radically break with the traditional Western and asks to be accepted as emblematic of the transformational genre is in its depiction of community. The common pattern, as we discussed above, is that the hero must at some point commit himself and his skills to the preservation of ways of civilization. In a dramatic, 180 degree turn from this element in the formula, John Dunbar commits to the Indian community and in fact takes up arms against "his own people." Consequently, conventional musical expectations, our competency in regard to the genre, will be challenged — and perhaps undermined — as we enter a more musically ambiguous terrain. Where Steiner has the "Homecoming" theme and other diegetic music such as "Yellow Rose of Texas" and "Shall We Gather at the River" provide the emotional underpinning for the activities of the settlers, Barry had an entirely different communal reality to deal with in *Dances with Wolves*: the better community, the community the cowboy must serve and defend, is the Sioux nation and not the military and the U.S.

government. Consequently, little of the music associated with forces of civilization — that used to underscore scenes of the war, that for the first fort he visits, and that for his final encounter with the military — resonates with any of the positive values we associate with the westward movement. In fact, we have very clear cues about the evil of the forces of civilization when Dunbar and the Lakota go into the Buffalo Killing Ground. The cue echoes the opening lift gesture of the Dunbar theme but it is scored in a minor key, signifying the tragic undercurrent in Western expansion and the threat to both the Native American and to Dunbar's own quest to be reconciled to the Lakota way of life. Finally, in the film's climax, Barry scores the John Dunbar theme in a minor key, first when he is captured and later when the soldiers kill Two Socks. This provides a stunning contrast to Two Socks's actual theme, which is played by a flute and emphasizes the pastoral:

Figure 5.28. "Two Socks — The Wolf Theme."

His one nod to the exotic is a later harmonic shift from A major to A minor and back to the home key of A major within the eight bars of the main theme.

Next, we have the love theme. In Westerns, the love theme can be seen as a key motif in signifying the values of civilization. On the surface, Barry's love theme is a classically conventional foray into the type, but it conversely problematizes the central conflict when we realize that Stands with a Fist (Mary McDonnell) is, in essence, a Sioux in spite of her white heritage. By taking her hand in marriage, moreover, Dunbar then commits to Kicking Bird's tribe and family and like his cowboy hero forebears signals his ultimate commitment to preserving the values of civilization through marriage (or at least some sort of film's-end commitment) to the heroine. Ironically, his commitment to the white captive seals his commitment to the preservation of the values of the savage wilderness. The theme itself wouldn't be out of place in any Western from any time period. It is a lyrical 3/4 time tune whose dominating gesture is an octave leap from the third beat to the downbeat that is then countered by a pastorally tinged bass accompaniment:

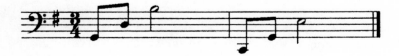

Figure 5.29. "The Love Theme."

The entire effect is indeed like the pastoral topic with only the leaps signifying the rising passions of the two lovers. Aside from the rolling, prairie-like feeling, nothing associated with the Native American way of life or anything expressive of the emotions of the Native Americans is present in the melody. It is finally a reminder that the lovers are indeed white, even though they are no longer committed to a life dominated by white values.

The final aural sign that the hero is no longer an agent of "civilized" values is that the music most often used to underscore the actions of the forces of civilization will be marked, minor key variations on the Dunbar theme, signifying that civilization itself is the threat. In this regard, Barry very much emulates Steiner, who scored the "Homecoming Theme" in a minor key to signify a threat to Martha (and by extension Ethan). For the final showdown between the forces of civilization and the savage wilderness, for instance, Barry opts for the "less-is-more" school of scoring. The cue is simply structured, relying upon a relentless four beat pulse in the bass and a tonally ambiguous harmonic progression of I-VI-IV-V,[5] with the opening, potentially heroic, chromatic mediant gesture leading to a striking and somber (read tragic) minor IV chord before returning to the dominant and back to the tonic and a repetition of the same pattern.

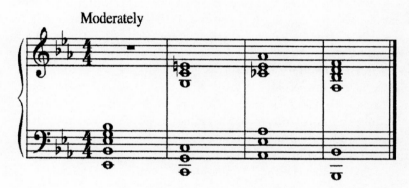

Figure 5.30. Harmonic progression for "Rescue of Dances with Wolves."

Significantly, here the melody is based on the same intervallic pattern of the buffalo hunt cue but, although the harmonic progression begins with what appears to be a root chord in E flat major, the melody outlines a triad (B♭-G-D) which for all intents and purposes sounds very much the minor (G minor to be exact). This tonal ambiguity, however, suits the scene very well by first signifying to the viewer the uncertainty of Dunbar's fate at the hands of the military; the marked variation of the key motif is also effective in signaling a change in the way of life for Dunbar and the Lakota by signifying the imminent threat of civilization. The relentless rhythmic regularity and circumscribed thematic development stand in dramatic counterpoint to the violent action unfolding on the screen. In a thoroughly appropriate reversal for this new Western, instead of the climax being Dunbar's commitment to one side or the other in the central conflict, it is the Lakota who must resort to violence in their commitment to him. In the process they invite the wrath of the American military, who, in the final frames of the film, are inexorably tracking them to what we may assume is the ultimate tragedy of Wounded Knee many years later. The music reminds us that, in keeping with the "new" Western, civilization does indeed stink!

This, however, is not the end. Dunbar's return to the camp brings with it dangers for his new community. They know that now the military will pursue those who have killed American soldiers. In what is probably the final irony in this "new" Western, Dunbar chooses not to stay with his new community but to return to civilization in the hopes of clearing himself and explaining what has happened. In short, he acts nobly, much as we would (should) expect the classic hero of the Western, who is supposed to represent the best of our civilized values — of course, he is actually behaving better than any of his civilized counterparts have (with the possible exception of the officer who gives him Cisco in the opening sequence). The music used to score the final camp sequence largely restates most of the motifs heard earlier, emphasizing the positive qualities of the Sioux and, perhaps as Claudia Gorbman suggests, leaving us with the impression that the Indians are indeed "the traditional Americans" ("Scoring the Indian" 249). I see it a bit differently: subtly — and perhaps perversely — the film finally validates *idealized* white, civilized ways. How? First, with Stands with a Fist's commitment to accompany Dunbar back to civilization and, second, with Dunbar's sacrifice: ostracizing himself from the community he has come to love and defend in the hopes of ultimately saving them. Ironically, like many of the great cowboy heroes of the past, he is ultimately excluded from the very community he has chosen to defend with his skills. Ethan must turn away from the open doorway through which his kith and kin have walked and return to the arid, hostile and lonely landscape that has shaped him. Similarly, Dunbar and his wife ride slowly away, backs to the camera, framed in a high angle, long shot with grey skies above and blowing snow whirling about them. The music underscoring their return to civilization is notable first for the classic lift gesture that begins the theme — a reminder of their heroic sacrifice — and second for the dark harmonic progression that dominates the scene (F minor-C♭ major (B major)-G♭ major-B♭ major-and back to F minor); the darkness is the result of the three successive unmarked major chords, which ever so tentatively seem to have brought the motif out of its initial tragic gesture (F minor) only to be thrust dramatically back to the marked minor and the tragic feeling. The music eventually leads into a restatement of the "John Dunbar Theme," reminding the audience, in the final analysis, that he is the hero of this film.

Conclusion

Like many other genres, the music of the new Western provided (provides?) composers with unique challenges and opportunities. Bruce Broughton's task in *Silverado,* for instance, was to create a score that hearkened to the glory days of the genre but still sounded fresh. Leigh Harline in *Warlock* had to reconcile classic Western topics with narrative elements that seemed to call for more marked and contemporary approaches to scoring (e.g., atonal elements, disjunctive rhythms). Each man's task, however, was somewhat less complicated than Barry's in *Dances with Wolves* because the central conflict they needed to score pitted white authority figures against white resistance to that authority (even though marginalized figures like women and African Americans are swept up in the power struggle). On the one hand, Barry's task was not appreciably different from that of his predecessors: he had to create motifs that aurally situate the hero as a marginalized figure in both communities. Like other cowboy heroes, Dunbar finds himself wholly integrated into neither civilized society nor the wilderness. The difference is in whose values he finally defends — and even here he remains a marginalized figure: he fights the military but he returns to civilization as a matter of honor.

Barry's solution is not necessarily to marginalize the conventions of classic Western scoring. He deftly manages to privilege marked musical elements, signifying the dominance of the Native American and the "exotic" locale while validating a positive role for the white man. However, he also is able to aurally signify the very important shift in the central conflict between the wilderness and civilization that is characteristic of the transformation of the Western genre. Were we to pull back from these two scores under consideration here and try to label and categorize cues on an unmarked-versus-marked scale or continuum, we shouldn't be surprised to see that Steiner's score privileges unmarked elements. Clearly dominant are those topics, gestures and motifs emphasizing standard tonality and conventional musical symbols drawn from the genre itself and from other genres (in regards to the hero, community, etc.). For instance, were we to do a simple count of how many times the "Homecoming Theme" is scored in major versus minor keys, we would find that it is predominantly scored in the major. Barry's score, on the other hand, is more ambiguous. Marked elements are more prominent but they do not necessarily dominate. Often, as I noted above, the presence of the two white leads forces an intrusion of unmarked elements into scenes where Native Americans should dominate, but their music is altered ever so slightly by marked musical elements and gestures that are not neatly pinned to conventional white values. It is significant, however, that the marked elements in the score are more prominent, and that is the key thing. Were we to do a similar count of the "Dunbar" theme, we probably would find that the ratio of unmarked to marked scorings is more evenly balanced. That reveals the central dilemma for the modern day cowboy-military hero: he is an avatar of the advance of civilization, but his quest is fraught with uncertainty. It is as if the score itself is singing *sotto voce* to the hero: civilization stinks; in wildness is the preservation of humankind.

6

From Swan Lake to Synthesizers

The Music of Horror Films

Some viewers claim that they are more disturbed by the "music" of horror movies than the images and that they cover, not their eyes but their ears in the "scary parts."— Carol Clover

Horror, Cultural Myth and Cultural Conflict

As is the case with most genres, the horror film attempts to work out some fundamental cultural conflicts. What those conflicts may be, however, is open to some debate. Stuart Kaminsky, for instance, states: "Horror films are overwhelmingly concerned with the fear of death and the loss of identity in modern society" (101). He goes on to add that "a recurrent motif of horror films is the struggle between good and evil within the individual — the recognition that it is not merely an external manifestation of evil we are seeing in the form of a monster, but something monstrous within ourselves" (104). In short, the major threat is the loss of one's individuality; we can lose it to science run amok, to madness, to our animal instincts, or even by, as Kaminsky notes, "sinking into total conformity" (106).

There are other schools of thought about the kernel conflict in horror, however. One such view sees the kernel conflict centering on the struggle between the normal and the abnormal. Yet another school of thought about the kernel conflict in horror focuses on sex. James Twitchell, for instance, sees horror being focused on sex — and incest in particular (93) — and goes so far as to suggest that the horror of incest may be the ur-myth of horror. Andrew Tudor, on the other hand, paints the conflict in broader strokes: "Though it is true that all horror movies are variations on the 'seek and destroy' pattern — a monstrous threat is introduced into a stable situation; the monster rampages in the face of attempts to combat it; the monster is (perhaps) destroyed and order (perhaps) restored — this general and abstract genre-model can be realized in a variety of ways and located in a range of possible settings" (81). He goes on to detail a number of oppositions that drive the horror narrative, all of which underscore a basic conflict between the known (good) and the unknown (bad), some of which would be:

1. Life vs. death
2. Secular everyday vs. supernatural
3. Human normality vs. alien abnormality
4. Normal sexuality vs. abnormal sexuality

5. Social order vs. social disorder

6. Health vs. disease

Twitchell supports this bipolar opposition when he states: "For if horror depends on occlusion, on not being able to know enough, then what makes the printed page and the flickering film so powerful is that the audience is always kept from complete knowledge, held in an almost hypnogogic state of suspended disbelief, in dreamland, in the dark" (26).

The view that informs my analysis of the music of the horror film, and one which I think subsumes the above mentioned concepts, is this: the individual (that is the individual as person and concept) is involved in a struggle with a monster (another form of the Other) who is simultaneously a by-product of and a threat to social institutions (of medicine, science, family, religion, politics, and education) and/or to the individual's identity and the individual's attempt to be reconciled to those institutions. Berenstein notes that the "sliding of gender traits" attracted her to the genre and led her to study "more closely the lures of fiends that terrorize men and women alike and threaten to dislodge some of American culture's most treasured possessions, including heterosexual matrimony, the law, medicine, and science" (3). In most of the films, a threat to one of the dominant social institutions is part and parcel of the individual's struggle with the monster. We lose ourselves to Dracula if our faith (i.e., religion or church) is too weak, we are threatened by Dr. Frankenstein's Monster because a scientist steps over a line (presuming to be God, or showing hubris), we become cat people because family or marriage is weak, Jason or Freddy (and others of the slasher ilk) are omnipresent (eternal!) threats because of the dual failure of the health professions, schools, and family. Like science fiction, the alien Other constantly threatens us; in science fiction, the threat is clearly exterior (or most often clearly exterior), in horror the threat is interior and, as suggested by Kaminsky, we must entertain the notion that we ourselves are the threat, and, like Nathaniel Hawthorne's Young Goodman Brown, that we ourselves are "the chief horror of the scene."

As we saw in science-fiction films, composers draw upon certain topics and gestures to underscore the antinomian nature of the social conflicts outlined above. Consequently, we should expect to encounter a duality in compositional decisions: on the one hand, there must be music to underscore the normal, stable or functional and, on the other hand, there must be musical motifs that signify the abnormal, unstable or dysfunctional. The drama of this kernel structure is enacted, moreover, by simple *dramatis personae*: monsters, heroes and victims, the three character groups that dominate most of the categories of horror films. The transformation of horror over the decades must then be studied in light of the different categories of films. Let us look briefly at some of the different critical categorizations of horror films so we have the necessary historico-cultural framework for generic transformation.

Andrew Tudor classifies the films by type and by narrative paradigm; his typology is defined by binary oppositions and is as follows:

- Supernatural vs. Secular
- External vs. Internal
- Autonomous vs. Dependent

His narrative paradigms, as one will see, are closely related to his typology:

- Knowledge narrative; this paradigm centers on the world of science, technology and knowledge and would include "mad scientist" films and those of the Frankenstein ilk (83–84).

- Invasion narrative; this paradigm seemingly grows out of the external vs. internal typology and centers on not only the threats from outer space but those which assume a more internal "invasion" as in the case of Dracula or *The Exorcist* (1974). They can be closed, in which the monster is destroyed and stability is restored, or they can be open, where the horror continues (90–91).
- Metamorphosis narrative; this paradigm reflects the autonomy vs. dependence struggle and centers on the transformation of the human into a monster, as in *Halloween* (1978), *Dr. Jekyll and Mr. Hyde*, or *The Night of the Living Dead* (1968).

In yet another vision of the genre, James Twitchell (59–60) divides the films into the following categories, which could easily be grouped into many of the same categories Tudor outlined above:

- Science-fiction horror (*The Fly*, 1958)
- Outer space horror (*The Thing*, 1951)
- Up-from-below horror (*The Creature from the Black Lagoon*, 1954)
- Horror of the neurotic woman (*Hush, Hush Sweet Charlotte*, 1965)
- Horror of the neurotic man (*Psycho*, 1960)
- Horror of neurotic children (*Bad Seed*, 1956)
- Horror of possession from without (*Invasion of the Body Snatchers*, 1956)
- Horror of possession from within (*The Exorcist*)
- Natural horrors (*Tarantula*, 1955)
- Cataclysms (*Earthquake*, 1974)

To these relatively conventional categories we can add the following three subgenres identified by Rhona Berenstein (10):

- "mad-doctor movies";
- "hypnosis films"; this includes films about vampires, mummies, and zombies;
- "jungle horror pictures."

Although not explicitly mentioned above, we also have the relatively recent phenomenon of the "splatter" film or what Ryan and Kellner call "slash and gash" films. The authors state that *Halloween* (1978) established "the template for the series: Young teens, especially girls, are show engaging in 'immoral' activities like sex and drugs. They are killed" (191). And according to John McCarthy, these films also possess the following characteristics: they 1) "present gore in a 'gleefully extended form' giving the audience a good look at the anatomically realistic effects of violence; 2) seek to mortify the audience rather than to scare them or keep them in suspense, and 3) present mutilation as the only message of these 'often illogical and inconsistent films'" (qtd. in Dika 11). From the standpoint of the kernel conflict and the musical elements that will be used to underscore the conflict, we need to be mindful of what Tania Modleski sees as the "increasingly open-ended" tendency of the films, that they "often delight in thwarting the audiences' expectations of closure" ("The Terror of Pleasure" 769). Another important characteristic of the splatter film is that, as Stuart Kaminsky notes, it is actually part of a trend beginning already back in the 1970s in which the films are "more pessimistic, more horribly confident that the dark side of man's nature will triumph, that our worst fears must be faced, and that the evil within us simply cannot be destroyed or controlled" (108).

The primary reason for mentioning the categories or sub-genres is that they are in some instances reflective of the transformational genre; consequently, we should also expect corresponding shifts in approaches to scoring within the sub-genres, at least in some small details. This, in turn, prompts us to wonder if, as in other genres, there is a corpus of relatively stable musical gestures and topics that function affectively within the conventions of the genre and of scoring itself or if generic diversity leads to a corresponding diffusion of motivic ideas. I believe that if we look across the various typologies, we see common threads in the generic conventions, which in turn, force composers into relying upon a conventional body of topics and gestures. For instance, there will always be a monster and the composer will always have to find appropriate musical analogues to underscore its actions. Second, at the heart of the genre's mythology is the tension between the threat to and the quest for (or perhaps need for is the better expression here) normalcy in everyday life and stability within our social institutions. Whether the stability is threatened and revalidated by filmmaker and composer or threatened and left in a dysfunctional state is a "transformational" issue to be worked out between director and composer.

Before looking at the conventions of the genre, I think it is important to address the issues of "effect" in horror, that is the psychological effect on the audience. Of course, in each genre the composer works toward using music to engender some emotional and, hopefully, palpable reactions to the visuals on the screen. In the Western, for instance, filmmaker and composer may attempt to take our breath away with the topography of the land, evoke an admiration for the cowboy hero or a sense of revulsion for the savage, etc. The composer of the horror film must sustain the elements of suspense and, if you will, revulsion, in a more sustained fashion. Carol Clover has written that "much of the art of horror lies in catching the spectatorial eye unawares — penetrating it before it has a chance to close its lid" (202). James Twitchell, similarly, finds the key to the effect of horror in the idea of helplessness. In analyzing Hogarth's "Gin Lane" (1751) he finds the key to horror in the "look on that toppling baby's face — a look so central to horror — the look of complete helplessness.... That wide-eyed, open-mouthed look is on the face of every victim in every gothic novel and horror film" (30). The composer's job is to complement that spirit of helplessness, to find the right musical topics and gestures that allow the camera to catch the "spectatorial eye unawares." We can perhaps generalize here and say that the composer's task is to suspend the audience's feelings, make them experience, like Emily Dickinson looking at a snake, "a tighter breathing/And Zero at the Bone." This state, however, is evanescent: we are fooled into not shutting our eyes in anticipation of the "horror," thus making all the more effective the moment when visually we must confront it — that moment when we feebly shut our eyes or watch helplessly. Perhaps we could say it is the composer's job to create the fear and the filmmaker's to render or reveal the horror.

Main Title Music

An intriguing challenge would be to try to find the threads of commonality in main titles, starting with the use of Tchaikovsky's music from *Swan Lake* for *Dracula* in 1931 and continuing up to the titles of present day slasher films. One thread would be the composer's efforts at establishing mood and tension in the music to create fear or at least a sense of foreboding. Another thread would be the domination of marked elements in the scoring. As with title music for the other genres, horror movie title music creates a mood, insinuating the viewer into this world where the normal and abnormal, the secular and the scientific, and the ordered versus the disordered collide. Tension is usually signaled, as it is with science fiction, by contrasts in volume and timbre and by compositional techniques that break with the conventions we associate with standard scoring topics and gestures in most genres and stress the marked and more modern schools of composition. Richard Bush, in his notes to the *The Bride of Frankenstein* soundtrack recording, observes that Franz Waxman relied a lot on "whole tone scales for the majority of cues" in the film; he goes on to add that they are characterized by a "'restless' feeling." We will also find composers relying upon timbral contrast and indeterminacy in melodic and harmonic structure in main-title music and in other cues as well. Seldom in horror will you find main titles that feature the clearly defined melodic contours of, let us say, "Tara's Theme" from *Gone with the Wind*, or the gentle rolling rhythms and elegant melodic line of Victor Young's main title for *Shane*. What, then, will one encounter in this main-title music?

One of the most common devices used by composers in horror and science fiction is the creation of tension and foreboding through timbral and motivic contrast. In the first instance, one may recall a main title that began with a tremolo in the high strings, and supported by a dissonant chord in the brass or by a meandering melody in the low brass or strings. In the second instance, composers create melodic lines consisting of tropes and seemingly unfocused gestures: three notes will outline an intervallic leap in the violins only to be followed by a stepwise pattern in the low strings or brass that seems to bear little relation to the initial motif; this might then be followed by a sustained dissonant chord shared by strings and brass while an ominous irregular rhythm is established by tympani. A third variation is one in which an ostinato (one could characterize it here ominously as a stalking topic or more benignly as a walking topic) is established — melodic range seems to be a secondary consideration — and then a theme, often of disjunctive character, is presented contrapuntally. This strategy emblematically conveys the spine of the horror film: the common, everyday routine is disrupted or is brought into uneasy relief by the presence of the disjunctive rhythms and dissonances in the melodic line and asymmetrical harmonic progressions. John Carpenter's theme for *Halloween* is an example of this technique. The ostinato pattern in F♯ (*Swan Lake* is never far away) minor carried by the piano in the upper registers that outlines an augmented fifth is countered by a simple three-note motif prominently featuring a minor third resolving to what a appears to be a major third. However, the ostinato pattern shifts down a half step to F major, consequently denying us a consonant resolution to a major third. The interval is instead a second, creating a dissonance and a sense of disequilibrium.

Figure 6.1. Main title, *Halloween*.

Some main titles, like those of Franz Waxman for *The Bride of Frankenstein*, will also announce a theme with a conventionally harmonized melodic line, this, apparently, to remind the viewer that the ordinary, the normal, is also part of this world. However, even in this example the music, which is the "Bride's Music," has an exotic, almost non–Western feel to it (some listeners will notice a similarity to Richard Rodgers's "Bali Hai").

Figure 6.2. "Bride," *The Bride of Frankenstein.*

Ironically, this is just the kind of theme we might associate with science fiction some twenty years later. In short, a common strategy is to wed an ambiguous tonal center to an equally ambiguous or disorienting thematic structure that deconstructs the anticipated logical structure the audience might expect from a conventional main title. The sense of disorientation, unease and/or fear then is established as the titles roll. However, should the composer choose to go the "tonal" route, relying upon a classically structured theme with a clearly defined tonal center and architectonically structured arrangement of motifs, we find a privileging of marked elements such as minor harmonies and melodies scored for lower strings or brass as well as more rhythmic complexity or combinations of all these elements. Patrick Doyle's recent score for *Mary Shelley's Frankenstein* (1994) features just such a strategy.

Setting

Like other elements of the horror film, the setting complements the oppositional or binary lines of the kernel conflict. We have the general setting of the film: the small town, turn-of-the-century London, Castle Frankenstein, Transylvania and so forth. Then there is a secondary setting, a smaller site where the evil flourishes (think of Henry Jekyll's lovely London flat which, significantly, houses the downstairs lab where Hyde is brought into being). Similarly, although reared in upper class wealth and the comfort of Castle Frankenstein, Henry removes himself to a dismal, remote tower to conduct his experiments. In later installments his nefarious lab may be housed in the bowels of Castle Frankenstein. Although Lugosi's Dracula will be preying upon Londoners, he takes up residence, coffins, brides and all, at Carfax Abbey in Essex.

Consequently, the music written to establish moods for the settings will also fall into two fairly conventional camps, exploiting unmarked and marked elements accordingly. The general setting, be it countryside, city, house, or summer camp, will normally feature tonal music befitting time and place, or it will feature diegetic music that communicates a sense of time and place. Hans Salter's "Frankenstein's Castle" from *The Ghost of Frankenstein* completely belies the horror that will emanate from that self-same setting. It is bucolic and almost lullaby-like in its gentleness, signifying the warm comforts of home and family.

Figure 6.3. "Frankenstein's Castle."

Even here, however, the horror is anticipated in the gestural sighing or tragic figures: for every upward leap there is a corresponding downward leap, the overall impression being one of descent rather than ascent, tragedy rather than victory. In more recent films, a radio in the background playing easy listening or light rock music signifies parental domain and authority; if we should hear a radio or stereo blasting rock, it may in actuality be an ironic comment: listening to the dangerous sounds of thrash metal anticipates immersion into a dangerous world, as if to say, the kids don't realize what evil forces lie out there ready to ensnare them. This last perfectly describes the scene from *Nightmare on Elm Street* where Nancy (Heather Langenkamp), Tina (Amanda Wyss), and Glen (Johnny Depp) are listening to hard rock music on the radio just prior to Tina's "visit" from her boyfriend, Rod, and a more terrifying subsequent visit from Freddy Krueger. The music foreshadows the danger that is imminent in the world of the teenager on Elm Street.

The music associated with the "site of evil" (for lack of better term) will, in contrast, exploit the marked elements of atonality and dissonance to communicate that sense of evil. Many of the same conventions that dominate the main-title music surface in creating atmosphere in setting. A camera panning the inside of a darkened laboratory or a misty wood on the night of the full moon will be accompanied by the suspense topic, the seemingly ever-present tremolo in the violins coupled with marked and disjunctive rhythms in low strings or brass. Visually, we are not given a lot of information, although we may have a sense of some danger lurking because of prior action in the film, and so it is left to the music to supply plenitude to the scene, to anticipate the horror and aurally generate fear and tension. In short, we will be feeling something about what might happen well in advance of something actually happening on the screen. One very common device used to generate this feeling is to employ the monster's music in scenes where the secondary site predominates, thus aurally correlating architecture with character and mood with conflict.

The Monster

One of the wonderful ironies of the horror film is that we largely go to see the monster. Where the alien Other in any other genre — with the possible exception of science fiction — functions in largely a supporting role or may serve as a foil for the virtues of the hero, in the horror film, the monster is front and center. It is all about him/her/it! Of course, even using the term monster immediately calls forth qualifiers in light of transformations in the genre over the last thirty to forty years. On the surface, Anthony Perkins's character in *Psycho* (1960) or even Jason in the *Halloween* series appear to share little kinship with Karloff's Monster, Lugosi's Dracula, or Chaney's Wolfman, but in the end their actions, their aberration from those norms alluded to earlier, sufficiently qualify them for monster status.

From the silent film creations of Lon Chaney, Sr., to the Freddy Krueger of Robert Englund, most great movie monsters share some similar characteristics: essentially, they represent an aberration from the norms and values of civilized society, resulting in their being physically deformed, or psychologically damaged; or they may diverge from their gender roles (Perkins dressing like Mother), or they may diverge from social roles — scientists, like the protagonist of *The Fly* (1958) who, in a later manifestation of the Frankenstein syndrome, pushes too far outside the bounds of "good" science and becomes, writ large, one of nature's more disgusting insects. Freddy Krueger transforms the normally harmless character of the school janitor into a living, breathing nightmare whose connection to the kids in his school has gone beyond maintenance of their social playground to a literal and lethal invasion of their homes and psyches.

Monsters can also be seen as a byproduct of the failure of certain social institutions. These failures, it must be noted, are from a distinctly American perspective: Frankenstein's Monster is the embodiment of the failure of science and education, the lesson being that we must respect the limitations of each or else; Dracula signifies the failure of politics, especially Old World (and in particular eastern European, c. 1897) aristocratic politics, and he may also possibly signify the failure of religion. Stuart Kaminsky has, in fact, noted that such villains represent "corruption in European society" (108). The Mummy can also be seen as a reflection of the failure of politics and power: governments cannot oppress human emotion and feeling; to do so is to unleash a monster on future generations. The Mummy may also be seen to be an indictment of modern science: some mysteries of life should perhaps remain undisturbed; to disturb history — or maybe more simply to just disturb the dead — is to invite monsters into our lives. Similarly, the Wolfman is the embodiment of the failure of human reason to control the animal in us and is a reminder of how imminent the corrupting influence of instinct is within us — that even the pure of heart may not be exempt from the curse of the werewolf. Humorously, I suppose, we might recall here the impact of having Freud's theories unleashed on the youth of the 1920s, turning them from respectable avatars of Victorian manners and morals into hip-flask toting party animals frequenting speakeasies and shocking Mom and Dad with the Charleston and the Black Bottom! Church, state and family were powerless in the face of this "horror."

Recent splatter films suggest that the monsters are the result of the failures of schools, family, marriage, etc. In these films, as Vera Dika notes, the killer

> is usually socially inept, or at least frozen at an earlier stage of development, one in which the overvaluation of a family ties dominates his/her psychology. For this reason the opposition *life/death* best separates the young community from the killer, but in a dynamic way, where life is meant to encompass the young community's acceptable social practice (both sexual and casual) as well as their physical attractiveness and perfection, and "death" is the simultaneous, actively opposing force to integrity [58].

Similarly, Tony Williams states: "Unlike Elm Street parents he [Freddy] can discipline and definitively punish his teenage victims" (229). One of the most interesting transformations in horror is the phenomenon of the teen protagonist. One will be hard pressed to find teens battling the forces of evil in the '30s and '40s Universal productions and the Hammer films of the '50s and '60s.

The seeming immortality of the monster is a dominant characteristic and one that for which composers need to find appropriate aural analogues. One of the very frightening aspects of monsters in horror films is that they appear nearly impossible to kill, defying the laws of nature, man and God. Not being subject to the same laws of life and death that we are means that all earthly attempts to destroy them are, moreover, futile and at times disturbingly absurd. Stuart Kaminsky notes that regardless of disease, death, and mortality, "the horror films share a common concern with man's fear of the unknown" (104). The monster's immortality is emblematic of that fear: it is seemingly beyond comprehension (read reason) and efficacious action and, consequently, is an unsettling and frightening phenomenon for the spectator. Another key element in the monster's immortality as it relates to the aberration of normality is that, as Kaminsky notes, "the curse of immortality is loss of feeling, being equated with the uncontrolled animal, at one extreme (*The Wolf Man, King Kong, Cat People*), or the mindless continuum of the living dead or loss of identity, at the other (*Invasion of the Body Snatchers, White Zombie, Night of the Living Dead, The Mephisto Waltz, The Possession of Joel Delaney*)" (102). As one can see, the struggle between mortality and immortality gives rise to some interesting thematic variations. We have what Stuart Kaminsky calls "the parasite theme, of living off others" that he sees as being related to the "horror of disease and its relationship to mortality" (102). The parasitic subtext provides us with a whole new dimension of existential dread as the monster, in his need to feed off of the living, actually moves toward some sort of ultimate state of alienation because of the taboos implied in the behavior. In the process we come face to face with the horror of alienation, of being cut off from all those institutions

Frankenstein. **Music for the Monster reinforces the audience's fear that the Monster may be indestructible.**

that help define us as human beings ("Why, it's not human!") and as civilized human beings. As Kaminsky has observed, immortality for some "was clearly a curse," and the price of that immortality is "alienation from the human world" (101). We might be reminded here of some of the Dracula characters who will on occasion express a desire to be "truly dead." The fear is intensified by the fact that often the monster seems to thrive, as Kaminsky observes, on destroying others so it may go on living (102). In each case, the monster threatens our humanity by not only posing a threat to our physical well-being but also by threatening the delicate balance between emotion and reason.

As I stated earlier, the music of horror films privileges marked elements. Consequently, one of the key features in the monster's music, as it was with the alien from outer space, is dissonance, leading composers invariably to create melodies that exploit atonal elements, including dramatic and unpredictable intervallic leaps and meandering melodies that emphasize minor seconds and tritones. Harmonically, one can expect loud, closed, crashing chords that prominently feature minor seconds and tritones. Franz Waxman's "monster" cue from *The Bride of Frankenstein* (1935) succinctly features all these elements:

Figure 6.4. "Monster," *The Bride of Frankenstein.*

One rather interesting motif we find in films of the two great classic horror periods is a descending (or alternately descending and ascending) three-note pattern, sounded predominantly in lower registers to signify the monster. It makes an appearance in the Universal Frankenstein films, an invention of either Hans Salter or Frank Skinner, and then in Hammer's *The Curse of Frankenstein* (1957). Skinner or Salter in a sense created the archetype with the scores they did for Universal in the late 1930s and early 1940s with motifs like this one from *The Wolf Man* (1941):

Figure 6.5. "Wolf Man Revived," *House of Frankenstein.*

The cue's effectiveness is attributable to the contrapuntal interplay of the gestures in the motif: on the one hand, we sense the tragic downward movement in the repetition of the three note figure; on the other hand, tension is created by having the figure repeated on an ascending chromatic scale. It is as though two musical impulses are warring, probably much like the impulses in the psyche of the monster. Similarly, in the Hammer films, Larson states: "Opening with a slow, plodding, three-note descending-then-ascending theme, [James] Bernard captures a darkly evil-sounding motif in low register. It's not a melody, but a progression of relentless dark chords suggesting terrible evil, their first 3 downward notes dominating the theme and suggestive of the syllables *FRANK-en-steinnn*" (Larson 21).

Figure 6.6. "Frankenstein."

What of the other great screen monster: Dracula? Hearkening to the archetypes in the genre, either consciously or subliminally, Bernard also relied upon a three note motif for the Dracula films he scored. Randall Larson notes that "as he did with *Curse of Frankenstein*, Bernard derived his main theme for *Horror of Dracula* from the three syllables of the word *Dracula*" (22). The motif (see m.3–4 of figure 6.8), a striking downward octave leap, preceded by variously a stepwise four note motif or a three note motif, features strong use of brass and low strings and suggests a kind of evil finality as though the viewer must submit to the power of the prince of the undead. There is also the potential in the motif for another referent: the use of a rhythmic, pounding gesture can signify a couple of different ideas, depending upon interpretants, most notably the plodding, relentless stalking topic of the monster and, conversely — and ironically — the act of driving the stake into the vampire's heart and thereby bringing an end to his evil and restoring order. The motif then signifies the life force and the seeds of destruction in the monster and simultaneously reminds us of the monster's tragic fate: he is doomed to live and he is doomed to die.

Another musical element associated with the monster is the privileging of dynamics in attack sequences, especially the crescendo from moderately loud to almost deafening and the use of crashing dissonances. Musical phrases for the monster are constructed out of simple materials and are given form largely through scalar sequences (either chromatically ascending or descending) that are accompanied by a corresponding rise in dynamic levels and generally punctuated by dissonant closed chords, especially at the moment of attack (or destruction).

Figure 6.7. Monster stalking music.

We see here the composer building suspense and impending horror through a stepwise ascending sequence complemented by increasing loudness in the orchestra. Similarly, Randall Larson describes a sequence from *Dracula, Prince of Darkness* (1965) that relies upon the same conventions:

> When Dracula vampirically seduces the woman, the Dracula theme starts out quietly as he slowly approaches her, all strings over ominous tympani rolls, growing in power and urgency and finally overcome by a climax of blaring trumpets as Dracula bites the woman's neck. Bernard continually demonstrates his penchant for these immensely dramatic and powerful musical moments, the orchestra surging slowly and inexorably into huge and dynamic crescendos, soft fluid surges of rhythm, mingling low, rolling waves of brass and strings with higher, urgent violin figures, all building toward a climactic dissonance [24].

As I stated at the outset, the monster's music is marked — in both musical and narrative terms — to remind us of his otherness and his threat to our humanity.

Heroes and Victims

One could, I suppose, easily isolate these two conventional character groups, but the more one focuses on the scores in the films the more one will be frustrated in any attempt to delineate clear musical motifs that signify the two groups. Andrew Tudor actually opts for the terms *experts* or *pursuers* rather than *hero* in his discussion of the genre. He notes that "indeed, the gap between 'pursuers' and 'victims' has been progressively eroded as the genre has developed" (22). Why? Because more often than not the hero can be a victim and vice-versa. Take one of the archetypes, Dr. Van Helsing. Ostensibly he is brought in to deal with the evil of Dracula; he alone seems to have some insight into the workings of the monster and, perhaps, some insight into how to rid society of the evil. For all his knowledge and skill in dealing with the monster (the use of crucifixes, mirrors, wolf's bane and the like), there are, however, a few moments where his heroic status is jeopardized. For instance, in the 1931 film, Van Helsing (Edward Van Sloan) confronts and exposes Dracula, informing the monster that he knows all about him, but Dracula is undaunted and eventually extends his claw-like hand and commands him to "Come here!" Van Helsing appears temporarily hypnotized and we see him waver ever so slightly toward the monster. Only through an incredible act of will does he pull himself back from the precipice and the inevitable neck punctures that will condemn to him life (death?) among the undead. The one distinction we can perhaps make, at least in the classic horror film, is that the hero will most often be a man, while the victims are women.

Dracula. Van Helsing and Dracula in a battle of wills and good and evil.

As to the character of the hero — be it man or woman — we can identify some dominant characteristics. Andrew Tudor notes that experts have some "capacity for autonomous action" (113). This quality would seem to be emblematic of positive aspects of Western society and, in a very conservative sense, human nature: we as individuals are supposed to be served by institutions dedicated to ensuring our freedom and autonomy. The hero, then, will defend our freedom and autonomy and not jeopardize those values through aberrant behavior. The monster is a threat to those values, compelling people to lock their doors, not to go out at night, to stay away from site X, and to adopt other forms of restrictive behaviors. The hero may as well be a defender of the moral values of the dominant culture, a person, according to Stuart Kaminsky, who may be "a religious figure, also from the old world" (108). It goes without saying that this hero is not just a representative of the dominant culture but an exemplar of that world and, in particular, of the very institution who has, either through evil or accident, spawned the threat, e.g., a doctor who values the Hippocratic oath, a scientist who understand the limits of science, a person of the cloth whose faith is unassailable, or city officials who generally have the good of the community in mind and not just their own political ambitions. One might also expect the person to be self-sacrificing; Kaminsky states, "In some films, the protagonist is permitted the dignity of dying, but only after he makes a sacrifice of himself for others, by giving up his life for the future because he has faith in the future" (110). A notable example of this is the death of the two exorcists (Max Von Sydow and Jason Miller) in William Friedkin's *The Exorcist* (1973).

One of the chief characteristics of the horror film hero is perhaps the quality of fallibility. Only in the rarest of cases will one find a superhero in the horror film. The reason is quite simple: the monster is the one superhuman presence in the films. Conversely, then, heroes will be drawn from the ranks of ordinary citizens or, as suggested above, will be exemplars of the various institutions that are under assault by the monster. But what links these hero figures is that they will be subject — some might say victimized — by their human weaknesses. How they respond to their all-too-human fallibility will be the measure of their heroism. In some of the classic horror movies they actually may be moved by pity in their dealings with the monster: they know the creature is evil but they also know that it may be a victim of evil, not inherently evil but a byproduct or avatar of some sort of social evil. It is for that reason that the killing of the Wolfman, for instance, is as much an act of mercy as it is an act of survival: poor Larry Talbot, who was basically pure of heart, just happened to have been bitten, and now he must be killed to be released from the agonizing transformation brought on by the appearance of the full moon.

Turning briefly to recent hero figures, we can observe some subtle changes taking place. Tudor and Kaminsky in their early studies of the genre anticipated the current trend, especially as exemplified in the slasher film. Kaminsky, for instance, notes that the hero's sacrifice may bring positive results, but he added that in some films the hero's death is "fruitless" (110). This, indeed, may summarize perfectly the efforts of the hero in horror since the 1980s. Rhona Berenstein suggests that many of the recent heroes are less than heroic, and, in fact, may be feckless: "over and over again heroes fail to dispatch the fiend — leaving that task to some other character — and are attacked and subdued by a creature.... Surprising as it may seem, given the genre's reputation, most of classic horror's heroes are feminized men" (5). Of course in the more recent "slash and gash" films we have the female hero, a character who at once embodies both victimhood and heroism. Tania Modleski states: "Importantly, in many of the films the female is attacked not only because, as has often been claimed, she embodies sexual pleasure, but also because she represents a great many aspects of the specious good — just as the babysitter, for example, quite literally represents female authority" (772). The lines between the hero as victim and the hero of efficacious agency become even more blurred. This heroic dilemma goes to the heart of the modern horror film, the postmodern condition cited by Paul Budra that the "'threat in postmodern horror ... is not the lurker on the threshold, but the very absence of thresholds'" (qtd. in Harris 98). The victories seem at best tentative, but more often than not there is no victory. The films may contain a character who stands at the center of the pursuit and destruction of the monster, and that person may die in the conflict, leaving it to someone else — and probably in a sequel — to take up the fight and hopefully triumph. And indeed this seems to be the most recent trend as evidenced in the movies of the *Scream* (1996) generation where the "Final Girl" emerges at the end more classically heroic than her 1970s and 1980s forebears. Valerie Wee writes: "In these early slasher films, female heroism is defined more in terms of the Final Girl's ability to survive and escape numerous attacks than in her ability to triumph independently over her tormentor(s). In the instances in which the female actually does triumph over her persecutors, Clover points out, that the victory comes at a price" (58). However, that has changed somewhat in the 1990s and 2000s. Wee observes that there is a "new treatment of the Final Girls, who emerge as women, are not defeated, do not die, and most important, continue to persevere against the various bogeymen/monsters that they encounter in their lives as depicted by each sequel" (59).

Finally, we should also mention those films that rely upon the collective-hero phenomenon, where it takes a group to (hopefully!) overcome evil. In *The Exorcist* (1974), for instance, the exorcism is only possible because of the cooperative efforts of the two priests. In some cases, the music may rely upon classic heroic topics or gestures, as in *The Vampire Lovers* (1970), where, as Randall Larson notes, a "Gregorian-like chant" theme is used to underscore the pursuit and destruction of the vampires: "Here it takes on almost heroic proportions as it accompanies the torch-bearing crusaders on their godly mission against evil" (108). Musically, however, if we go looking for classic heroic topics like those in other genres, we are bound to be disappointed. There are those, like the abovementioned *The Vampire Lovers*, that evoke the heroic gestures of other, but in the case of *The Bride of Frankenstein*, the effect is almost comedic because nothing up to this point has prepared us for the heroically musical flourishes so reminiscent of the music of the swashbucklers and other adventure movies of the period. The gesture seems larger than the action, and in fact is, as the pursuit degenerates into quasi-slapstick and ultimately does not succeed in its mission to rid the community of the monster. That we would not have the larger than life topics and gestures should not be surprising. The horror film trades on vicitimization, including the vicitimization of the hero. Consequently, the music associated with societal forces in conflict with the monster would stress more unmarked elements and gestures that signify innocence and, possibly, goodness. The motif "Family Theme" from Jerry Goldsmith's score for *The Omen* (1976) is a good example of scoring that correlates innocence and goodness with unmarked elements:

Figures 6.8. "Family Theme, *The Omen* (Darby and DuBois 507).

The use of sixths and thirds exploits the archetypal "feminine" significations with the third and lends a gentleness and wistful innocence to this simple theme. Placed in contrast to the unmarked elements in the remainder of the score, it is a reminder of the family's role as not only defender of domestic virtues and values but also of their precarious position as protectors of those selfsame virtues and values.

Another type of theme that is crucial to the monster-victim dichotomy is the love theme for the hero and heroine (although some may argue that the designation heroine is problematic because, more often than not, she will be the archetypal victim). Here we can expect the classic gestures to emerge in archetypally transgeneric fashion. Sweeping melodic lines, poignant gestures, classic romantic harmonies, and soothing doses of sentimentality are effective analogues for the innocence and optimism of the lovers.

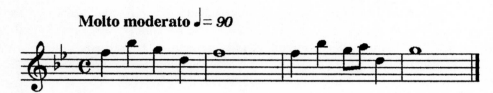

Figure 6.9. "Romance: Young Love," *Taste the Blood of Dracula.*

In keeping with generic scoring practices, however, the horror film score needs to aurally articulate the basic conflict in the film and situate the hero in relation to monster. As is the case with most other genres, the gestures and topics associated with the hero feature unmarked musical elements. Conventionality must predominate in the face of aberration and/or dysfunction. A filmmaker may opt for a strategy that minimizes the underscoring for the hero, and by extension draws more attention to the monster's threat, but more often than not the composer will provide the hero and the community with music. About the only generalization one might be able to make about the music for hero figures is that it is relatively unobtrusive. Randall Larson makes an interesting observation about such a motif and the way it is handled in one of the Dracula series films:

> Bernard balances the *DRAC-u-la* theme, which represents vampiric evil, with an emotionally weaker motif representing Van Helsing and the "good" people on which Dracula preys. This second motif, a five-note theme for strings, is given many more variations than the vampire's theme, which remains relatively unchanged (as does the malevolent vampire) throughout most of the film. The Good motif is continually assaulted by the vicious Dracula theme, dominated in counterpoint and trampled upon by the pervasive vampire music [23].

One will find this convention cropping up in more than just the Hammer films. One of the most convincing ways to suggest the power of the monster is by having a theme associated with a strong character consistently being altered in the course of the film. We have, of course, seen this strategy in other genres where the hero's music will be rescored in a minor key to signify a threat to his values or an alteration in his values. In such cases, the common strategy is to alter harmonies, incorporating more dissonance or shifts in key (e.g., major to minor, using polychords). In classic horror films, the triumph of the hero will be signaled by the return of the motif to its home key — generally a major key, we should add — and it will often be scored in a fashion that communicates a sense of strength, hope and finality. In the transformational genre, we can also expect composers to take such strategies and patterns of expectation and subvert or deconstruct them to leave the filmgoer with a sense of weakness, insecurity, and ambiguity.

In Depth: The Horror of Dracula *(1958) and* Nightmare on Elm Street *(1984)*

The films *The Horror of Dracula* and *Nightmare on Elm Street*, like others in the genre, contribute to the mythology of our modern condition by exploiting cultural, ideological, and intellectual dichotomies or antinomies: the normal vs. the abnormal; the natural vs. the unnatural; the living vs. dead; science vs. superstition; rationality vs. emotion (or possibly sexuality). True to the nature of the transformational genre the resolution of the conflict itself becomes conflicted over the years with doubt reigning over certainty and flux triumphing over, well, resolution. The struggle in all the films, moreover, is complex; and what is striking about it — and this holds true for many of the genres — is the level of violence that is demanded to resolve the conflict. This should not be surprising. A great deal is at stake. The monster's threat is a threat to body and soul and mind. There is in fact a dual threat centering on possession and destruction: first, there is the threat that the monster will possess us and rob us, while living, of some portion of our humanity, and, second, there is the threat that then he will destroy us — or that the possession is but a preface to destruction. Poe's tale "Fall of the House of Usher" offers us an interesting template: if Roderick is symbolic of the mind and the House symbolic of the body, then it follows that if the mind goes the body will follow, which is exactly how Poe structures the narrative. Similarly, in the *Horror of Dracula*, the count seduces or hypnotizes his victims, bites them, and relegates them to an eternal walking death, devoid of peace and satisfaction. In *Nightmare on Elm Street*, on the other hand, Freddy controls the dreams — ironically, something the kids (or any of us) can't really control; once he is in their dreams (the subconscious or unconscious, if you like) then he can destroy the body and often in the most violent manner. Death is the ultimate horror: if you lose your soul, or lose your identity, then you lose your life. In spite of their similarities, these two tales of the undead reveal some marked differences, and the music of each provides us with some significant insights into the transformational genre.

Main Title

The main title of *Horror of Dracula* suggests that violence is going to play an important role in the film. The centrality of the monster to the myth is made manifest by the presence of the Dracula theme in the main title. The main titles begins with a low angle shot of a statue of a bird of prey — a bird with some very dragon-like features — against a blue sky on the right and a portion of a castle in the background on the left; as the music plays, the camera moves to the right until we see the castle fully in the background. Then the camera pans left and downward, finally focusing on the door to Dracula's crypt. A threatening atmosphere of violence is achieved through a simple three note slashing or perhaps hammering gesture (m.3-4) initiated by an octave drop that dominates the main title — the notes serving as an aural analogue for *Drac-u-la*. The dramatic octave leap downward and the "impact" of the 16th and the half note, resolving to the tritone harmony that ends the motif, portend the violent threat of Dracula (Christopher Lee).

Figure 6.10. Main title, *The Horror of Dracula*.

This may be one of the most overtly violent main titles in all of filmed horror. But what of the other dimension of this monster, the subtler, more seductive threat posed by this aristocratic predator who would possess us before destroying us? Although the insistent and plodding quarter note rhythm in the bass and percussion that supports the motif could be read as signifying the count's relentless, inexorable pursuit of his victims, I believe it could also signify the Count's Old World conservatism, a sort of perversion of a stately court march or anthemic rhythm. This is countered by the more melodically disjunctive elements in the brass and strings, where Bernard scores a theme that, by virtue of it alternating time signatures, resists regularity and valorizes markedness and otherness. This rhythmic dislocation is a nice metaphor for the count: the regularity of the bass line correlates to his stately title and class; the rhythmic irregularity and violent downward gestures are an analogue for his threat to the very civilized values of which he should indeed be an exemplar.

Bernstein's main title for *Nightmare on Elm Street* is quite different. The stress here is almost totally on atmosphere as opposed to anticipating the violence that is endemic to Freddy's clashes with the kids, even though it will figure in the attacks forthcoming in the film. It also hard to characterize it as Freddy's (Robert Englund) theme in same way the main title for *Horror of Dracula* is the Count's leitmotif. The theme, however, is structurally aligned to the basic conflict in the film, because it is used to anticipate attacks and to create tension. It is this theme that Bernstein is I believe referring to when he states:

> There were a lot of little tricks in *Nightmare on Elm Street*. I had a theme and also a sub-theme (or a counter-theme), and one was evocative of this dream villain that appears in the dreams of these teenagers, and I could bring that sound in. It wasn't as obvious as the shark sound in *Jaws*. Therefore, it was quite, "Oh-oh, here comes Freddie." But there was a sense of being able to somewhat manipulate the audience into feeling his presence when he wasn't on the screen — to indicate his imminent arrival [qtd. in Karlin and Wright, *On the Track* 184–185].

Consequently, hearing the theme when Freddy is not in the scene, in essence places Freddy in the scene and fills that moment with foreboding — as Clover suggests, one has a tendency at these moments not to close one's eyes but to stop one's ears. And it is in this sense that the two main titles function quite similarly: they are both used to underscore the threat of the attack. Where they differ is, significantly, that Bernard's theme speaks to the simultaneous finality of the monster's attack and his own tragic fate; Bernstein's, on the other hand, relies upon the dominating gesture of the downward sigh, first of a half step in m.2 and then of a 6th, but the 6th does not sound major or like a finished period but hangs in the air like an uneasy feeling of something not yet realized but threatening nonetheless and something that exists inside and outside of time and space.

Figure 6.11. Main title, *Nightmare on Elm Street*.

Setting

The *Horror of Dracula* opens with a carriage making its way through the Transylvania countryside. A soothing, wistful melody with a somewhat meandering quality plays in the background. The unmarked elements in the theme stress simplicity and innocence, much in keeping with pastoral topics we hear in science-fiction films.

Figure 6.12. Opening theme.

It seems a perfect aural analogue for the bucolic Transylvanian countryside — in the daylight hours. Correlations with characters who represent the good in the good vs. evil quotient are emphasized throughout the film, as variations of the theme appear when these characters are investigating or pursuing Dracula. There is nothing particularly heroic about the music; it is just an aural reminder of the values of normalcy, gentleness, simplicity and innocence and the faint hope that evil can be kept at bay or driven out of their lives. Other than some music from a music box in a Transylvania inn, there is little other music to convey a "normal" atmosphere in the film. However, in keeping with the conventions of the genre, the sense of civility and repose conveyed in this theme and the brief snatches of source music establish a context for the intrusion of the abnormal in the form of the monster into the lives of these ordinary folk.

The music used to create mood, atmosphere and setting in *Nightmare on Elm Street* is similar in some ways to that of classic horror films but offers some interesting ironies. First, there is the jump-rope melody sung by girls playing jump rope early in the film that bears strong resemblance to the old rhyme, 1-2 buckle your shoe, 3-4 etc. Clearly we can label this a childhood or nursery rhyme topic, signifying the innocence of the small town setting as a whole and, more particularly, the youth who dominate this film — although rather quickly we will see that these kids are not so innocent, not nearly as innocent in fact as all the supporting characters in *Horror of Dracula*. The other irony is that it is also associated with Freddy in that he is referenced finally in the lyrics. There is a wonderful dissociation of sensibility and dialogical counterpoint here: the hopelessly juvenile lyrics suggest a trivialization of Freddy's threat while the visuals and other motifs remind of us his unrelenting quest to destroy the days and nights of the townspeople — striking at them through that which they *should* love most: their kids. The singsong rhyme seems a totally inadequate talisman against the monster. The irony is further intensified because it also figures in the music used to underscore Freddy's pursuit of the victims, varied in a triad quaver gesture and used as a countermelody with the main title.

Figure 6.13. "Jump Rope Theme."

For all intents and purposes, Bernstein creates a trope here with the introduction of the marked countermelody, which in turn subverts the motif, rendering meaningless its innocence and transforming it into something decidedly more portentous. A similar strategy was adopted by Roy Webb in his score for *Cat People*, where his motif "Cat People" alludes to a nursery rhyme reminiscent of "Rain, Rain, Go Away" to suggest the corruption of the innocent by the monster.

Figure 6.14. "Cat Theme."

In addition to the non-diegetic score, *Nightmare* also uses occasional source music to culturally situate the victims of the nightmare. The two blatant cases where hard rock or heavy metal figure in a scene are, first, when Glen (Johnny Depp) and the girls are listening to metal on the stereo at the sleep-over prior to first attack and, second, when Glen is listening to rock in bed prior to his death. I am hesitant to draw a conclusion about the role of source music here as corollary for the (morally ambiguous) values of the kids in town, because of the ubiquitous nature of rock in the lives of young adults. However, the brief appearance and sound of rock music, which stands in dramatic counterpoint to the jump-rope tune and Freddy's music, mark it for significance. Although perhaps a bit of a stretch, I believe the music in essence is a topic, call it the "rock topic" if you will, to suggest a music that signifies youthful rebellion and resistance to adult manners, norms, and mores. Does it suggest here a breakdown in family values and parental influence — especially positive influence — or is it just a reminder that these kids are beyond the pale of parental control and that they are venturing into an adult world of dysfunction and fears, an adult world that creates Freddy Kruegers? The difference in the two films is that *Nightmare* does not provide the viewer with tidy and straightforward musical analogues for normalcy; instead, its topics and tropes suggest that the corruption and the evil is pervasive and touches every nook and cranny of life in the small town — even little girls in white playing jump-rope.

Dracula, Freddy and Their Victims

We have seen previously that different monsters represent different threats. But do similar monsters represent the same kind of threat? In the case of Dracula and Freddy, they are both avatars of the undead and their modus vivendi is to "feed" off of the living. One, of course, literally feeds off the living in order to sustain his existence; the other "feeds" off the living to sustain his vengeance and hatred, which, in a manner of speaking, are the things that keep him "alive." Their feeding is accomplished through violent means and, in general, they seem to seek out the innocent or possibly the youthful. They, however, belong to different sub-genres and, consequently, we should be looking for differences as well. As we explore those differences, we might well get some insight into the psycho-cultural nature of their threat. The monster's music, then, should tell us something about the nature of the threat, while the music for the victims — which in actuality is the music accompanying the monster's attack — should tell us something about their innocence or lack thereof, about their tragic struggle to ward off threats beyond their knowledge and earthly powers.

In general, the threat in *Horror of Dracula* is rather subtle: Dracula's threat is predicated as much on his ability to seduce as on his physical power. Unlike the Universal Draculas, the Hammer Dracula is not afraid to flex his muscle, and routinely there will be a scene where he handily flings the hapless hero or some unwitting victim across the room or into a wall, rendering the poor sod unconscious. But at heart, he is a classic eastern European aristocrat surrounded by all the trappings of civilization. David J. Skal has noted that "the twentieth-century image of Dracula is a distinct hybrid, combining Stoker's Count with character traits borrowed from the brooding antiheros of Gothic romances, from *Don Juan, Wuthering Heights,* and elsewhere" (*Monster Show* 83). Under the aristocratic exterior and "brooding" Gothic hero figure, however, is a subtle predator; his aristocratic exterior, moreover, enables him to wield a special kind of power. Van Helsing compares his power to drug addiction, pointing out that his victims, once seduced, are then repelled by future attacks but are helpless to defend themselves, so completely are they in his thrall. Traditionally, Dracula's ability to victimize is linked to his charm, his Old World manners, or possibly his class (he is an aristocrat and those encountering him are generally from the professional class like Van Helsing or the bourgeois class like Harker); these qualities manifest themselves in the monster's ability to hypnotize, the act that precedes the attack. Once the victims' blood has been taken and has mingled with his they are under his spell and, like addicts, they will have no peace as they are forced to seek out their own victims to remain amongst the undead. In this way, this

Horror of Dracula. **The count's aristocratic veneer masks a violent predator.**

version of the Dracula myth is consistent with those of preceding decades in Hollywood for, as Skal notes of the 1931 *Dracula,* "among many other things, *Dracula* is a story about a particularly destructive and compulsive form of drinking; in the ensuing decades vampire stories would be colored increasingly by the metaphors of addiction" (124).

Starting with the opening titles, Bernard's music seems to want to rip the aristocratic veneer off the Count and expose the violent nature of his assault on civilized values. To achieve this, Bernard stresses brass instruments and music scored in the lower registers combined with a throbbing, regular four-beat pulse in the percussion and lower register instruments; the plodding rhythm is a reminder of the relentless threat of the undead while the strident timbres and irregularity of the melodic line reminds us of the ominous nature of the monster.

In the film itself, the motif is sometimes used, almost like a whispered warning, to foreshadow the Count's appearances. The first statement occurs as Harker (John Van Eyssen) approaches the castle in the opening scene and as he looks at the cellar door (which contains Dracula's coffin). We hear it next, shortly after this, when the camera reveals the family crest over the fireplace, and then it is stated a bit more loudly when Harker reads a note from Dracula. The most dramatic statement, however, occurs when Dracula makes his actual entrance; the scene begins with a dramatic low angle shot of Christopher Lee at the top of the stairway, a dark ominous silhouette in a lighted doorway. During the ensuing scene with Harker, Bernard reintroduces the theme almost in echo of his earlier use as Dracula leaves Harker; the camera tracks him

Figure 6.15. Main title, *The Horror of Dracula.*

as he walks to the door, zooming in to a close-up of his hand on the door, and then we hear it again. In subsequent scenes, the Dracula theme will be used whenever Dracula threatens someone or the filmmaker wants to suggest an imminent threat — in short, we may hear the theme even when Dracula is not on the screen, suggesting that his presence now is pervasive and imminent.

The music for the attack in horror films shares many similarities to the music for the attack in science-fiction films. Topics and gestures that signify a threat or tension will be yoked to gestures signifying violence, thus producing a new topic, the attack topic. If we were to yoke the figures below with something like the cue "The Thing Strikes," figure 2.10 in the science-fiction chapter, we would have a complete attack trope. *The Horror of Dracula* relies upon a couple of different motifs to suggest the pursuit.

Figure 6.16. Stalking motifs, *The Horror of Dracula.*

For instance, one of the first attacks in *Horror of Dracula* occurs when Harker admits Dracula's consort into his room. She tells her tale of woe and, as he comforts her, the camera shifts to her face and especially her eyes as they look at this throat. The accompanying music is a low trilling note played by strings and winds that swells and leads to a half note ascending pattern based on measures 1 and 2 above as she prepares to bite his neck. Only Dracula's intervention saves Harker from the attack — at least for the time being, for upon waking, Harker discovers to his horror that he has become a victim of Dracula. The music reveals the status of the victim: as Harker pulls out the mirror to examine his neck, Bernard begins with a trilling gesture in the low strings and then begins building the motif until it crescendos in a high trilling gesture as Harker realizes that he has been "infected" by Dracula himself. As he slumps to the floor, we hear a loud, crashing, percussive chord that echoes the ending of the Dracula theme.

Another example occurs later when Dracula attacks Lucy (Carol Marsh). The scene begins with Mr. and Mrs. Holmwood tucking Lucy into bed for the night. Bernard has a sweet little quasi-lullaby melody playing under this scene, creating an illusion of familial warmth and security. After the couple leaves, the music changes dramatically: Bernard introduces an ostinato pattern played by celeste and vibraphone as Lucy, in an almost zombie-like state, goes to open the veranda doors and then returns to her bed in almost erotic anticipation of Dracula's visit. The music cleverly sustains the innocent feel of the preceding action and serves as an antecedent trope for the next motif, which, using strings and winds, relies upon a three note pattern in an ascending sequence, the classic monster-stalking topic (see figure 6.16), a topic that bears strikingly similarities to similar tension topics in science-fiction and detective films. The camera cuts to the open doors and we see Dracula, his presence announced by the Dracula theme. As he approaches her bed, Bernard uses the trilling three-note ascending pattern. The camera tracks him as he approaches her bed, focusing on his back as he hovers over her; as he bends down, raising his cape to black out the attack and providing closure to the scene, we hear the Dracula theme again. The effectiveness of these scenes lies in the subtle juxtapositions hinted at earlier: the Count's aristocratic and mannered exterior merely cloaks a violent predator; the innocence of family and home (the lullaby) is overwhelmed by the monster's presence in the household (the Dracula theme).

Bernard's score, then, draws upon the archetypal topics and gestures of the genre to communicate the nature of the monster's threat. The suspenseful trilling wedded to the relentless half-step monster topic are the key motifs in the music. Bernard invests the monster's music with gestures and topics signifying overt violence, the kind of gestures we associate more with "living" monsters like Frankenstein's and the Wolfman, whose threatening nature is predicated on physical prowess rather than the subtler class and psychological subtexts that inform the Count's attacks. The Hammer-Bernard monster, then, is a heady mix of seduction and violence, qualities derived from the older Universal series but married to a post–*film noir* consciousness steeped in violence.

Bernstein's music for Freddy, on the other hand, is an apt aural analogue for this postmodern stalker of youth, featuring a heady combination of nursery rhyme, pounding, aggressive rhythms, and archetypal monster dissonances. Bernstein's music juxtaposes worlds by relying upon gestural tropes: the world of childlike innocence that actually precedes adolescence, the world of the blue-collar maintenance worker, and the world of adult fears and latent violence. Freddy, of course, either subverts these worlds or makes them painfully real. To exploit the trope-like intensity of these juxtapositions, Bernstein relies upon sharp contrasts in timbres whenever an attack by Freddy is imminent or actually occurs. For instance, when Freddy makes the "phone call" to Nancy, Bernstein relies upon a contrasting texture of a deep bass scored against high synth strings. Similarly, in Nancy's daydream-nightmare at school, Freddy's cue develops by fits and starts, relying upon sustained strings mixed with tone clusters and fragments of the main title to create suspense; when Freddy's actual pursuit of her begins, Bernstein employs a vigorously syncopated rhythmic figure, which nonetheless conveys a relentlessness in its regularity.

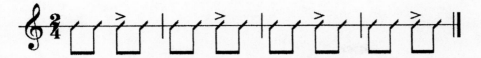

Figure 6.17. "Freddy Stalks Nancy."

When Freddy eventually becomes a central presence in the film his pursuit of the kids is at times a surrealistic blend of violent and innocent musical materials. One example of this is his attack on Tina. The scene actually begins by showing Nancy asleep while above her head the crucifix falls off the wall in a portent of the evil to come. When this happens Bernstein relies upon the common suspense gesture of a sustained note in the high strings; as she falls back to sleep, we hear the "Jump Rope Theme." It is an ironic moment, because the audience is slowly becoming conditioned to expect this motif as a harbinger of Freddy's imminent appearance on the screen, but it also is an aural analogue for the innocence of childhood, an innocence about to be crowded out by the nightmare of Freddy Krueger. Next, there is a cut to Tina, and we see the camera tracking toward the house accompanied by a sustained note in high strings followed by a single chord played by piano and low strings. Then Bernstein introduces the Jump Rope motif played accelerando. The camera cuts back to Nancy and we hear high strings as we see the impression of Freddy pressing out against the wall over her head; we hear a variation on the main title and then a triad eighth-note pattern in a minor key as the wall seems to engulf her:

Figure 6.18. *Nightmare on Elm St.*, main title variation.

This turns into the stalking topic supported above by sustained strings followed by a variation on the main title as she taps the wall; the cue closes with a slow downward glissando. Cut back to Tina, who has now boldly (some viewers might say, stupidly) ventured out into the yard to try and track down the sound she heard from her room. She asks, "Somebody there?" and, to the accompaniment of a prepared piano and strings, we hear Freddy's scratchy reply, "Tina!" As Freddy stalks her in the alley, Bernstein relies upon the triad quaver that had been suggested in the preceding scene with Nancy and disjunctive rhythms in lower registers of the synthesizer to build tension and portend the threat. The triad quaver, like the bass line in the Dracula main title, signifies the relentlessness of the attacker and the overwhelming odds the victim is up against. Once the actual attack begins, the music almost drops out, leaving only the sounds of a fight for survival filling the theatre. Throughout such cues there is a strong suggestion of violence with slashing synth-chord stingers and wave-like dynamics; the percussive elements are not as overtly violent as the Dracula theme but more subtextual, and, melodically, the materials seem to be signifying shifts in psychological states.

We hear an interesting element in two other attacks in the film, on Nancy and Glen respectively, Bernstein, like his "classical" Hollywood forebears, relies upon a regular beat in the bass line to suggest the relentlessness of the attack. This regularity offers an effective counterpoint (literally and figuratively) to devices like the stinger glissando that underscores Freddy's hand coming up through the bed to grab Glen and later, in the same attack, the *Psycho*-like grace notes that presage the incredible bloody geyser that gushes from the heart of his bed; or the arpeggiated strings (set against the regular bass) that accompany the attack on Nancy. The structure of the motifs, then, correlates perfectly with the kernel conflict in the genre by counterposing the marked elements against unmarked ones: the world of childhood innocence versus the world of adult dysfunction and evil.

In general, both composers rely upon similar conventions in the monster's attack. Suspense topics and gestures associated with the violent and tragic are the key ingredients. The combined elements of minor or dissonant harmonies, rapid rhythms, and half-tone ascending melodies create tension in the music and thus build tension under the visuals. There are some differences, however. On the one hand, we have the imminent and clearly focused finality of Dracula's threat, while, on the other, we have the indeterminate pervasiveness of Freddy's threat. Bernard relies upon a simple and aggressive motif to signal the imminence of Dracula's threat; there is little mystery and an almost overwhelming sense of inevitability here: we know how he gets his victims and that he will get them. Bernstein, on the other hand, relies upon a combination of the tonally ambiguous main-title motif and the "Jump Rope Theme" (or a variation of it often scored with dissonant harmonies) and sustained tones or clusters in the high strings and synthesizer (a la *Psycho*) to keep us off balance: as with Dracula, we know Freddy will strike, but unlike with Dracula we really don't know what form the attack will take.

Figure 6.19. Main title variation, *Nightmare on Elm Street.*

Ryan and Kellner note of films like *Nightmare*, "Indeed, the strategy of the conservative rhetoric of these films, like the projection of nihilism in certain horror films that seems to imply a call for a strong antidote of meaning and leadership, is to represent the world as a paranoid's paradise of fear and distrust that is beyond rational redemption. What is most significant about this world is that the violence seems unmotivated" (192). This is not to say that there is not violence when Freddy attacks, but the question in *Nightmare* is "What will happen?"; the question in Dracula is "When will it happen?" However, when the monster begins his attack, the music for both monsters settles into a familiar groove where violence is the dominant musical emotion. Consequently, the attack motifs both employ dramatic timbral contrasts, driving and relentless rhythms, tremolos and other high string figures, and finally the crushing percussive effects from drums, pianos, and low brass.

The Hero and Final Confrontation

In *The Horror of Dracula*, Van Helsing's (or for that matter, anyone else's) pursuit of Dracula prior to the finale is underscored using a five note motif that was introduced in the opening scene; this motif is, moreover, often coupled with classic suspense gestures (tremolos, half-step ascending patterns, etc). The five note motif signifies the struggle the forces of normality face in their encounters with the almost overwhelming power of the abnormal, symbolized by the monster.

Figure 6.20. "Van Helsing in Pursuit."

It is interesting to note, however, that the five note motif is not employed in the final showdown between hero and monster, but all the other conventions of the genre come into play to heighten the drama and violence in final battle between the forces of normalcy and those of the abnormal or unnatural. We can, I believe, read this as the composer and filmmaker's way of saying that civility has no place in this life and death violent struggle with the monster.

Horror of Dracula. Van Helsing (Peter Cushing) equipped with one of the weapons in his struggle with the monster.

Van Helsing tracks Dracula to his residence but finds himself trapped. As Dracula stalks Van Helsing, Bernard relies upon a classic stalking topic as the monster prepares to bite his victim's neck. Van Helsing, however, is able to fool Dracula into thinking that he is nothing now but a helpless victim, and then, as Dracula relaxes for the attack (a rather interesting notion), Van Helsing hurls him off and moves away. However, Dracula is back on the attack, assured of his victory. As he stalks his prey, the stalking topic is heard again, but the camera cuts to Van Helsing eyeing the window. He leaps on the banquet table and scampers toward the window, underscored by a Mickey-mousing triplet figure. He leaps and drags the curtains away from the window, exposing Dracula to the morning light. The camera cuts to Dracula as the sunlight streams over him; as it does, and as we see him sink under the harsh but life-affirming rays of sunlight, Bernard states the Dracula theme, employing dissonant and closed chords. Bernard cleverly builds an element of suspense into the monster's death by repeating the motif on progressively descending scale tones, capped off with single descending notes as a close-up reveals the monster's chest, now nothing more than an ashen mass, caving in on itself in a final destructive image. The camera cuts to Van Helsing at the window bathed in sunlight and, of course, unharmed by it. Bernard then introduces a variation of his opening theme played sweetly by the strings. There is a cut to Holmwood and his wife seated outside Dracula's castle and a close-up of her hand. We see the burned image of the cross gradually disappear as the opening theme is played. The mellow tones of viola accompany Mr. Holmwood kissing his wife's hand. These physical gestures combined with the music strongly suggest a return to normalcy and the restoration of the family unit; the marriage is no longer threatened by Dracula, and all is forgiven. The camera cuts back to the floor and there is a close-up of the dust that was Dracula now being blown away by a gust of wind, leaving only his ring. The three-note Dracula motif is stated once more but this time on the same note, implying that he is dead and no longer a threat.

Of course, one dramatic difference between the classic Universal or Hammer horror film and some more recent films is that women are often the heroes in the dramas, and such is the case with *Nightmare*. Nancy indeed comes off as a dynamic hero in the film as she prepares to take on Freddy. The music for the final confrontation begins with a variation of the stalking topic, this time featuring a dynamic rhythmic pattern of a sixteenth, quarter and four sixteenths:

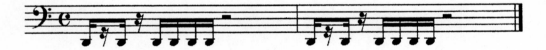

Figure 6.21. "Nancy Prepares."

Over this figure Bernstein layers a sustained note played by an electric guitar and then introduces a quaver built on a minor triad as Nancy takes Freddy's glove out of the furnace in her basement.

Figure 6.22. "Freddy Attacks Nancy."

As she climbs down the ladder into the boiler room, Bernstein states the main title and then shifts to a low sustained note—an aural representation of her descent into Freddy's domain—and then begins an ostinato pattern played by a synthesizer that is similar to the familiar triad quaver used in other stalking sequences. The music lends a strong degree of suspense through irony: we are watching Nancy stalking Freddy but the music is telling us quite

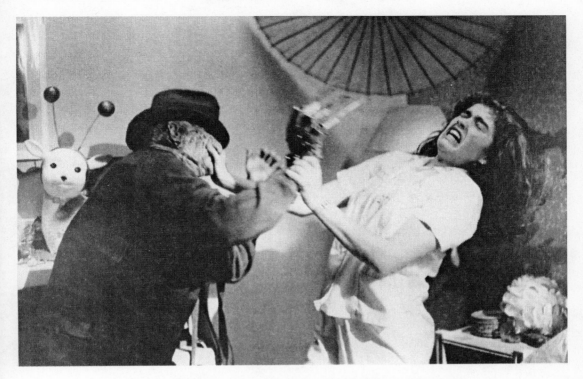

Nightmare on Elm St. **"Final Girl" Nancy fearlessly takes on Freddy.**

the opposite; that no matter her intent, Freddy is still the master stalker. As Nancy picks up Glenn's headphones (the ones he was wearing when killed by Freddy), Bernstein introduces the classic stalking topic as the winds play an ascending half-step pattern in the lower registers. Bernstein employs the classic stinger as Freddy pops out to attack Nancy. Then a low bass begins a regular beat, but this gives way to a strong syncopated rhythm picked up by other instruments and, as she taunts him into her trap, we hear the familiar triad quaver. Freddy's actual "death" is underscored by a rapid figure played by the bass guitar, and then Bernstein uses a glissando stinger to punctuate the images of Freddy dissolving. It is interesting to note here that the death of both monsters is marked by disintegration of some sort; this is a final reminder of their nonhuman status — they are very real but immaterial: the ultimate horror. The music used to underscore their deaths, moreover, is quite similar. The difference lies in the fact that Freddy's death, unlike Dracula's, is an illusion, and the sense of triumph and closure will be short lived.

Freddy's dead, and as happy Mom and Nancy emerge from the house into gauzy sunlight, we see Glenn, Tina and Rod driving up to pick her up and go to school. Things are back to normal; it all was just a bad dream — or was it? As Glenn's car drives off, the windows shut, the convertible top — now the color of Freddy's striped sweater — traps the kids in the car and the camera tracks the car as it moves out of the frame. The camera then stops and focuses on the girls dressed in white playing jump rope and singing,

1, 2 Freddy's coming for you
3, 4 better lock your door...
9, 10 never sleep again.

The last image we have as the song is sung is of Freddy's hand punching through Nancy's front door and grabbing the seraphically happy Mom and dragging her back into the house, now not so happy but screaming hysterically. Finally, Freddy has a victim besides the kids; his revenge is complete as takes the whole family. 9, 10 never sleep again! Music and image work contrapuntally here and are in marked contrast to the final musical cues in *The Horror of Dracula*, where the pastoral topic underscores the denouement and a return to normalcy. Here the nursery rhyme is horribly ironic — maybe even cynical, as it is so innocently sung under the ambiguous and unsettling final images.

Conclusion

In the world of contemporary horror, monsters don't die easily — in fact they don't seem to die at all. Of course, you may say, wasn't this also the case with the Universal and Hammer films; didn't they have sequels that brought the monsters back for encores? They did indeed, but the films themselves brought a sense of closure each and every time, lulling us into thinking that the monster had been confronted and dispatched. Frankenstein's Monster is destroyed at the end of *Frankenstein*, and he is destroyed again at the end of *The Bride of Frankenstein* and at the end of *The House of Frankenstein*. In a sense, prior to the 1980s one might posit that the monster is not the point, it is the state of the society at the film's end. In each of the abovementioned Universal films and in most of the Hammer films, social order (or at least a portion of the social order) is restored. In the *Horror of Dracula*, for instance, the reintroduction of the opening scene pastoral topic, heard in the opening as the carriage makes its way through the lovely natural countryside, is a reminder of our desire for a return to serenity and an uncorrupted, untainted world.

Nightmare on Elm Street's ending, on the other hand, reminds us that we cannot dispatch our demons so easily; the problems run deeper and the irony of the "Jump Rope Theme" further drives that point home. That the girls are still singing about Freddy, even in the context of play, is emblematic of his pervasive presence and of our youth's feeble attempts to ward off the corruption that their parents have willed to them through their own failings.

Part Two

Gender/Genre

Heroism in Sports Films and the Woman's Film

7

"The best there ever was in the game"

Musical Mythopoesis and Heroism in Film Scores of Recent Sports Movies

They don't want to know how it "really is." ... *they want the metaphor, they want to see hard work, discipline, teamwork, sacrifice, and heroism succeed.*—Commissioner of the NBA, David Stern (1985)

In retrospect, Commissioner David Stern's comments seem to be an almost perfect explanation for the rise in popularity of a group of sports films made since the mid–1980s that hearken back to the classic sports films of Hollywood's golden age. After a number of years of cynical and critical (read negative) views of sports in American life by filmmakers, the 1980s saw a resurgence of films that unwittingly made Commissioner Stern into a prophet. Filmmakers seemed willing to once again reaffirm our deeply held belief in the efficacy of the sports hero, that sports are indeed a metaphor for the American Dream and the American Myth of Success, and that sports can regenerate our communities or at least reconcile that classic American dilemma of the individual vs. the community. It is, in fact, these three themes that inform this examination of the role of film music in the construction of a mythology of the sports hero in three films drawn from the three major sports: *The Natural* (1984)—baseball; *Rudy* (1993)—football; *Hoosiers* (1986)—basketball. I will be dealing solely with classic Hollywood scores and not diegetic (i.e., source) music or popular songs from other sources that might be used to underscore filmic sequences.

Up until the 1960s, the sports hero was a staple in American films. Sports films celebrated the achievements of exemplary athletes, their rise to fame, and their struggles to overcome social or physical odds on their path to glory and a place in their respective halls of fame. Films about Lou Gehrig (*Pride of the Yankees*, 1942*)*, Babe Ruth (*The Babe Ruth Story,* 1948), Monty Stratton (*The Stratton Story*, 1949), Grover Cleveland Alexander (*The Winning Team*, 1952), and Jim Thorpe (*Jim Thorpe, All American*, 1951), to name just a few, dealt with Alger-like heroes rising up from humble origins, the perfect embodiment of the American Myth of Success. They were, moreover, classic American heroes, individuals possessed of some exceptional talent, who advocated hard work and clean living, who validated the devotion of their fans, who displayed the requisite courage needed to overcome whatever challenges they were confronted within their professional and personal lives, and who were able to transform or regenerate their communities through their heroic efforts.[1] In regard to this last mentioned heroic attribute, they share similarities, as Kent Cartwright and Mary McElroy note, to the quest heroes of classic legends: "The basic challenge of the Quest hero — Sir Galahad, Sir Perceval, Sir Gawain, or the antecedent heroes of the ancient Vegetation rites — is to restore the sick or maimed Fisher King to health through the accomplishment of a task and thereby to relieve the Waste Land from infertility, drought, and desolation" (50).

The 1960s led to a reevaluation of most of our cherished myths, and the sports hero was not spared this critical interrogation. The sports films that followed were less willing (in a paraphrase of John Ford's line in *The Man Who Shot Liberty Valance*) to print the legend. Films like *North Dallas Forty* (1979), *The Longest Yard* (1974) (albeit set in a prison), and *Slap Shot* (1977) were often downright cynical in their depictions of the fallibilities and foibles of athletes, stressing, moreover, the athlete's complicity in the corruption underlying the business of sports. The protagonists were reminiscent of Hemingway's boy-men, unable to grow up and, at heart, ineffectual under their seeming sports prowess. This trend continued into the 1980s and 1990s with films like *Dead Solid Perfect* (1988), *Cobb* (1994) and *Any Given Sunday* (1999), and to a lesser extent, *Bull Durham* (1988) and *Tin Cup* (1996). During this same time period, however, some films emerged that reaffirmed the power of sports to create genuine heroes, films that seemed to suggest that sports were indeed a reflection of what was best about the American spirit, and that our popular mythology was not completely exhausted. In general, the heroes of *The Natural, Hoosiers,* and *Rudy* can readily be summoned as exemplars of the major tenets of the American Myth of Success: they worked hard, were men of integrity, and with a little bit of luck achieved fame and/or fortune.

One of the most compelling aspects of the reification of American sports heroes in film is the music that accompanies — or perhaps better underscores — their achievements. As in the case of most genres that feature strong hero figures, composers working in this genre rely upon tried and true musical motifs, topics, and gestures to reinforce the mythological stature of the heroes. In the case of underscoring heroic action, composers oftentimes rely upon gestures that employ vigorous or driving rhythms, dramatic intervallic leaps, especially of a fourth or fifth or an octave, or soaring melodic patterns which exploit chords outlining the fifth (1-3-5) or octaves or ascending melodic lines to underscore the exploits of the hero.[2] Let's look at a couple of examples of heroic musical themes that employ these gestures. The first comes from Richard Strauss's tone poem *Don Juan* (1889) (figure 7.1), and the next two notable examples are drawn from Korngold's music for *Captain Blood* (figure 7.2) and Miklos Rosza's theme for the Cid from *El Cid*.[3]

Figure 7.1. *Don Juan.*

Figure 7.2. *Captain Blood*, main title.

Figure 7.3. *El Cid,* "El Cid Theme."

These three examples share a couple of common characteristics: first, the opening gesture in each either directly or indirectly features a leap of a fourth or fifth within the first two measures; second, the melodic line is characterized by an upward stepwise movement. The repeated use of these gestures over time (in a variety of musical settings) and played by certain types of instruments (brass, massed strings, etc.) primes the audience to respond in a certain way when they hear them. As we shall see, the gestures cited above, along with others, are still part of the composer's musical arsenal in forging a musical mythology to underscore and reinforce the "heroic" visuals in sports films. Let's begin with the film that initiated this renaissance of classic film scoring in sports genre films, *The Natural.*

One might argue that *The Natural* and Randy Newman's score have become the archetype for athletic heroic splendor in the late 20th and early 21st centuries. The main-title theme is almost as ubiquitous as Richard Strauss's simple opening motif for *Also Sprach Zarathustra,* so effectively used in Stanley Kubrick's *2001: A Space Odyssey. The Natural* was a lushly photographed and decidedly more heroic interpretation of Bernard Malamud's novel. At the center of the film is Roy Hobbs (Robert Redford), a perfect example of that boy-man referred to earlier: a baseball player of childlike innocence, prodigious talent, and tragic flaws. Malamud's novel validates William Carlos Williams's line about there being no second acts in American life; Levinson's film, on the other hand, gives the lie to Williams: there can be a second act and a splendid one at that; one can come back and achieve apotheosis. In fact, Roy, as Cartwright and McElroy note, "is the aging fertility hero of Western myth. He is rural, of the land; he comes in the dry season; and his task is to renew the king, save his people, and restore the waters" (50). Roy also might be seen as what Robert Ray calls a "two-sided character," a hero who is "designed to appeal to a collective American imagination steeped in myths of inclusiveness" and who reconciles "the most significant pair of competing myths: the outlaw hero and the official hero" (qtd. in Dickerson 8). Randy Newman brought just the right note of Coplandesque optimism, folk-like vibrancy, foursquare musical values and classic film music gestures to underscore the triumph of this "two-sided" hero.

The first musical motif that we associate with Roy is one I call the "Promise" motif because it often accompanies or anticipates some heroic event. It is a classic heroic musical gesture: often it begins with the arpeggiated figure you see in figure 7.7 and then is followed by a simple fanfare, beginning with a four note motif featuring an opening leap of 4th followed by one of a 6th and then one of a fifth. Initially, it bears a significant resemblance to another heroic motif, the "Donner Motive" at the opening of "The Entrance of the Gods into Valhalla" from Wagner's *Das Rheingold* (see figures 7.4 and 7.5).

Figure 7.4. "Donner Motive."

Figure 7.5. *The Natural*, "The Promise."

This motif will often be followed by a simple but more animated motif that is reminiscent of the pastoral topic, featuring regular rhythms and a repeated sequence that evokes the sights of rolling prairies and farmland (figure 7.6). Kent Cartwright and Mary McElroy note that "we have for a long time, of course, thought of baseball in terms of the pastoral," and they mention elements like the "seasonal cycle" and observe that the game is "perennially concerned with age and youth and renewal," that the heroes are "country folk at heart," and that the game itself is "played in a meadow that appears, always, unspeakably green" (49) This motif, reminiscent of themes one finds in the later movements of Ives's Symphony no. 2 and in Copland's *Rodeo* and *Billy the Kid*, seems to capture those pastoral elements outlined by Cartwright and McElroy.

Figure 7.6. *The Natural*, "Success."

Newman uses these motifs to simultaneously create tension within a scene and to portend heroic achievement; for instance, we hear it early in the film as Roy prepares to toss the third strike to the Whammer (Joe Don Baker) and later in the film's climax just prior to his game-winning homer in the pennant game. In contrast to *Hoosiers* and *Rudy*, *The Natural* makes less of the work ethic and more of the promise of the hero to elevate the community of team, fans, and family. Roy, after all, is a "natural"; he does not need to learn hard work, just character. Peter Turchi says of this dimension of the hero's development, "But while his baseball life is finished, his real life — his life as a man, Malamud would tell us — has reached a new, glorious plateau" (156). This motif reminds the viewer that heroism is only a promise until it is married to character.

The other motif, which I will call the "Heroic" motif, is actually the central theme from the main title, and it features musical gestures that we often associate with heroic figures: an opening dramatic leap of a 6th followed by a descending three note phrase that outlines an octave.

Figure 7.7. *The Natural*, "Heroic Motif."

This motif, like the one previously discussed, is cast in an "American" mode. By that I mean that the musical materials are closer, in their harmonic and melodic language, to the folk-classical elements we find in the work of American composers such as Copland, Ives, and Roy Harris, who drew upon combinations of folk and popular musical elements in creating their large scale works. Here is a brief passage from Copland's *Fanfare for the Common Man* (1942):

Figure 7.8. *Fanfare for the Common Man.*

Like the Copland piece, Newman stresses open intervallic leaps in both themes. We hear echoes of measure three of *Fanfare for the Common Man* in measures six and seven of Newman's "Promise Motif" and of measures two and three in *Fanfare* in measures two, three and four in Newman's main title. Additionally, in his use of dramatic intervallic leaps, Newman conforms to practice in serious music and that of the Korngold and Steiner "school" we saw earlier where the dramatic leap, be it of a fourth, fifth or sixth, becomes the gesture we most often associate with heroic effort. To this, however, he adds some distinctly American ideas to fill out his motifs by relying upon angular rhythms and melodies with gently rolling, economic melodic lines of narrow range (the pastoral topic) that help us equate Roy's ultimate triumph with his farming roots.

Levinson and Newman want us to see Roy as a heroic avatar of a version of the Myth of Success in this film: the poor boy from humble roots who rises to the top of his sport. Levinson leavens Malamud's dark vision with Hobb's triumph and the team's winning the pennant and defeating the forces of evil (the Judge, Gus the Gambler, and Memo the seductress). The gestures mentioned above work in tandem throughout Roy's rise and fall and rise to be "the best there ever was." For instance, the first time we hear the "Promise" motif in the context of the baseball setting is in the pitching contest with the Whammer; the motif is sounded as Roy goes into his windup to deliver strike three; the sun is setting, bathing him and outlining him in silhouette. The motif in concert with the low angle shot and slow motion photography heightens the tension in this penultimate moment prior to delivery. Once the ball almost magically cracks in Sam Simpson's glove and Mercy (Robert Duvall) declares "Strike Three. You're out," Newman follows it up with a very Ives-or Copland-like theme that in its shanty-styled rhythms evokes a feeling of Roy's country roots as much as victory. He does not use the main title at this point, reserving that gesture for Roy's heroic exploits with the Knights. It is not at all coincidental that the "Heroic" motif is almost exclusively associated with the home run, that most dramatic and heroic of all hits in the game.[4]

The most important use of the motifs in tandem occurs during the film's finale, the pennant championship game. Winning this game ultimately defines success for Roy and the Knights (especially Pop, who declares that this all he ever wanted, even more than a World Series victory). It is Roy's chance to redeem his character, to not be felled by the corrupting values of the Harriet Birds, Guses, and Judges of the world, and to lift up those whose hearts

The Natural. **Roy Hobbs at bat in his quest to be "the best there ever was in the game."**

and motives (i.e., a love of the game) are true. Consequently, Newman relies on a similar pattern of motivic development to construct this ultimate heroic act. As the rookie Pirate pitcher prepares to deliver the make-or-break pitch, Newman underscores the scene with a version of the "Promise" motif, thereby building tension and cuing the audience that Roy is standing on the threshold of greatness. He may not be the greatest of all time but he will achieve a kind of apotheosis in this moment. As the ball rockets off his bat toward the lights above, Newman states the main title (i.e., "Heroic" motif) theme. Then, as Roy rounds the bases and the ballpark is alternately pitched into darkness and lit up with fragments of fireworks-like light, Newman states the "Success" motif (figure 7.6), which was used earlier in the pitching contest scene, but this time it is less brash and youthful and more elegiac but nonetheless equally triumphal, with strings carrying the melodic weight. The warm autumnal timbre of the accompanying brass and the more stately rhythms in this iteration of the "Heroic" motif also suggest that character has finally triumphed. He may not be the "best there ever was" but he certainly is on this cool autumn evening.

The convergence of these themes in a harmonious whole in the finale functions as an aural analogue for the hero's ability to reconcile his individual achievement with the hopes of the community and in the process renew the community: Roy's farming roots are finally reconciled with the dynamism of the ballpark in the city. This point is emphasized in the final frames of the film where Levinson tracks the ball as it flies away from the ballpark, accompanied by the ostinato pattern in figure 7.7, en route to the glove on the hand of Roy's son as they play catch in the golden twilight of a rich field (a mirror of the opening frames of the film), while the music shifts to an elegiac rendering of the "Promise" motif (figure 7.5) on the trumpet. The music here underscores an affirmation of his dad's caution that it takes more than talent to be great. As Peter Turchi notes, "The film ends not with the homerun of mythical proportions, but with Roy and his son playing catch in a field of golden wheat, Iris looking on. The life cycle has been renewed" (156). Roy's heroics, his boon, to use Campbell's language, enable him to simultaneously regenerate his family, make the Knights function as a team, and allow the fans to partake of the Myth of Success. All differences — age, racial, sexual, and religious — disappear in the glow of fireworks and the efforts of one man. The individual is the community and the community is the individual. Peter Turchi states, "The true hero must be a part of his community even as he rises above it" (156). Newman, and others as we shall see, use the main title or hero's theme to signify the role of the hero in the renewal of the community.

Moving from *The Natural* to *Hoosiers* we encounter a slightly different perspective on heroism in sports. Ostensibly, coach Norman Dale (Gene Hackman) is the protagonist in the film, but it becomes clear as the narrative unfolds that the triumph is a collective effort and the team (coach and players) is the hero. At some point in the film each member of the team and other outsiders in the community, like Shooter (Dennis Hopper), will rise to the occasion to help win a game and, ultimately, the state championship. Like *Rudy* and to a lesser extent, *The Natural*, it is also a story about the underdog and quite literally the "little guy" triumphing against Goliath-like odds (Roy, to a degree, conforms to this model by merit of his being a kid from the farm, a "huckleberry," as the Whammer describes him at one point). Jerry Goldsmith's masterful score captures perfectly the journey of the coach, the boys, and the town to the ultimate destination in Indiana high school basketball: the state championship.

Like the protagonists in the other two films, Coach Dale is an outsider. A volatile coach booted out of college ball for striking a player, he is trying to rehabilitate his career and Hickory High School is his last chance. This loner status is established musically in the main-title music where we hear a solo trumpet playing the theme over a gentle string accompaniment as Coach Dale wends his way through the Indiana countryside on his way to an impossibly

Hoosiers. The team as collective hero: Coach Dale and his players.

small town called Hickory. Darby and DuBois say this about the theme: "This expansive music, redolent of farming country and the presumably slower and simpler life of rural America, thus comes to stand for the central character in moments of crisis" (511). This description would suggest the presence of a strong pastoral topic in the theme and, indeed, the visuals working dialogically with the theme give credence to this perception. The theme, however, draws on the gestural language of classic heroic themes of the past by accentuating intervallic leaps of the fourth and fifth. The melody, after an initial downward leap of a fourth, echoes the examples from Strauss, Korngold, and Rosza cited earlier, by seemingly straining upward over an octave (stressing leaps of a fourth and fifth) as though it is trying to rise above or overcome, a feeling that is further intensified in the second measure with a four note motif that also outlines a fifth:

Figure 7.9. *Hoosiers*, "Coach."

As was the case with both *The Natural* and *Rudy*, the myth of success is the narrative subtext for heroic achievement in *Hoosiers*. The myth is clearly musically enunciated throughout the film by merit of Goldsmith's motifs for practices and game sequences. The dominant musical characteristic here is rhythm: drums and vigorous bass lines emphasizing a pattern reminiscent of a disco beat are the key elements. When Jimmy rejoins the team the montage of winning is underscored by two examples: the first, dubbed "Victory" (figure 7.10) by Darby and DuBois, was introduced at the team's first practice with Coach Dale and suggests work and striving; the other, which I call "Winning," is used in tandem with "Victory" and is associated with the team's winning streak.

Figure 7.10. *Hoosiers*, "Victory."

Figure 7.11. *Hoosiers*, "Winning."

The contrast between these motifs and the main-title music ("Coach") is notable: where "Coach" often features the solo trumpet, which aurally suggests the coach's quest to pull the team together and make them winners, these two motifs, on the other hand, emphasize the brass "choir" or other orchestral ensembles (e.g., strings) befitting music for a team. The first time we actually hear a suggestion of the "Winning" motif is in the main title, where Goldsmith uses a fragment of it as a countermelody to musically foreshadow the major conflict facing the coach when he arrives at Hickory High. One slight variation on the "Winning" motif occurs at the regional championship when more syncopated rhythmic elements combine with a simpler melodic motif to give the music a very Western feel, reminiscent of the hoe-down music from Copland's *Rodeo*. Significantly, in both *Hoosiers* and *Rudy*, Goldsmith uses the "Victory" motif and "Success" variation motifs respectively to underscore both practice and game scenes, thus aurally drawing a connection between work (practice) and winning the game (success).

As the film progresses and we begin to see the town coming together in homage and loyalty to the team's winning ways, Goldsmith varies "Coach" to suggest the slow symbiosis of hero and community. For instance, one such variation occurs in the subplot featuring Coach Dale and Myra Fleener (Barbara Hershey), the English teacher and Jimmy's guardian. Cold to him at first, she is symbolic of the town's changing attitude toward this outsider taking over the team as she is won over by his sense of ethics and his attempts to help people in the town. Prior to the finale they have a scene where Goldsmith varies the main title, softening it and diminishing its heroic tenor by easing the tempo and featuring strings and winds in the orchestration. In yet another variation, Goldsmith also uses the theme in the reconciliation scene between Shooter and his son. Both of these scenes anticipate the finale at the state championship.

Just as Randy Newman did in *The Natural*, Goldsmith brings all the themes together in the finale, the state championship sequence. The rhythmic motifs ("Victory" and "Winning") predominate in the sequence, emphasizing not only the action of the game itself but also the struggle of the team to comeback and defeat the Goliath-like big city team. The comeback is underscored using all three motifs. After a timeout, in which Dale not so subtly gets the team to stop being intimidated by the South Bend team, they take the floor, with "Winning" underscoring the initial stages of the comeback. Goldsmith next brings in "Victory" as the team narrows the gap in the score, leaving them just one shot away from their impossible dream. As noted earlier, it is significant that this is the same music that was used earlier to underscore practice sequences (as a reminder of the efficacy of hard work) and the team's gradual odyssey from down-and-out "hick" team through districts and regionals to the ultimate prize, the state championship. What is striking here is that, aside from crowd noise and an occasional snippet of coaching advice, the music is the dominant aural element in this sequence — at one point in fact, it is the only sound we hear over the victory celebration. As Jimmy hits the final shot at the buzzer, the "Winning" motif (figure 7.11) is stated triumphantly by brass and then we hear the "Coach" motif, this time transfigured, no longer a solitary trumpet or elegiac love theme, but a soaring victory anthem. It is carried by strings and horns with high strings suspending the harmonies above, giving the whole scene a transcendent feeling as the camera moves from the team to the crowd, isolating some of the figures who were initially hostile to the coach (Myra and George and the police chief) but who are now cheering and celebrating this victory of the outsider over his demons and of the underdog over what were seemingly insurmountable odds in their quest for an impossible dream. Darby and DuBois note of the music in this scene, "When they finally win the game, Goldsmith's theme for the region and for Dale [i.e., figure 7.9, "Coach"] rises out of the victory music as if to assert that the contest has been won by forces and individuals beyond the actual team members" (511). It is, as one of the players says, a victory for all the little towns that might never get to the state tournament — in short, it is not just Norman Dale's comeback victory but also a victory for the community.

In a way, it is appropriate to end with *Rudy* because it is a little bit of *The Natural* and little bit of *Hoosiers*. Made by the same director as *Hoosiers*, the film uses the fabled football program of Notre Dame to tell its story of a small town boy who, unlike the "natural" Roy Hobbs, must rely on the traditional values of grit, hard work, dedication, and an undying belief in a dream to achieve Rocky-like success. Based loosely on the real-life exploits of Rudy Ruettiger, it is a story that would have made Horatio Alger proud because it chronicles a working class kid rising above the meager expectations of his class and reaffirming the myth that in America anything is possible with hard work and character.

The aural centerpiece in the creation of Rudy's heroic persona is the main-title music, which is also the theme for Rudy (Sean Astin). It is a Gaelic-tinged 3/4-time melody whose main (A) theme is one of simplicity, grace and longing; the contrasting B theme has a slightly more heroic cast, moving upward through a simple three-note pattern (not unlike *Hoosiers*). Here is the first part of the A theme:

Figure 7.12. *Rudy*, main title.

The melody is often played in the film by a solo flute, which suggests simplicity, modesty, and diminutive stature, and it has a folk-like quality, which is mildly suggestive of Rudy's Irish, working class background. I would also say that it captures perfectly the dream-like quality of Rudy's quest, like a siren's song from afar calling to him. Not surprisingly, that siren's voice is an Irish one, that is, the Irish of Notre Dame. The theme's ability to signify Rudy's dream is brought home dramatically in the scene where his best friend, Pete, gives him a Notre Dame jacket from the second-hand store. As they talk about Rudy's dream to play football for Notre Dame, the melody plays gently in the background and seems the perfect accompaniment to Pete's line about how dreams make "life tolerable."

Rudy, like *Hoosiers*, wraps the heroic quest around the Myth of Success, and in this film, Goldsmith relies upon the motif, which I call the "Success Motif," to signify the success myth, especially the work ethic component. Structured on a simple four-note pattern, the motif emphasizes an intervallic leap of a fifth downward followed by a dramatic octave leap upward, both gestures that we traditionally associate with hero figures in film. The intervallic leaps and Goldsmith's favorite device of a brief ascending figure that seems to end in a quasi-suspension heighten the feelings of desperation and hope that are warring in Rudy:

Figure 7.13. *Rudy,* "Success Motif."

The first full statement of the "Success" motif occurs when Rudy arrives on the campus and approaches the football stadium. The main title gently plays in the background as he wanders through the campus and then is foregrounded more when he sees the stadium. As he quickens his pace toward the stadium, Anspaugh shifts to a shot from inside the tunnel entrance looking out with the library in background; Goldsmith uses tremolo in the strings to heighten tension in the scene. Then as the camera shifts to Rudy's point of view looking out to the field, Goldsmith brings in the "Success" motif. He uses brass — horns in particular — recalling the grand heroic gestures of post–Romantic music. The repeated four-note gesture, supported by a counter-melody derived from the main title and played by a flute, is like an echo of something dreamed. Throughout, the bass line is deep and resonant. This more fully developed use of the motif here simultaneously recalls his speech to his father at the bus station and portends his Alger-like quest to suit up for a Notre Dame football game. This motif or some variation of it will be used in all the future practice sequences and the final game sequence.

As Rudy struggles to bring his grades up at Holy Cross and get admitted to Notre Dame, Anspaugh underscores his hero's quest by alternating and balancing his use of the main title with a variation on the "Success" motif.

Figure 7.14. *Rudy*, "Success Motif Variation."

As he did in *Hoosiers*, Goldsmith endows this variation on the "Success" motif with strong driving rhythms and simple melodic lines, two musical gestures that the filmmaker and composer would have us associate with work and effort. The variation perfectly underscores the tryouts and the scenes on the practice field, which vigorously blend the romantic with the realistic: atmospheric shots in morning haze are juxtaposed with crushing hits and bloodied warriors who are struggling to make the team. This alternating of the romantic main title with the more aggressively rhythmic variation on the "Success" motif underscores the success mythology of the film as Rudy first struggles to overcome his dyslexia, make good grades, and get admitted to Notre Dame and then as he struggles on the practice field in his quest to dress for a game. As we shall see, this alternation of motifs anticipates their coda-like convergence in the film's final sequence.

Before the big game, however, Anspaugh constructs a sequence out of two related scenes that musically set up the film's finale. After finding out he will not suit up for the final game,

Rudy threatens to quit the team but is hectored by his friend Jim who tells him how important he has been to the second team. Next, the head groundskeeper, Fortune (Charles Dut-
ton), sternly lectures Rudy, telling him not to quit and reminding him of the things he has
already achieved (an education; sticking it out with the best team in the nation, etc.). He
goes on to remind Rudy that if he quits he will regret it his whole life, confessing his own
regrets for quitting the team years before. The scene then shifts to the final practice. Anspaugh
intercuts overhead long shots and medium shots of the team and the coaches running drills
in a final practice before the big game. Then the camera cuts to a long shot of the team, and
Goldsmith underscores Rudy's entrance into the frame with a stinger; this is immediately followed by the "Success" motif as Rudy dons his helmet and merges into the midst of his team-
mates who begin to clap in unison, a gesture of acclamation for their hero.

Next, in a rather moving scene, players turn up at Devine's (Chelcie Ross) office to ask
that Rudy play in their places. The main title is used to underscore the scene, signifying
Rudy's role as inspiration and heart of the team. It is in fact the reference to Rudy's heart
which is its own leitmotif in the film: earlier in the film, his high school coach remarked that
his heart is greater than his talent, and later Ara Parseghian (Jason Miller) dresses down one
of his star athletes by telling him that if had half of Rudy's heart he would really be a great
player. Significantly, this is the first time that Rudy's theme is used to accompany an action
by the team, signifying that the team has found its heart prior to any actual football action.
The crowning moment in the scene comes when star defensive back Roland Steele, when
rebuked by Devine with the line "You're an All-American and our captain, act like it," courageously tells the coach, "I believe I am," implying that the best thing for the team (as a team)
is for Rudy to suit up. Goldsmith wisely replicates the same musical motifs for the final game

Rudy. At practice, Rudy shows Coach Parseghian what "heart" in football is all about.

sequence. Goldsmith's cue suggests that the first step in the regeneration and reintegration of the community has been accomplished. All that remains for the hero is apotheosis.

We should not be surprised that for the finale of *Rudy*, Goldsmith relies upon the same structuring of musical gestures and motifs as he did in *Hoosiers*. The game footage itself employs the "Success Motif Variation" (figure 7.14), which throughout most of the scene emphasizes a slower, grinding rhythm with the strings maintaining an ostinato figure while the horns carry the dominant melody. After Rudy enters the game and gets his tackle, Goldsmith states the "Success" (see figure 7.13) theme again, but this time it is bigger and more dynamic, with the final (fourth) note sustained for effect. And then in grand fashion he brings in Rudy's theme (the main title). This time, however, it is less filled with longing and more with triumph, as the brass and strings give the theme a grandly sweeping quality. As Goldsmith introduces the main title's B theme, the horns carry the melody giving it a far-off but warmly romantic and heroic feeling; the timbre and texture of the brass echo the brass textures that we have heard previously in the "Success" motif. During the playing of the main title, the camera ranges through the crowd locking on his family, then his "loser" friend D-Bob (John Favreau), all celebrating and sharing in his victory. As in *Hoosiers,* the underdog has shown his ability to bring the community together, to break down the differences and hostilities that might exist there, and lift team and community up in a moment of triumph. Like a real hero, he is one of us, and yet for this brief moment he is greater than us. The "truth" of this part of the myth is validated by Goldsmith's scoring of the hero's theme in this scene.

In the 1988 film *Bull Durham*, heroine Annie Savoy (Susan Sarandon) comments: "Walt Whitman once said: I see great things in baseball. It is our game — the American game. It will repair our losses and be a blessing to us." Were Whitman alive and able to see these films and hear these scores he might well revise his statement to include all three sports. The scores of these films aurally construct a mythology of American sports that suggests that heroic individualism is still an American virtue, that the "little guy," the outsider, can triumph over almost insurmountable odds, that hard work and teamwork are the hallmarks of success, and that success (i.e., the victory) has the power to regenerate and reintegrate our communities. The scores are a siren's song, a musical mythology, calling to us, seducing us into once again believing and embracing the inchoate desire that these games will indeed repair our losses and be a blessing to us.

8

"I always thought I was"

Heroism and Music in Three Women's Films

HE: Aren't you glad?
SHE: Not glad and not not glad.
HE: I should think a baby would make you happy.
SHE: Will it, Louis?
HE: It ought to. Why should you be different from any other woman.
SHE: I always thought I was. Now I'm like all the rest. — *Beyond the Forest* (1949)

In a sense, every woman's film is about the protagonist struggling with a desire to be like all the rest and a desire to not be like all the rest. Some filmmakers resolve this conflict by having us believe that the protagonist's conformity is indeed a victory, as Jeanine Basinger writes: "The woman's film was successful because it worked out of paradox. It both held women in social bondage and released them into [a] dream of potency and freedom. It drew women in with images of what was lacking in their own lives and sent them home reassured that their own lives were the right thing after all" (6). Molly Haskell sees three divisions in the woman's film. First, there are films about *extraordinary women*. "Their point of view is singular, and in calling the shots they transcend the limitations of their sexual identities" (160). Next, there are films about *ordinary women*: "The purpose of these fables is not to encourage 'woman' to rebel or question her role, but to reconcile her to it, and thus preserve the status quo" (161). Finally, she notes, "Between these two, there is a third category, one to which the better women's films aspire: It is the fiction of the 'ordinary woman who becomes extraordinary,' the woman who begins as a victim of discriminatory circumstances and rises, through pain, obsession, or defiance, to become mistress of her fate" (161). The films under consideration here are about women forced to make choices and who through their actions choose not to be like all the rest and emerge heroic at the end.

What I will be suggesting in my analysis of three women's films is that when we speak of heroism in the women's film we need to redefine the concept in light of feminist criticism. In short, classic definitions of heroism, conditioned as they are by patriarchal models and concepts, may not be sufficient to understand the heroism of the protagonist in the women's film. The concepts of subjectivity and interiority are central to discussion of character and conflict in much feminist criticism and, I believe, it is in the notion of interiority that we will find the key to heroic behavior in many women's films. Let me begin with a basic definition of the women's film and then discuss the role of myth and the kernal conflict in the genre as it relates to those myths.

The Women's Film

Mary Ann Doane defines the women's film as follows:

> The label "woman's film" refers to a group of Hollywood films produced from the silent era through the 1950s and early 60s but most heavily concentrated and most popular in the 1930s and 40s. The films deal with a female protagonist and often appear to allow her significant access to point of view structures and enunciative level of the filmic discourse. They treat problems defined as "female" (problems revolving around domestic life, the family, children, self-sacrifice, and the relationship between women and production vs. that between women and reproduction), and, most crucially, are directed toward a female audience [3].

Doane's choice of women's films, moreover, is "largely determined by their tendencies to activate the specifically cinematic structures of subjectivity — primarily the voice-over, point-of-view shots, and the marking of certain sequences as dreams, hallucinations, or flashback memories — in relation to a female character. Films which attribute a narrative or story-telling agency to the woman (e.g., *Possessed, Rebecca, The Gay Sisters*) are particularly important" (35). The "problems" that inform the central conflict of the women's film are, moreover, deeply rooted in cultural myth. Throughout this study we have focused on the myths that inform the different genres and with the women's film we have a richly layered mythology. The myths, moreover, reinforce the narrative dynamics at work in the kernel conflict in the films.

One body of myth has its genesis in the ancient and powerful notions of hearth and domesticity, a mythology that places the woman as the center of the home and as a defender of the values signified by home and hearth. One of the most potent and pervasive myths deriving from the domestic realm is the "Cult of True Womanhood," which, according to E. Ann Kaplan, accentuates four qualities: "piety, purity, domesticity and submissiveness," qualities, she adds, that "closely mimic qualities of Rousseau's Sophie" ("Mothering, Feminism and Representation" 116). Closely related to this is the Victorian "cult of domesticity." According to Maria LaPlace, "more than just a term to describe settings and plot concerns, it refers to a strain of nineteenth-century feminism which valorized the domestic — defined by the values of love, support and shared responsibility — over the brutal, masculinist values of early industrial capitalism" (152). Molly Haskell sees this as emblematic of "middle-classness":

> Central to the woman's film is the notion of middle-classness, not just as an economic status, but as a state of mind and relatively rigid moral code. The circumscribed world of the housewife corresponds to the state of women in general, confronted by a range of options so limited she might as well inhabit a cell. The persistent irony is that she is dependent for her well-being and "fulfillment" on institutions — marriage, motherhood — that by translating the word "woman" into "wife" and "mother," end her independent identity. She then feels bound to adhere to a morality which demands that she stifle her own "illicit" creative or sexual urges in support of a social code that tolerates considerably more deviation on the part of her husband. She is encouraged to follow the lead of her romantic dreams, but when they expire she is stuck [159–160].

In a sense, these myths are ones we associate with the traditional woman, the housewife, the mother. Her domain is the home and she is the goddess of the hearth — whether, as Haskell suggests, she likes it not.

Another body of myth situates the woman outside the home and attempts to explain what happens to one who would wander from the hearth. Here we have the myth of the fallen woman or the loose woman. These are the women who stray from the circumscribed duties and values of the "true woman." Other female protagonists, such as career women, who have a different mythology surrounding them, would also fit into this camp: traditionally, the career woman pursued a career, chose an occupation over love and, generally, found herself lonely (and perhaps lost) at the end of the narrative. In a sense, the women's film is a social arena where these competing mythologies struggle for possession of the woman's soul. Patricia White notes that "from the perspective of genre theory, the woman's film could be seen as performing 'cultural work'—speaking, if displacing, genuine social conflicts—between women's economic dependence and desire for autonomy, between heterosexual and maternal ideology and sexual self-definition" (120). Succinctly, the conflict as E. Ann Kaplan notes is between domestic and public spheres (129). Will the woman resist the "calling" of home and family (and their attendant mythologies) and seek a career that will enable her to define herself in very existentialist terms?

The power of the conflict, which Ibsen recognized in *A Doll's House*, is located in culturally constructed notions of duty. Almost everyone is encouraged to follow the dictum "to thine own self be true" and to take advantage of that inalienable right to the pursuit of happiness. Simultaneously, both men and women are then conditioned and socialized to accept another duty. For men, the task has traditionally been easier, because they were presented with a multiplicity of choices. Women, on the other hand, were constrained, as Helmer reminds Nora, by a duty to husbands and children; in short, you are free to pursue happiness as long as it is within the home or within a career that entails nurturing and/or service (hence, the primacy of occupations like schoolteachers, nurses and secretaries for women in previous decades). Where men are the masters of their own fate, women are servants to everyone else. As the myths remind us, however, there is an odd status that attends the duty: the woman is the protectoress of the hearth, responsible for the maintenance of the moral code that serves as the cultural glue that binds the family together. Should she fail, the family fails; if the family fails, the fabric of society is rent and imperiled.

The women's film deals with choice. The very thing that makes a man's life exciting and full of promise fills the woman's life with the specter of existential dread. Not surprisingly, the women's film exploits a crucial iconographic dichotomy that is also important for film music composers. Where the male hero, in the spirit of Campbell's hero with a thousand faces, is sent out into the vast world, space, as Mary Ann Doane notes, "is constricted in the woman's film, usually to the space of the home. The opposition between inside and outside in relation to the house attains a significance which it rarely reaches in other genres" (179). Lea Jacobs notes that "good" women are situated in "traditional décor," signifying an "ideal of domesticity." On the other hand, the fallen woman or the more socially mobile woman, those women Jacobs describes as displaying more "female aggressivity," will appear "in increasingly lavish and exotic settings, greatly attenuating the severity of the fall. It is as if Eve were admitted to the Garden of Eden *after* having tasted the apple" (15). Ironically, the setting the woman enters, when she is outside the home, is the man's world: she competes with him for work and must act in aggressive ways to achieve economic security or freedom. In the three of the films under review here the element of materialism in the woman's choice is crucial, and that materialism is, as we shall see, is not a blessing but a trap.

The iconography of the women's films under review here also underscores the central conflict of the film. In each case, the home is the central iconic and dramatic space, but each film also features a secondary site. The secondary site, moreover, is central to the conflict because it suggests an alternative, another choice if you will, to the home, and in each case the secondary site plays an important role in the choice the woman will make on her path to heroism. In *Rebecca,* the secondary site is the cottage by the sea. It is here where the truth about Maxim and Rebecca is revealed and where the second Mrs. de Winter is forced to choose: to escape Manderley and Maxim or remain by his side during his crisis. In *All That Heaven Allows* it is Ron's mill, and it is here where the leads realize their feelings for one another. The mill is also interesting because Ron transforms it into a home that reconciles their philosophies and worldviews: there is the material and artistic beauty of Wedgwood married to the natural beauty of the wilderness and the deer. Finally, in *The Piano* it is Baines's cottage where the piano ultimately ends up being housed and where Ada can escape to free her spirit. It is also the site, like Ron's mill, where he wins her love.

Heroism

It is noteworthy that as we begin a discussion of heroism, we almost unconsciously gravitate towards texts like Joseph Campbell's *Hero with a Thousand Faces*, so much a staple is it of our understanding of the whole concept of heroism in Western literature and film. Of course Campbell's classic study deals primarily with male heroes in myth, legend, and literature. Women heroines are indeed present in literature but are relegated — some may prefer the term marginalized — to specific genres: the occasional tragedy, domestic drama, gothic romance, and, later, detective fiction — but, significantly, not hard-boiled fiction until V.I. Warshawsky in the '80s. The archetypal male hero is a man of action, his heroism defined by that action and by his willingness to risk; in genres, we can also add the element of exteriority to the pattern of action. By that I mean that the hero's actions are not undertaken to resolve existential dilemmas but to solve larger sociocultural conflicts. The cowboy helps bring civilization to the wilderness, the detective helps rid the city of crime, the scientists helps kill the monster threatening society, the swashbuckler is defending freedom for all men (and some women). The journey the hero takes, his quest, is also quite similar in each genre. The diagram on the following page is a from Campbell that illustrates the journey of the hero.

The hero, as you can see, is called to action, is tested, is aided in his quest by "helpers," faces the spectre of "fight or flight," confronts his adversary, and then must bring a boon back to the community; aside from the brief moment when he must decide if will fight or run — of course, the outcome of this existential tussle is a foregone conclusion for most audiences viewing most genres — resolving interior issues is not what he is about.

The woman hero in the women's film is I think something distinct from the archetypal male hero. Jeanine Basinger, in her discussion of Lucille Ball's TV character, locates female heroism in action, and she is right in one regard: the woman cannot become a hero through passivity; some action is demanded. Where I think we have to look, however, is not in overt action but in interiority. Kaja Silverman, commenting on Jacqueline Suter's ideas on female authorial voice, states: "Her theoretical model thus closely replicates the Hollywood model, which identifies the male voice with enunciative exteriority and the female voice with diegetic interiority" (393). Similarly, Maria LaPlace notes, "The basic narrative pattern of women's fiction is a 'heroine's text,' a story of a woman's personal triumph over adversity. The dominant variation features a young woman who is forced, because of circumstances beyond her control, to endure a series of hardships completely on her own. As she struggles to survive and build a satisfactory life for herself she finds the inner resources — will, courage and

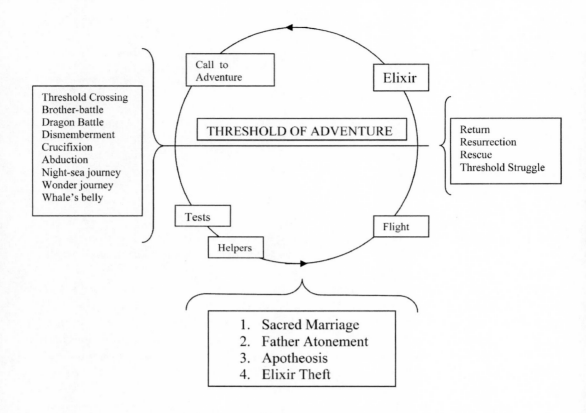

Figure 8.1. The Hero's Journey.

intelligence — that permit her to succeed" (151). These inner resources are, moreover, employed in the service of making a choice; where the male risks his body, the woman, in choosing, literally risks her identity, her inner self. Jeanine Basinger states:

> Every movie female has to confront the major action of the woman's film: making a choice. This means showing a viewer two opposite directions for a character to take, and that means giving substance to some form of liberation. First, the woman's film makes a woman important, and, last, it reminds her that her problem is that she *is* a woman; she can't escape the fact and thus ought to accept love. In between, however, comes the conflict and contradiction in the form of a visualized Other [19].

Basinger goes on to identify qualities and characteristics of different women heroines:

- A woman who defies conventional rules and redefines her life on her own terms, even if she opts to become a wife and mother (the process of questioning is what is of value)
- A woman who defies not just convention but society itself, never settling for less than possession of her own life, even if she is destroyed in the fight (a man who fights this way is called a hero; why not a woman)
- A woman, who, by choice or by accident, finds herself in a situation or profession that would be commonly restricted to male participation, and who functions ably in this situation (she must not be caricatured as choosing this endeavor because she is "unwomanly" or "frigid")
- A woman who forms and maintains a positive sisterly relationship or a healthy mother-daughter relationship [43–44].

With the possible exception of the third, choice and interiority are key elements in all these depictions of the woman as hero. The notion of defining self, of coming to an understanding of "who I am," is central to defining what makes the protagonist a hero in the women's film. And so it is with the films under consideration here.

The Men in Their Lives

Before we look at the music for our women heroes, I think a word about the men in their lives is in order. The ability of the women to define self must be assessed in light of the patriarchal hegemony at work in the films and in light of the men's roles as antagonists, foils, or allies in the women's struggle. Maxim, Ron, and Baines, in a sense, are not typical of the men we might assume to find in the women's film, that is, men who are rigidly authoritative, oppressors who demand that the woman attend to functions of the hearth and who ultimately make final choices for the women. Although we might have difficulty in labeling them as feminists or liberators, they at least may be characterized as integrators, characters who aid the women in their own quest for self-actualization.

Maxim (Laurence Olivier) comes perhaps the closest to the stereotypical male in his desire to find a wife who possesses the qualities Rebecca lacked: kindness, honesty, a lack of affectation, and, most importantly, a deep affection for Maxim himself. In short, at heart he seems to want a companion and someone who genuinely loves him for himself. Frank Crawley, in fact, identifies what makes the second Mrs. de Winter special: he says she has kindliness, sincerity and modesty; and these things, he adds, are "more important than wit and beauty" — Mrs. Danvers would disagree, but the second Mrs. de Winter's heroic triumph will indeed be predicated on these relatively simple values. At the same time, flashes of the old patriarchy are clearly evident in the film, with Maxim's assuming a very parental stance toward her at times, like someone who is addressing a child; there is, however, no cruelty in his words or even evidence that he renders her childlike to enhance his status as master of the manor to exercise male power.

Ron (Rock Hudson), in *All That Heaven Allows*, is a man who has largely freed himself from the conventions and attendant evils of middle class suburban (or small town) life by merit of his Thoreau-like connection to nature and his Emersonian espousal of self-reliance. He is a gardener with dreams of owning a tree farm and retreating from the hurly-burly to a sylvan mill away from town. It is hard to imagine Ron sitting around in his dotage, like Prufrock wondering if he should eat a peach or worrying about his bald spot; we, in fact, can imagine him hearing the mermaids singing! As the plot of the film unfolds, Ron's character almost gets subsumed into emblem, as he becomes for Cary more than just the man of her dreams but a living and viable symbol for freedom from the crippling conformity and deadening pettiness of the country club set. In fact, it is Ron who reminds Cary that it is her choice whether she wishes to conform to the expectations of her friends (enemies!) and children or listen to her own heart.

Baines (Harvey Keitel), like Ron, is also close to nature, living in a small hut contiguous to Stewart's estate. He, moreover, appears to have "gone native," sporting the distinctive markings of the Maori. Like Ron's warm mill in contrast to Cary's cold suburban house, Harriet Margolis notes that Campion offers "the blasted setting for Stewart's house, in pointed contrast to Baines' more ecologically integrated living quarters" (17–18). And, although he receives some sexual benefit upon Ada's visits by allowing her to play the piano in his hut, he also offers her release and a taste of freedom — expressed very nicely, as we shall see, through the music she performs. One significant aspect of Baines's relationship to Ada has to do with the prosthetic finger he crafts for her towards the film's end. In the context of the role of music in the film, this act is central to Ada's heroism, because he is helping her keep her art alive so she can continue to make music, so she can, in other words, be herself.

The Heroic in Film Music

In previous chapters, I outlined some of the dominant gestures and topics that have informed the underscoring of male heroes in genre films. Vigorous rhythms, lift gestures (especially of the fifth), ascending and aspiring melodic lines have dominated the musical vocabulary of the hero in both the concert and film music worlds. In the previous chapter on heroes in sports films, we saw that post romantic archetypes like Strauss's *Don Juan* or motifs from Wagner's ring cycle are often hearkened to and thus remain viable aural analogues for male heroism. Can we make similar generalizations about women and heroism in music? If we attempt to, we first are confronted with a fairly narrowly circumscribed body of texts to work from: women have figured prominently in opera, but in those roles they are often tragic heroines; they also figure but largely as minor characters in some religious works (Mary Magdalene, Salome, the Blessed Virgin). In short, the collective wellspring of women hero figures in music is significantly shallower than that of male heroes. But are there any conclusions we can draw from the music for the various women characters that might figure in the musical mythology of women in film? Susan McClary makes an interesting statement about one type of melodic gesture that could have relevance here, when she reminds readers of "the old semiotic principle that movement by fifths is strong (i.e., masculine), while movement by thirds is weak (i.e., feminine)" (77). She also speaks of the "heavily gendered legacy of these paradigms" (16) and discusses chromaticism: "Similarly, chromaticism, which enriches tonal music but which must finally be resolved to the triad for the sake of closure, takes on the cultural cast of 'femininity'" (16). In film genres, we have already observed that chromatic topics and gestures are often associated with characters like the *femme noir* in the detective film and the "other" woman in Westerns and historical romances. If chromaticism is a dominant principle in women's music we can see this as signifying transgression, resisting the dominance of tonality, rigidity and stability, and validating movement, desire, and perhaps something inevitably tragic if it must resolve the triad or, worse, the root. McClary characterizes Carmen as "the dissonant Other" (57), and similar things could be said of other such independent tragic heroines. We can see this as well in music written for women heroines like Charlotte Vale in *Now, Voyager*. Kate Daubney notes that Max Steiner used the tension between the diatonic and chromatic in the score as an analogue for Charlotte "treading a narrow path between unfortunate victim and deliberate adultress" (49). Similarly, Anahid Kassabian, in citing the research of Tagg and Kalinak, notes that "the features to which Tagg attributes the musical meaning 'pastoral' are the features that Kalinak says represent the virtuous wife: no syncopation, directional classical harmonies, and legato phrasing" (32). Consequently, one might be led to look for more dissonance in female heroes as emblematic of the transgressive nature of their desires. But this is not the case with women heroes in film, with perhaps the exception of the fallen woman.

I would suggest that if we are going to look for musical correlatives for the heroic that might transfer to the screen it might be in characters like Tosca or Madama Butterfly. Both are women who defy certain standards, Tosca by merit of her art and by merit of her sexuality and Butterfly by merit of her sexuality and her breaking with the conventions of Japanese society. Each has a stunning, character defining aria, which at once speaks to aspiration, desire and tragedy. In Tosca's aria "Vissi d'arte" ("I have lived for art"), she sings of how she has devoted her life to music and piety and asks why God repays her with misery. Gesturally, the first part of the aria privileges tragic gestures, emphasizing downward stepwise movement and downward leaps of the third and fourth. A reversal takes place as she begins singing "Diedi gioielli della Madonna," and we find more upward leaps especially in the climax of the song where in quick succession the aria features a leap of a fifth and then an octave (on "perchè, perchè, Signor") as she challenges the heavens to tell her why she is not rewarded for the gifts

l'o-ra del do-lor   per - che, per - che, Si - gnor, ah,

Figure 8.2. "Vissi d'arte."

she has offered. Madame Butterfly's aria "Un bel di" also relies heavily upon the intervals of the third and fourth in the opening. Even in the dramatic conclusion as she inexorably works her way up the staff to her high B♭, Puccini relies upon the interval of the third to build tension into her dramatic statement of belief that Pinkerton will return, concluding with a final leap of a sixth on "l'aspetto" ("I with faith unshaken await him!"). Were I asked to posit a theory for how desire is expressed musically in these arias, I would say that it is the combination of sighing gestures, used heavily at the outset, offset by inexorable upward movement as the themes are developed and culminating in final dramatic statements characterized by corresponding dramatic leaps. These are women who yearn, hope, struggle against patriarchal attitudes, and forcefully declare their desires to the world. We may also see them as transgressing against the conventions of their given societies, Tosca by challenging God and Butterfly by falling in love with a *gaijin*. Let us now see what sorts of gestures and topics film music composers use to capture desire and heroic behavior in three women's films.

Rebecca

Rebecca presents the critic and commentator on the women's film with an interesting dilemma. The film's title implies that Rebecca indeed should be the protagonist and not merely a ghostly presence insinuating herself into the central conflict. Rebecca herself, as she is described, would seem to be in many ways a perfect exemplar of the whole concept of female heroism: she clearly rebels against the staid and deadening strictures of upper class life. In one sense, she is an example of what Linda Woodbridge describes, in reference to the Duchess of Malfi, as a "hero of desire" (162), as she seeks pleasure — especially sexual pleasure — wherever she may find it. But, of course, she is quite unlike the Duchess as well because she is also an example of the notion of conspicuous consumption endemic to the fallen woman of which Lea Jacobs speaks. She, in essence, was a woman who, confronted with the opportunities of freedom and sexual liberation and the constraints of the hearth, clearly transgressed against the norms of her society and rejected the hearth. Yet she is not our protagonist. That title belongs to the "Second Mrs. de Winter," who, on the surface, is a somewhat demure, plain-looking, mousey, shy, and seemingly easily intimidated young woman; a woman, significantly, whose name is never spoken and who will only be known to us as the Second Mrs. de Winter (Joan Fontaine). The film, however, is about her triumph, and I think it is fair to call it a triumph. Because for all her retiring qualities, she, like our other heroes, must make a choice and then live with that choice. The choice she makes is, moreover, not an easy one, and it is one fraught with danger. Franz Waxman's score brilliantly outlines the subtleties of the film's rather complex conflicts.

The central conflict in the film is one that mines the dueling mythologies of the 20th century woman. One the one hand, we have Rebecca and her materialistic and morally ambiguous values; and on the other, we have the Second Mrs. de Winter, who, as we shall see, possesses values almost diametrically opposed to those of Rebecca. Rebecca, however, casts a shadow over all the events in the film. As I stated earlier, from a feminist perspective her life is almost a template of the classic heroine's struggle in the women's film. But she is a secondary character here, functioning as a symbol of certain largely negative feminine and social characteristics. As the story unfolds, we discover that she is strong willed, beautiful and witty. But we also find that she is careless (one senses that du Maurier, like Fitzgerald, hated this characteristic in people), restless and rootless, concerned about surface niceties of her class — in short, she maintained the veneer — and sexually active; the thought crossed my mind that were this a Restoration comedy, she would be the equivalent to a rake. Not surprisingly, Waxman's theme for her is a brilliant trope, consisting of, first, a gesture signifying aspiration but followed by a tragic, sighing gesture.

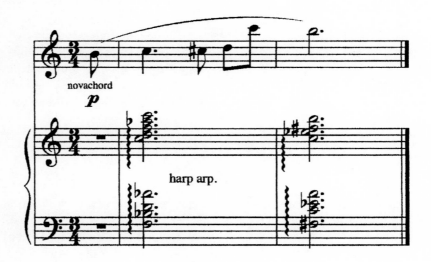

Figure 8. 3. "Rebecca."

It captures perfectly her struggle to break away from the strictures of her class and her tragic legacy, a legacy that the Second Mrs. de Winter must struggle against herself. Rebecca's legacy and her role as antagonist to the Second Mrs. de Winter is made palpable by two plot elements. First, there is the setting of Manderley, the epically proportioned gothic home of the de Winters that positively reeks of class and excess, the kind of excess that Rebecca seemed prey to. The Manderley leitmotif is particularly effective in aurally establishing the potentially tragic environment our heroine is about to inhabit. Like other motifs for women's films the motif is a trope with aspiring gestures being countered by tragic ones. The overall effect, however, the cue being scored in B minor, is tragic by virtue of the dramatic downward leaps and the final sighing-tragic gesture, which significantly is a leap of a minor third:

Figure 8.4. "Manderley," *Rebecca.*

And then there is Manderley's housekeeper and keeper of the legacy of Rebecca, Mrs. Danvers, played by a prodigiously frightening Judith Anderson. Danvers makes no bones about her adoration for Rebecca. She clearly revels in remembering how the first Mrs. de Winter thumbed her nose at the rigid moral conventions of her class and she vicariously revels in the material excesses of Rebecca's life. Danvers has her own motif, but Rebecca's motif, played on the novachord, is also used in scenes with Danvers. Christopher Palmer writes: "And

Rebecca. The Second Mrs. de Winter's heroism in defined by her struggle with the memory of Rebecca and the reality of Danvers.

because the malevolent spirit of the drowned Rebecca lives on in Mrs. Danvers, the nova-chord comes to stand as musical symbol for the latter also; its sinister purr seems to deepen the undercurrent of lesbianism and necrophilia through which the past contrives to poison the present" (103).

The Second Mrs. de Winter, then, emerges on the scene, seemingly quite the polar opposite of the first. I can easily see how one could have a hard time imagining her as anything remotely resembling a hero, so demure, insecure, and seemingly helpless does she appear. But over the course of the film, we come to see that she is locked in a struggle for her own identity. She must resist becoming like Rebecca, she must resist the temptations of the class, those temptations that result in moral vacuity and carelessness. She, in short, must indeed become the Second Mrs. de Winter and become her own woman in the process. How does she do that, and what musical cues give us clues into her ultimate victory?

Waxman employs two themes associated with Maxim and the second Mrs. de Winter, the first a light and jaunty melody that usually accompanies their courting scenes and signifies a freeing up of both of the personalities: his from the memory of Rebecca and hers from the subservience to an affected lady of leisure and from her own timidity. The other theme is one we associate more with the two as lovers. It shares many of the same characteristics of the "classic" love theme we hear in other genres. It serves as a perfect analogue of the second Mrs. de Winter's struggle and ultimate triumph because it begins with a dramatic downward leap only to be countered by the classic aspiring gesture that is shared by heroic topics and love themes in film.

Figure 8.5. "Love Theme," *Rebecca.*

It is perhaps significant that the intervallic leaps in the motif are of the sixth or the third, which seem to validate McClary's quote about the "old semiotic" of the third being feminine. In this case, we can perhaps make the case that, even though feminine, when contextualized in the *mise-en-scène* the third may achieve an heroic dimension. It also mirrors the two arias discussed earlier in the trope-like pattern of downward vs. upward movement, signifying the struggle between the tragic and the triumphant. In terms of its use, the theme is important in the confession scene and fireplace tableau when Maxim informs her that he may have been responsible for Rebecca's death and that she will have to decide if she will remain constant or if she will flee him. In the film's climax, as the second Mrs. de Winter seeks out Maxim in the midst of the fiery chaos enveloping Manderley, Waxman scores the love theme in most dramatic form, replete with brass and vigorous rhythms and, as Christopher Palmer notes, in a "climactically triumphant A major (one of the brightest keys)" (103). She has survived both the fire and the long shadow that Rebecca cast over Manderley and their marriage, and she has steadfastly remained committed to Maxim. If we reflect back on the film's opening where she returns to Manderley, we can see the burned out shell of a mansion being overtaken by the natural undergrowth as a metaphor for the Second Mrs. de Winter's triumph and her heroism: nature — or should we say a more natural way — triumphs over the materialistic, superficial and vacuous values of the dominant culture. Not ironically, much the same mythology is at work in *All That Heaven Allows* and *The Piano*.

All That Heaven Allows

Sirk's film masterfully explores the classic conflict of the woman having to choose between a safe, conventional, and ultimately vacuous middle class life consisting of children, the country club, and gossiping acquaintances or a younger, non-conformist man whose lifestyle stands in direct opposition to middle class norms and values but who can offer her true love. Cary, in classic heroic style, is asked to "risk it all" by choosing Ron (Rock Hudson). What makes Sirk's film so profoundly entertaining is that the choice is not one that pits adultery and/or true love against conventional or married love but one that pits true love against social conventions. Cary is indeed a "hero of desire," like the Duchess, as she finds herself torn between two conflicting cultural imperatives. Sirk gives us, on the one side, a mythology of the suburbs or small town, against which he counterposes a mythology of nature or the "natural" that is derived from Emerson and Thoreau. It is a conflict between those leading lives of quiet desperation and those who wish to crow like a rooster greeting the new day. He himself admitted that *Walden* was a subtext and "ultimately what the film was about. The picture is about the antithesis of Thoreau's qualified Rousseauism and established American society" (*Sirk on Sirk* 99). Frank Skinner underscores this conflict in a most unusual manner. His entire score is almost entirely borrowed from the repertoire of Romantic composers, in particular Liszt, Schumann and Brahms.

Cary's dilemma is that she is a widow who lives in a fashionable (but not necessarily ostentatious) neighborhood that, iconographically, signifies an upwardly mobile middle class or lower upper-class lifestyle. Her friends are the stereotypical country club set: vacuous, gossipy, philandering, and mean-spirited. She falls in love with Ron, a younger man who inherited his father's nursery and landscaping business but who wants to go out on his own and start a tree farm. Through him and, perhaps more importantly, through some married friends of his (who have escaped the rat-race of corporate and suburban life), she learns something of his character: he is totally unconcerned with the ways of the middle class and instead enjoys the outdoors and the simplicity of nature; he wants a business that will not necessarily yield huge profits but will instead provide him personal satisfaction. Barbara Klinger says of Ron's character:

> *All That Heaven Allows* accentuates the essential simplicity and uncluttered rightness that lay at the center of Hudson's particular kind of masculinity. His character, Ron Kirby, is overtly lined with nature both by his gardening vocation and his lifestyle. Kirby is presented as the "natural man" — earthy, generous, soft-spoken, and unassuming. As someone who rejects social artifice, preferring the woods and down-to-earth friends, he stands in contrast to the cronies of his beloved, Cary Scott (Jane Wyman) [*Melodrama and Meaning* 100].

Klinger's reference to Ron's "particular kind of masculinity" is important here because it might be precipitous for us to automatically associate the idea of someone close to nature with a form of masculine heroism. Kay Armatage in a fascinating study of Nell Shipman links her heroism with her close communion with nature: "In Shipman's case her extraordinary communication with the world of nature is an essential element in the constitution of heroic hyper-femininity" (136).[1] To this end, Skinner employs a motif from the introduction to the 4th movement of Brahms's Symphony no. 1 when Ron is in his natural habitat. The motif emanates warmth by merit of its generally being scored for a horn and its graceful downward sighing gesture.

Figure 8.6 Fourth Movement, Brahms's Symphony no. 1.

It is a gesture that does not signify the tragic, however, but instead conveys a sense of the heroic or a sense of nobility by virtue of the many leaps of the fifth contained in it. The sighing gesture, however, puts in the camp of the arias mentioned earlier, with the four-note descending pattern bearing some similarities to the descending gesture in "Vissi d'arte." In this way, it seems to bridge the topical characteristics of both love themes and the kind of "classical" heroic gestures we might encounter in historical romance films. Clearly, Skinner's strategy is that the music cues us to perceive Ron's "natural" way, the way that leads from the constricted and petty ways of the city, as something admirable and something that Cary should aspire to. Molly Haskell notes: "Hudson's little log cabin in the woods, with its fourteen-square-foot plate glass window at which deer nuzzle amiably, is hardly a picture of the rugged life, and it is not as if Wyman were marrying a black. But in terms of middle-class security and conditioning with which Sirk makes us understand her, her choice could not be more radical" (274–75).

The primary love theme — and ultimately the motif associated with Cary's triumph or her heroism — is also the dominant theme from the main title, Liszt's "Consolation No. 3." This theme is most often employed to suggest the bond between Cary and Ron and the hope, promise, and triumph of their love. It appears in scenes where their mutual commitment is discussed or expressed through their actions, ranging from their first kiss, to the scene where Cary is given pause by the prospect of riding to the country club in Ron's woodie (complete with company name on the side — he sees no reason why his work vehicle is not acceptable for social occasions as well!) to the final scene where she returns to him and vows not to leave — in spite of what her family and the entire community might say or think (of course, she does not say that — she doesn't have to, the music and mise-en-scène do that for her). The theme follows some archetypal motivic contours in relationship to film music: its strongest gestural characteristic is its upward yearning movement, a characteristic we find in both love

All That Heaven Allows. **Cary is torn between stifling social conventions and family and Ron's more natural and independent lifestyle.**

themes and heroic themes. Its more narrowly circumscribed range, however, sets it apart from the classic lift gestures of heroic themes; instead it moves away from the tonal center, initiated by an insistent repeated note, only to seek resolution.

Lento Placido

Figure 8.7. "Consolation No. 3."

The yearning correlates to her feelings for Ron (and vice versa) and the return to the tonic signals a validation of this yearning but not necessarily a return to "home" in the conventional sense of the term (which would mean her cold and expansive house). In fact, Ron is "home," real home, the home symbolized by the mill, far away from the club, the straitlaced dress, and the desperation of middle class life.

How then is the conflict underscored to make the "Consolation" theme the statement of Cary's heroism? Secondary themes or motifs in a sense act contrapuntally, stressing elements different from the main theme and consequently clarifying the emotional subtext of "Consolation." The first of these, Robert Schumann's "Warum?," the third piece from his op. 12, *Fantasiestücke*, for piano, is often used when Cary is confronted with choices. It works particularly well because its main motif seems almost resistant to resolution, beginning as it does on an altered chord (II6/4) and resolving as it does for two measures on the third scale degree of the tonic.

Langsam und zart

Figure 8.8. "Warum?"

This theme is used in a number of scenes with Ron where Cary must wrestle with her desire to be with him or her desire to conform (mostly for the sake of family). The most notable example is in the break-up scene, but the theme is used also in a scene with Harvey, where he tenders an offer of marriage in the most unromantic way imaginable. In this instance, Schumann's title is significant: "Why?" The motif is most often used when Cary is confronted with choice or finds her allegiance to her middle class status quo challenged and when she is tempted to flee back to the security of that lifestyle. The melody's dramatic leap of a sixth suggests a similar pattern we have observed in the hero's music elsewhere, but it is not the "male" fifth but the "feminine" third that predominates, seen in the D against the B♭ in the first measure and the F against the D♭ in the third. Thus, in the women's film the presence of the feminine third, then, may not always signify a sort of consonance or resolution to the tonic but may be used transgressively to suggest underlying dilemmas in consonance and resolution. That this resistance to resolution in the music should work so effectively in Sirk's film may be explained by Molly Haskell's comments on Sirk's heroines: "Salvation for Sirk's heroines, contrary to the practice of most women's films, is not in the sacrifice of oneself to children or social codes, but in the refusal to make that sacrifice" (272).

The second important musical motif is heard in Cary's confrontation with Ned after the debacle at the country club. In a *tour de force* exposure of the corrosive and deadening influence of country club and home, Sirk brings into dramatic relief the dangers of losing one's identity to either of these social forces. Cary escapes one part of a wretched evening only to stumble into the middle class version of hell upon her return home. The climactic scene occurs in the living room, in an almost *film noir* setting, as her priggish son Ned confronts her about her "affair" with Ron. Ned is perhaps the most strikingly frightening male image in the entire film: the "perfect" epitome of the 1950s male *Weltanschaung*, mixing equal parts greed, sexism, power, untrammeled consumerism, self-centeredness and boyish immaturity. He confronts Cary with much the same arguments that Helmer used to try and coerce Nora to remain with him in the climax of *A Doll's House*, most notably reminding her of her "duty" to her social set and the memory of his father — who Helmer is sure would never have approved of the match. This is the most darkly scored portion of the film — as one might imagine — with Skinner relying heavily upon motifs scored for the bass register of the piano. Earlier in the film, Cary had been playing the Liszt "Consolation" on the piano, signifying her hope for happiness and contentment with Ron; now the sound of the piano is ominous, filled with foreboding, tragedy and just a suggestion of violence.

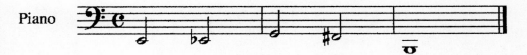

Figure 8.9. Confrontation with Ned.

The tragic gesture is thematized throughout the scene, with the music seemingly always seeking lower notes.

In contrast to both "Warum?" and the music used in the mother-son confrontation, Skinner employs Liszt's "Consolation No. 3" to underscore the romance itself and Cary's movement toward resolving the conflict in her life. There are a couple of topical-gestural elements at work in the piece that make it work well in the film. First, the accompaniment features a repeated bass note (almost like a pedal point) against which Liszt supplies an arpeggiated triplet pattern that hearkens to the pastoral. These two elements speak, first, to a need for stability and resolution, and, second, to the pastoral and, by extension, unaffected lifestyle represented by Ron. The melody itself contrasts a tendency to repetition with two types of yearning gestures, one a gentle stepwise ascent to a repetition of the third scale degree in echo of the opening and then a later yearning gesture that employs a lift gesture before it resolves to the dominant, in short not a complete resolution. The music communicates Cary's conflict and her triumph: the repeated notes are the call from society to maintain the status quo, but the call to something more meaningful is signified in the ascending gestures. Throughout the theme, moreover, one senses a tendency to reach beyond and to break away from that initial repeated pickup-downbeat figure. Consequently, when Cary finally commits and goes to Ron after his accident, the theme resonates with a clear sense of the rightness of her choice, a choice to embrace something natural and genuine and to reject the artificiality of the life she had once known. Jeanine Basinger notes of Cary and of Barbara Stanwyck's protagonist in *My Reputation* (1946): "Neither woman caves in to pressure from family, and, although their choices are men and love, they are questioning the traditional lives women are asked to lead and exhibiting bravery in rejecting these lives" (44). This is the second time we have a theme that relies upon yearning to signify feminine heroism.

The Piano

The Piano is, needless to say, the most musical of all the films here — although, were one to do timings, I think one would find that the films use almost an equal amount of music. But music is very central to this film because it is Ada's primary mode of expression and it is clearly, in form, content and use, a sign for desire and subjectivity. It also correlates beautifully with the interiority of her struggle and triumph. It is, moreover, a plot device that helps us discriminate between modes of patriarchy. Ann Hardy states that patriarchy in *The Piano* "is not only divided into two, into Baines and Stewart (as female characters have so often been divided in film); in the person of Stewart it is also divided against itself" (82). Baines, as I suggested earlier, shares some similarities with Ron in his closeness to nature (going native, if you will) and in the fact that he does not exercise power and authority but instead seems to encourage Ada (Holly Hunter) to choose and to choose of her own free will. Baines's role as facilitator or integrator in Ada's quest for self is most evident in the scene when he finally sets Ada free of their agreement by saying he will not make her a whore; Ron's scene is more direct, as he tells Cary she must choose between her family and her social circle or him. Interestingly enough, both women seemingly deny desire and retreat from making a choice only to recant later and follow their hearts.

Stewart (Sam Neill), on the other hand, is, like Ned in *All That Heaven Allows*, all repressed sexuality, business, material acquisition, and power. His abandonment of the piano on the beach as he comes to retrieve his wife-to-be is all one needs to know of his character. This is especially pointed because, prior to this, Campion shows us how inextricably linked the piano and *her* music is to desire when, as the piano sits crated up on the beach, Ada breaks off a piece of the crate to get access to the keys so she can play. The hand is constricted by the space but her soul will not be denied. Stewart will try to constrict her (music and body) but will find that her hand will find the keys; in the end, Baines will even craft a prosthesis that will enable her to find the keys when it appears that that facility will be lost to her.

One gets a full sense of the struggle in Ada through two cinematic elements, one visual and one aural. The visual is her stare — maybe we could term it her gaze, in counterpoint to the concept of the male gaze. We are introduced to it early in the film as she confronts a woman in her house and withers her with nothing but her stare. It is hard, defiant, suggesting she will not be dominated, and she will have her way. She immediately sits down at the piano and is almost magically transformed, when, as she begins to play, the hard edge of the stare gives way to a contemplative and loving expression and to supple, sensuous, and flowing movement throughout her body. Much is made of the fact that Ada does not play music from the standard classical repertoire but plays her own music. Her music, however, is a wonderful blend of Romanticism and folk-like simplicity. The Romantic undercurrent of her music is most evident in the inner voicings of the music, where we find broken chords and arpeggiated figures predominating. This is especially true and significant in her main theme (titled in the sheet music, "The Heart Asks Pleasure First"),which features an accompaniment pattern reminiscent of some of Schubert's lieder and his famous "Impromptu in G flat major" (op. 90, no. 3). When the piano and the music are removed from her, the gaze once again becomes the dominating visual analogue for her struggle and figures prominently in her interaction with other characters. It is an absolute barrier to her soul, and it is all that Stewart will experience of her. Baines, who saves the piano and ultimately saves her — not *from* anything but *for* herself— is allowed to experience her gentler facial expressions, her movements and to share in the release of her spirit. In the process, they are, ironically, both set free, released from the tired progress of industry and acquisition symbolized in Stewart's plantation.

Ada's music beautifully underscores the kernel conflict in the drama by emphasizing a persistently repeated note against the flowing accompaniment. If one were to isolate the

The Piano. Ada and Baines's bond is predicated on her ability to express herself through the piano.

melody line one could feel the urge to move but would finally be struck by the static nature of the line. Add the accompaniment, however, and the melody's sense of movement seems more purposeful. It is a movement against stasis and repression and an urging of the soul to escape, a portent of her triumph over those very forces of stasis and repression.

Figure 8.10. "The Heart Asks Pleasure First."

The other theme that appears with some regularity and that initially seems peripheral to Ada's struggle and triumph but actually figures in the resolution of the conflict is a simple folk-like melody that we hear her daughter sing on occasion:

Figure 8.11. "Silver-fingered fling."

It is a theme that we are supposed to associate with home and contentment and, in fact, it is the final piece of music heard in the film, thence perhaps its titling of "Silver-fingered Fling" in the published sheet music. What are we to make of this? Ada's free spirited, romantic music is seemingly finally abandoned at the end as we see her in a warm embrace with Baines and trying to learn to speak. Has she become the very thing she resisted earlier in the film? That one might reach this conclusion is perfectly logical. Earlier, upon leaving Stewart's planta-tion, she indeed does attempt suicide when she allows her foot to get entangled with the piano that she has ordered to be tossed over the side of the dingy. She follows the piano over the side and allows it to drag her into the murky darkness of the sea. As she looks around at the bleak underwater landscape, she has an epiphany as she seemingly realizes that if she drowns she loses not just the piano but the music — and by extension herself— and that, as she says, there is "silence in the grave." At the last, she rejects silence and the grave, wrestles with the line, frees herself, and swims to the surface and sunlight; she chooses life. The final images of the film confirm her triumph and the wisdom of her choice: Baines again supports her art by crafting a metal prosthetic finger so she can do that which she loves most — not so she can do that which serves him best or keeps her in a position of submission to his will. She also chooses to learn to speak, once again defying the grave and, ultimately, defying the spirit of Stewart and a form of patriarchy that would silence the woman's soul. In this scene, she is, moreover, happy and contented. Like Cary, Ada in choosing Baines has followed a natural route, and, although at the end she appears to be in a fairly conventional setting, we can justifiably argue that she has defied social convention and foiled societal expectations for what a woman *must* do. Musically, Nyman nicely captures the struggle and triumph. In the attempted suicide sequence he employs a minor key variant of "The Heart Asks Pleasure First," signifying the potential loss of her spirit (via the loss of her art, symbolized in the piano). The music, which had earlier soared and gamboled like her fingers on the keys, now is darker and slower, emphasizing oppression instead of liberation. This is countered, however, in the final scene described above by Nyman's using the "Silver-fingered fling" theme, with Ada beginning the cue by playing the theme using her prosthetic finger. Like "Consolation" in *All That Heaven Allows*, this theme features a movement upward and away only to gently return to "home." But in this case, home is configured in something different than conventional terms because the home is one of her choosing and her learning to speak is her decision, so the music correlates perfectly with a new Ada who has unconventionally embraced tradition.

There are those who probably would take more comfort in her suicide, seeing her tragedy as a more apt expression of feminism, or in her rejecting both men just because they are that, men! But I think Campion's film, in a sense, is a good barometer of the women's film today because the focus in on interiority. Ada's choice is clearly that: Ada's choice and no one else's. She indeed demonstrates throughout that she can pursue the path of tragedy or the path of rebellion, but she chooses love, home, and family. And Campion's film suggests that that is OK, as long as you knowingly and, if you will, critically make that choice. In a sense, were she to follow the tragic path it would be a betrayal of her spirit because it would be capitulating to the world of silence symbolized by Stewart and even the Maori tribe and would ultimately kill the music; she loses the piano but she does not lose the music — that is saved and so is she. You don't need a piano to have music and to be free!

Conclusion

In each of the films under consideration here, we see women struggling with issues of identity, and in each case the music serves as an excellent analogue for that interior journey. Molly Haskell states: "But in the distinguished women's films, the combination of director and star serve the same function as the complex perspective of the novelist: They take the woman out of the plural into the singular, out of defeat and passivity and collective identity into the radical adventure of the solitary soul, out of the contrivances of puritanical thinking in the enlightened self-interest" (162). And so we see that in the women's film, the motifs associated with the protagonist's ultimate triumph are not cut from the same cloth as that of our standard male heroes. There is an elegiac and reflective quality to the music we associate with the woman's desires, with the various themes relying upon aspiring/ yearning gestures and consonant resolution to the home key. Each motif, as well, functions like a trope by juxtaposing a sense of movement with a sense of stasis to signify that interiority. What remains somewhat paradoxical is that the women transgress the normal patriarchal order but their music does not transgress — i.e., the music does not privilege non-traditional elements, atonality, or chromaticism. Instead, like the women themselves, the music recasts tonality and feminine musical semiotics in new ways, heroic ways, and ironically in the process transgresses by giving us a new definition of the woman as hero in film.

Discography

This discography contains recordings cited in this book and some that I found
particularly useful during my research into the music of film genres.

Science Fiction

Arnold, David. *Independence Day.* Original motion picture soundtrack recording. RCA Victor/Twentieth Century–Fox/BMG Classics 09026-68564-2. 1996.

Elfman, Danny. *Men in Black.* Columbia/Sony music soundtrack CK 68859. 1997.

Goldsmith, Jerry. *Frontiers.* Royal Scottish National Orchestra, Jerry Goldsmith, cond. Varese Sarabande VSD-5871. 1997. Collection of Goldsmith's music from science fiction films including *Star Trek, Alien, Logan's Run, Capricorn One, Total Recall,* and others.

_____. *Logan's Run.* Original motion picture soundtrack. MGM Records MG-1-5302 (vinyl).

_____. *Outland* and *Capricorn One.* Original motion picture soundtracks. GNP/Crescendo GNPD 8035. 1993.

_____. *Planet of the Apes.* Original motion picture soundtrack. Cond. Jerry Goldsmith. Varese Sarabance/Fox Classics VSD-5848. 1997. Includes suite from *Escape from the Planet of the Apes.*

_____. *Star Trek: The Motion Picture.* Music from the original soundtrack. 30th anniversary collector's edition. 2 CDs. Columbia Legacy C2K 66134 JS. 1979, 1998.

The Greatest Themes from the Films of Arnold Schwarzenegger. The City of Prague Philharmonic, cond. Nic Raine; electronic music produced by Mark Ayres. Silva America SSD-1041. 1995. Includes themes and selections from *Predator, Total Recall, Terminator,* and *The Running Man.*

Herrmann, Bernard. *The Day the Earth Stood Still.* Original motion picture soundtrack. 20th Century–Fox Records 07822-11010-2. 1993.

Journey to the Stars: A Sci-Fi Fantasy Adventure. Hollywood Bowl Orchestra, John Mauceri, cond. Philips 446 403-2. 1995. Includes themes and music from *The Day the Earth Stood Still, Star Trek, Forbidden Planet, 2001: A Space Odyssey, Things to Come, Star Wars,* and others.

Monstrous Movie Music. Radio Symphony Orchestra of Cracow, cond. Masatoshi Misumoto. Monstrous Movie Music MMM-1950. 1996.

More Monstrous Movie Music. Radio Symphony Orchestra of Cracow, cond. Masatoshi Misumoto. Monstrous Movie Music MMM-1951.

Polidouris, Basil. *Starship Troopers.* Varese Sarabande VSD-5877. 1997.

Rosenman, Leonard. *Star Trek IV: The Voyage Home.* Original motion picture soundtrack. MCA Records MCAD-6195.1986.

Silvestri, Alan. *The Abyss.* Original motion picture soundtrack. Varese Sarabande VSD-5235. 1989.

_____. *Contact.* Music from the motion picture. Warner Brothers 9 46811-2. 1997.

Space and Beyond. The City of Prague Philharmonic, cond. Nic Raine. Silva America SSD 1065. 1996. Two CD set containing music and themes from *2001, Apollo 13, The Right Stuff, Species, Alien, Capricorn One, Cocoon, The Black Hole, Enemy Mine, Close Encounters of the Third Kind,* and the *Star Wars* and *Star Trek* series.

Themes from Classic Science Fiction, Fantasy and Horror Films. Orchestra cond. Dick Jacobs. Varese Sarabande VSD-5407. 1993. Includes themes and selections from *The Mole People, This Island Earth, The Incredible Shrinking Man, It Came from Outer Space, Tarantula, The Deadly Mantis* and *The Creature from the Black Lagoon.*

2001: A Space Odyssey. Original motion picture

soundtrack. Rhino Movie Music R2 72562. 1996.

Williams, John. *Close Encounters of the Third Kind.* The collector's edition soundtrack. Arista 07822-19004-2. 1977, 1998.

_____. *The Empire Strikes Back.* Original motion picture soundtrack. 2 CDs. RCA Victor 09026-68747-2. 1997.

_____. *Return of the Jedi.* Original motion picture soundtrack. 2 CDs. RCA Victor 09026-68748-2. 1997.

_____. *Star Wars.* Original motion picture soundtrack. 2 CDs. RCA Victor 09026-68746-2. 1997.

The Detective Film

Bernstein, Elmer. *Twilight.* Original motion picture soundtrack. Edel America Records 0038002EDL. 1998.

Deutsch, Adolph. *The Maltese Falcon and Other Classic Film Scores by Adolph Deutsch.* William Stromberg, cond. Moscow Symphony Orchestra. Marco Polo 8.225169. 2000.

Goldsmith, Jerry. *Basic Instinct.* Varese Sarabande VSD-5360. 1992.

_____. *L.A. Confidential.* Varese Sarabande VSD-5885. 1997.

Mancini, Henry. *Touch of Evil.* Varese Sarabande VSD-5414. 1993.

Murder Is My Beat: Classic Film Noir Themes and Scenes. Rhino R2 72466. 1997.

Rozsa, Miklos. *Double Indemnity, The Killers, Lost Weekend.* Koch International Classics 3-7375-2-H1. 1996.

Schifrin, Lalo. *Bullitt.* Aleph Records 018. 2000.

Steiner, Max. "The Big Sleep." On *Now Voyager: Classic Film Scores of Max Steiner.* Charles Gerhardt, conductor and the National Philharmonic Orchestra. RCA Victor 0136-2-RG. 1973.

Historical Romance

Burwell, Carter. *A Knight's Tale.* Columbia /Legacy/ Sony Music Sountrack CK 85947. 2001.

Captain Blood: Classic Film Scores for Errol Flynn. Charles Gerhardt and the National Philharmonic. RCA Victor 0912-2-RG. 1974. Contains selections from *The Adventures of Don Juan, The Sea Hawk, Captain Blood,* and *The Adventures of Robin Hood.*

The Crimson Pirate: Swashbucklers of the Silver Screen. The City of Prague Philharmonic, Paul Bateman, cond. Silva America SSD 3009. 1997.

Dudley, Anne. *Tristan and Isolde.* Original motion picture soundtrack. Varese Sarabande 302 066 713 2. 2006.

Glennie-Smith, Nick. *The Man in the Iron Mask.* Original motion picture soundtrack. Milan 73138 35846-2. 1998.

Goldsmith, Jerry. *First Knight.* Original motion picture soundtrack. Epic Sountrax EK 67270. 1995.

Horner, James. *The Mask of Zorro.* Music from the motion picture. Sony Music Sound SK 60627. 1998.

_____. *Troy.* Warner Reprise Records 48798-2. 2004.

Kamen, Michael. *Robin Hood, Prince of Thieves.* Original motion picture soundtrack. Morgan Creek Music 2959-20004-2. 1991.

Jarre, Maurice. *Dr. Zhivago.* Original motion picture soundtrack. Rhino Movie Music R2 71957. 1965, 1995.

Korngold, Erich Wolfgang. *The Adventures of Robin Hood.* Original motion picture score. Varujan Kojian, conductor, and the Utah Symphony Orchestra. Varese Saradbande VSD-47202. 1983.

_____. *The Adventures of Robin Hood.* Film score, 1938. Score restorations by John Morgan. William Stromberg, conductor, and Moscow Symphony Orchestra. Marco Polo 8.225268. 2003.

_____. *Erich Wolfgang Korngold: The Warner Bros. Years.* 2 CDs. Rhino Movie Music; Turner Classic Movie Music R272243. 1996. Contains original motion picture soundtrack music for *The Adventures of Robin Hood, Captain Blood, The Sea Hawk, Anthony Adverse, The Private Lives of Elizabeth and Essex* and other films.

_____. *The Private Lives of Elizabeth and Essex.* World premier recording of the complete score. Carl Davis, cond., with the Munich Symphony Orchestra. Varese Sarabande VSD-5696. 1998.

_____. *The Sea Hawk.* Original film score. Varujan Kojian, cond. The Utah Symphony Orchestra. Varese Sarabande VSD-47304. 1940, 1988.

Morross, Jerome. *The War Lord.* Original soundtrack album. Joseph Gershenson, cond. Varese Sarabande VSD-5536. 1994.

Newman, Alfred. *The Prisoner of Zenda.* Turner Classic Movie Music. *Film Score Monthly FSM* vol. 7, no.1. 1952, 2004.

_____. *Wuthering Heights: A Tribute to Alfred Newman.* Richard Kaufman, cond. New Zealand Symphony Orchestra. Koch International Classics 3-7376-2 H1. 1996. Includes selections from *Wuthering Heights, Prince of Foxes, David and Bathsheba, Dragonwyck, Prisoner of Zenda,* and *Brigham Young March.*

North, Alex. *Cleopatra*. Original motion picture soundtrack. 2 CDs. Varese Sarabande 302 066 224 2. 2001.

Raksin, David. *Forever Amber*. Original motion picture soundtrack. Alfred Newman, cond. Varese Sarabande /20th Century–Fox VSD-5857. 1998.

Rosza, Miklos. *Ben-Hur: A Tale of the Christ*. Original motion picture soundtrack. 2 CDs. Rhino Movie Music (Turner Classic Movie Music). R2 72197. 1959, 1996.

_____. *El Cid*. Music from the Samuel Bronston Production. Sony Music Special Products AK 47704. 1991.

_____. *Ivanhoe*. Cond. Bruce Boughton. Intrada (The Excalibur Collection) MAF 7055D. 1994.

_____. *Miklos Rosza at M-G-M*. Motion picture soundtrack anthology. 2 CDs. Rhino Movie Music R2 75723. 1999. Includes selections from the original motion picture soundtracks for *Ivanhoe*, *Knights of the Round Table*, *Beau Brummel*, *The King's Thief* and others.

Shearmur, Ed. *The Count of Monte Cristo*. Original motion picture soundtrack. RCA Victor 09026-63865-2. 2002.

Waxman, Franz. "Prince Valiant." *Sunset Boulevard: The Classic Film Scores of Franz Waxman*. Charles Gerhardt, conductor, and the National Philharmonic. RCA Victor 0708-2-RG. 1974.

Steiner, Max. *Gone with the Wind*. Original motion picture soundtrack. 2 CDs. Rhino Movie Music (Turner Classic Movie Music) R2 72269. 1939, 1996.

The Western

Barry, John. *Dances with Wolves*. Original motion picture soundtrack. Epic Associated ZK 46982. 1990.

Bernstein, Elmer. *John Wayne*. Vol. 2. Elmer Bernstein, cond., and the Utah Symphony Orchestra. Varese Sarabande VCD 47264. 1986. Includes selections from the scores for *The Shootist*; *Big Jake*; and *Cahill, United States Marshall*.

_____. *The Magnificent Seven*. Original motion picture soundtrack. Ryko RCD 10741.1960, 1998.

Best of the West. Ryko/MGM RCD 10721. 1998. Selections from original motion picture soundtracks including *The Big Country*, *The Unforgiven*, *The Wonderful Country*, *The Scalphunters*, *The Return of a Man Called Horse*, *The Hallelujah Trail*, *Hour of the Gun* and others.

Broughton, Bruce. *Silverado*. Intrada MAF 7035D. 1985, 1992.

_____. *Tombstone*. Intrada MAF 7038D. 1993.

Friedhofer, Hugo. *Broken Arrow*. Complete original motion picture soundtrack. Brigham Young Film Music Archives. FMA-HF 105. 1999.

Goldsmith, Jerry. *Wild Rovers*. Original motion picture soundtrack. Turner Classic Movie Music. *Film Score Classics/FSM* vol. 6, no. 15. 1871, 2003.

Harline, Leigh. *Broken Lance*. Original motion picture soundtrack. Film Score Golden Age Classics. *FSM* vol. 4, no. 18. 1954.

_____. *Warlock*. Original motion picture soundtrack. Lionel Newman, cond. Intrada; 20th Century–Fox. Intrada Special Collection, vol. 27. 1959, 1955, 2005.

How the West Was Won. Classic Western Film Scores 1. Nic Raine, cond., and the City of Prague Philharmonic. Silva America SSD 1058. 1996.

Howard, James Newton. *Wyatt Earp*. Original motion picture soundtrack. Warner Bros. 9 45660-2. 1994.

Lonesome Dove. Classic Western Scores 2. Nic Raine, cond., and the City of Prague Philharmonic. Silva America SSD1061. 1996.

Morricone, Ennio. *A Fistful of Dollars*. Original motion picture soundtrack. BMG/Razor and Tie 7930182171-2. 1998.

_____. *The Good, the Bad and the Ugly*. Original motion picture soundtrack. EMI Manhattan CDP7 48408 2. 1985.

_____. *The Legendary Italian Westerns*. The Film Composers Series, vol. 2. RCA Victor 9974-2-R. 1990. Includes selections from soundtracks for *A Fistful of Dollars*, *A Gun for Ringo*, *For a Few Dollars More*, and *Once Upon a Time in the West*, among others.

_____. *Once Upon a Time in the West*. Original soundtrack recording. RCA 4736-2-R. 1972.

Morross, Jerome. *The Big Country*. Tony Bremner, cond., and the Philharmonia Orchestra. Silva America SSD 1048. 1988.

Newman, Alfred. *How the West Was Won*. 2 CDs. Original soundtrack. Rhino Movie Music (Turner Classic Movie Music) R2 72458. 1962, 1997.

Newman, Randy. *Maverick*. Original film score. Reprise 9 45816-2. 1994.

North, Alex. *Cheyenne Autumn*. Original motion picture score. Label "X" LXCD 4. 1987.

Polidouris, Basil. *Lonesome Dove*. Original soundtrack. Sonic Images Records (Hallmark Entertainment) SID-8816. 1998.

Tiomikin, Dimitri. *The Alamo*. Original soundtrack. Columbia/Legacy CK 66138. 1995.

_____. *The Western Film World of Dimitri Tiomkin*.

Laurie Johnson, cond., and the London Studio Symphony Orchestra. Unicorn-Kanchana UKCD2011. 1988. Includes selections from *Red River, Duel in the Sun, High Noon, Night Passage,* and *Rio Bravo.*

Steiner, Max. "Dodge City." On *Captain Blood: Classic Film Scores for Errol Flynn.* Charles Gerhardt and the National Philharmonic. RCA Victor 0912-2-RG. 1974. Also contains selections from *They Died with Their Boots On.*

———. *The Lost Patrol, Virginia City* and *The Beast with Five Fingers.* William Stromberg, cond., and the Moscow Symphony Orchestra. Marco Polo 8.223870. 1995.

———. *They Died with Their Boots On.* Restored by John W. Morgan. William T. Stromberg, cond., and the Moscow Symphony Orchestra. Marco Polo 8.225079. 1998.

True Grit: Music from the Classic Films of John Wayne. Paul Bateman, cond., and the City of Prague Philharmonic. Silva America SSD 1037. 1994. Includes selections from *Stagecoach, She Wore a Yellow Ribbon, The Searchers, The Alamo, How the West Was Won, True Grit,* and *The Cowboys.*

The Wild West: The Essential Western Film Music Collection. 2 CDs. Paul Bateman and others, cond. The City of Prague Philharmonic. Silva America SSD 1099. 1999.

Williams, John. *The Cowboys.* Original motion picture soundtrack. Varese Sarabande VSD-5540. 1972, 1994.

Young, Victor. *Johnny Guitar.* Original motion picture soundtrack. Varese Sarabande VSD-5377. 1993.

———. *Rio Grande.* Original motion picture soundtrack. Varese Sarabande VSD-5378. 1993.

———. *Shane: A Tribute to Victor Young.* Richard Kaufman, cond. New Zealand Symphony Orchestra. Koch International Classics 3-7365-2 H1. 1996.

Horror

Bernard, James, Harry Robinson, and others. *The Hammer Film Music Collection,* vol. 1. GDI Records GDICD002. 1998.

Bernard, James, Harry Robinson, and others. *The Hammer Film Music Collection,* vol. 2. GDI Records GDICD005. 1999.

Bernard, James and others. *Hammer: The Studio that Dripped Blood.* 2 CDs. Silva America SSD 1137. 2002.

Bernstein, Charles, Christopher Young, and others.

Freddy's Favorites: The Best of A Nightmare on Elm Street. Varese Sarabande VSD-5427. 1993.

Carpenter, John. *Halloween.* 20th anniversary edition. Varese Sarabande VSD-5970. 1998.

Doyle, Patrick. *Mary Shelley's Frankenstein.* Original motion picture soundtrack. Epic Sountrax EK 66631. 1994.

Goldsmith, Jerry. *The Mephisto Waltz* and *The Other* (suite). 20th Century–Fox Classics/ Varese Sarabande VSD-5851. 1971, 1972, 1997.

A History of Horror: From Nosferatu to The Sixth Sense. Silva America SSD 1111. 2000.

Legendary Horror Films. Soundtrack Factory. 33566. 2002. Original themes from classic Universal horror movies.

Morricone, Ennio. *Wolf.* Columbia CK 64231. 1994.

Salter, Hans J., and Frank Skinner. *The Monster Music of Hans J. Salter and Frank Skinner.* Marco Polo 8.223747. 1995. Includes scores for *Son of Frankenstein, The Invisible Man Returns,* and *The Wolf Man,* reconstructed and orchestrated by John Morgan.

———, and ———. *Universal's Classic Scores of Mystery and Horror.* Orchestrated by John Morgan and William T. Stromberg. William T. Stromberg, cond. Slovak Radio Symphony Orchestra. Marco Polo 8.225124. 1999. Includes selections from *The Ghost of Frankenstein, Son of Dracula, Black Friday, Man Made Monster,* and *Sherlock Holmes and the Voice of Terror.*

Salter, Hans, and Paul Dessau. *House of Frankenstein.* Complete film score, 1944. William T. Stromberg, cond. Moscow Symphony Orchestra. Marco Polo 8.223748. 1995.

Waxman, Franz. *The Bride of Frankenstein.* Kenneth Alwyn, conductor, with the Westminster Philharmonic Orchestra. Silva America SSD 1028. 1993.

Webb, Roy. *Cat People: Classic Music for the Val Lewton Films.* Score reconstructions by John Morgan. William T. Stromberg, conductor, with the Slovak Radio Symphony Orchestra. Marco Polo 8.225125. 1999.

Sports Films

Goldsmith, Jerry. *Best Shot (Hoosiers).* That's Entertainment Records (import). CDTER 1141. 1987.

———. *Rudy.* Varese Sarabande VSD-5446. 1993.

Newman, Randy. *The Natural.* Warner Brothers 25116-2. 1984.

Shaiman, Marc. *61*.* Jellybean Recordings JBR-5048-2. 2001.

Tyler, Brian. *The Greatest Game Ever Played*. Hollywood Records 2061-62541-2. 2005.

The Woman's Film

Classic Film Scores for Bette Davis. Charles Gerhardt and the National Philharmonic Orchestra. RCA Victor 0183-2-RG. 1973.

Korngold, Erich Wolfgang. *Devotion*. Marco Polo 8.225038. William T. Stromberg and the Moscow Symphony Orchestra. 1999.

Newman, Alfred. *All About Eve* and *Leave Her To Heaven*. Film Score Monthly. *FSM* vol. 2, no. 7. 1950, 1945.

Nyman, Michael. *The Piano*. Virgin Records 07777 7 88274 2 9. 1993.

Waxman, Franz. *Rebecca*. Joel McNeely with the Royal Scottish National Orchestra. Varese Sarabande 302 066 160 2. 2002.

_____. *Rebecca*. Film Score, 1940. Viktor Simcisko and the Slovak Radio Symphony Orchestra. Naxos 8.557549. 1991, 2005.

Chapter Notes

Chapter 1

1. The progression from "I Got Rhythm" is so often used that it literally has its own name: "Rhythm Changes." For instance, the progression for the first four measures of Gershwin's "I Got Rhythm" goes like this: $B^{\flat}\backslash Gm\backslash Cm\backslash F^{7}$; the progression for Charlie Parker's "Anthropology" goes like this: $B^{\flat 6}\backslash G^{7}\backslash Cm^{7}\backslash F^{7}$. Melodically the two tunes could not be more different, with Gershwin accentuating Charleston-like rhythms and Parker accentuating a continuous and rapidly played eighth note figure.

2. A very similar point is made by Ernst Cassirer in his *Myth and Language*, pp. 60–69.

3. See Roger Manvell and John Huntley, *The Technique of Film Music* (London: Hastings House, 1957); Tony Thomas, *Music for the Movies* (New York: A.S. Barnes, 1973); Roy Prendergast, *Film Music: A Neglected Art*, 2nd ed. (New York: Norton, 1992); Claudia Gorbman, *Unheard Melodies: Narrative Film Music* (Bloomington: Indiana University Press, 1987); Kathryn Kallinak, *Settling the Score: Music and the Classical Hollywood Film* (Madison: University of Wisconsin Press, 1992); Royal Brown, *Overtones and Undertones: Reading Film Music* (Berkeley: University of California Press, 1994); Fred Karlin, *Listening to Movies: The Film Lover's Guide to Film Music* (New York: Schirmer Books, 1994); Irwin Bazelon, *Knowing the Score: Notes on Film Music* (New York: Van Nostrand Reinhold, 1975); George Burt, *The Art of Film Music* (Boston: Northeastern University Press, 1994); Anahid Kassabian, *Hearing Film: Tracking Identifications in Contemporary Hollywood Film Music* (New York: Routledge, 2001).

4. Musical cue is the term most often used to describe a musical segment or passage in a movie.

5. These two topics are taken from a list in V. Kofi Agawu's *Playing with Signs*, p. 30.

6. Aaron Ridley, in his *Music, Value and the Passions*, makes a useful distinction between music being an "expression" of something ("Passions *are* attributed to somebody") and music that is "expressive of" of something ("passions that are ascribed to nobody"; both quotes from page 18. The power of film music may indeed be ascribed to its ability to accomplish both of these functions; we may not see the music as an expression of the composer but we could conceivably see the music as coming from the character on the screen as a reflection of their mental or emotional state; on the other hand, there are times in a film when the music may not be connected directly to character and then we may see the music as being expressive of some emotion or value.

7. Robert Hatten uses the terms "marked" and "unmarked" in his analysis of style and meaning in Beethoven's music. They are concepts he borrowed from linguistics. He states: "The marked term specifies phonological, grammatical, or conceptual information which is not made specific by the more general, unmarked term; thus, the unmarked term may be used either when the opposition does not matter or when the exclusion of marked information is required" (*Musical Meaning in Beethoven* 34). Thus the term "cow" is unmarked and the term "bull" is marked, and in musical terms major would be unmarked — owing to frequency and more widespread usage in classical music — and minor would be marked by merit of its narrower expressive range (36).

8. Terasti discusses the usefulness of Barthes's approach to myth in "studying the connecting points between myth and music, especially the case in which myth subordinates music, retaining it as a substance in its own sign system" (*Myth and Music* 27).

9. Quotes are taken from Robert Fagles translation of *The Odyssey* (New York: Penguin Books, 1996).

10. Terasti writes of the opening of Smetana's *Vysehrad*: "Consequently, what is involved here is a musical sign which acquires its mythical character from its position in the composition's syntagma; on the other hand, the timbre and harmonies make this sign refer to a sort of 'mythical past,' to an ancient prehistoric time" (*Myth and Music* 67).

11. This second case is in actuality what I would call "Tin Pan Alley" or "Gershwin Blues," referring to the tradition of using blues materials in standard AABA Tin Pan Alley songs. The introduction of blues elements into popular music evolved slowly from minor usage in the early days of the Alley (1880–1918) to vigorous and inventive usage beginning with Gershwin's dominance of the musical scene in the 1920s; his "Stairway to Paradise" being, as David Ewan has suggested, a watershed work for the incorporation of blues elements into American popular song. Film music composers employ blues elements in much the same fashion in their scores. For instance Alfred Newman's "Street Scene."

12. A good example of this is Lidov's list of "the famous chain of interpretants" for *La Traviata*, including the novel, the play as interpretant of the novel, the opera as interpretant of the play, and, as he says, "Garbo's movie as an interpretant of all of it," plus biographies of Dumas and Duplessis (*Is Language a Music?* 167).

13. See James Buhler, "*Star Wars*, Music, and Myth," in *Music and Cinema,* ed. James Buhler, Caryl Flinn, and David Neumeyer (Hanover: Wesleyan University Press, 2000), 33–57; and Justin London, "Leitmotifs and Musical Reference in the Classic Film Score," in *Music and Cinema*, ed. James Buhler, Caryl Flinn, and David Neumeyer (Hanover: Wesleyan University Press, 2000), 85–96, for more discussion of the leitmotif debate.

14. Once again, we may be seeing the influence of Adorno here; he states: "The leitmotif is not supposed merely to characterize persons, emotions, or things although this is the prevalent conception." He notes that Wagner conceived its purpose as the endowment of the dramatic events with metaphysical significance so that, for instance, the Valhalla motif is meant to "connote the sphere of sublimity, the cosmic will, and the primal principle. The leitmotif was invented essentially for this kind of symbolism. There is no place for it in the motion picture, which seeks to depict reality" (5). If, as I have suggested, we view genre films as repositories of myth and fantasy wish-fulfillment, then, ironically, Adorno's thought on the leitmotif are still relevant to genre films — a thought that I somehow feel he would find troubling.

15. Recent research in the cognitive effect of film music has yielded some interesting observations relevant to this point. Annabel Cohen, for instance, states: "Music adds information that is both consistent and inconsistent with the narrative. The affective quality is consistent; the acoustical aspects of the music are not.... In the case of background music, it seems that the affective meaning of the music reaches consciousness but the acoustical musical surface does not, at least in the stream focusing on the visual interpretation" ("Film Music" 373–74).

16. Another powerful example of this is supplied by Carolyn Abbate in her analysis of "The Sorcerer's Apprentice" where she states that elements in the opening of the piece suggest "some 'cardinal functions'.... In this description, the sequence is again a string of musical items, now read as executions of gestures codified by musical convention, and enclosed within a musical web" (41).

17. Zuckerkandl (98) illustrates the relative stability and instability of tones using a curve to signify a tonal dynamic field with 5 being situated at the apex of the curve.

18. A wonderful example of this from the realm of popular music is George Gershwin's "The Man I Love."

19. For an excellent introduction to semiotic analysis of topics the reader is encouraged to read V. Kofi Agawu's *Playing with Signs.*

20. According to Cumming, "A 'legisign' is 'a law that is a Sign ... usually established by men' and includes any kind of regular ('law-governed') relationship, interpreted as a sign" (94).

21. Related to this is Caryl Flinn's suggestion that the return to the tonic signifies a return to nostalgia (*Strains of Utopia* 93–94).

22. One of the most notable examples of this is Max Steiner's well-chronicled battle with studio executives over the use of "As Time Goes By" in the score for *Casablanca*; I have summarized some of this battle in my article "'You know what I want to hear': The Music of Casablanca," *The Journal of Popular Film and Television* 32.2 (2004): 90–96.

23. This wonderful quote is attributed to Alfred Newman and was taken from the liner notes to *David Raksin Conducts Laura, The Bad and the Beautiful, Forever Amber* (RCA ARL1-1490).

Chapter 2

1. I am indebted to the liner notes from the album *Monstrous Movie Music* for supplying the instrumentation in this description.

2. Vivian Sobchak's comments about the musical impulses in science-fiction films are particularly relevant here: "The two predominant musical sounds one remembers hearing in the wide spectrum of SF films are heavenly choirs and rock music, the first closely connected with the promise of a new Eden and of the post-nuclear holocaust film, the second blared from the car radios before a 'thing' attacks the necking victims, or played before us by a 'live' group on a beach or at a dance, again prior to an alien attack" (212).

3. See my article "Kubrick vs. North: The Score for *2001: A Space Odyssey*," in *The Journal of Popular Film and Television* 25 (Winter 1998): 172–182.

4. This example is from George Burt's *The Art of Film Music*, p. 125.

5. The names for these cues come from the album *Journey to the Stars*; see the discography for complete information.

6. Trope, as defined by Robert Hatten, is "the bringing together of two otherwise incompatible style types in a single location to produce a unique expressive meaning from their collision or fusion" (*Interpreting Musical Gestures* 68). It can also be fusing two gestures, as in this example, where the downward ascending tragic or sighing gesture is fused with the lift gesture.

7. While listening to a recording of the musical cue "Charge" from the film on an album entitled *Historical Romances*, I was struck by how well I could specifically recall the details of this sequence by just hearing the music again.

8. Vivian Sobchak, in citing a *Sight and Sound* interview with Herrmann, offers a slightly different summary of the instrumentation used in the score: "electric violin, electric bass, two high and low electric Theremins, four pianos, four harps, and very strange section of about 30-odd brass" (211). Similarly, Leydon has noted, "Indeed, one of the principal means by which Herrmann evokes of sense of the paranormal is by dispensing altogether with the convention of a large string section" (40).

9. The titles of the musical cues used in the analy-

sis are taken from the original soundtrack album on Twentieth Century–Fox Records; see discography for complete details.

10. If readers wish to see some of these motifs in complete orchestral or conductor score formats, they can be found in the first edition of Karlin and Wright's *On the Track*, on pages 88, 182, 269, and 287.

11. Fred Karlin nicely outlines the many influences at work in Williams's score in his *Listening to the Movies*, p. 130.

12. Some may find more satisfying Neil Lerner's astute (if somewhat astringent) assessment of how the conflict is underscored and resolved through the music: "The score thus sets up the more experimental musical style as strange by associating it with the aliens, and ultimately it rejects this modernist musical language, substituting tonality for atonality just as it substitutes a nondescript heavenly existence for middle–American materialist banality" (102).

Chapter 3

1. Roy Prendergast cites Goldsmith's wishes for orchestrating the score for *Chinatown*: "'when I first saw the film *Chinatown* I immediately got a flash as to the orchestral fabric that I wanted. I of course had no idea musically what it was going to be but there was a sound in my mind and I wanted to use strings, 4 pianos, 4 harps, 2 percussion, and a trumpet'" (159).

Chapter 4

1. Darby and DuBois make an interesting comment about the use of the love theme at the film's end, implying that it might have been a misstep on Newman's part. However, if we subscribe to the idea that one of the genre's main themes is "love conquers all" and that romantic love is eternal, the use of the theme makes perfect sense: indeed Colman's character will leave the queen to her proper king, but it is clear that the affection they share for one another is an almost transcendental phenomenon and it validates the myth of romantic love that true love lasts forever.

2. In his *Listening to Movies*, Fred Karlin identifies this motif as "Robin Hood's theme" (98). Throughout this analysis I will be referring to Karlin's titles as I discuss the cues in the film; in some cases, I will use his appellations.

3. See Royal Brown's discussion of the interweaving of themes in Korngold's *The Sea Hawk* and Steiner's *King Kong* in *Overtones and Undertones: Reading Film Music*, pp. 101–17.

Chapter 5

1. This moral ambiguity, it should be noted, is probably made all the more problematic for the viewer by virtue of the fact that the protagonist is James Stewart, an actor known for his portrayals of kindly, competent, and even classically heroic individuals.

2. My thanks to Tony Bremner for helping me reconstruct the orchestration for this theme. For more on the use of pentatonic scales in Western scores, see Tony Bremner's liner notes for his recording of the score for *The Big Country* (Silva America SSD 1048, 1988).

3. Philip Loy notes that discussions of post–1955 Westerns feature words like ambiguity, neurotic, self-doubt, "emotional eccentricity" (Jon Tuska), obsessed and laconic (37–39).

4. A number of commentators have written about this, and I summarize most of their research in my article "'You Know What I Want to Hear': The Music of *Casablanca*," in *The Journal of Popular Film and Television* 32.2 (2004): 90–96.

5. The markedness of this progression is all the more telling when we consider that the more diatonically familiar progression would be I-VI-IV-V, a progression common to much popular music from Richard Rodgers's "Blue Moon" to countless Doo-Wop and Brill Building tunes in the late '50s and early '60s.

Chaper 7

1. These heroes are, in fact, very much cast in the mold or may be seen as a hybrid of what Joseph Campbell describes the hero of the monomyth, who is "a personage of exceptional gifts. Frequently, he is honored by his society, frequently unrecognized or disdained. He and/or his world in which he finds himself suffer from a symbolic deficiency. ... Typically, the hero of the fairy tale achieves a domestic, microcosmic triumph, and the hero of myth a world-historical macrocosmic triumph. Whereas the former — the youngest or despised child who becomes the master of extraordinary powers — prevails over his personal oppressors, the latter brings back from his adventure the means for the regeneration of his society as a whole" (*Hero with a Thousand Faces* 38).

2. See Deryck Cooke's discussion of Beethoven's *Eroica Symphony* in *The Language of Music* (New York: Oxford University Press, 1959), 228.

3. The musical figures for *Captain Blood*, *The Natural* (main title), *El Cid*, and *Rudy* (main title) are from published sheet music; the figures "Coach" and "Winning" from *Hoosiers* are from Fred Karlin and Rayburn Wright, *On the Track: A Guide to Contemporary Film Scoring* (New York: Schirmer Books, 1990); "Victory" from *Hoosiers* is from Fred Karlin and Rayburn Wright, *On the Track: A Guide to Contemporary Film Scoring*, 2nd ed. (New York: Schirmer Books, 2004). The remaining musical figures are the author's own transcriptions. I wish to thank composer and conductor Mr. Tony Bremner for his help with the "Promise" cue from *The Natural* and my son Andy Scheurer for his valuable assistance and advice on the transcriptions I did myself.

4. Although Joe Don Baker's portrayal of the Wham-

mer owes a lot (in both his look and behavior) to the actual Babe Ruth, it is Roy's home runs that are actually more evocative of the Bambino's contribution to the game after the Black Sox scandal of 1919. F.R. Lloyd in his article "The Home Run King" extensively analyzes the importance of home runs in Babe Ruth's career, noting that they "could have been evaluated as sources of wealth and celebrity, for their cathartic regenerative effects on the game of baseball and its fans, and for their apparent affirmation of qualities like strength, self-sufficiency, gallantry and even destructiveness" (181); later he notes that Ruth and his home runs "were identified widely as the authors of a profound change in the offensive philosophy of the game of baseball, and this change was evaluated positively as a kind of regenerative force" (184).

Chapter 8

1. Kay Armatage writes: "In *Back to God's Country*, the construction of feminine subjectivity operates upon Shipman's intuitive communication with animals and nature, and this natural connection is relayed to a level of heroic defiance of social convention. As character and as a star, Shipman doffs the fetters of ladylike decorum to cavort not only in natural but *au naturel*" (137). In a slightly less dramatic sense, Sirk achieves a similar thing with Cary choosing Ron and his "communication with animals and nature" (the reader may recall there is a scene where he is feeding a deer) and, consequently, achieves a sort of "heroic defiance of social convention" in doing so.

Bibliography

Film Studies and General Criticism

Altman, Rick. *Film/Genre*. London: BFI Publishing, 1999.

_____. "A Semantic/Syntactic Approach to Film Genre." In *Film Genre Reader*, ed. Barry Keith Grant, pp. 26–40. Austin: University of Texas Press, 1986.

Barthes, Roland. "Introduction to Structural Analysis." In *A Barthes Reader*, ed. Susan Sontag, pp. 251–295. New York: Hill and Wang, 1982.

_____. "Myth Today." In *A Barthes Reader*, ed. Susan Sontag, pp. 93–149. New York: Hill and Wang, 1982.

Bordwell, David, and Noel Carroll, eds. *Post-Theory: Reconstructing Film Studies*. Madison: The University of Wisconsin Press, 1996.

Braudy, Leo. "Genre: The Conventions of Connection." In *Film Theory and Criticism: Introductory Readings*, ed. Leo Braudy and Marshall Cohen, pp. 663–679. 6th ed. New York: Oxford University Press, 2004.

Braudy, Leo, and Marshall Cohen, eds. *Film Theory and Criticism: Introductory Readings*. 5th ed. New York: Oxford University Press, 1999.

Browne, Nick, ed. *Refiguring Film Genres: Theory and History*. Berkeley: University of California Press, 1998.

Campbell, Joseph. *The Hero with a Thousand Faces*. Bollingen Series 17. Princeton: Princeton University Press, 1949.

_____. *The Masks of God: Creative Mythology*. New York: Viking Press, Compass Books, 1968.

Cassirer, Ernst. *Language and Myth*. Trans. Susanne K. Langer. New York: Dover Publications, Inc., 1946, 1953.

Clynes, Manfred. *Sentics: The Touch of Emotions*. Garden City, NY: Doubleday/Anchor Press, 1977.

Duff, David. Introduction to *Modern Genre Theory*, ed. David Duff, pp. 1–24. Harlow, UK: Longman Critical Readers, 2000.

Easthope, Anthony. "Classic Film Theory and Semiotics." In *Film Studies: Critical Approaches*, ed. John Hill and Pamela Church Gibson, pp. 49–55. Oxford: Oxford University Press, 2000.

Grant, Barry Keith, ed. *Film Genre Reader*. Austin: University of Texas Press, 1986.

_____. *Film Genre: Theory and Criticism*. Metuchen, NJ: The Scarecrow Press, 1977.

Harmon, Gilbert. "Semiotics and the Cinema: Metz and Wollen." In *Film Theory and Criticism*, ed. Leo Braudy and Marshall Cohen. 5th ed. New York: Oxford University Press, 1999.

Hess, Judith Wright. "Genre Films and the Status Quo." In *Film Genre Reader*, ed. Barry Keith Grant, pp. 41–49. Austin: University of Texas Press, 1986.

Kaminsky, Stuart M. *American Film Genres: Approaches to a Critical Theory of Popular Film*. New York: Pflaum Publishing, 1974.

King, Noel. "Hermeneutics, Reception Aesthetics, and Film Interpretation." In *Film Studies: Critical Approaches*, ed. John Hill and Pamela Church Gibson, pp. 210–221. Oxford: Oxford University Press, 2000.

Klinger, Barbara. "'Cinema/Ideology Criticism' Revisited: The Progressive Genre." In *Film Genre Reader*, ed. Barry Keith Grant, pp. 74–90. Austin: University of Texas Press, 1986.

Levi-Strauss, Claude. *Structural Anthropology*. Trans. Claire Jacobson and Brooke Grundfest Schoepf. Garden City, NY: Doubleday Anchor Books, 1963, 1967.

Marsden, Michael, John G. Nachbar, and Sam L. Grogg, eds. *Movies as Artifacts: Cultural Criticism of Popular Film*. Chicago: Nelson-Hall, 1982.

Mast, Gerald, and Marshall Cohen, eds. *Film Theory and Criticism: Introductory Readings*. New York: Oxford University Press, 1974.

Michaels, Walter Benn. *The Shape of the Signifier: 1967 to the End of History.* Princeton: Princeton University Press, 2004.

Mulvey, Laura. "Visual Pleasure and the Narrative Cinema." In *Feminism and Film Theory,* ed. Constance Penley. New York: Routledge, 1988.

Neale, Steve. *Genre and Hollywood.* London: Routledge, 2000.

Nimmo, Dan, and James E. Combs. *Subliminal Politics: Myths and Mythmakers in America.* Englewood Cliffs, NJ: Prentice-Hall, 1980.

Nye, Russel. *The Unembarrassed Muse: The Popular Arts in America.* New York: The Dial Press, 1970.

Penley, Constance, ed. *Feminism and Film Theory.* New York: Routledge, 1988.

Robertson, James Oliver. *American Myth, American Reality.* New York: Hill and Wang, 1980.

Ryan, Michael, and Douglas Kellner. *Camera Politica: The Politics and Ideology of Contemporary Hollywood Film.* Bloomington: Indiana University Press, 1988.

Schatz, Thomas. *Hollywood Genres: Formulas, Filmmaking, and the Studio System.* New York: Random House, 1981.

_____. "The Structural Influence: New Directions in Film Genre Study." *Film Genre Reader.* Ed. Barry Keith Grant, pp. 31–101. Austin: University of Texas Press, 1986.

Solomon, Stanley J. *Beyond Formula: American Film Genres.* New York: Harcourt Brace Jovanovich, 1976.

Wollen, Peter. *Signs and Meaning in the Cinema.* 3rd ed. Bloomington: Indiana University Press, 1972.

Wood, Michael. "Ideology, Genre, Auteur." In *Film Theory and Criticism,* ed. Leo Braudy and Marshall Cohen, pp. 717–726. 6th ed. New York: Oxford University Press, 2004.

Music and Film Music: General

Abbate, Carolyn. *Unsung Voices: Opera and Musical Narrative in the Nineteenth Century.* Princeton: Princeton University Press, 1991.

Adorno, Theodor, and Hanns Eisler. *Composing for the Films.* New introduction by Graham McCann. London: The Athlone Press, 1947, 1994.

Agawu, V. Kofi. *Playing with Signs: A Semiotic Interpretation of Classical Music.* Princeton: Princeton University Press, 1991.

Bazelon, Irwin. *Knowing the Score: Notes on Film Music.* New York: Van Nostrand Reinhold Co., 1975.

Brown, Royal S. "Film Music: The Good, the Bad, and the Ugly." *Cineaste* 21.1-2 (1995): 62–67.

_____. *Overtones and Undertones: Reading Film Music.* Berkeley: University of California Press, 1994.

Budd, Malcolm. *Music and the Emotions: The Philosophical Theories.* London: Routledge and Kegan Paul, 1985, 1992.

Buhler, James. "*Star Wars,* Music, and Myth." In *Music and Cinema,* ed. James Buhler, Caryl Flinn, and David Neumeyer, pp. 33–57. Hanover: Wesleyan University Press, 2000.

Buhler, James, Caryl Flinn, and David Neumeyer, eds. *Music and Cinema.* Hanover: Wesleyan University Press, 2000.

Burt, George. *The Art of Film Music.* Boston: Northeastern University Press, 1994.

Clement, Catherine. *Opera, or the Undoing of Women.* Trans. Betsy Wing. Minneapolis: University of Minnesota Press, 1988.

Clynes, Manfred. *Sentics: The Touch of Emotions.* New York: Doubleday; Anchor Press, 1977.

Cohen, Annabel J. "Film Music: Perspectives from Cognitive Psychology." In *Music and Cinema,* ed. James Buhler, Caryl Flinn, and David Neumeyer, pp. 360–377. Hanover: Wesleyan University Press, 2000.

Cooke, Deryck. *The Language of Music.* Oxford: Oxford University Press, 1959.

Cooper, Grosvenor, and Leonard B. Meyer. *The Rhythmic Structure of Music.* Chicago: The University of Chicago Press, Phoenix Books, 1960.

Cumming, Naomi. *The Sonic Self: Musical Subjectivity and Signification.* Bloomington: Indiana University Press, 2000.

Dahlhaus, Carl. *The Idea of Absolute Music.* Trans. Roger Lustig. Chicago: University of Chicago Press, 1978, 1989.

Dallin, Leon. *Techniques of Twentieth Century Composition: A Guide to the Materials of Modern Music.* 3rd ed. Dubuque, IA: Wm. C. Brown Company Publishers, 1975.

Darby, William, and Jack DuBois. *American Film Music: Major Composers, Techniques, Trends, 1915–1990.* Jefferson, NC: McFarland, 1990.

Donnelly, K.J., ed. *Film Music: Critical Approaches.* New York: Continuum International Publishing Group, 2001.

Flinn, Caryl. *Strains of Utopia: Gender, Nostalgia, and Hollywood Film Music.* Princeton: Princeton University Press, 1992.

Goodman, Nelson. *The Languages of Art.* Indianapolis: The Bobbs-Merrill Company, 1968.

Gorbman, Claudia. *Unheard Melodies: Narrative Film Music.* Bloomington: Indiana University Press, 1987.

Hagen, Earle. *Scoring for Films.* Revised ed. Los Angeles: Alfred Publishing Co., 1971.

Hatten, Robert. *Interpreting Musical Gestures, Topics and Tropes: Mozart, Beethoven, Schubert.* Bloomington: Indiana University Press, 2004.

_____. *Musical Meaning in Beethoven: Markedness, Correlation, and Interpretation.* Bloomington: Indiana University Press, 1994, 2004.

Kalinak, Kathryn. *Settling the Score: Music and the Classical Hollywood Film.* Madison: The University of Wisconsin Press, 1992.

Karlin, Fred. *Listening to Movies: The Film Lover's Guide to Film Music.* New York: Schirmer Books, 1994.

Kivy, Peter. *Sound Sentiment: An Essay on the Musical Emotions.* Philadelphia: Temple University Press, 1989.

Karlin, Fred, and Rayburn Wright. *On the Track: A Guide to Contemporary Film Scoring.* New York: Schirmer Books, 1990.

_____. *On the Track: A Guide to Contemporary Film Scoring.* Revised 2nd ed. New York: Routledge, 2004.

Kassabian, Anahid. *Hearing Film: Tracking Identifications in Contemporary Hollywood Film Music.* New York: Routledge, 2001.

Keil, Charles. *Urban Blues.* Chicago: University of Chicago Press, 1966.

Lidov, David. *Elements of Semiotics.* New York: St. Martin's Press, 1999.

_____. *Is Language a Music? Writing on Musical Form and Signification.* Bloomington: Indiana University Press, 2005.

London, Justin. "Leitmotifs and Musical Reference in the Classic Film Score." In *Music and Cinema,* ed. James Buhler, Caryl Flinn, and David Neumeyer, pp. 85–96. Hanover: Wesleyan University Press, 2000.

Lyons, John. *Noam Chomsky.* New York: Viking Press, 1970.

Mache, Francois-Bernard. "Method and System." In *Musical Signification: Essays in the Semiotic Theory and Analysis of Music,* ed. Eero Tarasti, pp. 3–9. Berlin: Mouton de Gruyter, 1995.

Marks, Martin Miller. *Music and the Silent Film: Contexts and Case Studies, 1895–1924.* New York: Oxford University Press, 1997.

Marmorstein, Gary. *Hollywood Rhapsody: Movie Music and Its Makers 1900–1975.* New York: Schirmer Books, 1997.

Mancini, Henry. *Sounds and Scores: A Practical Guide to Professional Orchestration.* Miami: Warner Bros. Publications; Northridge Music, Inc., 1973, 1986.

May, Elizabeth, ed. *Musics of Many Cultures: An Introduction.* Berkeley: University of California Press, 1980.

McLary, Susan. *Feminine Endings: Music, Gender and Sexuality.* Minneapolis: University of Minnesota Press, 1991.

Meyer, Leonard. *Emotion and Meaning in Music.* Chicago: University of Chicago Press, 1956.

Monelle, Raymond. "Music and Semantics." In *Musical Signification: Essays in the Semiotic Theory and Analysis of Music,* ed. Eero Tarasti, pp. 91–107. Berlin: Mouton de Gruyter, 1995.

Murtomaki, Veijo. "The Problem of Narrativity in *En Saga.*" In *Musical Signification: Essays in the Semiotic Theory and Analysis of Music,* ed. Eero Tarasti, pp. 471–494. Berlin: Mouton de Gruyter, 1995.

Neumeyer, David and James Buhler. "Analytical and Interpretive Approaches to Film Music (I): Analysing the Music." In *Film Music: Critical Approaches,* ed. K.J. Donnelly, pp. 16–38. New York: Continuum International Pub. Group, 2001.

Palmer, Christopher. *The Composer in Hollywood.* London: Marion Boyars, 1990.

Prendergast, Roy M. *A Neglected Art: A Critical Study of Music in Films.* Second ed. New York: New York University Press, 1992.

Ratner, Leonard. *Classic Music: Expression, Form and Style.* New York: Schirmer Books, 1980.

Ridley, Aaron. *Music, Value and the Passions.* Ithaca: Cornell University Press, 1995.

Scheurer, Timothy E. "'You know what I want to hear': The Music of Casablanca." *The Journal of Popular Film and Television* 32.2 (2004): 90–96.

Skinner, Frank. *Underscore.* New York: Criterion Music Corp., 1950.

Simms, Bryan R. *Music of the Twentieth Century: Style and Structure.* New York: Schirmer Books, 1986.

Sloboda, John. *The Musical Mind: The Cognitive Psychology of Music.* Oxford: Clarendon Press, 1985.

Smart, Mary Ann. *Mimomania: Music and Gesture in Nineteenth-Century Opera.* Berkeley: University of California Press, 2004.

Swain, Joseph P. *Musical Languages.* New York: W.W. Norton, 1997.

Tarasti, Eero. *Myth and Music: A Semiotic Approach*

to the Aesthetics of Myth in Music, Especially That of Wagner, Sibelius and Stravinsky. The Hague: Mouton Publishers, 1979.

Thomas, Tony. *Film Score: The View from the Podium.* New York: A.S. Barnes and Co., 1979.

Timm, Larry. *The Soul of Cinema: An Appreciation of Film Music.* Upper Saddle River, NJ: Prentice Hall, 2003.

Zuckerkandl, Victor. *Sound and Symbol: Music and the External World.* Trans. Willard R. Trask. Bollingen Series XLIV. Princeton: Princeton University Press, 1956, 1969.

Genre —

Science Fiction

Agel, Jerome, ed. *The Making of Kubrick's 2001.* New York: Signet Books, 1970.

Blish, James. "On Science Fiction Criticism." In *SF: The Other Side of Realism: Essays on Modern Fantasy and Science Fiction,* ed. Thomas Clareson, pp. 166–170. Bowling Green, OH: Bowling Green University Popular Press, 1971.

Butor, Michel. "Science Fiction: The Crisis of Its Growth." In *SF: The Other Side of Realism: Essays on Modern Fantasy and Science Fiction,* ed. Thomas Clareson, pp. 157–165. Bowling Green, OH: Bowling Green University Popular Press, 1971.

Ciment, Michel. *Kubrick.* Trans. Gilbert Adair. New York: Holt, Rinehart and Winston, 1980.

Haspel, Paul. "Future Shock on the National Mall: Washington, D.C., as Disputed Ideological Space in Robert Wise's *The Day the Earth Stood Still.*" *Journal of Popular Film and Television* 34:2 (Summer 2006): 62–71.

Hodgens, Richard. "A Short Tragical History of the Science Fiction Film." In *SF: The Other Side of Realism: Essays on Modern Fantasy and Science Fiction,* ed. Thomas Clareson, pp. 248–262. Bowling Green, OH: Bowling Green University Popular Press, 1971.

Hogan, David, ed. *Science Fiction America: Essays on SF Cinema.* Jefferson, NC: McFarland, 2006.

Kagan, Norman. *The Cinema of Stanley Kubrick.* New York: Grove Press, 1972.

Kuhn, Annette, ed. *Alien Zone: Cultural Theory and Contemporary Science Fiction Cinema.* London: Verso, 1990.

Lerner, Neil. "Nostalgia, Masculinist Discourse, and Authoritarianism in John Williams' Scores for *Star Wars* and *Close Encounters of the Third Kind.*" In *Off the Planet: Music Sound and Science Fiction,* ed. Philip Hayward, pp. 96–108. Bloomington: Indiana University Press, 2004.

Leydon, Rebecca. "Hooked on Aetherophonics: *The Day the Earth Stood Still.*" In *Off the Planet: Music Sound and Science Fiction,* ed. Philip Hayward, pp. 30–41. Bloomington: Indiana University Press, 2004.

Nelson, Thomas Allen. *Kubrick: Inside a Film Artist's Maze.* Bloomington: Indiana University Press, 1982.

Phillips, Gene D. *Stanley Kubrick: A Film Odyssey.* New York: Popular Library, 1975.

Scheurer, Timothy E. "Kubrick vs. North: The Score for *2001: A Space Odyssey.*" *Journal of Popular Film and Television* 25:4 (Winter 1998): 172–182.

Sobchak, Vivian. *Screening Space: The American Science Fiction Film.* Second ed. New York: Ungar, 1987.

Stevenson, Lionel. "The Artistic Problem: Science Fiction as Romance." In *SF: The Other Side of Realism: Essays on Modern Fantasy and Science Fiction,* ed. Thomas Clareson, pp. 96–104. Bowling Green, OH: Bowling Green University Popular Press, 1971.

Telotte, J.P. *Replications: A Robotic History of the Science Fiction Film.* Urbana: University of Illinois Press, 1995.

Walker, Alexander. *Stanley Kubrick Directs.* New York: Harcourt Brace Jovanovich, Inc., 1971.

Detective Films

Chandler, Raymond. "The Simple Art of Murder." In *The Simple Art of Murder.* New York: Ballantine Books, 1950, 1972.

Eaton, Michael. *Chinatown.* London: BFI Publishing, BFI Film Classics, 1997.

Leitch, Thomas. *Crime Films.* Cambridge: Cambridge University Press, 2002.

Palmer, R. Barton. *Hollywood's Dark Cinema: The American Film Noir.* New York: Twayne Publishers, 1994.

Telotte, J.P. "Talk and Trouble: *Kiss Me Deadly*'s Apocalyptic Discourse." *Journal of Popular Film and Television* 13 (Summer 1985): 69–79.

Thomson, David. *The Big Sleep.* London: BFI Publishing, BFI Film Classics, 1997.

Willett, Ralph. *The Naked City: Urban Crime Fiction in the USA.* Manchester: Manchester University Press, 1996.

Historical Romance

Elley, Derek. *The Epic Film: Myth and History.* London: Routledge and Kegan Paul, 1984.

Grindon, Leger. *Shadows on the Past: Studies in the Historical Fiction Film.* Philadelphia: Temple University Press, 1994.

Hoffman, Carl. "The Evolution of a Gladiator: History, Representation, and Revision in *Spartacus.*" *Journal of American and Comparative Cultures* 23.1 (Spring 2000): 63–70.

Landy, Marcia. *Cinematic Uses of the Past.* Minneapolis: University of Minnesota Press, 1996.

Lenihan, John H. "English Classics for Cold War America: MGM's *Kim* (1950), *Ivanhoe* (1952), and *Julius Caesar* (1953)." *Journal of Popular Film and Television* 20.3 (1992): 42–51.

Rapee, Erno, arranger. *Motion Picture Moods for Pianists and Organists: A Rapid-Reference Collection of Selected Pieces.* New York: G. Schirmer, 1924.

Richards, Jeffrey. *Swordsmen on the Screen: From Douglas Fairbanks to Michael York.* London: Routledge and Kegan Paul, 1977.

Taves, Brian. *The Romance of Adventure: The Genre of Historical Adventure Movies.* Jackson: University Press of Mississippi, 1993.

The Western

Berg, Chuck. "Fade-Out in the West: The Western's Last Stand." In *Film Genre 2000,* ed. Wheeler Winston Dixon, pp. 211–225. Albany: State University of New York Press, 2000.

Bremner, Tony. "Liner Notes" for his recording of Jerome Moross's score for *The Big Country.* Tony Bremner, cond. The Philharmonia Orchestra. Silva America SSD 1048. 1988.

Browne, Nick. "The Spectator-in-the-Text: The Rhetoric of *Stagecoach.*" In *Film Theory and Criticism,* ed. Leo Braudy and Marshall Cohen, pp. 118–133. 6th ed. New York: Oxford University Press, 2004.

Buscombe, Edward. *The Searchers.* London: British Film Institute, BFI Film Classics, 2000.

Cawelti, John. *The Six-Gun Mystique.* Bowling Green, OH: Bowling Green University Popular Press, 1971.

Countryman, Edward, and Evonne von Heussen-Countryman. *Shane.* London: British Film Institute, BFI Film Classics, 1999.

Coyne, Michael. *The Crowded Prairie: American National Identity in the Hollywood Western.* London: I.B. Taurus, 1997.

DeLoria, Philip J. *Playing Indian.* New Haven: Yale University Press, 1998.

Dowell, Pat. "The Mythology of the Western: Hollywood Perspectives on Race and Gender in the Nineties." *Cineaste* 21.1-2 (1995): 6–12.

Gorbman, Claudia. "Scoring the Indian: Music in the Liberal Western." In *Western Music and Its Others: Difference, Representation, and Appropriation in Music,* ed. Georgina Born and David Hesmondhalgh, pp. 234–253. Berkeley: University of California Press, 2000.

Jackson, Richard, ed. *Popular Songs of Nineteenth-Century America: Complete Original Sheet Music for 64 Songs.* New York: Dover Publications, 1976.

Kalinak, Kathryn. "'The Sound of Many Voices': Music in John Ford's Westerns." In *John Ford Made Westerns: Filming the Legend in the Sound Era,* ed. Gaylyn Studlar and Matthew Bernstein, pp. 169–192. Bloomington: Indiana University Press, 2001.

Lenihan, John H. *Showdown: Confronting Modern America in the Western Film.* Urbana: University of Illinois Press, 1980.

Loy, R. Philip. *Westerns in a Changing America, 1955–2000.* Jefferson, N.C.: McFarland, 2004.

Maltby, Richard. "A Better Sense of History: John Ford and the Indians." In *The Book of Westerns,* eds. Ian Cameron and Douglas Pye, pp. 34–49. New York: Continuum, 1996.

McAllester, David P. "North American Native Music." In *Musics of Many Cultures: An Introduction,* ed. Elizabeth May, pp. 307–331. Berkeley: University of California Press, 1980.

Mitchell, Lee Clark. *Westerns: Making the Man in Fiction and Film.* Chicago: The University of Chicago Press, 1996.

Nachbar, Jack, ed. *Focus on the Western.* Englewood Cliffs, NJ: Prentice-Hall, Spectrum Books, 1974.

Prats, Armando Jose. "His Master's Voice(over): Revisionist Ethos and Narrative Dependence from *Broken Arrow* (1950) to *Geronimo: An American Legend* (1993)." *ANQ* 9.3 (Summer 1996): 15–29.

Silber, Irwin, ed. *Songs of the Great American West.* New York: Dover Publications, 1967, 1995.

Tompkins, Jane. *West of Everything: The Inner Life of Westerns.* New York: Oxford University Press, 1992.

Horror

Berenstein, Rhona J. *Attack of the Leading Ladies: Gender, Sexuality, and Spectatorship in Classic*

Horror Cinema. New York: Columbia University Press, 1996.

Brunas, Michael, John Brunas, and Tom Weaver. *Universal Horror: The Studio's Classic Films, 1931–1946.* Jefferson, NC: McFarland, 1990.

Clover, Carol. "The Eye of Horror." In *Viewing Positions: Ways of Seeing Film,* ed. Linda Williams, pp. 184–230. New Brunswick: Rutgers University Press, 1995.

Dika, Vera. *Games of Terror: Halloween, Friday the 13th, and the Films of the Stalker Cycle.* Rutherford: Farleigh Dickinson University Press, 1990.

Edmundson, Mark. *Nightmare on Main Street: Angles, Sadomasochism, and the Culture of Gothic.* Cambridge, MA: Harvard University Press, 1997.

Evans, Walter. "Monster Movies: A Sexual Theory." In *Movies as Artifacts: Cultural Criticism of Popular Film,* ed. Michael T. Marsden, John G. Nachbar, and Sam L. Grogg, pp. 129–137. Chicago: Nelson-Hall, 1982.

Freeland, Cynthia. *The Naked and the Undead: Evil and the Appeal of Horror.* Boulder, CO: Westview, 2000.

Harris, Martin. "You Can't Kill the Boogeyman: *Halloween III* and the Modern Horror Franchise." *Journal of Popular Film and Television* 32:3 (Fall 2004): 98–109.

Larson, Randall D. *Music from the House of Hammer: Music in the Hammer Horror Films, 1950–1980.* Lanham, MD: The Scarecrow Press, 1996.

Meikle, Denis. *A History of Horrors: The Rise and Fall of the House of Hammer.* Filmmakers Series no. 51. Lanham, MD: Scarecrow Press, 2001.

Modleski, Tania. "The Terror of Pleasure: The Contemporary Horror Film and Postmodern Theory." In *Film Theory and Criticism,* ed. Leo Braudy and Marshall Cohen, pp. 764–773. 6th ed. New York: Oxford University Press, 2004.

Rosar, William. "Music for the Monsters: Universal Pictures' Horror Film Scores of the Thirties." *Quarterly Journal of the Library of Congress* 40. 4 (Fall 1983): 390–421.

Russell, David J. "Monster Roundup: Reintegrating the Horror Genre." In *Refiguring American Film Genres: History and Theory,* ed. Nick Browne, pp. 233–254. Berkeley: University of California Press, 1998.

Sanjak, David. "Same as It Ever Was: Innovation and Exhaustion in the Horror and Science Fiction Films of the 1990s." In *Film Genre 2000,* ed. Wheeler Winston Dixon, pp. 111–124. Albany: State University of New York Press, 2000.

Skal, David J. *The Monster Show: A Cultural History of Horror.* New York: Faber and Faber, Inc., 1993, 2001.

_____. *Screams of Reason: Mad Science and Modern Culture.* New York: W.W. Norton, 1998.

Svehla, Gary J., and Susan Svehla, eds. *Bitches, Bimbos, and Virgins: Women in the Horror Film.* Baltimore: Midnight Marquee Press, 1996.

Tudor, Andrew. *Monsters and Mad Scientists: A Cultural History of the Horror Movie.* Oxford: Basil Blackwell, 1989.

Twitchell, James B. *Dreadful Pleasures: An Anatomy of Modern Horror.* New York: Oxford University Press, 1985.

Wee, Valerie. "Resurrecting and Updating the Teen Slasher: The Case of *Scream.*" *Journal of Popular Film and Television* 34.2 (Summer 2006): 50–61.

Williams, Tony. *Hearths of Darkness: The Family in the American Horror Film.* Teaneck: Farleigh Dickinson University Press, 1996.

The Sports Film

Campbell, Joseph. *The Hero with a Thousand Faces.* Bollingen Series XVII. Princeton: Princeton University Press, 1949, 1972.

Cartwright, Kent, and Mary McElroy. "Malamud's 'The Natural' and the Appeal of Baseball in American Culture." *Journal of American Culture* 8 (Summer 1985): 47–55.

Dickerson, Gary. *The Cinema of Baseball: Images of America, 1929–1989.* Westport, CT: Meckler, 1991.

Lloyd, F.R. "The Home Run King." In *The Popular Culture Reader,* ed. Jack Nachbar and John Wright, pp. 180–192. Bowling Green, OH: Bowling Green University Popular Press, 1977. Reprinted from *The Journal of Popular Culture* 9 (1976): 983–995.

Turchi, Peter. "Roy Hobb's Corrected Stance." *Literature/Film Quarterly* 19 (1991): 150–156.

The Woman's Film

Armatage, Kay. "Nell Shipman: A Case of Heroic Femininity." In *Feminisms in the Cinema,* ed. Laura Pietropaolo and Ada Testafieri, pp. 125–145. Bloomington: Indiana University Press, 1995.

Auerbach, Nina. *Woman and the Demon: The Life of a Victorian Myth.* Cambridge: Harvard University Press, 1982.

Basinger, Jeanine. *A Woman's View: How Hollywood Spoke to Women, 1930–1960.* New York: Knopf, 1995.

Daubney, Kate. *Max Steiner's Now, Voyager: A Film Score Guide.* Film Score Guides number 1. Westport, CT: Greenwood Press, 2000.

DeLauretis, Teresa. *Technologies of Gender: Essays on the Theory, Film, and Fiction.* Bloomington: Indiana University Press, 1987.

Doane, Mary Ann. *The Desire to Desire: The Woman's Film of the 1940s.* Bloomington: Indiana University Press, 1987.

Elsaesser, Thomas. "Tales of Sound and Fury: Observations on the Family Melodrama." In *Home Is Where the Heart Is: Studies in Melodrama and the Woman's Film,* ed. Christine Gledhill, pp. 43–69. London: BFI, 1987.

Hardy, Ann. "The Last Patriarch." In *Jane Campion's The Piano,* ed. Harriet Margolis, pp. 59–85. New York: Cambridge University Press, 2000.

Haskell, Molly. *From Reverence to Rape: The Treatment of Women in the Movies.* New York: Penguin Books, 1974.

Jacobs, Lea. *The Wages of Sin: Censorship and the Fallen Woman Film, 1928–1942.* Berkeley: University of California Press, 1995.

Kalinak, Kathryn. "The Fallen Woman and the Virtuous Wife: Musical Stereotypes in *The Informer, Gone with the Wind,* and *Laura." Film Reader /5* 82: 76–82.

Kaplan, E. Ann. "Mothering, Feminism and Representation: The Maternal in Melodrama and the Woman's Film, 1910–1940." In *Home Is Where the Heart Is: Studies in Melodrama and the Woman's Film,* ed. Christine Gledhill, pp. 113–137. London: BFI, 1987.

Klinger, Barbara. *Melodrama and Meaning: History, Culture and the Films of Douglas Sirk.* Bloomington: Indiana University Press, 1994.

Lacan, Jacques. *Ecrits: A Selection.* Trans. Alan Sheridan. New York: W.W. Norton, 1977.

LaPlace, Maria. "Producing and Consuming in the Woman's Film: Discursive Struggle in *Now, Voyager."* In *Home Is Where the Heart Is: Studies in Melodrama and the Woman's Film,* ed. Christine Gledhill, pp. 138–166. London: BFI, 1987.

Margolis, Harriet. "Introduction: 'A Strange Heritage': From Colonization to Transformation?" In *Jane Campion's The Piano,* ed. Harriet Margolis, pp. 1–41. New York: Cambridge University Press, 2000.

Modleski, Tania. *The Women Who Knew Too Much: Hitchcock and Feminist Theory.* New York: Methuen, 1988.

Mulvey, Laura. "Visual Pleasure and Narrative Cinema." *Film Theory and Criticism,* ed. Leo Braudy and Marshall Cohen, pp. 837–848. 6th ed. New York: Oxford University Press, 2004.

Pietropaolo, Laura, and Ada Testaferro, eds. *Feminisms in the Cinema.* Bloomington: Indiana University Press, 1995.

Rodowick, David N. "Madness, Authority and Ideology: The Domestic Melodrama of the 1950s." In *Home Is Where the Heart Is: Studies in Melodrama and the Woman's Film,* ed. Christine Gledhill, pp. 268–280. London: BFI, 1987.

Silverman, Kaja. "The Acoustic Mirror." In *Feminisms,* ed. Sandra Kemp and Judith Squires, pp. 390–395. Oxford: Oxford University Press, 1997.

Sirk, Douglas. *Sirk on Sirk (Interviews with Jon Halliday).* New York: Viking Press, 1972.

White, Patricia. "Feminism and Film." In *Film Studies: Critical Approaches,* ed. John Hill and Pamela Church Gibson, pp. 115–132. Oxford: Oxford University Press, 2000.

Williams, Linda. "Film Bodies: Gender, Genre, and Excess." In *Film Theory and Criticism,* ed. Leo Braudy and Marshall Cohen, pp. 727–741. 6th ed. New York: Oxford University Press, 2004.

Woodbridge, Linda. "Queen of Apricots: The Duchess of Malfi, Hero of Desire." In *The Female Tragic Hero in English Renaissance Drama,* ed. Naomi Conn Liebler, pp. 161–84. New York: Palgrave, 2002.

Index